BYRON IN ENGLAND

HIS FAME AND AFTER-FAME

S.Phillips R.A.pinx.   Walker & Cockerell.ph.sc

Lord Byron.

BYRON IN ENGLAND

HIS FAME AND AFTER-FAME

BY SAMUEL C. CHEW

WITH A PORTRAIT

> Though he may have no place in our own Minster, he
> assuredly belongs to the band of far-shining men, of whom
> Pericles declared the whole world to be the tomb.—
>   JOHN MORLEY

NEW YORK

RUSSELL & RUSSELL · INC

1965

FIRST PUBLISHED IN 1924

REISSUED, 1965, BY RUSSELL & RUSSELL, INC.

BY ARRANGEMENT WITH LUCY E. CHEW

L. C. CATALOG CARD NO: 65-17883

PRINTED IN THE UNITED STATES OF AMERICA

PREFACE

" THE pageant of his bleeding heart " which Byron bore across Europe resembles other pageants in that behind it one finds a litter of paper and odds and ends ; bibliographers, those patient sweepers, have been busy gathering them up ever since, yet, despite their efforts to collect them into proper receptacles, many scraps are still blowing about the world. In these unconsidered trifles, as in all the relics that humanity leaves behind it on its stormful journey across the astonished earth, I find something of interest, something of pathos. That so many books have been written about Byron is not an objection to this one ; rather it is the very reason that I have written it. The history of a great writer's fame and after-fame, of the changes and fluctuations in critical estimates of his achievement, is a part of the history of criticism that has not yet been fully investigated. Certain phases in the history of Shakespeare's reputation have been studied ; and Milton, Spenser, and Pope have received attention from this point of approach. Sir Sidney Colvin has written a graceful, though incomplete, account of Keats's after-fame. Other examples of this sort of inquiry might be adduced. The value of an investigation into the history of the contemporary and posthumous renown of Byron, apart from the consideration that it involves the compilation of a full bibliography, is that the fluctuations in this poet's renown go hand in hand with changes in current thought and cast some light upon shifting ethical standards, religious tenets, political opinions, and literary tastes. This I shall endeavour to make apparent. I would not, however, press unduly the importance of this side of my investigation, and prefer that it be regarded as a contribution at once to Byronic bibliography and to the age-long history of the curiosities of literature and the calamities of authors.

The bibliography of editions and selections of Byron's writings compiled by the late Mr. E. Hartley Coleridge is an admirable piece of work, despite various omissions which will be supplied in the bibliography promised by that great expert, Mr. Thomas J. Wise. But no list of English Byroniana with any pretence to completeness exists anywhere. I cannot claim that mine is exhaustive; but it is far fuller than any other. Though my theme is the history of Byron's fame in England, I have avoided the pedantic consistency of never referring to writings on the poet published in other countries. For a full treatment of Byron's reputation and influence in France I refer to Monsieur Estève's admirable treatise; for his influence in Germany, to Dr. Ochsenbein; in Italy, to Signor Muoni and Dr. Simhart; in Spain, to Mr. Churchman. These writers, with others who treat of similar aspects of Byron-study, are referred to in my Bibliography. I would especially mention Professor W. E. Leonard's monograph, *Byron and Byronism in America*.

No complete collection of Byroniana exists anywhere in the world. I have examined hundreds of books, pamphlets, and magazine and newspaper articles, and to assemble my notes have had to make use of the resources of the British Museum; the libraries at Oxford and Cambridge; the Bibliothèque Nationale; the libraries of Harvard, Yale, Columbia and Johns Hopkins Universities; the Public Libraries of Boston and New York; The Boston Athenaeum, and the Library of Congress, besides various smaller public libraries. I am indebted to Mr. Huntington and Mr. Morgan for permission to make use of their Byron collections. My visit to Mr. Herbert C. Roe, of Nottingham, is a delightful memory; I profited much from the examination of his splendid collection of Byroniana. It is a pleasure to record various visits to Mr. Wise, in whose wonderful Ashley

Library is the unique copy of *The Illiberal*. Mr. John Murray generously permitted me to examine his collections.

The late Dr. Gertrude H. Campbell most kindly copied for me some material at Oxford. Miss Marie Corelli presented to me the manuscript of her unpublished lecture on Byron, for which I am very grateful. Mr. Alfred Ela, Professor C. H. Page and Professor W. L. Phelps called my attention to some allusions to Byron that might have escaped my notice. Mr. W. C. Bullitt, Jr., and Dr. Alan C. Woods have loaned me rare books. To Mrs. Chew I am indebted for much careful copying and for her unfailing interest in my work.

The reader must be forewarned that the nature of the theme made it impossible to make the story of the beginnings of Byron's reputation, as distinct from the beginnings of his career, as interesting as its later developments. Not until 1816 do picturesque and interesting matters enter into the history of his fame.

The miserly saving of space effected by the constant use of abbreviations in references has not been thought worth while. I must note, however, that the letters " LJ " stand throughout for the definitive edition of Byron's *Letters and Journals*, edited by Mr. Rowland E. Prothero (now Lord Ernle). Fuller information as to all works referred to in my foot-notes will be found in the Bibliography.

S. C. C.

CONTENTS

BYRON IN ENGLAND

HIS FAME AND AFTER-FAME

CHAPTER I

IN WHICH THE SUBJECT IS INTRODUCED

" WHERE is the Greek heart that forgets the land that gave us Byron ? " The question was put by a minister of the Greek government in the days immediately before the entrance of Greece into the Great War. " Our thoughts," he said, " have more often turned towards England and France than towards Germany. The concrete, scientific achievements of the latter have not been lost upon us, but where is the Greek heart that forgets the land that gave us Byron ? " As I strolled through the Royal Gardens, vociferous with nightingales, at Athens, while the full May moon rose over Hymettos, I came, near the Arch of Hadrian, upon Falguière's monument that bears the inscription " *Hellas to Byron*," and I wondered whether Greece indeed remembers the leader who came to her from the islands of the West. And standing on the Acropolis by the temple of Nike Athena I thought again of Byron, as the setting sun—

> Not as in Northern climes obscurely bright,
> But one unclouded blaze of living light—

sank over Salamis' unconquered gulf, turning to purple the far heights of the Morea. The English poet lived again in memory on the broad plain of Marathon, and on Sunium's marble steep, and when, coasting by night along the Gulf of Corinth, I saw dimly the lights of Missolonghi twinkling

1

across the water.   Nor is it Greece only that is haunted by the memory of this passionate personality.

As one strolls on the Lido, Byron and Shelley, galloping up and down the sands, seem far more real than the hotels and piers and bathing-houses.   And in forlorn Ravenna one may sit and meditate at the little *caffe* on the " Piazza Byron " that was once the poet's home, within a stone's throw of Dante's tomb—

> Ravenna ! where . . . at twilight-time
> Through the pine-forest wandering with loose rein,
> Wandering and lost, he had so oft beheld,
> (What is not visible to a poet's eye ?)
> The spectre-knight, the hell-hounds and their prey.

The Pineta, now so sadly ravaged by repeated conflagrations, harbours a more tremendous ghost than that of the huntsman of Onesti's line.   Byron's spirit is present in the prisons of the Ducal Palace and in the dungeons of the Estes at Ferrara.   He seems to mingle with the holy ashes of Santa Croce, and to gaze still, " drunk with beauty," at the Venus of the Uffizi.   He broods over the Coliseum and the Palatine.   Standing, once, on deck as our boat entered the Bay of Naples, I watched the golden sunrise behind Vesuvius, and the transcendent beauty of the scene brought to memory that Byron, as he passed there for the last time, on his way to Greece, had said, characteristically : " If events are of a serious nature they shall go into a fifth canto of *Childe Harold ;* if they are comic they shall go into *Don Juan.*"

Wherever he went he left the impress of his personality. Amid the crowded associations of Lake Leman one remembers him side by side with Voltaire and Rousseau and Gibbon and Shelley.   To the Jungfrau one brings memories of *Manfred.*   The Rhine recalls him ; and it is his verse that gives added vividness to the experience of standing on the lion-surmounted pyramid at Waterloo.   To England—and rightly—he does not seem to belong so much as to Europe ; and though one passes his monument in London and notes the memorial tablets upon houses once occupied by him, he is there seldom present in one's thoughts. At Harrow, yes ; but hardly at Cambridge, despite Thorwaldsen's statue in the library of Trinity. Only around Nottingham do associations cluster thickly about him ; and no lover of English poetry can pass unmoved the hill " crowned with a peculiar diadem," on the way from Newstead Abbey, past Annesley, to the drab and dirty mining town of Hucknall Torkard where, in the chancel of the little church, folding back the worn and soiled carpet that covers the floor, one comes upon the tomb marked simply BYRON. The irony of fame speaks in the fact that facing on the dingy square opposite the church there is a wretched plaster statue of the poet set in the wall of " The Byron Chip and Fish Saloon."

> Nay, Byron, nay ! not under where we tread,
> Dumb weight of stone, lies thine imperial head !
> Into no vault lethargic, dark, and dank,
> The splendid strength of thy swift spirit sank.

It was on the vanity and irony of fame that Byron was himself wont to meditate. Fame, he says, " will scarce reanimate the clay " of those who gamble their lives for it. To be glorious he considered " a foolish quest," for " fame is the thirst of youth " and the grave hides alike

> Obscurity and Fame—
> The Glory and the Nothing of a Name.

In one mood or another, now lofty, now mocking, he returns to this idea. In *Don Juan* he moots the question and replies :

> What is the end of Fame ? 'tis but to fill
> A certain portion of uncertain paper. . . .
> For this men write, speak, preach, and heroes kill,
> And bards burn what they call their " midnight taper,"
> To have, when the original is dust,
> A name, a wretched picture, and worse bust.

The same thought is expressed rhetorically in this passage :

> That mighty heap of gathered ground . . .
> By nations raised, by monarchs crowned,
> Is now a lone and nameless barrow !
> Within—the dwelling-place how narrow !

> Without—can only strangers breathe
> The name of him that *was* beneath ?
> Dust long outlasts the storied stone ;
> But Thou—thy very dust is gone !

Such quotations might be multiplied, for the thought is never far below the surface of Byron's consciousness. It was in a not altogether characteristic moment that he expressed his hopes of being remembered with his land's language ; and in another mood he turns upon himself, translating from Martial :

> While living
> Give him the fame thou wouldst be giving ;
> So shall he hear, and feel, and know it—
> Post-obits rarely reach a poet.

Whether or not this is true of Byron the subsequent pages are to show.

CHAPTER II

THE MORNING OF FAME

On May 4, 1812, Elizabeth, Duchess of Devonshire, told a friend[1] that Lord Byron "continues to be made the greatest fuss with"; and on May 12:

He continues to be the greatest attraction at all parties and suppers. The ladies, I hear, spoil him, and the gentlemen are jealous of him. He is going back to Naxos, and then the husbands may sleep in peace.

A little later she writes that *Childe Harold*

is on every table, and himself courted, visited, flattered, and praised whenever he appears. He has a pale, sickly, but handsome countenance, a bad figure, animated and amusing conversation, and, in short, he is really the only topic of almost every conversation—the men jealous of him, the women of each other.

About the same time, the little girl who was to become Mrs. Browning "used to think seriously of dressing up like a boy and running away to be Lord Byron's page." The inclinations of various older, but not wiser, ladies found other and less innocent expression.

With the morning on which Byron "awoke famous" the history of his fame and after-fame commences. Before his first journey to the East he was not utterly unknown; but the ridicule with which *Hours of Idleness* was greeted would have been quickly forgotten had he accomplished nothing more; and even the notoriety of *English Bards and Scotch Reviewers* would have soon died out had his

[1] Vere Foster, *The Two Duchesses*, pp. 361, 364, 376.

5

attempt to suppress that satire been successful and had he
then abandoned the writing of verse. At most the satire
would now be remembered merely as the best of the large
number of such things that appeared during the last years
of the waning influence of Pope. The notice of Byron's
first volume in *The Edinburgh Review* [1] is part of literary
history, but it, too, would have long since been forgotten
had it not aroused Byron's spleen and latent genius. Nor
would one, for its own sake, ever turn, for instance, to
the review of the same collection of juvenile pieces that
appeared in *The Satirist*.[2] This gibes at the rhymes and
sentiments and pretensions of the book. The reviewer
declares :

The verses completely prove, that although George Gordon
Lord Byron, a minor, may be a gentleman, an orator, or
a statesman, unless he improves wonderfully, he can never
be a poet.

The same periodical returned to Byron in a later number,
when it published the following lines, the first of many
satires directed against him :

Lord B—n to his Bear. To the Tune of " Lo Chin y gair."

I.

Sad Bruin, no longer in woods thou art dancing,
    With all the enjoyments that Love can afford ;
No longer thy consorts around thee are prancing,
    Far other thy fate—thou art slave to a Lord !

II.

How oft when fatigued, on my sofa reposing,
    Thy tricks and thy pranks rob of anguish my breast,
Have power to arouse me, to keep me from dosing [*sic*],
    Or what's the same thing, they can lull me to rest.

---

[1] Vol. xi, January 1808, 285 f. The review begins : " The poesy of this
young lord belongs to the class which neither gods nor men are said to
permit." It is reprinted in LJ, i, Appendix ii, pp. 344 f. For excerpts
from other notices of *Hours of Idleness* that are more favourable than the
Edinburgh's, see LJ, i, 171, notes 1–4.

[2] For this and the following quotations see *The Satirist*, i, October 1807,
77 f. ; ii, June 1808, 368 (cf. p. 489) ; iii, August 1808, 78.

III.

> But when with the ardours of Love I am burning,
> I feel for thy torments, I feel for thy care ;
> And weep for thy bondage, so truly discerning,
> *What's felt by* a Lord *may be felt by* a Bear !

In the same number we find the remark that if every one followed the pursuits in which nature destined him to excel,

then might Mr. Sheridan be respectable as a mountebank, . . . Mr. Walter Scott excellent as a compiler of nursery tales, and George Gordon Lord Byron, a minor, might obtain some admiration and applause as the keeper of a beargarden.

Poor stuff ; but genuine wit was seldom part of the equipment of those who attempted to cross swords with Byron.

For any sincere interest in Byron in these early days we must look to his friends, and the only one of them who expressed that interest in print was Francis Hodgson. In 1809 he published the poem " Energy " [1] which begins :

> B—n ! since rank's discordant tone
> Allows the friendly sound—
> B—n ! in energy alone
> Can genuine bliss be found.

Hodgson appeals to his friend to awake to the voice of glory and to assume his responsibilities as an hereditary legislator :

> Mid listening senates boldly stand,
> Thy country's firm support.

In another poem, written just before Byron's first departure from England, Hodgson bids him farewell and offers him advice on matters of religion.

Childe Harold was published on March 10, 1812.   Years

---

[1] In *Lady Jane Grey*, pp. 188–9 ; reprinted in the *Memoir* of Hodgson, 1878, i, 160.   There, too, will be found part of the second poem mentioned in my text, with the statement that it was published in *Lady Jane Grey ;* but I have not found it there.   Edgcumbe (*N. & Q.* 7th Series, ii, 3) records " five fugitive pieces addressed to Lord Byron at various intervals " by Hodgson.

afterwards Samuel Rogers told [1] how Byron sent the proof-sheets to him before the poem appeared.

I read it to my sister. " This," I said, " in spite of all its beauty, will never please the public : they will dislike the querulous repining tone that pervades it, and the dissolute character of the hero." But I quickly found that I was mistaken. The genius which the poem exhibited, the youth, the rank of the author, his romantic wanderings in Greece—these combined to make the world stark mad about *Childe Harold* and Byron.

Francis Jeffrey noticed the poem in *The Edinburgh Review*.[2] He at once admits the success it has attained despite the many sentiments expressed in it that are opposed to " our national passions and most favoured propensities." He notes its " freedom and boldness, both of thought and expression " ; and its originality, in which quality Byron excels Scott. After criticizing the occasional tame and prosaic passages, he concludes, not unwisely, that the poem is

rather a proof of the author's powers, than an example of their successful exertion. It shows the compass of his instrument and the power of his hand ; though we cannot say that we are very much delighted either with the air he has chosen, or the style in which it is executed.

The notice in *The Quarterly Review* [3] is more carping. By a " happy accident," says the reviewer, Byron has hit upon travel as the theme for poetry. Reasonable objections are raised to the " group of antiques " that is introduced in the opening stanzas, and to the archaic diction. There follows a passage that throws light upon the way in which war was regarded a hundred years ago. Harold, if not a " craven," is " at least a mortal enemy to all martial exertions." The reviewer condemns Byron's satire against war.

---

[1] *Table-Talk*, p. 229.   [2] Vol. xix, February 1812, pp. 466 f.
[3] Vol. vii, March 1812, pp. 180 f. (by George Ellis).

The joys of a triumph, it may be said, are mere illusions ;
but for the sake of such illusions is life chiefly worth having.
When we read the preceding sarcasms on the " bravo's
trade," we are induced to ask, not without some anxiety
and alarm, whether such are indeed the opinions which a
British peer entertains of a British army.

The famous opening stanzas of the second canto—on Death—
are quoted with the following comment :

The common courtesy of society has, we think, very justly
proscribed the intrusive introduction of such topics as these
into conversation ; and as no reader probably will open
Childe Harold with the view of inquiring into the religious
tenets of the author, . . . we cannot but disapprove, in
point of taste, these protracted meditations.

The causes of the success of *Childe Harold* were various
and numerous. For nearly twenty years most Englishmen,
unless they were fulfilling a military or diplomatic function,
had been shut off from the Continent by the almost uninterrupted succession of wars. This lack of opportunities for
travel made attractive a poem that dealt with wanderings
in foreign lands ; and Byron was the originator of this poetic
genre. Moreover, there was a special interest in Spain
because of England's choice of the peninsula as the field
of her chief military activities against Napoleon. Added
to this was the fascination which " orientalism " in literature
exercised, and for many years had exercised,[1] over many
readers. The vogue of the Orient was one cause of the
popularity of Byron's narrative poems that succeeded
Childe Harold ; it prompted Thomas Moore's advice to
Byron to " stick to the East." The many imitators of
Byron often laid their tales in lands bordering on the remoter
parts of the Mediterranean. And *Childe Harold* was connected not only with the current " orientalism " but also
with the novel of the " school of terror," for its hero, the
melancholy Childe, was an adaptation of the hero of the

---

[1] See Conant, *The Oriental Tale*, index, *sub* " Byron."

Radcliffian tradition.[1] There was also the traditional and
genuine English love of liberty, stimulated by years of war
and admirably expressed by the new poet. And, lastly,
there was the attraction of Byron's personality ; he was
endowed with " youth, genius, and an ancient name " ;
he had dared in his satire (now recalled to mind) to attack
many mandarins of literature ; he had wandered through
romantic and perilous lands ; strange things were whispered
about his private life.

Two copies of verses, prompted by the poem, bear good
counsel to Byron. One is called *Lines to Harold* [2] (1812),
sixteen stanzas of well-meant banality said to have been
written by one Granville Penn. The other is entitled :
" Lines written on perusing Lord Byron's poem entitled
Childe Harold." [3] Its exceptionally early date, rather than
any intrinsic merit, justifies the quotation of it entire :

> Titles exalt, but cannot give renown,
> From rank alone no man can truly shine ;
> The ray of genius springs from mind alone,
> And only that defies the hand of Time.
> Was each man equal in this state of things,
> And ev'ry mortal emulous of Fame ;
> Byron's bold thoughts, borne on Apollo's wings,
> Would from their beauties gild their master's name.
> Accept then, Byron, from an humble pen,
> Another laurel round thy form to wave.
> Titles and wealth may be forgot by men,
> The works of genius live beyond the grave.
>
> J. C. BLABY, Jan. 12.

The success of *Childe Harold* and Byron's subsequent
enormous social prestige carried with them, among other

---

[1] See Kraeger ; and Sir Walter Raleigh, *The English Novel* (Scribner,
1910), p. 230.

[2] The British Museum does not possess a copy of the original edition,
the only one I know being in the Boston Athenæum. In that copy is
written : " Very scarce. . . . Privately printed at Stoke Park, Buckinghamshire." The " Lines " obtained some circulation in the newspapers ;
a clipping containing them is in the British Museum scrap-book of
Byroniana, vol. ii ; the catalogue ascribes them to Granville Penn. They
were reprinted in 1815, 1829, and 1841 ; see Bibliography, *sub* " Penn."

[3] From a newspaper clipping, bearing no indication of its source, in
the B. M. scrap-book, vol. i. It is there dated in handwriting, 1813.

emoluments, the invitation to compose the *Address at the Opening of Drury-Lane Theatre*, which was delivered on October 10, 1812. Leigh Hunt's commendation of this *Address* in *The Examiner* of October 18, opens the story of Hunt's relations with Byron, a matter to which we shall return later. The story of the *Rejected Addresses* (1812) by Horatio and James Smith is well known. The fourth piece in that amusing collection is " Cui Bono ? By Lord B." It consists of twelve stanzas in the moodily sententious, misanthropic vein of *Childe Harold*, and has been described by Oliver Elton [1] as " a poem which the author of *Childe Harold* might easily have dreamt was his own, and which rivals the ditty assigned by Peacock to his ' Mr. Cypress.' " There are two other offshoots of Byron's poem. One is a serious *Critique on the Address*, apparently the anonymous production of one of the unsuccessful competitors. The other is *Accepted Addresses* (1813). The seventeenth Address is " Lord B—n to J. M—y, Bookseller." These halting octosyllabics feebly satirize the " disjointed fragments " of *The Giaour*, the amount of money that Byron has received from Murray for his poems, the number of readers he has won, and the tears which his verses call from the eyes of ladies.

Not so well known as the *Rejected Addresses* is the subsequent volume by the brothers Smith entitled : *Horace in London* (1813). This has sometimes been described as containing satiric allusions to Byron, but it does not. Ode xv, " The Parthenon. On the Dilapidation of the Temple of Minerva at Athens," attacks Lord Elgin ; Minerva, meeting Elgin's ship at sea as he is carrying off the marbles, upbraids him and prophesies :

> Soon a titled bard from Britain's Isle,
> Thy country's praise and suffrage shall engage,
> And fire with Athens' wrongs an angry age.

The reference here is probably to *Childe Harold* (ii, 10–15), though the Smiths may have seen the privately printed

[1] *Survey*, ii, 281.

quarto edition of *The Curse of Minerva* (1812). Somewhat similar to *Horace in London* is *Sortes Horatianae : A Poetical Review of Poetical Talent* (1814). In this satire some lines on Byron express compassion for his misanthropy and " jaundiced eye," and confess the poet's power " to sway the feelings of the throbbing heart."

Between June 1813 and August 1814, Byron was " the grand Napoleon of the realms of rhyme." *The Giaour, The Bride of Abydos,*[1] *The Corsair,*[2] and *Lara* appeared at intervals of several months. Without attempting to survey all the reviews of these immensely successful poems I have selected a few typical notices from the more influential organs of opinion, together with some out-of-the-way references that cast light upon the reception of these Eastern tales.

In his notice of *The Giaour*[3] Jeffrey praises the striking originality of the hero and the beauty of the passage " He who hath bent him o'er the dead " ; but insists that energy of character and intensity of emotion combined with guilt form a corrupter of our moral nature ; and Byron's poetry " is full of this perversion." He urges the poet to turn to subjects " less gloomy and revolting." Reviewing *The Bride of Abydos* and *The Corsair*[4] he notes once more Byron's energies and exaltations, and the struggles in the souls of his characters.

---

[1] *The Bride of Abydos* was dramatized three times : by William Dimond, by "W. O.," and by Henry J. Byron. Dimond's tragedy used material from *The Corsair* as well as from *The Bride*. In a foreword " W. O." states : " The groundwork, and almost the entire structure of the story, are Lord Byron's. . . . The humble individual who says this, feels, and condemns from his heart, the presumption—the absurdity of blending himself . . . with a Poet, whose only adequate praise is the silence of unutterable adoration." He adds : " To *The Bride of Abydos* of Drury Lane [*i.e.* Dimond's play] he is not indebted for one idea, one word, or one incident." H. J. Byron's piece is a burlesque. Here may also be mentioned J. W. H. Payne's *The Unfortunate Lovers*, a tale based on *The Bride*. This I have not seen ; it is listed by Intze. Another offshoot is a parody called *The Outlaw*, by " Erasmus " ; this, too, I have not seen. It is mentioned in *N. & Q.* 2nd Series, ii, 48.

[2] *Conrad, the Corsair*, by William Hone (1817) is a prose romance adapted from Byron's poem. Cf. *The Corsair. Libretto for Grand Opera.* By W. V. Herbert, 1906.

[3] *The Edinburgh Review*, xxi, July 1813, pp. 299 f.

[4] *Ibid.*, xxiii, April 1814, pp. 198 f.

It is by this spell, chiefly, . . . that he has fixed the admiration of the public ; and while other poets delight by their vivacity, or enchant by their sweetness, he alone has been able to *command* the sympathy, even of reluctant readers, by the natural magic of his moral sublimity, and the terrors and attractions of those overpowering feelings, the depths and the heights of which he seems to have so successfully explored.

Jeffrey then attempts to demonstrate that Byron is the voice of an age wherein security has bred a new " avidity for strong sensations " and in which " the more powerful spirits will awaken to a sense of their degradation and unhappiness."

The poet who has devoted himself most exclusively, and most successfully, to the delineation of the stronger and deeper passions, is likely to be its reigning favourite.

There follows an interesting review of the attempts made by contemporary poets—Scott, Southey, and Campbell—to introduce a " strong " element into the scenes and personages of their poetry. This element Byron possesses in full measure, " superadding the charm of enchanting landscape to that of interesting recollections." This is a by no means contemptible formula for arriving at an explanation of Byron's earliest appeal. There follows a long analysis of the two tales ; and then Jeffrey continues :

We still wish he would present us with personages with whom we could more entirely sympathize. At present he will let us admire nothing but adventurous courage in men, and devoted gentleness in women. . . . We . . . suggest to him to do away the reproach of the age, by producing a tragic drama of the old English school of poetry and pathos.

The conclusion reached in *The Quarterly's* notice [1] of *The Giaour* and *The Bride of Abydos* is that the " tide of success " has had a beneficial rather than a mischievous effect upon the new poet ; the successive revisions of *The Giaour* show increasing care ; the same care is evident

[1] Vol. x, January 1814, pp. 331 f. (by George Ellis).

in *The Bride* as compared with the first oriental tale.[1] The same review's notice,[2] also by George Ellis, of *The Corsair* and *Lara* is more interesting.

Conrad is a personage so eccentric, so oddly compounded of discordant qualities, and so remote from common nature, that it is difficult to sympathize in his feelings.

The critic advances the queer notion, based on Conrad's affinity to the Giaour and Harold, that all three pieces are separate fragments of one poem. He denies that Byron's popularity has depended upon the " growing appetite for turbulent emotions." True, the last twenty years have been full of unrest, but the inciters of that unrest were " certainly not legitimate arbiters of taste "—a remark that shows a total unawareness of the fact that Byron was essentially a voice of revolutionary sentiment. Continuing, the critic rebukes Byron for prying into the " secret sensibilities " of the soul : in so doing he exceeds " the legitimate pretensions of poetry " and invades " the province of metaphysics."

The Champion in 1814 printed as the sixth of a series of " Portraits of Authors " an article on Byron, signed " Strada." The writer attacks the pernicious sentiments of *Childe Harold*, particularly the mock melancholy that pollutes the fairest scenes of nature with " the breathings of discontent." But hopes are drawn from Byron's subsequent poems in which there are a descriptive power, a rapidity of narration, and a sense of feminine loveliness, etc., that promise excellent things to come. Byron's announced determination to wait some years before again coming before the public will, the reviewer thinks, give time for his passions to cool, and he will be able to accomplish something " deserving the praises of the wise, as well as the stupid admiration of the vulgar and unthinking."

It was just at this time that John Keats, who, if not unthinking, had not yet shaken off some taint of vulgarity,

---

[1] Byron, remembering the actual circumstances of the composition of *The Bride*, must have been amused by this judgment.

[2] Vol. xi, July 1814, pp. 428 f.

composed the astonishingly feeble " Sonnet to Byron," [1] in
which the poet is addressed as a dying swan who tells " the
tale of pleasing woe." Quite as feeble are some " Lines
occasioned by reading *The Bride of Abydos*," which appeared
in *The Gentleman's Magazine* in 1814.[2] The writer declares
that Byron has purloined his flowers of immortal bloom from
some " Peri height " or " charmed grove " ; and that his
verse is the saddest child that ever sprang from the union of
Poetry and Melancholy. But how far more beautiful
would the strain be if religion inspired the " holy Minstrel."
From the same pen are some " Lines occasioned by reading
The Giaour." [3] The author read it after perusing *The
Bride;* not till his " heart had mourn'd . . . o'er the dying
Giaour " did he know the full power of Byron.

> With pride I hail thee Chief of Bards on Earth,
> And joy that favour'd Britain gave thee birth.

Similar raptures introduce Thurston's *Illustrations to The
Corsair* (1814)—six copper-plate engravings with an opening
sonnet " To Lord Byron," that lauds his " lyre," his " power-
ful tones," his " beam of genius," and his " sweet vibrations."
There were many other such extravagances ; but those that
I have cited are amply sufficient as specimens.

A reaction was bound to follow. Rumours of Byron's
loose living disturbed his more respectable followers, but the
immediate cause of his sudden decline in popularity in
February 1814 was political. Certain " Stanzas on a
Lady Weeping," attacking the Prince Regent, had been
published anonymously in *The Morning Chronicle*, March 7,
1812. These were republished gratuitously in the second
edition of *The Corsair*, February 1814, when Byron's authorship was consequently revealed. Immediately there was
an outcry from the Tory press, while Byron was defended by
the journals of the opposition. This political scandal, in
which Byron was berated for his anonymous attack upon

---

[1] *Poems*, ed. E. de Selincourt, N. Y., Dodd, Mead and Co., 1909, p. 347.
[2] lxxxiv, Part 1, 592 (signed "H.S.B."
[3] *Ibid.* This periodical published many poems on Byron.

Royalty, paved the way for the more serious outbreak of hostility two years later.[1]

His wedding (January 2, 1815) was greeted in *The Gentleman's Magazine* by some lines " On the Recent Marriage of a Noble Lord." [2] The gist of these twenty-five lines is that Harold, no longer wandering in lonely misanthropic gloom through foreign lands, has found Happiness at home, and holds " a heaven of inspiration " within his " circling arms " which will " prompt the efforts of his Patriot Muse " to defend the honour of his country. The writer obviously meant well, but he was not endowed with foresight.[3]

With the year 1815 Byroniana become more prevalent and more significant. James Hogg, " the Ettrick Shepherd," dedicated *The Pilgrims of the Sun* to Byron in a stanza that explains the dedication as due, not to the poet's politics or lineage or virtues, but to his " bold and native energy " and to the soul that overflies all bounds, and ranges " through Nature on erratic wing." [4]

T. N. Talfourd's *Attempt to Estimate the Poetical Talent of the Present Age* begins with a general sketch of the history of poetry and then introduces " characters " of the chief living poets : Southey, Crabbe, Scott, Moore, Byron, Campbell, Coleridge, and Wordsworth. Byron is unique among poets, says Talfourd, for he comes from the " sunny elevations which lie near the summit of society." The critic notes the rapid extension of his faculties in the period between his earliest effusions and *Childe Harold*, and laments the darkness of Byron's spirit (which reminds him of Salvator Rosa) and his unbelief. The very repulsiveness of his poetry captivates the multitude by its novelty ; but " a milder light is at length breaking in upon his genius."

---

[1] All biographies of Byron give some account of this incident. See especially Mayne, i, 293 f. Courthope (*Hist. Eng. Poetry*, vi, 239) stresses the importance of this political prejudice. Prothero (LJ, ii, Appendix vii.) collects the principal newspaper attacks on Byron at this time.

[2] Cf. *ibid.*, lxxxv, Pt. 1, 350; Pt. 2, 356; lxxxvi, Pt. 1, 447 f., 616, etc.

[3] Byron's only publication during this year of married life was the *Hebrew Melodies*, which Jeffrey (*Edinburgh Review*, xxvii, December 1816, p. 291) rightly pronounced " obviously inferior " to the poet's previous works.   [4] The stanza is quoted in LJ, iii, 270, note 1.

In July 1815 *Colburn's New Monthly Magazine* published " Some Account of the Right Hon. George Gordon, Lord Byron." This very laudatory but entirely insignificant piece of journalism is typical of the sort of sketches which from now on appeared in the periodicals in such numbers that I shall not attempt to catalogue them all.

More important is *The Modern Dunciad* (1815). This anonymous satire—well known to bibliophiles from the fact that the frontispiece is by George Cruikshank—is by George Daniel, the Shakespearean scholar.[1] It contains the following passage on Byron :

> The town is pleased when Byron will rehearse,
> And finds a thousand beauties in his verse ;
> So fix'd his fame—that write whate'er he will,
> The patient public must admire it still ;
> Yes,—though bereft of half his force and fire,
> They still must read,—and, dozing, must admire ;
> While you and I, who stick to common sense,
> To genius, taste, and wit, have no pretense,
> Throughout the whole we toil to understand ;
> Where'er we tread—'tis strange, 'tis foreign land ;
> Nay, half the thoughts and language of the strain
> Requires a glossary to make them plain.
> Beauties there are, which candour bids me own,
> Atone for these—for more than these atone :—
> Beauties—which e'en the coldest must admire—
> Quick, high-wrought passion—true poetic fire—
> Bold, energetic language—thoughts sublime—
> And all the artful cadences of rhyme.

What begins satirically thus ends as a tribute. The lines are typical of the opinions expressed by more thoughtful people at the time of Byron's marriage, and before the scandal of 1816, and the consequent notoriety, opened the floodgates of pamphleteering against the poet.

There is much information on the state of literature in 1815 in a curious satiric poem entitled : *Scribbleomania ; or, The Printer's Devil's Polichronicon. A Sublime Poem. By Anser Pen-Drag-On.*[2] This is a jog-trot satire on all

---

[1] The authorship was admitted when the poem reappeared in 1835.

[2] In *Byroniana und Anderes,* Erlangen, 1912, this satire is ascribed to W. H. Ireland. The catalogue of the British Museum, however, uses

kinds of authors and publications : science, politics, art, novels, poems, and so forth. Among those mentioned are Coleridge, Wordsworth (who is respectfully treated), Southey (who is not), Lewis, Scott, and Byron. Byron is said to possess much fancy, but he should throw off the " harlequin dress," the obsolete words and tortured language, of *Childe Harold*. His power as a " didactic writer " is admitted, but he cannot soar into " the heaven of heavens " of poetry. He is urged to apply his abilities to some topic of sterling and lasting quality, and to obliterate from his thoughts all recollections of the new school of verse.

The last bit of Byroniana that belongs to 1815 is a quaint little book entitled : *Lines Addressed to a Noble Lord ; (His Lordship will know why)*. *By One of the Small Fry of the Lakes*.[1] Be wiser, this person counsels Byron ; the burden of guilt will grow as you grow older ; be content with simple happiness ; " learn to reverence thy Betters."

There is little noteworthy during 1816 apart from the pamphlets of the separation to which the next chapter is devoted. J. Wedderburne Webster's *Waterloo and other Poems* contains some " Lines on Lord B——n's Portrait," from which four may be quoted as a specimen of the whole :

> The sense of feeling and the soul of thought,
> On Earth unteachable—by Heaven untaught :
> Long may the spirit of thy varied Page,
> Redeem from infamy this lifeless age.

These lines are dated 1813 ; in view of Webster's personal relations with Byron, so cynically set forth in Byron's letters to Lady Melbourne,[2] it is interesting to find him publishing them so late as 1816.

merely the pseudonym of the title-page.   Ashbee (*Index Librorum Prohibitorum*, p. 474) commends the book for the interesting information that may be gleaned from it, but sheds no light on the authorship.   On the title-page is a woodcut of a goose with wings spread, be-spectacled, and wearing a bottle of ink and a quill pen slung around its neck.   See the article on Ireland in *The Dictionary of National Biography*.

  [1] According to the catalogue of the British Museum this piece is by " Miss Barker." Byron may have known why she should address him ; I do not.

  [2] See *Lord Byron's Correspondence*, edited by John Murray, 1922, vol. i, *passim*.

CHAPTER III

THE PAMPHLETS OF THE BYRON SEPARATION

HAVE, happily, to deal in this chapter not with the old, unhappy, far-off story of the separation of Lord and Lady Byron, but with the comment, set forth in quaint, shabby little pamphlets, that the separation evoked.[1]

The strain of vulgarity in Byron which shocked Matthew Arnold was mixed with an even more repellent strain of what our ancestors called "sensibility." Something of both these qualities went to the making of the poem "Fare thee well!" into which Byron poured his overwrought feelings in the spring of 1816, at the time of the separation, and which, unwisely, he printed for private circulation among his friends. I do not think that he intended to publish these verses, nor the companion satiric *Sketch* of Lady Byron's housekeeper and companion ; but the two pieces were piratically printed in the *Champion* newspaper of April 14, 1816, and from its columns were widely copied in the press. There followed immediately a number of pirated editions of Lord Byron's *Poems on his Domestic Circumstances*, among the publishers being R. Edwards and the redoubtable William Hone, both of them men whose names occur frequently in connection with Byron's early reputation. An incredible number of these issues came from various presses,[2] Hone's pamphlet alone going

---

[1] This chapter is an enlargement and revision of my article on "The Pamphlets of the Byron Separation," *Modern Language Notes*, **xxxiv**, March 1919, pp. 155 f.

[2] The list of these editions in Mr. Coleridge's bibliography is far from complete. For example : *Poems on his Domestic Circumstances by Lord Byron . . . to which is prefixed, The Life of the Noble Author.* London :

through fifteen editions in 1816. And as they grew in number these collections increased also in size, taking on accretions in the shape of various spurious poems, political and personal, that were audaciously attributed to Byron. These forgeries I shall describe in a later chapter.

Public opinion was against Byron, the more so because the private scandal was mixed up with a revival of political attacks occasioned by certain poems that were thought to betray an unpatriotic sympathy with Napoleon.[1] Macaulay's rhetorical flourish about Byron being the periodical scapegoat required by the British public is well known. More philosophical is an article on "Lord Byron and the British Conscience," by William Haller.[2] Mr. Haller traces the development of feudalism into the social system of the Regency. The moral code in high life required that gentlemen, having sown their wild oats, must "settle down" after marriage. Byron did not reform after his marriage, and was, moreover, disgusted with his stupid, irreproachable wife. "Multiply," says Mr. Haller, "by Byron's dynamic force the disgust which those of us who are young and healthy feel towards one of Scott's heroines, and we shall understand what happened in this unfortunate household." Byron refused to live in hum-drum respectability with the prim prude who was, he knew, a product of the system that was secretly quite as immoral as he was openly. In attacking her satirically he was guilty of bad taste, and this breach of etiquette the British public did not forgive.

The matter, however, is not quite so simple as Mr. Haller

Richard Edwards, 1816, is omitted, notwithstanding that by 1818 this piratical issue had gone through eighteen editions. Another edition of the *Poems* is that with a statement of the facts of the separation by the Rev. J. Nightingale. Of this I have seen the second edition. The memoir therein is chiefly concerned with Byron's ancestors; the "statement" is very favourable to Byron. The story of the presence of a Drury Lane actress in Byron's house is advanced in a very mild form as an explanation of the separation. The kindly clergyman pleads for justice to the exiled poet.

[1] See Courthope, *Hist. Eng. Poetry*, vi, 244, who as usual emphasizes the political aspect of the case. It is noteworthy that in Hone's pirated collection these political poems are associated with the domestic pieces. The theme of *Parisina*, which appeared just before the separation, made that tale share the odium of the "domestic pieces." See further, on the newspaper attacks on Byron at this time, E. H. Coleridge, *Poetry*, iii, 534.

[2] *The Sewanee Review*, January 1916.

puts it. " He had been posing," says Leslie Stephen,[1] " as
a rebel against all the domestic proprieties. . . . But when
a Lara passed from the regions of fancy to 13 Piccadilly
Terrace, matters became more serious." It is now well
known that malign rumours were afloat at the time respecting
Byron and Mrs. Leigh. " Probably the specific scandal
which Lady Byron had been compelled to disavow was never
taken seriously outside Lady Byron's immediate circle,"
says Mr. Gribble ; [2] but Henley says : [3] " By specifying
nothing, and so suggesting the unspeakable, she captured the
general imagination." When Shelley heard that Lady
Byron and Mrs. Leigh were living together, he wrote to
Byron : [4]

I felt much pleasure in this intelligence . . . as affording a
decisive contradiction to the only important calumny that
ever was advanced against you. On this ground at least,
it will become the world hereafter to be silent.

The truth is that Lady Byron was a good, well-meaning
and (*pace* her few admirers) odious creature. " She should
have married Wordsworth," Henley once remarked ; " he
would have had plenty of opportunity to learn ' how awful
goodness is.' " The public that had lately rallied to the
defence of Queen Caroline now backed Lady Byron against
the fallen idol. They rushed into print at once.[5] Richard
Edwards, having helped to pour oil on the fire by pirating

---

[1] *Dict. Nat. Biog.* viii, 143.
[2] Francis Gribble, *Love Affairs of Lord Byron*, p. 228.
[3] *Works*, iv, 174.
[4] September 29, 1816 ; *Letters*, ed. Ingpen, ii, 522. In *The Day and
New Times* of June 23, 1817, there was a long critique of *Manfred* with
what a friend of Lady Byron's called " dreadfully clear " allusions to Mrs.
Leigh. No copy of this newspaper is in the British Museum, and I have
failed to find any elsewhere. See Lovelace's *Astarte*, ed. 1921, p. 69 and
note 2. In none of the reviews of *Manfred* that I have read, and in none
of the pamphlets on the separation, is there so much as a hint of this crime.
But Shelley's letter and the passage quoted in *Astarte* are proofs that such
rumours were more or less current, and they may have helped to prejudice
Byron's case.
[5] Many of these pieces, despite the diligence of various workers, especially Elze and Kölbing, have first been described by me. It is strange that
they have been almost altogether ignored by Byron's biographers, for they
cast much light on the state of English feeling at the time of his departure
from his country.

Byron's indiscreet verses, published *Lady Byron's Responsive
" Fare thee well,"* which is described in an introductory
note as " the offering of a common friend of the persons
most nearly concerned." The poem is in 23 four-line stanzas
and is dated April 29, 1816. Lady Byron is made to assert
her continuing love for her husband and to declare that she
and her lord were parted by treachery. In the future she
will renew in her child's face her husband's " thrice dear
lineaments." [1] " Every glimpse of future gladness " has
vanished from her ; but her doubts, fears and woes would
cease if she knew that Byron was at peace. This production
is followed by nine stanzas called " Conciliator to Lady
Byron " [2] in which she is urged to

> put forth a hand
> The more than classic head to raise.

A son of Phœbus must be expected to roam wide ; Daphne
and Thetis must both be loved ; Christian forgiveness
(despite the confusion of theologies) must be practised.

> I countenance no debauchees ;—
> I urge no justifying prayer ;—
> I joy to see him on his knees ;
> But wilt thou not receive him there ?
>
> So shall the darling of the Nine
> Bless thee with unremitting love :—
> So shall the little darling join
> In chorus with the blest above.

This volume attained at least a third edition, in which there
are some additional poems and a new preface which speaks
of the demand for the book.

As unctuously charitable as this is *A Reply to Fare thee
Well ! ! ! Lines addressed to Lord Byron* (Kirby, 1816). This
is a hoax, the pretended author being Lady Byron, who
declares that Love, if nursed by fond affection, endures
forever, but that neglect and insults kill it. Yet she has

---

[1] An interesting anticipation of the opening lines of *Childe Harold*, iii.
[2] This title is followed by the initials " S. P. D." Unless these are the
writer's, I have no idea what they mean.

compassion on Byron's frailties and admits his " matchless talent." What a pity that he allowed himself to be led astray ! " The tender pledge of soft affection " will " oft revive fond recollection " ; perhaps the prayers of mother and daughter will gain pardon for Byron's errors ; he is already forgiven by his wronged wife. This piece is followed by " To a Sleeping Infant," " by the same." The theme of this poem is that if " the pledge of love " knew how " that breast is fraught with woe " she would refuse to be fed " from sorrow's stream." [1]

A third *Reply to Lord Byron's " Fare thee Well "* (Hodgson, 1817) is in a different tone, its hostility towards the poet being unmixed with any charitable interpretation of his faults. " Talk not of sever'd love," exclaims the author (who signs herself " C "), while you boast of your errors. You have the

> sceptic's art
> To *charm* the fancy—but *corrupt the heart.*

A companion piece from the same press, in the same year, and (judging from the style) by the same hand, is : *Lines Addressed to Lady Byron.* In this mawkishly sympathetic effusion her Ladyship is advised to trust in God in Whom peace will be found, and to find consolation in that " little form rear'd on thy bosom." A great deal of " sensibility " was evidently expended by worthy people upon the infant Ada, future Countess of Lovelace ! [2]

---

[1] See further on this : E. Kölbing, " Byron-Literatur," *Eng. Stud.* xxvi, 1899, p. 68. This is one of the pamphlets of the separation that Elze had noted.

[2] The *Lines Addressed to Lady Byron* are by Mrs. Cockle, and are to be found bound up in a volume of her *Poetical Works* in the British Museum. The other pieces bound in this volume are elegies on the Princess Charlotte and on King George III. She was also author of " Important Studies for the Female Sex, in Reference to modern Manners ; " of an "Elegaic Tribute to the Memory of Sir John Moore," and of much else. Bertram Dobell (*N. & Q.* 6th Series, vi, 17) records, without a publisher's name, this title : *Lady Byron's Reply to her Lord's Farewell, with Referential Notes to the Lines in Lord Byron's Poem particularly alluded to by her Ladyship,* 1825. H. Sculthorp (at the same reference) says : " A gentleman . . . hazarded the assertion that [these lines] were composed for Lady Byron by Campbell, the poet." It is unlikely that a new *Reply* was published for the first time so late as 1825 ; the piece may be a new edition of one of the *Replies* of

Byron's satiric *Sketch from Private Life* (on Mrs. Clermont, Lady Byron's companion) occasioned the bitter parody : *A Sketch from Public Life* (1816), which was published and perhaps written by that picturesque firebrand William Hone.[1]   A prose foreword notes that this Sketch is designed as " an antidote to the poison " of Byron's lines.   In the verses themselves " Harold " is called " a base, un-loved, un-loving, sordid elf " who feels only for himself. The public has been " gulled into admiration of a knave." His song shall not protect him :

> Injured power of Virtue ! come along !
> And crush the worm through all its slime of song.

The fallen weak are merely pitiable ; but derision and contempt follow the great who are vile and base.   They shall live

> and wish in vain to die,
> Scorched in the burning sun of infamy.

A sane and moderate account of the affair is contained in the prose *Narrative of the Circumstances which attended the Separation of Lord and Lady Byron* (1816).   It declares that Byron, exposed by his talents to the " shafts and sarcasms of pretenders," has foiled all their attacks upon his poetry.   These jealous rivals now attempt to deform his character.   There follows a long account of the methods employed by such assailants.   The public has a right to know the true explanation of the separation.   Byron's stormy youth and the " calm domesticity " of Miss Milbanke's " maiden days " are contrasted.   Incompatibility of temperament was unavoidable.   Byron devoted to " the Muse " hours that should have been spent with his wife. A fairly accurate account follows of Lady Byron's departure from her home and of her suddenly announced resolution (following more than one friendly letter) not to return there.

1816.   But I have been unable to discover a copy.   As for Campbell's authorship—that is possible, for Campbell was a friend of her Ladyship, and later on ill repaid the favours done him by Byron by blackguarding his memory at the time of the appearance of Moore's biography.
[1] This piece is reprinted by Kölbing, *Eng. Stud.* xxvi, 1899, 70–3.

" The panders to a depraved taste " who have perverted this plain tale are denounced ; and the pamphlet ends : " Recall him, recall him, noble Lady; be yours the gentle hand stretched out to save him ; recall him to your heart," etc.

Byron's departure for the Continent created a new sensation, one result of which was the publication of some extremely censorious *Lines on the Departure of a Great Poet from his Country* (1816). The preface begins :

However great the poetical merits of that celebrated person may be, who has for some years past been wearying the public with the waywardness of his fancies, and the gloom of a misguided imagination, the blemishes of his character are equally glaring.

The author's object is to give " at least one public expression " to the sentiments which are generally held concerning these blemishes ; the justification for such personalities may be found, he claims, in Byron's own publication of his domestic pieces.

In the writings of that Poet, no good feeling is expressed, no moral sentiments inculcated, . . . and a turn of mind is everywhere indicated, manifestly incompatible with all religious feeling whatever.

The poem begins :

> From native England, that endur'd too long
> The ceaseless burden of his impious song,
> His mad career of crimes and follies run,
> And grey in vice when life was scarce begun ;
> He goes . . .

Does he leave friends behind ? No ; all " suppress the generous tear." Genius still dwells in that sinful mind, but she holds a barren court there. Byron may scorn these lines, but his heart must confess the truth of this " plain picture of [his] guilt and woe." The poem closes with an appeal to him to repent :

> Wert thou advanc'd beyond all bards in fame,
> In wit unrivall'd—as thou art in shame—
> How would it profit thee in time to come,
> When summon'd to thy last most dreaded home,

Tho' praise should dwell upon thy latest verse,
Tho' mournful Muses should adorn thy hearse,
To be recorded, when thy race is run,
England's best Poet, and her guiltiest Son ? [1]

Two sets of spurious poems accompanied Byron's departure from England : *Lord Byron's Farewell to England* and *Reflections on Shipboard, by Lord Byron* (both 1816). These shall be described in my chapter on " The Byron Apocrypha." There, too, will be found an account of some other pieces that are more remotely connected with the separation.

As the sensation caused by the private scandal died away, adverse criticism turned to Byron's impiety and immorality for subjects of attack. Disregarding strict chronological order, however, I shall consider the literature that grew up around *Don Juan* and *Cain,* and shall return thereafter to the miscellaneous Byroniana that appeared in the years between his departure from England and his death.

[1] According to Bertram Dobell's book-catalogue, number 300, item 93, these *Lines* are by Charles Thomson. *The Critical Review,* July 1816, well described the *Lines* as " an abusive effusion on the emigration of Lord Byron, published on an occasion when a generous mind would least of all have been disposed to be prodigal of censure. The poetry has no merit to compensate for our disgust at the purpose of the writer."

CHAPTER IV

THE RECEPTION OF *DON JUAN* [1]

As to the estimation of the English which you talk of, let them calculate what it is worth, before they insult me with their insolent condescension. I have not written for their pleasure. If they are pleased, it is that they chose to be so ; I have never flattered their opinions, nor their pride ; nor will I. . . . I have written from the fulness of my mind, from passion, from impulse, from many motives, but not for their " sweet voices." —(*Byron to John Murray*, 1819).

FEW books have had a stranger history than *Don Juan*. When the manuscript of the first two cantos arrived in London a group of Byron's friends assembled in conclave at John Murray's office, and after examining the poem were unanimous in advising its suppression. Murray sent word of the verdict to Byron, who, oddly enough, at first seemed to acquiesce, but presently, as opposition stirred up resentment in him, decided that fifty copies should be privately printed for circulation among his friends, and then within a few weeks determined to publish his work. In the end he was proof against even such tactful pleading as Hobhouse's (" *Carissimo*, do review the whole scene, and think what you would say of it as written by another ") ; and he consented only to the suppression of the anonymous dedication to Southey, certain anonymous stanzas upon Castlereagh, and one " damn." His ire was extreme when, in the published form, he found in the place of four stanzas or parts of stanzas rows of asterisks.

Previous to its appearance, the newspapers carried for several days the mysterious and arresting advertisement :

[1] This chapter and the next are based, with revision, correction, and large amplifications, upon my article, " The Centenary of *Don Juan*," *American Journal of Philology*, xl, April–June 1919, pp. 117–152.

" In a few days—*Don Juan*." [1]   It came into the world unacknowledged by its father.   John Murray, " the most timorous of God's booksellers " and of literary midwives, brought it shamefacedly before the British public, a burly bastard in large quarto, dignified with all the adornments of fine printing and broad margins, yet finding a foster-mother only in Thomas Davison, the printer, who was prosecuted for his pains.   The bar sinister upon its escutcheon was an invitation to publishers of low repute to issue pirated editions.   Not until it was evident that his offspring was making its way in the world did its father do the honourable thing and recognize it.   Then it appeared among the " Works of Lord Byron."

It is unfortunate for the good name of *Don Juan* that Canto One is the first canto, for many people know the poem merely from the opening episode—witty, sprightly, entertaining, vulgar.   Moreover, the reviewers of 1819 had not the advantage we possess of being able to set the incident of Donna Julia's bedroom and the seemingly heartless narrative of the shipwreck in the entire context, thus reducing these scenes to natural proportion in relation to the whole survey of life.

" You will certainly be damned for this," Hobhouse, to whom it was submitted, wrote on the manuscript.   The process of damnation began betimes.   In a famous passage comparing himself to Napoleon, Byron admits that " Juan was my Moscow."   He did not retreat, but in 1819 he faced a strong coalition.   As in the case of the domestic scandal of 1816, there is some evidence of division along the lines of political opinion, the more liberal journals venturing to support Byron ; but at first the hostility was almost unanimous.   *The Edinburgh Review* preserved a stony

---

[1] *Don Juan* was published July 15, 1819.   *The Literary Gazette*, July 17, 1819, remarks that the public mind had been strangely agitated by announcements in the newspapers.   It now appears that no calamity was foretold, but simply " the publication of an exceedingly clever and entertaining poem."   On the other hand, the Newcastle Literary and Philosophical Society at once ordered *Don Juan* to be removed from its library as an immoral publication.   (See a clipping, undated, from the *Newcastle Chronicle* in the B. M. scrap-book, vol. ii.)

silence. Gifford, in the *Quarterly*, could not well condemn the poem, since his review was published by Murray; therefore he, too, was silent. The attack was led by *Blackwood's* in some lengthy " Remarks on *Don Juan*." [1] " Maga" admits that Byron " has never written anything more . . . triumphantly expressive of the greatness of his genius " ; " our indignation, in regard to the morality of the poem, has not blinded us to its manifold beauties." But the assertion is made that " a more thorough and intense infusion of genius and vice—power and profligacy " there has never been than *Don Juan*.

Impiously railing against his God—madly and meanly disloyal to his Sovereign and his country—and brutally outraging all the best feelings of family honour, affection, and confidence, . . . it appears . . . as if this miserable man . . . were resolved to show us that he is no longer a human being, even in his frailties ;— but a cool unconcerned fiend.

To have " a calm careless ferociousness of contented and satisfied depravity . . . this atrocious consummation was reserved for Byron." These are strong words ; they drew from Byron that " Reply to Blackwood's Edinburgh Magazine " which he addressed to Isaac D'Israeli, but which was not published till after his death. In the following November, being in better humour, " Maga " printed some verses by William Maginn called " Don Juan Unread," [2]

---

[1] Vol. v, August 1819, pp. 512 f.
[2] Vol. vi, November 1819, pp. 194 f. The verses are reprinted in *The Odoherty Papers*, i, 179 f. The great torrent of British resentment was poured upon the first two cantos of *Don Juan*. *Blackwood's* review of the next instalment (ix, August 1821, pp. 107 f.) was more favourable. But by April 1822, John Wilson and his colleagues were again hard upon the " noble poet " in a " Letter from Paddy " (xi, 461 f.) which berated Robert Southey severely at the same time with Byron. Southey had recently branded his opponent as the leader of the " Satanic School " of poetry. The various notices in *Blackwood's* are cleverer than, but typical of, the comments that *Don Juan* inspired among the journals of the period. Extracts from other early reviews of the poem will be found among the notes to the first volume of *Don Juan* in the " Lyceum edition " of Byron's *Works*, edited by R. H. Stoddard (London and Boston : F. A. Niccolls, n.d.). Gendarme de Bévotte's *La Légende de Don Juan* (chap. xi.) supplies further information regarding the reception of Byron's poem.

an amusing parody on " Yarrow Unvisited," of which one
stanza will serve as a sample :

> " O ! rich," said I, " are Juan's rhymes,
>   And warm its verse is flowing !
> Fair crops of blasphemy it bears,
>   But we will leave them growing.
> In Pindar's strain, in prose of Paine,
>   And many another Zanny,
> As gross we read, so where's the need,
>   To wade through Don Giovanni ? "

From 1816 till his death pamphleteers followed Byron
as jackals trail after a wounded lion.   Don Juan gave them
occasion for hounding him anew.   I note first : *Remarks,
Critical and Moral, on the Talents of Byron, and the Tendencies
of Don Juan* (1819).[1]   The anonymous author's hostility
to Byron is not unmitigated ; the fourth canto of *Childe
Harold*, for example, he considers " *the sublimest atchieve-
ment of mortal pen.*" [2]   But he holds that the beauties
of *Don Juan* do not atone for its evil character.   " Alas !
the poison is general, the antidote particular."

Byron might have been not only the best, but the greatest
poet of past or present times, with the exception of Shakespeare alone ; he has chosen to be the most mischievous
and dangerous without any exception. . . . We envy him
not the fiend-like satisfaction of shining, only to mislead.

He especially attacks the Donna Julia episode, the blasphemy
of the poetical commandments, and the heartlessness of
the narrative of the shipwreck.   He considers that the
most charitable view to take is that the poet is not in earnest,
lack of sincerity being in this case a virtue.   *Don Juan*
is " a bold experiment, made by a daring and determined
hand, on the moral patience of the public."

---

[1] This piece is by Charles Caleb Colton, one of the minor victims (as
some of my readers may chance to remember) pilloried in the *Noctes Ambrosianæ*.   See *Blackwood's*, xvii, March 1825, 369.   Another edition of Colton's
diatribe has the title : *Remarks on the Talents of Lord Byron ;* the copy of
this in the British Museum is bound up with Colton's *Lacon : or Many
Things in Few Words*, 1820.

[2] Colton's italics, spelling, and style !

A diatribe of a different sort is *Don Juan : with a Biographical Account of Lord Byron* . . . *Canto III* (1819), This is a poem in 144 stanzas in *ottava rima ;* but despite the fact that it is labelled " Canto III " it is not properly to be grouped among the continuations of Byron's poem. It is a grossly false and hostile review of Byron's life, pretending to come from Byron himself, who leaves Juan slumbering in the arms of the frail Haidée and now " draws from himself." Byron is variously called " Lord Harold," " Lord Beppo," and " Lord Squander." The story of his career includes a fantastic account of his love-affair with " a fisher's or a corsair's daughter " whom he met in Greece, roamed around with, had a child by, and then abandoned. This yarn occurs repeatedly in early Byroniana. There is a bitterly hostile narrative of the marriage and separation. The most interesting portion of the poem is the account of the group of expatriated Englishmen at Geneva who numbered among them the greatest of English lyric poets. A sidelight upon contemporary opinion of Shelley is thrown by these lines :

> In rival conclave there and deep divan
> He met and mingled with the Vampyre crew
> Who hate the virtues and the form of man,
> And strive to bring fresh monsters into view ;
> Who mock the inscrutable Almighty's plan
> By seeking truth and order to subdue—
> Scribblers, who fright the novel-reading train
> With mad creations of th' unsettled brain.

> There Frankenstein was hatched—the wretch abhorred,
> Whom shuddering Sh—y saw in horrid dream
> Plying his task where human bones are stored,
> And there the Vampyre quaffed the living stream
> From beauty's veins—such sights could joy afford
> To this strange coterie, glorying in each theme,
> That wakes disgust in other minds—Lord Harold
> Sung wildly too, but none knew what he carolled.

The poem ends with a threat to " Lord Beppo " that should he not mend his morality another canto shall scourge the wretch " who toils for vice and spreads corruption wide." Another attack was prompted by very definite *animus.*

William Hone, the publisher whose name has already occurred several times in this book, was a rather remarkable character who has an honourable place in the history of the long fight for a free press. He now published, and may have been the author of, "*Don John,*" or *Don Juan Unmasked* (1819).[1] He describes the author of *Don Juan* as " grasping with one hand the thunderbolts of Olympus, and groping with the other in a filthy jakes " ; combining " the gaiety of the ball-room and the gloom of the scaffold." An analysis of the poem follows. He then declares that he has penetrated its anonymity (which, indeed, every one did), and proceeds to abuse " Don John " (that is, John Murray) for publishing such a work. All Murray's literary friends come in for their share of vilification, but the inspiration of the attack is seen when Hone centres his fire upon the famous series of literary commandments : [2]

[1] The following facts must be understood if the purpose of Hone's pamphlet is to be clear. Hone had published a number of satires against the Tory government ; and on three separate charges was tried for publishing the bold and, as it was held, blasphemous parodies : *The Late John Wilkes's Catechism ; The Sinecure's Creed ;* and *The Political Litany.* His trials (December 17–19, 1817) occasioned great excitement, and when he was acquitted on all three charges there were public celebrations in his honour. He published separate accounts of each trial ; and collected them in *The Three Trials of William Hone,* 1818. (These have been reprinted with introduction and notes by W. Tegg, 1876.) In 1818 Richard Carlile, another radical publisher—it was he who by the publication of *Wat Tyler,* a drama of Southey's anti-monarchial youth, had put the poet-laureate in an awkward position in 1816—reprinted Hone's suppressed parodies and also an edition of Paine's works. He was tried on six indictments, and in November 1819 sentenced to pay a heavy fine and to three years in prison. It was while Carlile's trial was pending (and also the trial of Russell, a Birmingham printer who had reissued *The Political Litany*), that Hone published " *Don John.*" See, further, F. W. Hackwood, *William Hone, His Life and Times,* London : Unwin, 1912, chapters v.–xi. Hackwood says nothing about " *Don John,*" which is, however, mentioned in " Hone's Famous Trials " in Augustus de Morgan's *A Budget of Paradoxes,* Chicago : The Open Court Publishing Co., 1916, i, 180–7. The full title of the *Litany,* a rare and curious piece, is : *The Political Litany, diligently revised ; to be Said or Sung, until the Appointed Change Come, throughout the Dominion of England and Wales, and the Town of Berwick-upon-Tweed. By Special Command. London : Printed for one of the Candidates for the Office of Printer to the King's Most Excellent Majesty, and sold by William Hone, 55, Fleet Street, and 67, Old Bailey, three doors from Ludgate Hill.* 1817. *Price Two-pence.* The authorship has been ascribed to one John Marshall.

[2] *Don Juan,* i, 205–6 : " Thou shalt believe in Milton, Dryden, Pope," etc.

Mr. Murray . . . actually publishes a Parody on the Ten
Commandments of God, whilst this prosecution is pending
. . . for a Parody on the Litany, which is an entirely human
composition. . . . Why did not Mr. Murray suppress
Lord Byron's Parody on the Ten Commandments ? . . .
Because it contains nothing in ridicule of Ministers, and
therefore nothing that they could suppose would be to the
displeasure of Almighty God.

Hone declares that Murray suppressed Byron's dedication
of *Don Juan* to Castlereagh on account of " delicacy to
Ministers." [1] He mockingly presents the sort of review of
Don Juan which Gifford will write :

It is open depravity against which *we* contend. . . . What
we blame in Mr. Murray is the *partial* concealment of the
fact, that he published *Don Juan*. . . . There is great
credit due to Mr. Murray for his *contrivance*, in getting the
booksellers to sell the book *openly*, which he did not choose
to publish openly.[2]

[1] The confusion here is doubtless due to some distorted rumour that
had reached Hone of the fact that a dedication to Southey and some
stanzas against Lord Castlereagh had been suppressed.

[2] William Hone's various satires on the court produced a number of
replies. One of these concerns our subject : *The Dorchester Guide ; or a
House that Jack Built* (n.d., *circa* 1820). A woodcut on the title-page
shows a pair of scales on which the Bible makes *The Age of Reason* and
The Principles of Nature kick the beam. The climax of this " House that
Jack Built " comes after Paine, Hone, and other radicals have been
satirized, and on page 31 there is a crude woodcut of a Peer in his robes
and coronet, with cloven left foot or hoof. The subjoined verses are as
follows :—

     And This is
          THE DEVIL
           to bring up the rear,
By mischief disguised in the dress of a Peer.—
Pursue the old method, you'll find out the cheat,
And the Imp stand confessed, if you look at his feet.
Distortion of Nature's the taste of the age,—
Make a Story obscene,—'twill be read ev'ry page.
His verses so sweet and harmonious appear,
The mind is corrupted while tickling the ear.
Fear or shame in this modern Leander's not found ;
The fate that decreed he should never be drowned
Formed his heart of materials harder than steel,
Which neither compunction nor pity can feel.

Byron is similarly grouped with other radicals in " Oxonian's " *The Radical
Triumvirate* (1820). This writer sounds a warning inspired by the dangerous signs of the times. A jury has recently acquitted a culprit who laughed

An anonymous pamphlet, the authorship of which has been ascribed to its publisher, John Stacy, appeared at Norwich in 1820 : *A Critique on the Genius and Writings of Lord Byron, with Remarks on Don Juan.* The writer describes himself as " a man advanced in life, and neither irascible or jealous." He sees a meteor rising, whose fiery hair shakes pestilence—this is Byron, " a phenomenon to whom the literature of no age can produce a parallel." He warns the " noble writer " that talents so depraved become crimes, that " immoral poetry was never long-lived." He attacks his sensual view of Love, and laments

> the mingled and chaotic gloom of infidelity, misanthropy, political scepticism . . . and the avowed and ostentatious abandonment of every moral principle, social duty, and domestic feeling

in Byron's writings. " It is incredible " to him " how females can peruse " his works. And he gives a recipe for composing a Byronic poem :

> I know nothing easier than to compose a poem à la Byron : take a (not) human being, load him with every vice ; . . . borrow as much pride, malignity, and blasphemy as Satan can afford ; . . . let him have a mistress ; . . . let her . . . be *insinuated* to be his *sister* ;

and so forth. There must be no narrative, and the " essence of the poem " must be wholly " physical." Stacy

---

at religion (the reference is evidently to Hone). This acquittal has encouraged Carlile to publish Paine's works. " Oxonian " contrasts former times " when Wisdom and Intelligence demonstrated the reasonableness of Christianity with almost mathematical precision." He gives a list of dangerous works, in which *Don Juan* figures along with the writings of Wollaston, Paine, and Hone. For not only in the lectures of philosophers and " the page of the Plebeian Republican " are dangers found ; a " titled Poet . . . tarnishes his title by publishing a poem fraught with ribaldry, licentiousness, and blasphemy." A long account of the poem follows. Then Byron is warned of the death-bed terrors that other men such as he have experienced. In conclusion " Oxonian " issues a call to Englishmen to rally around the throne and altar of their fathers. It should be added that the " radical triumvirate " are " Infidel Paine," Lord Byron, and Surgeon Lawrence (who had claimed to demonstrate that " the soul is only the brain ").

concludes : " I have detained public attention too long
with a subject which derives its importance only from its
mischief." [1]

Before the appearance of the second instalment of *Don
Juan* there was published a very curious piece entitled :
Gordon. A Tale. A Poetical Review of Don Juan (1821).
This is described in the preface as " partly a burlesque
parody on the style of *Don Juan* ; partly a sacrifice of
praise at the shrine of talent, and partly arguments proving
its immoral tendency." Lacking the personal motive of
Hone's pamphlet and the evidently sincere indignation of
Stacy's, it is a dreary piece of cheap wit and cheaper moralizing. In the first canto the writer tells how he read *Don
Juan* by his fireside and meditated upon the range of Byron's
genius. Praise gradually gave way to blame, and he
ended with the " distressing thought " that the poet's
intellect " serves but to infect." The second canto is a
bit more lively. As the fireside reader closes *Don Juan*
in pious disgust a tall stranger enters the room. The two
men fall into conversation, which presently leads to Byron
and his poem. The stranger defends it, and as the other's
criticism becomes more severe, turns from pale to red and
back again, and finally, losing all patience, becomes " a
dreadful goblin." A vision of eternity in hell passes before
the moralizer ; a crowd of fiends rushes towards him ; and
then all disappear and he finds himself alone in his room,
his strange guest gone, and the fire and candles burning as
usual. Sad rubbish !—but with an echo of the theme of
retribution—" There is no debt that is not paid "—which
was present in Tirso de Molina's drama, and became the

---

[1] The " Remarks on *Don Juan* " which follow are reprinted from
Blackwood's, August 1819. To this note may be consigned a reference to
An Expostulary Epistle to Lord Byron. By Joseph Cottle (1820). This
is an inflated attack, especially against *Don Juan.* I quote six lines :

> Disastrous man, from dreams of death arise !
> No longer tempt the patience of the skies !
> Confess, with tears of blood, to frowning Heaven
> The foul perversion of his talents given !
> Let none, at death, despairing charge on thee
> Their blasted peace, in shuddering agony.

leading motive, even the title, of a later Spanish version of the legend of Don Juan.[1]

Another burlesque satire directed against Byron's poem is a piece in two cantos ironically entitled *An Apology for Don Juan* (1824). This appeared just before Byron's death. It opens with the customary praise of Byron's genius, and this leads to a comparison between the poet-traveller and the writer's stay-at-home self ; thence to a glorification of English scenery and to the proofs of religion afforded by the majesty of nature ; and the circle is completed by a return to Byron to deplore his lack of faith and the lamentable sight of

> A towering genius, a gigantic mind
> By vice enslaved.

Byron is compared to Lucifer ; and the resemblances between *Don Juan* and *Cain* are cited as one proof of the authorship of the former anonymous poem. Its anonymity is made the subject of strictures that are certainly justified :

> More respect, I'm certain, had been shown thee,
> If that thy author had not blushed to own thee.

The satire then grows keener. Byron, it is declared, exploits immorality as a means of filling his pocket. The poet's doubts as to immortality suggest a disquisition on faith and virtue, closing with this severe chastisement :

> What is the poet's fame, who sometimes drolly
> And sometimes with dark scornful language shows his
> Aversion to whate'er is pure and holy,
> While his own pen his wretchedness discloses ;
> Who oft with equal wretchedness and folly,
> Contemns the Gospel and the books of Moses,
> And in despite of conscientious qualms,
> Perverts the Prophets, and profanes the Psalms ?

The second canto contains a rather amusing parallel between Byron's and Juan's career ; a survey of Byron's travels and ideas ; and the expression of a pious hope that, since " the noon of life is not yet past away," Byron, like Boccaccio

---

[1] Cf. *The Imperial Magazine*, May 1822.

and Rochester, may ultimately repent. The whole closes
with a confession that the author's

> ambition reaches
> To hope that, side by side, on the same shelf
> This work and his will rest.

After hearing of Byron's death he published a second edition,
to which he added eight elegiac " Stanzas on the Death of
Lord Byron " (one of the innumerable tributes of that
kind), lamenting " the mighty bard," " the wayward, moody
child." [1]

The most drastic of all contemporary pamphlets directed
against Byron's writings in general and *Don Juan* in
particular just synchronized in date of publication with
Byron's death. This is *Cato to Lord Byron on the Immorality
of his Writings* (1824).[2] The most interesting part of this
long splenetic diatribe is a review of the causes of Byron's
contemporary popularity.

What is beautiful in description, or sweet in numbers,
or soothing in sentiment, or provocative of passion, is not

[1] A third edition, " to which is added a third canto, including remarks
on the times," appeared so late as 1850. The author's name was now
revealed : John W. Thomas, who was, it seems, a clergyman, translator
of *The Divine Comedy*, and author of *The War of the Surplice*, a Hudibrastic
satire on the Oxford Movement. (See *N. & Q.* 4th Series, v, 329.) There
are several interesting changes from the two earlier editions. A stanza
that had prophesied the unpopularity of *Don Juan* is omitted, as is the one
that condemns the poet who " contemns the Gospel and the books of Moses "
—in 1850 it was no longer convenient to risk the Gospel and the Pentateuch
standing or falling together. The new third canto gives a summary of
progress since Byron's day : science, politics, the discovery of new gold-
fields, steam, telegraphy, and much else. Where now is Byron ?

> Gone—to the land where all things are forgot !
> Ah, what avail his genius and his wit ?
> The call of glory now can rouse him not ;
> His race is run, and—what is writ is writ.

In 1855 this third edition was reissued almost verbatim, but with the title
changed to *Byron and the Times ; or an Apology for Don Juan*.
[2] According to the catalogue of the British Museum this book is by
the Rev. George Burges (and under his name I list it in my bibliography).
A letter in Mr. Murray's possession confirms this entry. Mr. Burges was
vicar of Halvergate in Norfolk, and author of *The Conservative Standard
of the British Empire*. The book was wrongly ascribed to the Rev.
G. Croly, D.D.

often, by careless or indifferent readers, rejected for any defect in morals.

" The peculiar nature of the times " is another cause, for " these half-philosophers and half-infidels who aspire to a literature at once cheap and worthless " admire Byron. The professional critics (like those of *The Quarterly Review*) who commend instead of condemning Byron, are partly responsible for his vogue. And Byron's condescension towards public curiosity by his self-revelations is a further cause. Most of " Cato's " book is devoted to an elaborate review of all the defects of subject-matter, character-drawing, versification, and general view of life set forth in Byron's writings, with a contrast between Byron and (of all poets !) Cowper. The writer ventures the prophecy that *The Task* will be read

when Harold for his pride, Cain for his blasphemy, and Juan for his licentiousness, shall have scathed the laurels of Lord Byron, and consigned his poetry to an early and loathed grave. . . . The garbage which the present generation luxuriates upon, posterity will nauseate and cast upon the dunghill.

After a hundred and twenty-eight pages of such abuse comes the threat that if Byron does not mend his ways " what I have already said is mercy to what I shall be constrained to say hereafter."

As instalments of *Don Juan* continued to appear there were not wanting those who ventured to defend the poem.[1] Though to Keats it was simply " Lord Byron's latest flash poem " ; though Wordsworth, who called it " that infamous publication," was " persuaded that *Don Juan* will do more harm to the English character than anything of our time " ; and though Southey, as would be expected, could not write of it without foaming at the mouth, in general the greater men of the time were quick to appreciate its greatness. Hazlitt was less acrid than customarily, and reserved his

---

[1] There is a clever little defence in an early pirated edition : *Don Juan, with a Preface by a Clergyman.* (London : Hodgson, 1822.) The clerical authorship of this preface is certainly open to question.

censure for the " flashy passages " and for its desecration of
serious subjects.   Leigh Hunt, of course, defended it warmly,
for the later cantos were published by his brother, John
Hunt.[1] Jeffrey recognized its worth while deprecating its
" tendencies." Scott, who, despite his sincere if shallow
orthodoxy, was large-minded enough to accept the dedication
of *Cain* to him, praised *Don Juan*.   Shelley, with the cha-
acteristic lack of jealousy that is apparent in all his references
to Byron, said of *Don Juan* that it

sets him not only above, but far above, all the poets of the
day—every word is stampt with immortality. . . . Something
wholly new and relative to the age, and yet surpassingly
beautiful. . . . I think that every word is pregnant with
immortality.

Praise of another sort is contained in a pamphlet which
is by far the most interesting of all contemporary bits of
Byroniana, and is the only one which, I believe, is worth
reprinting.   This is *A Letter to the Right Hon. Lord Byron.
By John Bull*. 1821.[2] The blatant hearty " high jinks "
of this typical piece of regency prose has something of the
flavour of a print by Pugin or Rowlandson.   It bears on the
title-page two amusingly appropriate mottoes, both from
Arbuthnot ; these are : " Some of Bull's friends advised
him to take gentle methods with the young Lord ; but John

---

[1] Byron's separation from Murray undoubtedly loosened Tory criticism
which Murray's influence, especially in the circle of the *Quarterly Review*,
had previously helped to hold in check.   (This suggestion was made in
Blackwood's, xvii, February 1825, 132.)   Byron's connection with the
Hunts harmed his popularity during the last two years of his life.

[2] A hoaxing review of this *Letter* in *Blackwood's* for July 1821 ascribed
the authorship to Jeremy Bentham.   Swinburne, in atrabiliar mood, wrote
of the *Letter* that it was " so adroitly extravagant in its adulation that an
' ill-minded man,' after study of Byron's correspondence and diary, might
be tempted to assign it to the hand which penned them.   But for that
hand the trick would have been too delicate and dexterous—though
assuredly not too pitiful and mean " (" Wordsworth and Byron," *Miscellanies*, p. 69).   E. H. Coleridge's copy of the *Letter* is now in the British
Museum.   It has pasted in it a letter, with the signature clipped off, specu-
lating on the authorship.   The knowledge of Edinburgh and of Scotch
literature shown in it ; the knowledge of German, and the good command
of the classics all point to John Black of the staff of the *Morning Chronicle*.
Mr. Coleridge's correspondent may have been Richard Garnett, who
contributed a note on the John Bull *Letter* to *The Athenæum* (1903, p. 304)
arriving at the same conclusion from the same, and similar, evidence.

naturally loved rough play "; and : " It is impossible
to express the surprise of Lord Strutt upon the receipt of
this Letter." The text begins with a discourse on humbug.
The writer contends that such people as William Bowles
(with whom Byron was in the midst of a controversy on the
merits of Pope's poetry) are unworthy of his powers.

Compare Lord Byron when he is describing a beautiful
woman, or when he is quizzing Southey or Sotheby with
Lord Byron when he is puffing old Samuel Rogers, the
banker, and pretending (what vile humbug!) to class him
among the great poets of England.

Byron well knows that Wordsworth with all his foibles has
put more genius into ten lines " than all the banker-poets
of Christendom " into all their works. But he knows also
that

the stamp-master is wrapped round in vanity . . . and
that the least touch of sarcasm . . . will probably put the
stamp-master's swaddling bands into such a flutter, that
he . . . shan't be able to compose himself for a single
" Mood of my Mind " during the rest of the season.

He reproves Byron for his attack on Coleridge, who gave
Byron " a great many very reasonable good puffs in prose,
both rhymed and unrhymed." [1]

Coleridge is naturally as clever a man as your Lordship, and
if he chose to give up his opium for a week . . . could avenge
himself abundantly, and give you, or any wicked wit in
Europe, a thrashing to your heart's content.

But Bowles ! . . .

Stick to *Don Juan :* it is the only sincere thing you have
ever written . . . written strongly, lasciviously, fiercely,
laughingly—everybody sees . . . that nobody could have
written it but a man of the first order both in genius and
dissipation. . . . Ten stanzas of it are worth all your
Manfred.

---

[1] To what can this refer ? Coleridge never " puffed " Byron.

" John Bull," in conclusion, urges Byron to bring Juan forthwith to England.

Byron read this *Letter* and wrote of it : " I have just read John Bull's Letter : it is diabolically well written, and full of fun and ferocity. I must forgive the dog, whoever he is." [1] Of all contemporary critics " John Bull " alone seems to me to fulfil Professor Elton's requirement concerning " the alert and mischievous sympathy, crossed with protest, which [Byron's satires] demand." [2]

I have now to note three plays founded on Byron's poem. The earliest of these is a melodrama entitled *The Sultana ; or a Trip to Turkey* (1822). The plot is a distortion of Byron's third, fourth and fifth cantos. It opens with Juan's being washed ashore after the shipwreck. The Haidée episode follows, ending with the return of Lombro. Juan is sold as a slave and is presently found in a Turkish seraglio. Haidée, however, did *not* die, and follows Juan disguised as a boy. (A hint was here evidently obtained from some of Byron's oriental tales.) The two lovers are at length happily reunited.

Don Juan. A Romantic Drama, in three acts, by J. B. Buckstone, was first performed at the Adelphi Theatre, December 1, 1828. It introduces Donna Julia ; the shipwreck ; the island (with Lombro and Haidée's death) ; the slave-market at Constantinople ; and the seraglio scene with Juan's rejection of Gulbeyaz's advances. Juan is rescued from the seraglio by the captain of an English ship ; and the play closes.

Buckstone wrote the words of *A New Don Juan !* a " burletta," the music of which was by G. H. Rodwell (1828). This comic opera was performed at the Adelphi. Act One is occupied with the Julia episode. Act Two opens with Haidée ; but the scene soon shifts to a London boarding-school for girls, whither Juan comes dressed as a girl and

---

[1] LJ, v, 315.

[2] *Survey*, ii, 180. A note following the title-page of the *Letter* states that it is the first of a series ; the second is to be to Campbell ; the third to the King ; " and the fourth also to Lord Byron." These later Letters were, however, never published.

where Pedrillo, who was not drowned, is an usher. It ends with Juan's marriage. There are numerous songs and dances. Rather clever use is made, where possible, of Byron's phraseology and dialogue.

A curious offshoot of Byron's poem, unlike anything that I have thus far described, is Alfred Thornton's *Don Juan* (1821), a book now much sought after by collectors because of its coloured plates. An advertisement at the commencement of this book declares that the adventures, intrigues, and fate of Don Juan have for nearly three centuries

been a fruitful source of instruction and delight. . . . In the midst of its recent attraction as a drama, a noble poet (Lord Byron) seized it as the theme of one of the most extraordinary poems ever written. . . . He has . . . done little more than demonstrate how far that interesting subject may be improved by making it the vehicle of amusement, blended with solid information, and uniting with the delight of romance the grave and important principles of morality.

The book is a sort of picaresque romance with touches of orientalism and gothicism ; the hero and his valet are taken through various countries and many licentious adventures, which are not rendered more tolerable by the thin veneer of " morality " spread over them. In telling of Juan's parentage and upbringing Thornton introduces many quotations from Byron's poem. A sequel, entitled *Don Juan. Volume the Second. Containing his Life in London,* appeared in 1822. Juan's adventures in the British metropolis give ample opportunity for satire upon English society : theatres, opera, gaming, boxing ; the military ; racing ; notorious resorts ; dog-and-monkey fighting, and so forth. The whole forms a vivid and repulsive view of regency life. In both Thornton's books the " Spanish tradition " of the character of the hero is followed much more closely than in Byron's poem.[1]

---

[1] Two works that are evidently offshoots of Byron's poem I have been unable to see. These are : (1) *The Italian Don Juan ; or Memoirs of the Devil.* Translated by H. M. Milner (1820). I know this only from an unidentified two-line newspaper clipping in the B. M. scrap-book, vol. i.

I close this chapter with the remarkably favourable estimate of *Don Juan* contained in the anonymous *Byroniana Bozzies and Piozzies* (1825) :

Don Juan, though it embraces every variety of poetry, from the sublime to the ridiculous, may be classed as the finest sample of comic poetry ever produced. The gems of a luxuriant fancy, brilliant thoughts, quaint conceits, shrewd remarks, and curious and droll reflections . . . will . . . be its passport to the eyes of posterity, and to a place on the same shelf with *Gil Blas, Tom Jones, Henry IV,* etc., which inimitable productions still continue to be read with pleasure and improvement by people of every rank, sex, and age, notwithstanding the too ample mixture of licentiousness.

Milner was a profuse theatrical writer and adapter (see Bibliography). I greatly doubt whether there was any Italian original from which he " translated." The book is probably a hoax. (2) *The British Don Juan.* By Henry Coates (1823). This I know from Ashbee's *Index Librorum Prohibitorum,* p. 140 f. The outline there given is indicative of the scabrous nature of the book.

CHAPTER V

THE CONTINUATIONS OF *DON JUAN*

NEITHER the sensation that the publication of *Don Juan* caused, nor the storm of abuse that greeted it, nor the approval that it won from the great contemporaries of Byron who were not blinded by prejudice to its merits, is the reason why at the beginning of the last chapter I spoke of the poem's "strange history." Trailing on behind its great fame, both in the intervals between the appearance of instalments and after *Don Juan* had been left a gigantic torso, came a crowd of imitations and "Continuations" without parallel, it is safe to say, in the history of literature. Such continuations are a fairly frequent phenomenon in literature ; some are efforts to complete an unfinished work ; others are sequels to works that, though complete in themselves, bear continuing. The attempts to complete Schiller's *Demetrius* [1] belong to the first order ; the sequels to *Le Misanthrope*,[2] portraying the later fortunes of Alceste, belong to the second. To place among their peers the long series with which we are concerned in this chapter I may remind my readers of a few of the more noteworthy examples of this sort of thing, limiting my instances, however, to English literature.[3]

---

[1] For the continuations of *Demetrius* by Franz von Maltitz and Gustav Kuhne, see *Demetrius, Schiller's Fragment, für die Buhne bearbeitet und fortgefuhrt, nebst einer litterar-historichen Abhandlung.* Von O. F. Gruppe. Berlin : Albert Bach, 1861.

[2] *La Conversion d'Alceste* by Georges Courteline (a pseudonym for Georges Moinaux) was performed at the Comédie française, January 15, 1905, as an after-piece to *Le Misanthrope*. This graceful little play may be found in the *Théatre de George Courteline* (ed. Flammarion), ii, 27 f. It is also in the edition of *Le Misanthrope* published by Edouard Pelletan, 1907.

[3] Digression is of the very essence of Byron's poem, and at the outset

To one who knows *The Canterbury Tales* well the experience is not without charm of coming for the first time upon *The Tale of Beryn*, in the prologue to which an anonymous follower of Chaucer tells with some liveliness of the fortunes of some of the pilgrims after their arrival at Canterbury. Lydgate [1] and Henryson [2] are among the poets who have attempted to carry on Chaucer's stories ; and Spenser himself was reluctant to let remain

> half told
> The story of Cambuscan bold.[3]

A delightful example of this kind of literary exercise is Fletcher's *Woman's Prize*, in which Shakespeare's Petruchio, after the death of Katherine, meets his match in a second

of my chapter I am tempted to digress. If one looked beyond English literature many interesting examples of such continuations could be cited. The *Roman de la Rose* and A. F. de Avellaneda's sequel to *Don Quixote* occur to mind. The most illustrious example of such sequels, and perhaps the only one where the sequel is more famous than the original work, is of course the *Orlando Furioso* which continues the *Orlando Innamorato*. Boiardo's high-hearted and chivalric poem was interrupted by the coming of the French into Italy—

> Mentre che io canto, o Dio redentore,
> Vedo l'Italia tutta a fiamma e foco
> Per questi Galli—

and in a very different mood Ariosto takes up the tale. Even within the limits of English literature far more examples might be cited than those I have mentioned in my text. For instance : a forged second part of *Hudibras* appeared in 1663 which Butler denounced in his genuine second part (Canto iii, line 1001 and annotations). There is also Joseph Peart's *Continuation of Hudibras* (1778) which has to do with the American Revolution ; and *The Modern Hudibras* (1831). The fact that John Bunyan had himself promised a third part to his masterpiece and had left that promise unfulfilled opened the way to continuators. As late as 1827 we have Joseph Ivimey's *Pilgrims of the Nineteenth Century ; a Continuation of The Pilgrim's Progress, upon the plan projected by Mr. Bunyan : comprising the History of a Visit to the Town of Toleration : with an Account of its Charter and a Description of the Principles and Customs of its Inhabitants, under the Similitude of a Dream.* And as late as 1911 there appeared *The Story of Matthew and Mary. Being a Third Part to Bunyan's Pilgrim's Progress.* By the Rev. James E. Walker.
[1] Such, at least, was my impression, but I do not find any such poem in a hasty glance through Lydgate. In place of him I may offer *The Tale of Gamelyn* and the two versions of *The Ploughman's Tale* (the one Lollard, the other perhaps by Occleve), which are attempts to fill in the incomplete cycle of the *Canterbury Tales*.
[2] *The Testament of Cresseid.*
[3] *The Faerie Queen*, Book IV, Cantos ii and iii. In 1630 John Lane published a continuation of *The Squire's Tale ;* and two hundred years later Leigh Hunt thought of writing a conclusion to it, but did not.

wife. Continuations of Shakespeare are, however, rare. Kenrick's *Falstaff's Wedding* and Renan's *Caliban* (together with the continuation of *Caliban* entitled *L'Eau de Jouvence*) occur to me. Samuel Richardson was much annoyed by the continuator who carried his Pamela into "high life," and, at the suggestion of Warburton, continued his book in competition with his anonymous imitator. Richardson himself enumerated some sixteen continuations of his novel. Fielding's *Joseph Andrews* was begun as a parodying supplement to *Pamela*. He was a wiser man than the stationer-novelist, and therefore, not taking himself so seriously, seems not to have been much bothered by the anonymous sequel to *Tom Jones* entitled *Tom Jones the Foundling, in his Married State*. Thackeray's charming burlesque, *Rebecca and Rowena*, is a continuation of *Ivanhoe*. Martin Tupper's *Geraldine*, a sequel to Coleridge's *Christabel*, is the boldest and most forlorn of all such efforts save possibly an attempt to complete *Kubla Khan* which I once saw in manuscript. G. W. M. Reynolds, one of the continuators of *Don Juan*, wrote a *Pickwick Abroad;* Henry Morford, another continuator of Byron's poem, was the author of *John Jasper's Secret*, one of the many attempts to complete *The Mystery of Edwin Drood*.

To such essays in ingenuity the great fragment of *Don Juan* lent itself well ; its fame and its incompleteness joined to make it a fit subject for speculation as to how the poet planned to finish his tale. The number of attempts to carry it on or round it off is extraordinarily large, and these waifs and strays are not without interest to the explorer in the bypaths of letters.[1]

Whether Byron ever had, even at the commencement of

[1] Before my article upon which this chapter is based had been published, there were two accounts of these Continuations : (1) " Ueber einige Fortsetzungen von Byrons Don Juan " by Hans Raab (*Byroniana und Anderes*, Erlangen, 1912), which notes seven items and describes four ; and (2) "The Rest of *Don Juan*," by H. S. Ashbee (*The Bibliographer*, iv, July 1883, pp. 25 f.), which is more meagre than Raab's article. I cannot hope that my list is exhaustive—Professor W. E. Leonard (*Byron and Byronism in America*, p. 65, note 1) mentions one version that exists in manuscript, and there are quite possibly more—but at any rate it is more than four times as long as Raab's.

his poem, any definite idea of burlesquing the Spanish legend of Don Juan is an open question. Wanting a hero, he takes

> our ancient friend Don Juan—
> We all have seen him, in the pantomime,
> Sent to the Devil somewhat ere his time.[1]

But as the poem grew under his hand into the great satiric picture of modern society that it is, this purpose of parody, if it ever existed, disappeared. " You ask me for the plan of Donny Johnny," he writes to Murray.[2] " I *have* no plan. . . . Do you suppose that I could have any intention but to giggle and make giggle ? " Gradually, however, his design shaped itself somewhat. In a later letter [3] he is quite explicit :

The fifth canto is so far from being the last of *Don Juan* that it is hardly the beginning. I meant to take him a tour of Europe, with a proper mixture of siege, battle and adventure, and to make him finish like Anacharsis Cloots in the French Revolution. . . . I meant to have made him a *Cavalier Servente* in Italy, and a cause for a divorce in England, and a sentimental " Werther-faced man " in Germany. . . . But I had not quite fixed whether to make him end in Hell, or in an unhappy marriage, not knowing which would be the severest. The Spanish tradition says Hell : but it is probably only an Allegory of the other state.

Byron told Medwin that he thought of introducing a scene of the plague, and that he planned that Leila was to be in love with Juan and he not with her. " He shall get into all sorts of scrapes, and at length end his career in France. Poor Juan shall be guillotined in the French Revolution."

---

[1] In a note on this passage (i, 1) E. H. Coleridge says that the pantomime referred to is Delpini's, founded on Shadwell's play, *The Libertine*. Gendarme de Bévotte, however (p. 351), our chief authority, states that this pantomime is directly from the Spanish. Byron may have been present at some performance in Italy of Mozart's *Don Giovanni*. Fitzmaurice-Kelly sees in Byron's " lady-killer of the regency " no connection with Juan Tenorio, nor does Swinburne ; but Gendarme de Bévotte devotes a chapter of his monograph to Byron's poem. Byron claims that he himself

> and several now at Seville
> *Saw* Juan's last elopement with the devil.

[2] LJ, iv, 342.   [3] *Ibid.*, v, 242 f.

The poem itself contains but few indications as to the probable future conduct of the story. Towards the end of the first canto Byron outlines his programme of love, war, wreck, " a panoramic view of hell," and so forth, all to be comprised in twelve books. This number is later increased to twenty-four, and finally he declares that " the first twelve books are merely flourishes " and that he proposes to " canter gently through a hundred." He had already written to poor Murray : [1] " Since you want *length*, you shall have enough of Juan, for I'll make fifty cantos." In Cephalonia, in October 1823, he told Dr. Henry Muir that he would write at least a hundred cantos.[2] On the way to Greece in the same year he had remarked that if the coming adventures were of a serious cast they should be material for a fifth canto of *Childe Harold ;* if comic, they should go into *Don Juan.* It would seem, however, that except for the few stanzas beginning the seventeenth canto, which were first published in 1905, he put *Don Juan* aside during the last phase of his life. At least, in a letter to Thomas Moore of March 4, 1824,[3] he contradicts newspaper rumours that he is engaged on a further instalment of the poem. Several continuators took advantage of such rumours, and stated that the poem which now appeared was from a manuscript in the possession of Thomas Medwin or of the Countess Guiccioli. Many years later, La Guiccioli categorically accused Moore of having destroyed five genuine cantos of *Don Juan :* [4]

---

[1] LJ, iv, 284.   [2] *Ibid.*, vi, 429.   [3] *Ibid.*, vi, 336.

[4] *My Recollections of Lord Byron*, p. 39, note. The rumour that La Guiccioli possessed two genuine cantos continuing *Don Juan* reached George Meredith in 1864 (see Meredith's *Letters*, i, 165). It reappeared, as we shall see later in this chapter, in 1880. According to another rumour that occurs from time to time, Byron's papers, after his death, passed, in part at least, into the hands of a Greek, who lost them in a retreat before a Turkish force. When the Countess Guiccioli died in 1873 she left directions in her will that the papers of Lord Byron in her possession were to be published fifty years after her death. The year 1923 has come, however, without bringing these papers to light. Whether she possessed any further cantos of *Don Juan* is exceedingly doubtful, especially in view of her statement quoted in my text ; but among her documents there must have been many interesting letters. It is a curious fact that although Byron passed nearly eight years in Italy, no letters written in Italian are included in the collected edition of the Letters and Journals. Yet there must still be many such in existence. Where are they ?

During his stay in the Ionian Islands, Missolonghi, he wrote five cantos of *Don Juan.* The scene of the cantos that followed was laid first in England and then in Greece. The places chosen for the action naturally rendered these last cantos the most interesting, and, besides, they explained a host of things quite justifying them. They were taken to England with Lord Byron's other papers ; but there they were probably considered not sufficiently respectful toward England, on which they formed a sort of satire too out-spoken with regard to living personages, and doubtless it was deemed an act of patriotism to destroy them. And so the world was deprived of them.

After this lengthy introduction we come to the spurious continuations. The earliest group of sequels appeared after Byron's first two cantos. Samuel Rogers wrote to him in 1820 urging him to give further instalments to the world, adding : " In the meantime a forgery or two is issuing from the press to gratify the most impatient." These hoaxes brought from Byron an imperious protest to Murray : [1] " You should not let those fellows publish false *Don Juans.*" Some of my readers may need to be reminded that at the close of Byron's second canto his hero, shipwrecked on one of the Isles of Greece, is found and ministered to by Haidée, the beautiful daughter of a pirate living there. At this point the continuators began their work, in sad contrast to Byron's wonderful third canto, which contains the account of the banquet at which Lombro, the pirate, discovers his daughter and Juan, with Haidée's death and Juan's departure from the island. That canto Coleridge selected as the summit of Byron's work. It is made immortal by the presence of the lyric " The Isles of Greece " and of the stanzas on the *Ave Maria.* . . . How did the parasites on Byron's fame try to anticipate his conduct of the tale ? [2]

(1) *Don Juan. Canto the Third* (London : William

---

[1] LJ, iv, 369–70.
[2] Reluctantly, for the sake of clearness, I have decided to set down my list of the Continuations numerically in the dry form of a catalogue. I should have preferred to group them according to methods of treatment and subject-matter. The chronological order, however, has obvious advantages.

Hone, 1819). This version is almost certainly by Hone himself.[1] After four opening stanzas of abuse directed against " Drab John " (*i.e.* John Murray) stanza v takes up the narrative. Juan, after many wanderings, comes to London to earn his living and to support his large family, for he has married Haidée, who has regularly borne him twins for six successive years. He considers the advantages of the law and the church, but decides upon politics, which he plans to enter through a career in journalism. This gives Hone the opportunity for a satiric digression upon various magazines. Juan becomes a radical journalist. Hone's tone becomes intensely serious in the stanza in which he sketches the political and social situation :

> It was the time when England's robe was rent,
> And famine's curse was blistering on her tongue ;
> When through her every limb strange shiverings went,
> And suffering held her every nerve unstrung ;
> When passion vainly strove to find a vent,
> When helplessly her maniac arms were flung
> To Heaven, and Heaven allowed unscathed to go
> The monsters who had wrought such utter woe.[2]

Juan starts a newspaper called " The Devilled Biscuit " which he advertises in an unusual way, namely, by singing the contents of each number to the passing throngs in the London streets, to the accompaniment of his guitar. He attends a political meeting and gives a report of the various speeches delivered there, including one by J. C. Hobhouse.[3] He is arrested and brought before the magistrate on the charge of treasonable practices. The examination is lively, and in the end bail is refused and Juan is taken to gaol. The author closes his poem with the hope that if the police

---

[1] It is ascribed to him in the *D. N. B.* and in the catalogues of the British Museum and the Harvard Library.

[2] The reference is evidently to the terrible suffering and social unrest of the years immediately succeeding Napoleon's overthrow ; and it seems to comport ill with the chronology of the genuine poem till we remember that it is not until Byron's seventh canto, which narrates Juan's adventures at the siege of Ismail, that the period of *Don Juan* is established as that of the French Revolution.

[3] This interesting, if unpretentious, survival of the satiric method of the *Satire Ménippée* is noteworthy.

spare this canto a fourth may soon appear. It is obvious that his central theme—the fortunes and misfortunes of radical journalists—is based upon Hone's own personal experiences, the shafts of satire being directed against his persecuting Tory opponents.[1]

(2) *A New Canto* (London : William Wright, 1819). The planlessness of Byron's thirteenth canto is here anticipated ; Juan's adventures are postponed to a future instalment ; and this canto is chiefly occupied with an account of Doomsday and of how it will affect various personages. This theme gives an opportunity for heterogeneous satire of a very stupid kind.

(3) *Don Juan. Canto XI* (London : Sherwood, Neely and Jones, 1820). In a foreword the author quotes Horace—

> Pictoribus atque poetis
> Quidlibet *audendi* semper fuit aequa potestas—

in justification of his leap from canto ii to canto xi. At the point where he takes up the story Juan has rejoined Donna Julia, and the pair have become desperate criminals. During their wanderings through Switzerland the overwhelming of a village by an avalanche suggests to Juan the indubitable and unavoidable nature of the punishment that awaits his lost soul. Later they approach Rome, which is described with much Byronish rhetoric. Juan moralizes on " man, lordly man, the being of a day." He and Julia sit by the seashore and presently witness a shipwreck, the ship taking fire and blowing up when the powder-magazine aboard explodes. There follows a dismal, lurid description of the sea giving up its dead at the Last Judgment. Juan, in the hardness of his heart, smiles at the ghastly wreck, when suddenly a woman's form is cast upon the shore. It is Haidée, who " muttered ' Juan ' in her agony." She dies, praying that Juan may be forgiven, though, betrayed and deserted by him, she had fled from her father and her home.

---

[1] There is also some literary satire, directed against the Lake Poets. Hackwood, strange to say, makes no mention of this continuation, which, though of no poetic value, is of some interest as a protest against the conditions which were leading on to the " massacre of Peterloo."

This dreadful consequence of his evil life shakes Juan's self-confidence :

> How doubly dreadful death such love to sever !
> And shall they never, never meet again ?   Oh ! never.

Immediately after, Juan is struck by lightning. Julia, who had been converted to atheism by Juan,[1] mourns over him ; and Juan, who, despite the fact that he has been struck by lightning, does not die for a whole day, rebukes her lawless passion, contrasts her probable fate in the next world with that of the innocent Haidée, affirms his belief in God and eternal punishment, and confesses his sins to a priest who by chance passes by. Julia goes mad and leaps to her death from a crag.

> " Then all is o'er," said Juan, as he gaz'd :
> He gasped—he gnaw'd the sand in agonies.
> Sudden the friar started, for earth blaz'd ;
> And dark clouds roll'd, and deadly-glaring eyes
> Shot forth on Juan ; laughter rent the skies
> Whilst yawn'd the ground, and down the body sunk,
> Fathomless, hell-deep, and * * * * * *

Thus, with a row of asterisks, the piece ends.[2]   Its grotesque extravagance makes one suspect that beneath the obvious moralizing there is a feebly burlesque intention ; but of this one cannot be sure, remembering that this is a product of the age that took seriously *The Monk* and *Bertram*. Such noisome weeds grow among the fine flowers of romantic unrestraint.

(4) *Don Juan. Canto III* (London :   R. Greenlaw, 1821).   The writer of this hoax hits upon something like the development of the story that Byron himself contrived. Juan and Haidée, left sleeping side by side at the close of Byron's second canto, are awakened by approaching footsteps. Haidée leaves hastily. Her father enters and grapples with Juan.   Juan strangles him, throws his body over a cliff, and hides again in the cave, which hunger at

[1] At this point there is a long digression on the close relation of chastity to the other virtues in women.
[2] The stanza employed is the Spenserian, in which respect the thing is unique among the sequels.

length forces him to quit. He is captured by Greek pirates and forced to board their ship. Presently they are attacked by another vessel, and a sea-fight follows that is described at tedious length. Juan falls out of a port-hole and manages to climb aboard the other ship, which proves to be Spanish. The pirates are vanquished, and Juan proceeds with his countrymen to Venice. The canto closes with the promise that the next instalment shall be devoted to Juan's adventures there.[1]

(5) *Don Juan. Cantos IX, X, and XI* (Albany, N.Y., 1823). This continuation is ascribed to Isaac Star Clason in Cushing's *Anonyms* (under " Don Juan "). I have been unable to discover a copy, despite careful inquiry. It is apparently different from the continuation by Clason described later in this chapter.

No more " false *Don Juans* " appeared until after Byron's death. The last canto of the genuine poem tells of a house-party at Norman Abbey, at which Juan, who has been for some time in England, is a guest. One night Juan follows down a corridor a figure which he takes to be a ghost but which turns out to be his fellow-guest, the Duchess of Fitz-Fulke. With his recognition of her *Don Juan* comes to an abrupt conclusion. This risqué and dramatic ending gave ample scope to the imagination of continuators. Earlier cantos afforded them a few hints as to how the story was to be conducted. The eleventh ends with speculations as to whether Juan would marry or be " taken in for damages " ; the twelfth with the remark that his good looks were bound to expose him to the temptations of London society. It is evident that Juan's Turkish ward, the little Leila, was not brought to England for nothing ; Byron is himself anxious as to the fate of Juan's hostess at Norman Abbey, the Lady Adeline ; [2] in later cantos Aurora Raby was evidently to become a character of importance ; about the fate of " her frolic grace Fitz-Fulke " there can,

---

[1] This is one of the longest cantos of all the continuations, extending to 204 stanzas.

[2] *Don Juan*, xiv, 99.

I fear, be little doubt. The hordes of imitators, though some of them " reform " Juan, never once strike what is obviously the most likely fashion in which Byron might have completed his poem, and which has been well summarized by Roden Noel : [1]

Yet would not the poet have concluded it, had he survived the liberation of Greece, with the hero's devotion of himself to the cause of human emancipation, after having exhausted self-seeking experience, and found the mere pursuit of personal pleasure unsatisfying to the truer self ? That, at least, was the history of his own career, and he is reflected faithfully in his work.

But, leaving such speculations, we must return to the continuators.

(6) *Continuation of Don Juan. Cantos XVII and XVIII* (London : Whittaker ; Oxford : Munday and Slater, 1825).[2] A short advertisement at the beginning summarizes the poem to the point where Byron left off. Canto xvii opens with a long elegy on Byron : his virtues ; his heroic death ; his defects, among which the choice of the theme of *Don Juan* bulks large. The writer declares that he does not feel bound, in carrying on the poem, to follow out what " the poet *meant* to do." His cautious procedure is at once apparent, for, we read, when Juan discovered that the duchess had played a practical joke on him he wisely retreated and " saved his character and went to bed." At breakfast the next morning her Grace cuts Juan dead ; he is further distracted by being placed at table next to the bewitching Aurora Raby. A letter is brought to him, on reading which he bursts into tears. In canto xviii we learn that this letter bears tidings of the death of his mother. Juan is remorseful because of his long absence from home. A long digression follows on the advantages of home, accompanied by advice

---

[1] *Life of Lord Byron*, p. 139.

[2] Though dated 1825, this book was really published in 1824. The character of the advertisements bound in, and a reference or two in the text, point to some Oxford student as the author. A review in *The Literary Gazette*, November 27, 1824, p. 755, states that the author is " a young Collegian."

to Englishmen to travel through their own country and enjoy
its charms before venturing abroad. That evening, when
nearly all the company are away at a dinner, Juan wanders
disconsolately in the garden. He hears some one singing
sweetly ; the lyric is given, but it is a very mediocre one and
I shall not quote it. The voice is Aurora Raby's ; and
hearing her, Juan's determination to return to Spain to
visit his mother's grave weakens. He goes to bed, but not
to sleep. In the middle of the night he is roused by a tumult,
and finds that Norman Abbey is on fire. All the inmates
escape safely except Aurora. Juan rushes back into the
burning building and finds her in her oratory on her knees,
for she has abandoned hope. He carries her to " th'
embattled walls," some twenty feet above the lake, for the
fire now prevents escape through the building. He jumps
into the lake with his fair burden, and bears " his drooping
charge uninjured to the shore." Thus the book ends. It
is an unsophisticated juvenile production, but not un-
pleasantly written.

(7) *Don Juan. Cantos XVII, XVIII* (London : Duncombe, 1825).[1] In striking contrast to the simple decency
of the poem I have just described, there is in this piece an
evident ambition to outdo the opening canto of Byron's poem
in outrageousness. It begins with a passage in praise of
intrigue. Juan engages in a brief amour with the duchess,
which is observed by her scandal-spreading waiting-woman.
In canto xviii the same mischief-maker overhears Juan
talking to his hostess, the Lady Adeline, and reports the
conversation to Lord Henry Amundeville, the lady's
husband. He surprises Juan and his wife in the midst of
an entirely innocent conversation, and manages to make
a considerable fool of himself. He offers to send his incon-
venient guest on a mission to Scotland ; Juan accepts
the offer, and with an account of the journey the book
closes. Throughout both cantos the narrative is constantly

---

[1] This version sometimes follows *Don Juan* in the 1823 issue of the
genuine poem, " with a preface by a clergyman," to which reference was
made in my fourth chapter. See p. 38, *ante*, note 1.

interrupted by digressions—in the approved Byronic fashion
—on scandal and political economy ; architecture and the
improvements in personal comforts effected by modern
inventions ; travel, immortality, blasphemy, blue-stockings,
critics, and many other quite unrelated matters, all in a
very dull fashion indeed.

(8) *Don Juan. Cantos XVII–XVIII* (New York :
Charles Wiley, 1825). This continuation is, I believe, by
I. S. Clason.[1] Unlike most of the sequels, it is a deliberate
hoax, purporting to be by Lord Byron. The most noteworthy thing in it is the opening statement as to the function
of *Don Juan* to pluck the scales from men's eyes and make
them see clearly and without cant. The story deals with
Juan's liaison with the duchess ; the inopportune arrival
of the ugly old Duke of Fitz-Fulke ; his jealous suspicions
of his spouse ; and the confirmation of those suspicions
by the revelations of a waiting-woman who had herself
loved Juan. The customary digressions are provided : on
Napoleon, love, marriage, the vanity of human wishes, and
so forth.

(9) *Juan Secundus. Canto the First* (London : John
Miller, 1825). As in the *New Canto* of 1819, there is no plot
to this piece. It contains many literary and personal
allusions of some interest, including a long review of the
poets of the age. From Campbell " the purest rays of
literature have shone." Byron was " the God of poesy."
Scott was

> The first to change the Author's desert way
> To all that's fair, from what was desolate—

whatever that may mean. There is praise for " modest
Rogers " ; but—

> Wordsworth, thou'rt the oddest of all codgers !

The writer has " a high opinion " of Milman ; but Southey—
" no, I don't like Southey." Tom Moore is his favourite.

---

[1] It seems to be the version referred to in Sabin's *Dictionary of Books
relating to America* (iv, 134) as by Clason.

This review finished, he apologizes to the ladies for the dryness of his subject.

> I have another canto, which I *guess*
> (As Mathews says) will come out by and by,
> More suited to your taste ; this, I confess,
> Is rather stupid, common-place, and dry—
> A sort of hodge-podge, which I can't express,
> But who the Devil cares for that ? not I ;
> I write just as I think, and never mind
> What's coming after, or what's left behind.

He promises to sing of heroes, mathematicians, authors, politicians, judges, divines, debutantes, and barristers.[1] For the present, however, he thinks that eighty stanzas are enough.

(10) *Don Giovanni. A Poem : in two cantos* (Edinburgh : Edward West, 1825). This piece, which is the first of a number of poems in the same volume, is not precisely a continuation of Byron's *Don Juan ;* but it is sufficiently close to being one to be included in this catalogue.[2] It begins : " A subject and a hero—both I want." The writer chooses a relation of " that wicked dear Don Juan," namely, the original Don Giovanni whom devils could not tolerate in hell and therefore sent back to earth. " And here he's come to cool himself in Scotland." In the sequel we hear very little of Giovanni and much of Scotland.[3] Giovanni had visited Drury Lane ; this visit suggests the question, " Where's the great Siddons ? " which in turn suggests a long series of " Where's ? " on the disappearance of many people and things, imitated from a similar passage in *Don Juan.* At length the story, such as it is, begins. Giovanni met the heroine of the tale in Charlotte

---

[1] Apparently this programme for a future canto was not a mere conventionality borrowed from *Don Juan,* for bound with the British Museum copy of this piece there is another little work that contains among the advertisements at the end one of the second canto of *Juan Secundus.* Of this second canto I have been unable to find a copy anywhere.

[2] The title-poem is in two short cantos, the stanzaic form being *ababcc.*

[3] The writer remarks that it is a hard task to write upon this theme, especially when one is engaged upon some novels that will " cut Sir Walter out." This suggests a passage on Scott, whose style has grown monotonous and who is urging himself beyond his strength.

Square, Edinburgh ; it would take a Tom Moore to describe her.[1] Nevertheless a long account of her follows ; hence to women in general ; then to Scotch women ; and so to Scotland and the faults and charms of that country. Isabel, the heroine, pined for love and was sent for a change of air to " Love's own vale, Roslyn." In canto ii. Giovanni's name, for no apparent reason, has become Henri. He sees Isabel at Roslin. She dies there, and on her tomb is an inscription to the effect that she loved not wisely but too well. This is all, literally all, the story ; and it is quite as disconnected and incomprehensible as my account of it.

(11) *The Seventeenth Canto of Don Juan* (London : W. Wilson, 1829). This sequel is one of the most nearly successful of the series, though in the scandalous nature of the subject-matter it eclipses Byron. The canto is no less than 260 stanzas in length, and begins :

> We all have seen, or heard, or read, of late,
> A story somewhat amorous and witty,
> Concerning the adventures and estate
> Of a young Spaniard, noble, gay, and pretty :
> And tho' his birth 'tis needless to repeat,
> I cannot help esteeming it a pity
> A tale so well begun, so fair, and clever,
> Should hang thus lopp'd, as 'twere, and scant, for ever.

There follows presently an invocation to Xenophon, Thucydides, Plutarch, Goldsmith, Smollett, Gibbon, Hume, and Rollin. Then, lest the writer be guilty of giving offence, the " immediate consequences " of Juan's meeting with the duchess are skipped over. The story centres in a love-affair between Adeline and Juan, after his successful efforts to rid himself of Fitz-Fulke, which results in a duel with Lord Henry Amundeville. The digressions are chiefly upon the hypocritical sort of morality practised by

> this canting, croaking, preaching clan,
> Those strainers at a gnat, those camel bolters,

---

[1] This remark introduces praise of Moore :
> I'd make thee poet-laureate ; for Southey,
> Tho' bright at times, is in the long run *mouthey*.

The writer has the audacity to call this rhyme a " new coinage."

whose first commandment is " Thou shalt not know on earth felicity." From one of the notes we learn that the author was an Irishman. Throughout the poem there is very evident admiration for Byron's genius, and nowhere any sign of disapproval of the morality of *Don Juan*.[1]

(12) The title-page of ι, volume of miscellaneous poems containing " Don Juan in Search of a Wife " is missing in the copy in the British Museum ; I have not seen any other copy.[2] The poem is written in the metre of *Venus and Adonis*, the less difficult approximation to *ottava rima* already adopted in *Don Giovanni* and by Halleck in *Fanny*. It is not narrative, but an expression of juvenile opinions on marriage and politics in satirical vein.

(13) " Stanzas in Continuation of *Don Juan* " are included in the volume *Rodolph : A Dramatic Fragment . . . and other Poems*. By a Minor (1832).[3] There is very little about Juan in this pathetically poor effort ; two lines will indicate the quality of the piece. At the close of a love-scene between Juan and the duchess—

> Whispering good-night, the fair one gently heaves
> Her sleeping lover from his pillow'd bliss.

There are hints of coming rivalry with Aurora—and that is all the story. A tribute to Byron comes at the beginning, with hopes expressed that he is reformed and happy in heaven ; and at the close there are two stanzas (in anapæstic lines) about Thomas Moore, " on whose loved page my lonely spirit dotes." I have read a good deal of poor verse in my time, but nothing more hopeless than this Minor's productions.

---

[1] At the close of a modestly expressed preface the author says : " I shall console myself with the consideration that some credit at least is due to the individual who can support even the character of Harlequin with success." Such consolation as it is, it may be granted him.

[2] The first canto of the title-poem is dated Oxford, 1825 ; the second, Rome, 1834. Therefore the conjectured date, 1830, in the catalogue of the British Museum cannot be correct.

[3] The title-piece, *Rodolph*, consists of two scenes in imitation of the opening of *Manfred*, with gothic " trappings," spirits, and so forth. The minor poems (in a volume where all are *minima*) are redolent of Byron. There is an " Ode on the Fall of Poland." A song begins : " The struggle's o'er, the spirit's free." (See also *N. & Q.* 3rd Series, ii, 229 ; 4th Series, i, 267.)

(14) *Canto XVII of Don Juan. By one who desires to be a Very Great Unknown* (London : James Gilbert, 1832). A frontispiece, crudely done, shows two lamps, labelled Partiality and Prejudice, burning before a pile of volumes the titles of which are : Medwin, Parry, Galt, Moore, Hunt, and Reviews. The writer describes himself as a " mere disciple " of Byron who will undertake to complete *Don Juan*. He tells vaguely of the conclusion of the Fitz-Fulke episode ; of Adeline's warnings to Aurora Raby to beware of the Spanish guest, of the duchess's jealousy of Aurora, and of the earlier stages of a love-affair between that young lady and Juan. The piece is unusually direct in narrative with comparatively few of the customary satirical digressions.[1]

(15) The next continuation belongs to about the year 1833. According to H. S. Ashbee, writing in 1883, " about fifty years ago " Charles Hervé, the painter of a miniature portrait of Byron as a youth, wrote in collaboration with his son, Charles Stanley Hervé, a conclusion to Byron's poem entitled *Don Juan Married*. This was in six cantos. The Hervés claimed that the first two cantos were based on information given them by Byron's valet Fletcher as to what Byron intended, " for it is affirmed that cantos xvii and xviii were written by Byron, read by Fletcher, and suppressed by Byron's executors." This continuation I have not seen ; nor, apparently, had Ashbee.

(16) Internal evidence places the next sequel [2] between 1834 and 1847. Of this piece but one copy is known to exist. That is in the library of the English Seminar at Erlangen, and is the second volume only, without any title-page. The missing first volume contained cantos xvii-xx ; volume two

---

[1] In an amusing review, *Fraser's Magazine* (vii, June 1833, 658) says of this piece : " It is idle to criticise trash so utterly helpless." The author is described as " a person who is totally devoid of poetic talent, information, humour, [and] ordinary command of the tongue in which he writes." The reviewer quotes several specimen stanzas, with the intercalated refrain : " O cockney, cockney ! "

[2] For an account of this continuation I am indebted to Raab's monograph mentioned above. In the Erlangen copy there is inserted a clipping from an old book-catalogue, which gives John Clark of Bridgewater as the author's name and states that the poem " was privately printed by the author and never published."

begins with canto xxi. Juan is there discovered in a fortress
in the Pyrenees ; an agent of the Inquisition orders that he
be taken to Rome for trial on a charge of heresy. Juan,
through a series of comical adventures, escapes from the
ship and manages to reach his native town of Seville. Not
feeling safe there from persecution, he returns to England
and pays a second visit to Norman Abbey during a house-
party at which the same visitors as on the former occasion
are assembled. Thence he goes to Paris, arriving at the height
of the Reign of Terror. He becomes involved in an attempt
to rescue the Dauphin ; is arrested, tried, and executed ;
and a rich Jewish friend obtains burial for his body. The
author has thus followed hints afforded by Byron's letters
and by Medwin. The narrative is intermingled with
philosophical speculations of a rationalistic variety.

(17) An anonymous volume entitled *Georgian Revelations*
(1838) contains, among other things, " Twenty Suppressed
Stanzas of *Don Juan* " which, the title-page states, are
" From a Manuscript in the possession of Captain Medwin,
warranted genuine." They are without doubt an impudent
forgery. The Irish problem, a theme often touched on in
the continuations, forms the entire subject of these stanzas.
They resume some incidents of Irish history together with
some ecclesiastical legends of Irish saints and various com-
plimentary allusions to Irish characteristics—all in an utterly
un-Byronic manner.[1]

(18) *Don Juan Junior : A Poem by Byron's Ghost.*
Edited by G. R. Wyther Baxter (1839). This piece contains much vague, confused, rambling satire on men and
manners. The tale is of a son of Byron's Juan.[2] He refuses
to marry a girl whom he has seduced, and she, dying, sends
him a lock of her hair. This affects him but momentarily,
for presently he goes to a ball where he sings a heartless
song about this love-affair. Scarcely is it finished when the

[1] These stanzas may possibly be by Charles Clark, at whose private press
at Totham, Essex, *Georgian Revelations* was printed. In 1845 the stanzas
were reprinted separately, with the title changed to *Some Rejected Stanzas
of Don Juan*, at the same press.
[2] Thus faintly anticipating Echegaray's *The Son of Don Juan*.

dead girl appears in a vision and upbraids her faithless lover. He faints, and the canto ends with some cynical comments on morality. The second canto opens with a long passage on the changes wrought by time, obviously imitated from a famous passage in the real *Don Juan*. This leads to the changes in the character of the elder Juan, who has become a " Catholic devotee," with pinched face and slovenly dress. He is still a bit too fond of the ladies, but is constantly doing penance for his sins and is absolutely under the thumb of his confessor. The character of this priest is drawn with some skill, and there is an amusing account of Juan's confession to him—really a review of the various amatory adventures recorded in Byron's poem. The course of Juan's life from the point where Byron left off is hinted at, particularly a liaison with Lady Adeline. The younger Juan is a chip of the old block ; the identity of his mother remains a mystery. This suggests the pity of indiscreet love, and a long passage follows on the " pity " of a great number of things, public and private, ending :

> Young Victoria ! lady of these isles !
> It's a pity you let that guzzling Melbourne
> Come shadowing so often.

Incoherent as most of this satire is, the piece is of unusual significance, for the character of the younger Juan, in its brutal, cynical faithlessness and egotism, is the nearest approach to the true Don Juan tradition that has appeared in England since Shadwell's *Libertine* and the Lovelace of Richardson.

(19) *Don Juan Reclaimed ; or His Peregrination continued from Lord Byron.* By W[illiam] C[owley] (1840). Byronism here appears in prim and prudish Early-Victorian garb. After his meeting with the duchess, Juan reforms and spends much of his time in prayer. The occupations of the house-party and the conversations in which they engage are set forth at quite intolerable length. On the Sabbath Juan goes to the Roman Catholic Church in his Russian coach, taking with him the duchess and Miss Raby. Juan's

conduct is invariably exemplary, a change which the poet ascribes to the elevating influence of virtuous female society. His habit is to rise early to view the beauties of nature; each morn he is more deeply impressed until finally, like the birds, he bursts into a spontaneous morning hymn—which I am, I am happy to say, under no obligation to quote. As a sample of this edifying production, the last stanza of all, describing Sunday after church, may be quoted :

> While dinner and dessert brief passed away,
> Though all were free, good humour'd, social, kind,
> Yet none appeared indiscreetly gay :
> Their topics of discourse shew'd them inclin'd
> To manifest a deference to the day,
> And tended to improvement of the mind,
> Till it was time their pillows should receive them,
> Where to delightful rest at present leave them.

Surely an interesting contemporary account of the kind of Sunday which, Ruskin said, spoiled for him three-sevenths of the week—Saturday by anticipation; Sunday itself; and Monday by remembrance.

(20) *The Rest of Don Juan.* By Henry Morford (New York, 1846).[1] This sequel is "inscribed to the Shade of Byron." A motto on the title-page gives the keynote : " If rough talk offend thee, we'll have very little of it." The poem is very long—645 stanzas divided into seven cantos. The digressions, save for a few allusions to American affairs, and some literary satire on Dickens, L. E. L., and a few other notables, are even more tedious than in most of the sequels. The first canto is introductory and tells of Byron's death, his grave, his sister's loyalty to him, and much else ; an elegy supposed to be sung by the Greeks is introduced. The story, setting aside the digressions, is summarily as follows. Juan's relations with the duchess and Lady Adeline get him into various troubles. Later he receives a command from the Empress Catherine to return to St. Petersburg. This order he obeys, accompanied by his Turkish ward,

---

[1] This book has escaped the wide drag-net of Professor W. E. Leonard's researches into Byronism in America.

Leila ; but on the way he is warned of dangers in Russia, and retracing his steps he goes to southern France. There he leaves Leila and returns to Paris in time to witness various scenes of the Revolution. He engages in a couple of love-affairs, and a cast-off sweetheart murders a wealthy woman whom he is about to marry. Disgusted with Paris, Juan goes to Seville, where he settles down to an easy, dissolute life until one night, at a banquet, a tall, dark stranger enters and beckons Juan away. The two depart together, while the lights burn blue and the guests smell brimstone. The next day Juan's body is found in a cemetery. For such a conclusion Morford found a hint in Byron's poem.

(21) *A Sequel to Don Juan.*[1] This piece has been ascribed to G. W. M. Reynolds, a writer of some little note in his day, though now forgotten. Except Morford's, it is the most elaborate of all the sequels. The book is embellished with a series of steel engravings in the style which we associate with old " annuals " like *The Keepsake* or *Friendship's Offering*. In his preface the author promises eleven more cantos, should they be called for, in order to bring his poem (which is in five cantos) to the same length as Lord Byron's. It would seem that there was no call for them. One can imagine Byron himself—that is, Byron at his worst morally and poetically—writing this sequel, for though vulgar and shoddy it does achieve something of the tone of *Don Juan*. The plot, which is complex, rather clever, and very repulsive, exaggerates the license of *Don Juan* into licentiousness. A new heroine, the governess of the little Turkish girl brought by Juan to England, appears. Juan is involved in a divorce suit, and later loses all his money. He then goes to Paris where he has various adventures in the Revolution and is thrown into prison. The method of his release, apparently borrowed from Voltaire's *L'Ingénu*, through the agency of a mysterious female, is sufficiently scabrous ; with that episode the

---

[1] This piece is undated. The catalogue of the British Museum queries " 1825 ? " but allusions in the text place it much later. *N. & Q.* 4th Series, i, 267, dates it 1842. I should place it nearer 1850. See also *N. & Q.* 3rd Series, ii, 439.

book ends. Throughout there are many digressions, chiefly
on politics. It is a violently Whig production, exhibiting
the Whig tradition of glorification of Napoleon, attacking
Peel's tariff reforms, and loudly praising modern education.
In lines that are the very essence of Philistinism it glorifies
the portion of society that came into power with the passage
of the Reform Bill :

> But if you look for virtue, seek it where
> The golden mean is found—the middle grade
> Of our society, with whom the care
> Exists of England's commerce and her trade.

Of literary satire there is little ; Dickens is roughly handled :

> Dickens full well, too, knows what humbug means,
> For he has built his fame upon that basis,
> By dint of sheer vulgarity.

An attempt is made to apologize for the license of the poem
on the ground that it is a " satire on abuses, not a eulogy on
vice." This excuse the author borrows from Byron ; but
the imitator is evidently disingenuous, whereas Byron was
profoundly sincere. Byron puts his pictures of moral abuses
into proper setting and proportion with other subjects of
satire ; in this sequel the emphasis is exclusive.

(22) In 1877 H. J. Daniel published the following statement : [1] " I wrote a seventeenth canto of *Don Juan* and
published it in London about twenty years ago. . . . I
believe that a few printed copies are still extant." This
description corresponds to no continuation that I have
seen. The piece must have appeared about 1857.

(23) " Don Juan. Canto Seventeenth." This appeared
in a volume of *Poems,* by Edward Wilberforce and Edmund
Blanchard (1857). This sequel is almost unique in quality,
for it possesses some real charm and can be read with
pleasure as well as with merely antiquarian interest. It
purports to have been written by Byron in the Elysian
Fields. Byron is there reconciled to Wordsworth and has
met the great poets of former times. The judgment pro-

---

[1] *N. & Q.* 5th Series, vii, 519.

nounced by the Greeks upon Thackeray, Dickens, and other
mid-nineteenth-century novelists is amusing. Byron thanks
Heaven that there are no women in Elysium. That pious
expression of gratitude leads by an easy transition to Juan.
Byron has been lectured by Milton on his immorality, and
has promised to reform his hero. He undertakes to bring
him to France in the period of the Revolution (Carlyle will
supply materials) and to arrange that he be beheaded by
the guillotine. With this outline of the future course of
the narrative the canto closes.

(24) *The Termination of the Sixteenth Canto of Lord
Byron's Don Juan.* By H. W. Wetton (1864). Alone
among the continuators Wetton stupidly fails to see that
Byron's sixteenth canto is complete, the artistic conclusion
coming with Juan's discovery of the duchess. The morning
after meeting with her, Juan takes a walk and encounters
a funeral, which gives rise to sober reflections. When he
returns to breakfast he finds that the Duke of Fitz-Fulke
has arrived at the Abbey. With some lamentable attempts
to reproduce table-talk, this poem, the poorest of the lot,
ends. The efforts at digression and satire are amazingly
feeble. Wetton assures us that should his readers despise
this first essay of his Muse,

> She will not grieve, as I have said before,
> But take the hint, and never trouble more.

Apparently she " took the hint," for no more appeared.

(25) *Don Juan. Canto XVII* (London : Thomas
Cooper, 1870). This version is made up in large part of
asterisks ; it might have been better if more such chaste
stars had taken the place of some of the stanzas printed.
The theme is the jealousy of the Lady Adeline and the
duchess, and the contrasting purity of Aurora Raby. There
are the usual desultory side-glances at literary, social, and
ethical matters.

(26) *Don Juan in Ireland.* By " Leon." This is
mentioned in *The Athenæum* of December 3, 1870 (p. 723),
as about to appear. I have been unable to discover a

copy ; nor do I know its connection, if it has any, with the suppressed forgery *Don Leon*, which I shall speak of in my chapter on the Byron Apocrypha.[1]

(27) *The Shade of Byron* (n.d. [1871]). There is very little plot to this sequel : the liaison with the duchess ; a breakfast scene the following morning ; a quarrel with Lord Henry ; and a duel. This thin story is strung out through six cantos, with many digressions on a great variety of subjects, especially Byron's character and career and various typically Byronic ideas. There are numerous allusions to the Byron-Stowe controversy.

(28) *The New Don Juan. The Introduction by Gerald Noel Byron, and the Last Canto of the Original Don Juan from the Papers of the Countess Guicciolli* [*sic*] (n.d. [1880]). This forgery, the whole of which was written by G. N. Byron, takes advantage of the long-current rumours, to which I have already referred, that the Countess Guiccioli had in her possession certain unpublished cantos of *Don Juan.* The narrative portion of the book tells how Juan's attentions to the Lady Caroline [*sic,* for Lady Adeline] involve him in a duel with Lord Henry in which Juan is slightly wounded. He is tenderly nursed by Aurora Raby, with whom he falls honourably in love. After some dispute with her guardian, the Lord Chancellor, they are married, and the canto ends with the departure of the happy pair for Spain.[2]

---

[1] The statement is occasionally met with that *Don Leon* is itself a continuation of *Don Juan*. This is erroneous. See, *e.g.*, *N. & Q.* 5th Series, viii, 59.

[2] The date, *c.* 1880, is fixed by an attack on the " apostate, titled Jew," Disraeli, and on England's friendship with the Turks. The " Introduction " is an attack, both generalized and specific, on modern civilization. Room may be found in this note for a specimen of this continuation at its best. Lord Henry speaks, kneeling mournfully at Juan's side, after wounding him in the duel :

> I had one thought—my honour and my pride,
> 'Twas all I cared for, and 'twas all I knew.
> I loved and cherished well my chosen bride,
> And doubted not that she at least was true.
> Nor did I dream such ill could e'er betide.
> The sin—my wrong—her crime was shared by you ;
> Yet had *your* bullet pierced my tortured brain,
> It were not wracked, as now, with endless pain.

(29) "Don Juan. Canto XVII," the last and best of the continuations, is included in a volume of poems, *To the End of the Trail*, by Richard Hovey (New York, 1908). It is certainly the most convincing reproduction of the spirit and movement of Byron's verse. It is supposed to be written by Byron in Hades, in this resembling the continuation by Wilberforce and Blanchard. Byron refuses to take up the poem at the point he had dropped it :

> Southey's forgotten ; so is Castlereagh ;
> But there are fools and scoundrels still to-day.

The satire refers to current topics : we hear nothing of Juan. The poet is full of curiosity as to events on earth :

> I've such a next day's thirst for information,
> I'd even be content to read *The Nation*.

On the whole, despite some scanty exceptions to the contrary, poverty of invention and servile imitation of Byron's mannerisms, with no ray of his genius, characterize the entire series of continuations. If Byron laughs at much upon which his contemporaries set store, it is in order that he may destroy abuses by ridicule ; his imitators laugh— or titter, or giggle, or snicker—simply because Byron laughed ; it is the thing to do in a poem of this kind. He digresses because he has much to say ; because his poem is a criticism of life. His imitators digress because he has set the fashion. Their divagations, even when not offensive, have not a particle of the psychological interest that Byron puts into his. They are never the products of a full mind following the train of thought wherever it may lead. Byron's lightning-like second-thoughts are reflected palely in their laboured and deliberate turnings from the point. The continuators chatter wearisomely, breaking the course of the story and contributing nothing in the way of observation and criticism of life. The contrast is quite as marked in the narrative portions of the sequels. Donna Julia, her bedroom and her letter ; Haidée, her innocent love and her

pathetic death ; politics and scandal ; the country mansion
and urban escapades ; adventures and misfortunes by land
and sea—all are imitated again and again in these faint, crude
copies of Byron's pictures of life. Except the sequels by
Wilberforce and Blanchard and by Hovey, not one merits
for its own sake even such feeble renewal of life as is given
it in this chapter. But they form part of the history of
Byron's fame—what torso in any literature rivals *Don
Juan* in the number of attempts made to complete it ?—and
have therefore been recorded here.

If the continuations of *Don Juan* are numerous, imitations
in the metre and manner of the poem are innumerable. I
shall not attempt an exhaustive catalogue of them, but
notes on a few will further illustrate the greatness of the fame
of Byron's masterpiece.

One of the earliest and most successful of these imitations,
though not in the exact metre of the original, was Fitz-
Greene Halleck's once famous poem, *Fanny* (1819), a satire
upon flashy New York society, with many digressions.
This piece is aptly characterized in the *Fables for Critics*.
Blackwood's, which assailed *Don Juan* so promptly and
fiercely, at once began to imitate it in *Daniel O'Rourke ;
An Epic Poem in Six Cantos, by Fogarty O'Fogarty, Esq., of
Blarney*. This ran through several numbers in 1820 and
1821. Leigh Hunt attempted to bolster up the failing
Liberal by two satires in the metre, and in feeble imitation
of the mood, of *Don Juan*. These are *The Dogs* and *The
Book of Beginners*.

During the eighteen-twenties John Moultrie wrote *Godiva*
and *Sir Launfal*, both closely imitated from *Don Juan*,
both turning well-known stories to a modern and satiric
purpose.[1] The long anonymous poem *Grafenstein* (1826)
is much in the manner of *Don Juan*, though the metre is
different. The narrative in it is weighed down with

---

[1] Moultrie's *Maimoune* and *The Witch of the North,* though written in
ottava rima, are more in the manner of Thomas Hood's graceful and half-
serious supernatural pieces. These poems, and those mentioned in my
text, are included in *Poems.* By John Moultrie (London : Macmillan,
1876), volume i.

digressions.[1]   J. R. Best repeatedly imitated Byron's poem. His *Cuma* (1831) is a Don-Juan-ish tale of Neapolitan passion, written in irregular stanzas.   *The Beggar's Coin* (also 1831),[2] in *ottava rima*, consists of two cantos and part of a third, on love, sentiment, travel (especially in Switzerland), and so forth, with numerous digressions, now serious, now burlesque.   Best's manner may be illustrated by the following stanzas :

> I choose this metre as the most compact,
> Pleasant to read, and suited by its rhyme
> To any part that I may wish to act,
> Whether the sentimental or sublime,

[1] Early in the poem there is a long tribute to Byron :

> Empty, alas ! remains poor Byron's chair,
> And all regret, but none replace him there.

Milk from the Muse's breast was mingled, the writer says, with the fatal poison of passion in him.   But if any foe, standing o'er Byron's corse, aims a blow at his memory, "The World, indignant, shall avenge the deed."

[2] In *Satires and The Beggar's Coin*.   By John Richard Best.   Best's " Modern Poetry.   A Satire " (pp. 89 f.) is of some interest as a contemporary view of the state of literature during the " interregnum " between the Romantic and the Victorian periods.   He repudiates the idea that this (the early eighteen-thirties) is not a poetic age.

> Not this the age for poetry, you say.
> Since when has closed that blissful age, I pray ?
> Surely, when Byron rose, full many a strain
> Asserted poetry's almighty reign ?

He calls the roll of " Moore, Campbell, Rogers, Coleridge and a host of minor spirits " ; and proceeds :

> Byron arose : o'ertopt the rest ; but still,
> Long as she sang, his Muse could ever thrill :
> The public ever owned her empire high
> And yielded up its soul to poesy.
> When Byron's Muse her glorious pinions furl'd
> The warm tears of a fascinated world
> Were shed in sympathy.

Best then well analyses the present state of poetry.   Metaphysics, sentiment, " colloquies sublime with prosy ghosts," and " pretty " books now distract the attention of poets.   If we consider Sir Henry Taylor and the early Browning, Tennyson's Margaret, Lilian and Adeline, L. E. L., *Festus*, and the simpering ringlet-adorned beauties of the " annuals," we shall see that this is a fairly accurate diagnosis of the case.

The same volume contains (pp. 159 f.) a prose dissertation on " The Infidelity and Catholicism of Lord Byron," which was prompted by Scott's remark that had Byron lived he would have become a Roman Catholic. Best reviews Byron's expressed opinions on religion ; considers that his *feelings* were religious, his *reason* anti-Christian ; and finds in his latest writings warrant for the hope that Byron was nearing " the Truth."   " For all will allow," he quaintly says, " that even Catholicism is better than infidelity."

> Or ludicrous my fancy may attract,
> Each in its turn may, in this stanza, chime ;
> And, if the reader should of either tire
> He'll read on, trusting to my changeful lyre.

> Think not that I would imitate *Don Juan :*
> Not such my boldness or humility ;
> That strain, indeed, was by no means a new one,
> Though tuned according to the Bard's ability.
> But therefore 'tis not fair that you should view one
> Bard as a copier, when the like servility
> Is not charged to the other ;—for that metre
> Was Tasso's, Pulci's, Ariosto's feature ;

> And there's a poem far too little known
> With which my German studies most delighted—
> 'Tis Wieland's graceful, elfin *Oberon :*
> The style of these four, Byron has united
> And robed in glory which was his alone—
> That searching fire by which his soul was blighted.
> But *Juan* ne'er was said from these to flow—
> Neither will I as imitator bow.

He protests too much, for the imitation is obvious.

An anonymous American poem, *The Pilgrimage of Ormond, or Childe Harold in the New World* (Charleston, S. C., 1831) is, as the title indicates, a continuation of *Childe Harold ;* but, though written in Spenserians, the manner is that of *Don Juan.* The Childe, reformed, visits America and travels widely through the Southern states. His adventures are mildly amusing ; they are intermingled with descriptive and meditative passages. Here is a typical allusion :

> Carroll ! he of Carrollton ! 'yclept,
> The only one, who still survives the day,
> Which as Columbia's Jubilee is kept.

A good example, cleverer than most, of the imitations is *Mischief* (1831)—this is the whole title—which very happily reproduces the tone of *Don Juan* in the metre of *Childe Harold.* The author has a knack in rhyming, as when he says of one of his characters :

> Of royal stock, both Tudor and Plantagenet,
> He vaunted much his genealogic table,
> In spite of, here and there, an ugly patch in it,
> And, now and then, a chasm, supplied by fable.

There is much of antiquarian interest (as may be gathered from the title) in *Verbum Sap, or Reflections on Times Passed in Coffee Houses, Hells, Theatres, &c. A Poem in Ottava Rima.* By Theodore Norton (1832). This is in the manner of *Don Juan,* and is concerned with subjects which Byron would probably have taken up had he ever elaborated the London phase of his hero's career. It is appropriately dedicated to " the Author of *Pelham.*"

A very lively imitation is *Humbug. A Satire. By the Author.*[1] It tells of the parents and birth of Anthony Humbug ; of his christening (with a long account of the people present at that ceremony and of the dinner that followed it) ; of his school days, and so forth ; and stops just as the hopeful Anthony is about to enter college. The author plans to go on to another canto, but that depends upon the reception of this one ; it may " wither 'neath the blast of critics." The unsympathetic catalogue of the British Museum supplies the brief comment : " No more published."

The Count and his Cotempors (1837) is a long and rather pointless satire imitated from *Don Juan. Don Juan at Athens* (1858) is an equally pointless satire on Edinburgh architecture, with slighting allusions to Ruskin. *To Whom It May Concern. A Poem on the Times,* by W. W. Western, uses the *ottava rima,* and tells in satiric vein of the actual adventures of two Confederate officers journeying to Liverpool. *Childe Archie's Pilgrimage.* By R. Gordon (1873), is much more an imitation of *Don Juan* than of *Childe Harold.*[2] . . . But I must make an end. Thomas Hood's " Friendly Address to Mrs. Fry in Newgate " owes something to Byron for its manner, and George Croly's *The Modern Orlando* much for its substance. In Sir William Watson's *The Eloping Angels,* and in various poems by Alfred Austin, there are faint survivals of the style. Mr. Gilbert Cannan's

[1] Undated ; but a reference to " the pranks shortly to be perpetrated by Halley's old *tail-bearer* " fixes the date as 1835 or shortly before, for Halley's comet appeared in November 1835.

[2] The author was Miss Rose Gordon ; in her preface she admits that she " adores Byron."

long, dull, satirico-metaphysical "epic" entitled *Noel* betrays its ancestry at a glance, though the broad, full stream of Byron's poem has run into sands and shallows.

I have adduced ample evidence of the enormous prestige and long-continued vogue of Byron's poem. I believe that it is now comparatively little read. This is a pity, for, granting that parts of it are tiresome and trivial, there is much that is wise and witty, much that is beautiful and tender, much that is sincere and strong, crowded together with some things that one might perhaps wish away, in its many pages. It is a special and preëminent example of Arnold's definition of poetry as a Criticism of Life. And it is from this point of view that many critics of the most varying shades of opinion have hailed it as the most characteristic English poem of the nineteenth century, even as "the modern epic." It is a brilliant picture of life and society in many climes and lands, furnished with a running commentary, generally satirical but not always so, upon the men, women and affairs which it seeks to illustrate. In fine contrast to almost all modern English verse it is magnificently anti-insular; there is a continental breadth about it. Into it Byron put his admirable gift of friendship; his disastrous sensual view of women; his cool, clear-sighted superiority to the fashions of society and the fads of the moment; his experience as a man of the world; his high and ardent political aspirations; his romantic wanderings in far climes; his titanic questionings of the universe; his poetic sense of the beauty and grandeur of nature and the pettiness of man. All life is there. Remembering this, we can understand, and understanding place in their proper order and proportion, certain features of the poem. There are spots reflected in the mirror, but the blame therefor must attach not to the glass held up but to the original reflected therein:

> These things are life,
> And life, some think, is worthy of the Muse.

When all is said, the voluptuousness and license and

vulgarity and indelicacy—unfortunately the best-known characteristics of the book—make up but a small part of its total content. It is a tremendously human book ; life is here in its various and most vital phases : love and joy ; suffering and hate and fear ; death in many forms. And it records what lies between these highest and lowest strata of human experience, the petty along with the great, the dull and prolix along with the terse and thrilling. It is a satire on society and social usage, on sham and cant and humbug, on pride of place, on the ostentation and vanity of glory, on the wickedness and needlessness of war, on the hypocrisies of conventional morality, on the innumerable little affairs of human life. Perhaps it is most interesting when regarded as a record of friendships and animosities. True to life or in the thinnest of disguises, we find friends and enemies of Byron : his wife, La Guiccioli, and other women ; Ali Pasha ; Castlereagh, Wellington, and other political personages ; Wordsworth, Southey, Coleridge, Keats, Moore, and other literary celebrities ; people of London society ; Spanish ladies and those of the seraglio ; followers of the Empress Catherine and that redoubtable woman herself (here Byron penetrates beyond the range of his own experience, and the interest consequently flags in these middle cantos) ; enslaved Italian opera singers ; cossacks, highwaymen, sailors, pirates, members of Parliament, tutors, and what not. All life is there. It is a poem of many moods, grave and gay, bitter and sweet, mocking and serious. The sudden changes in the mood are accompanied by the constant surprises in the rhymes. The stanza employed lends itself, in this deft handling, imitated with such originality from Pulci and Berni, to all these tones. It is perhaps best adapted to satirical purposes where a situation can be summed up in the sestet and the required epigrammatic comment rendered in the concluding couplet. The great narrative metre of Italian poetry of the Renaissance, it is not so well fitted to that use in English ; but in Byron's verse the story flows easily and swiftly along when the poet does not wilfully hinder it by digression. We become

accustomed to regard the serio-comic as the most characteristic mood of the verse, but we must not forget Byron's
oft-quoted confession :

> And if I laugh at any mortal thing
> 'Tis that I may not weep.

The evil of the world is sensed not the less keenly because
the corrective furnished is that of ridicule.   And on occasion
the volleys of the Comic Muse give way, and the poem is
flooded with romantic sunshine or clouded over with philosophic speculation.   Even the fitful flashes of wit can be
suppressed in proper season.   There is, for example, the
sombre, magnificent, and incomparable description of the
shipwreck, so strangely misunderstood and abused by Byron's
contemporaries ;   or the Shelleyan picture of idyllic love
by the sea under southern skies ;   or the exquisite and tender
meditation upon the " Ave Maria " bell, followed by the
address to Hesperus ;   or the pathos of Haidée's death ;   or
the fierce denunciations of war ;   or the solemn questionings
about death in the narrative of the commandant's assassination.

   Don Juan will never be forgotten ;   nor can it be ignored
by the judicious.   It has entered upon its second century
of fame as that work which has more than anything else
of Byron's achievement stood the test of disparagement and
notoriety and imitation and time ;   which has grown in
renown when his fame grew, and has kept its place when his
fame suffered temporary but almost total eclipse ;   which has
come to be regarded as his greatest contribution to literature ;
which is a wonderful memorial of a society " gone glimmering
through the dream of things that were " ;   and which yet
remains—and this is the final mark of its greatness—in all
essentials still applicable to the life of to-day.

CHAPTER VI

THE RECEPTION OF *CAIN*

BYRON himself said—the metaphor had not then been worn threadbare—that *Cain* was his Waterloo.[1] Yet from his great contemporaries he received high praise for his " Mystery." Goethe said [2] that " its beauty is such as we shall not see a second time in the world." Scott, in a letter to John Murray, gratefully accepted the dedication to him of " the very grand and tremendous drama of *Cain*," and declared that Byron had " matched Milton on his own ground." Shelley said : [3] " It contains finer poetry than has appeared in England since the publication of *Paradise Regained. Cain* is apocalyptic—it is a revelation not before communicated to man." Goethe and Scott and Shelley were blind with the excess of light shining from Byron's personality ; but though we cannot subscribe to their extraordinarily favourable judgments, they were not more wrong than were the crowd of reviewers and pamphleteers and miscellaneous literary *canaille* who abused or threatened Byron and his publisher. Of course in this throng of hostile critics there were some whose indignation was undoubtedly sincere.

[1] The forthcoming appearance of the play had been advertised in *The Morning Chronicle*, November 24, 1821 ; and it was published in a volume along with *Sardanapalus* and *The Two Foscari* on December 19, 1821. In considering the adverse criticisms of *Cain* it must be borne in mind that reviewers and pamphleteers were further prejudiced by the voluptuousness, the scepticism and the anti-military spirit of *Sardanapalus* and by the political opinions implicit in *The Two Foscari*. The brunt of criticism was, however, directed against *Cain*.

[2] *Conversations*, ed. 1874, p. 261. This remark and the passages from Scott's and Shelley's letters are cited by E. H. Coleridge, *Poetry*, v, 204.

[3] In a letter to Gisbourne, April 10, 1822 ; *Letters*, ed. Ingpen, ii, 955.

Of the many journalistic critiques, I choose for analysis the pronouncements of Reginald Heber and Francis Jeffrey. A large part of Heber's article, in the *Quarterly* of July 1822, deals with Byron's lack of dramatic talent. His judgment of the three plays published together is severely adverse, *Sardanapalus* being considered (and rightly) the least unsatisfactory. Heber riddles *Cain* with theological arguments, directed chiefly against Byron's emphasis upon the Evil Principle in Manicheeism.[1] The remarks introducing the detailed criticism of the plays are the most important part of the review. It is several years, says Heber, since the *Quarterly* has noticed Byron's works ; during that period the *Quarterly* has witnessed,

with deep regret and disappointment, the systematic and increasing prostitution of those splendid talents to the expression of feelings, and the promulgation of opinions, which as Christians, as Englishmen, and even as men, we were constrained to regard with abhorrence.

The *Quarterly* had hoped that experience, deeper knowledge, and religious principles would " render him . . . such a poet as virgins might read, and Christians praise, and Englishmen take pride in." But *Don Juan* seemed hopeless. These dramas give cause for new hope.

Even . . . *Cain*, wicked as it may be, is the work of a nobler and more daring wickedness. . . . It is better that Lord Byron should be a manichee, or a deist, . . . a moral and argumentative atheist, than the professed and systematic poet of seduction, adultery and incest ; the contemner of patriotism, the insulter of piety, the raker into every sink of vice and wretchedness to disgust and degrade and harden the hearts of his fellow-creatures.

Heber denies that Byron's theological views are to be taken seriously ; the poet's arguments are a mere exhibition of

---

[1] See *Lord Byron's Cain und seine Quellen*, by Alfred Schaffer (Strassburg, 1880) and my *Dramas of Lord Byron* (Göttingen, 1915), pp. 119 f.

dexterity. The review closes with an appeal to Paley's
Evidences.[1]

Jeffrey [2] makes comparatively little of the theological
aspect of the case, and takes *Cain* and (in less degree) its
two companion plays as a text for an exhortation and rebuke
to Lord Byron. His critique is on the whole unfavourable,
though there are qualifications of his strictures in the case
of *Sardanapalus.* He remarks upon

> the want of dramatic effect and variety, . . . something
> in the character or habit of Lord Byron's genius which will
> render this unattainable, . . . too little sympathy with the
> ordinary feelings and frailties of humanity, to succeed well
> in their representation.

Then follows the complaint which had been part of the
stock-in-trade of reviewers from the time of the publication
of Byron's Eastern tales :

> His Childe Harold, his Giaour, Corsair, Lara, Manfred, Cain,
> Lucifer—are all one individual. There is the same varnish
> of voluptuousness on the surface—the same canker of
> misanthropy at the core, of all he touches. . . . The world
> will weary at last of the most energetic pictures of misan-
> thropes and madmen—of outlaws and their mistresses.

While recognizing its power, Jeffrey regrets that *Cain* should
have been published, and calls it " a scandal and offence."
" Philosophy and Poetry," he goes on to say (not very
profoundly), " are both very good things in their way ; but,
in our opinion, they do not go very well together." Byron's
complaints of detraction Jeffrey declares are totally un-
founded ; " we cannot recollect a single author who has
had so little reason to complain of his reception." From
the first, says Jeffrey, Byron offended principles and shocked
prejudices. Yet he was applauded.

---

[1] The *Quarterly* had already published (xxvii, April 1822, 123 f.) a
narrative of the cases of Walcot *vs.* Walker, etc., concerning the refusal by
Lord Eldon of an application to have *Cain* and *Don Juan* (among other
works, including Southey's *Wat Tyler*) protected from piracy.

[2] *The Edinburgh Review*, xxxvi, February 1822, 413 f.

As he grew in fame and authority, he aggravated all his offences . . . and only took leave of Childe Harold to ally himself to Don Juan ! That he had since been talked of . . . with less unmingled admiration—that his name is now mentioned as often for censure as for praise—and that the exultation with which his countrymen once hailed the greatest of our living poets, is now alloyed by the recollection of the tendency of his writings—

that these things are so is the fault of no one but himself. Jeffrey sums up this change in public opinion as " this decline of his popularity—or rather this stain upon its lustre—for he is still popular beyond all other example." The critic disclaims any personal *animus* in his strictures (and this Byron, in a famous passage in *Don Juan*, admitted), and declares

We are not bigots or rival poets. We have not been detractors from Lord Byron's fame, nor the friends of his detractors ; and *we* tell him . . . that . . . the great body of the English nation . . . consider the tendency of his writings to be immoral and pernicious. . . . We do not charge him with being either a disciple or an apostle of Satan.

Jeffrey is " glad to testify " to the dignity, tenderness, sublimity, and beauty of a portion of his poetry ; yet he repeats that the general tendency of that poetry " is in the highest degree pernicious." If Byron's work had been composed of " gaudy ribaldry and flashy scepticism " the mischief had been less. His charge is that Byron exhibits " profligate heartlessness in the persons who had been transiently represented as actuated by the purest and most exalted motives." [1] He concludes with a contrast :

---

[1] Jeffrey singles out as an example of this " heartlessness " the shipwreck in *Don Juan*, canto ii. Contemporary critics over and over again fell afoul of this scene. Keats in particular expresses his disgust at the episode. Apparently there was no awareness of the fact that juxtapositions of the sublime or tragic with the ludicrous or grotesque are an essential characteristic of the genre. Even at Roncesvalles, Pulci, though moved to real eloquence by the death of his hero in the dolorous valley, does not resist the temptation to introduce an occasional burlesque turn of thought.

How opposite to this is the system or the temper of the great author of *Waverley*— the only living individual to whom Lord Byron must submit to be ranked as inferior in genius.

In all this there is not much about *Cain*.

This critique called forth some good-natured satiric remarks in *Blackwood's* [1] upon Jeffrey's constant puffing of Byron and his belated protest against *Don Juan*. In the first instalment of the *Noctes Ambrosianæ* the same journal had already published [2] an amusing conversation on *Cain* from which I quote these remarks :

Editor [*i.e.* John Wilson] : As to *Cain*, I entirely differ from the Chancellor. I think, if *Cain* be prosecuted, it will be a great shame. The humbug of the age will then have achieved its most visible triumph. . . . The Society might have had some pretence had they fallen on *Don Juan*.

Odoherty [*i.e.* William Maginn] : Have you seen Lord Byron's letter on the subject to Mr. Murray ? . . . It was written originally in verse, but Murray's friends thought it would have more effect if translated into prose ; and a young clergyman, who writes for the *Quarterly*, turned the thing very neatly, considering. I believe I have a copy of Lord Byron's own letter in my pocket.

There follows Maginn's clever versification of Byron's famous letter to Murray from Pisa in defence of *Cain* (February 8, 1822). As the poem is long and easily accessible I do not quote it here.[3]

I turn now to the crowd of pamphlets that were inspired by the " Mystery." [4]

A Remonstrance addressed to Mr. John Murray, respecting

---

[1] *Noctes Ambrosianæ*, iii ; *Blackwood's Magazine*, xi, May 1822, 609 f.
[2] Vol. xi, March 1822, 376 f.
[3] It may be found in *The Odoherty Papers*, ii, 125 ; *Noctes Ambrosianæ* (N.Y., Redfield, 1855), i, 139 f. ; and in LJ, vi, 13, note 2.
[4] I omit the other reviews, which with less weight of authority repeated or anticipated the general drift of the arguments pronounced by Heber and Jeffrey. Thomas Moore recorded that " *Cain* has made a sensation " and that press and public were alike hostile (quoted by Coleridge, *Poetry*, v, 204). Coleridge also quotes (from *The Examiner*, February 17, 1822) the statement that His Majesty King George the Fourth " expressed his disapprobation of the blasphemy and licentiousness of Lord Byron's writings."

a *Recent Publication* (1822), bears on the title-page this motto from *Paradise Lost :*

> Whence,
> But from the author of all ill, could spring
> So deep a malice ?

The Remonstrance is signed at the end, " Oxoniensis." [1] The writer thinks it hopeless to appeal to Byron to change his ways and opinions ; he is alien from all civilized standards of conduct. He therefore addresses Murray in an endeavour to prevent him henceforward " from becoming the agent of so much mischief." Murray must not in extenuation plead gratitude to Byron for former favours, for when *Don Juan* appeared he showed that he could exercise discretionary powers, and his name did not appear on the title-page of that book. " This piece of mischief [*Don Juan*] was loaded under your own eye, though you left it to your Printer to pull the trigger." Surely the publication of *Cain* was another occasion for the exercise of at least that much discretion ; yet Murray's name now appears.[2] Only a recognition of "the peculiar temper of the times " would allow the prosecutor of Hone to let Murray escape with impunity. He is warned that his great and powerful patrons will turn against him if he continues to print attacks upon their " triple pillar "—religion, morality, and law. " Oxoniensis " affirms that Murray's only criterion has been the problem whether the book would sell well ; but—

Your noble employer has deceived you, Mr. Murray ; he has profited by the celebrity of his name to palm off upon you obsolete trash, the very offscourings of Bayle and Voltaire,

---

[1] According to Coleridge (*Poetry*, v, 202) this pamphlet is by the Rev. H. J. Todd.

[2] Byron wrote to Kinnaird (LJ, vi, 9) : " I know nothing of [the] *Remonstrance* by the ' eminent Churchman ' ; but I suppose he wants a living." With regard to Murray's keeping his name off the title-page of *Don Juan*, thus exposing himself to the strictures of " Oxoniensis," Byron wrote (LJ, vi, 18) : " As for what the clergyman says of *Don Juan*, you have brought it upon yourself by your absurd half and half prudery, which, I always foresaw, would bother you at last. An author's *not* putting his name, is nothing—it has been always the custom to publish a thousand anonymous things ; but *who* ever heard before of a *publisher's* affecting such a Masquerade as yours was ? "

which he has made you pay for, as though it were first-rate poetry and sound metaphysics.

It is a pity, the writer thinks, that Byron did not read Milton and Gessner more recently ; Gessner's devotional spirit and Milton's powerful mind grapple with the difficulties that have overcome him. Byron's motives in publishing *Cain* are then subjected to an analysis into which allusions to the poet's domestic troubles are gratuitously dragged. First, to make money ; second, to " mislead the ignorant, unsettle the wavering, or confirm the hardened sceptic in his disbelief " ; third, to gain " the satisfaction of insulting those from whom he differs both in faith and practice." Certain " pestilent sophistries, framed to mislead the weaker sex " are especially condemned. Among the people whom Byron now affronts are many who watched his earlier career with interest and admiration, though even in those days there was a cloud on the horizon.

A moral gloom hung over the most brilliant effusions of the imagination which every one was ready to lament, though most of us were sanguine enough to hope that it would be dispersed by the improving influence of reason and religion. How deplorably have their hopes been disappointed ; this portentous cloud has spread itself on all sides and involved his whole intellect in its fatal gloom. Nothing can pierce it, the flashes of wit and the bright blaze of imagination are alike ineffectual ; and the name of Lord Byron, who might (it would be a cruel effort of the imagination even to suggest what he might have been) [1] serves now only to point a moral.

Byron is talented but profane ; a Briton yet a scorner of his country. He has taken as his motto, " Evil, be thou my good." Will Byron find in you, Mr. Murray, a willing instrument to spread his poison ? Your " courtly locality and connections " will not protect you long.

You challenge a heavy responsibility. . . . You are responsible to that society whose institutions you contribute to

---

[1] The punctuation is that of the pamphlet.

destroy. . . . Hone, it is true, escaped with legal impunity ; but Carlile and his miserable associates are in gaol.

Attacks of this sort threw Murray into such a state of nerves that, hesitating, he postponed the publication of manuscripts sent him by Byron, and the severance of his connection with Byron was the outcome. For the present, however, the poet was not without a champion.

In February 1822 there appeared *A Letter to Sir Walter Scott, Bart., In Answer to the Remonstrances of Oxoniensis.* This is signed at the end "Harroviensis." The writer addresses Scott who, since *Cain* is dedicated to him, has a special concern in it. His object is to vindicate the Mystery from abuse, especially the abuse of "Oxoniensis." That pseudonymous clergyman is rebuked for the bad taste of accusing Byron of mercenary motives and for dragging into the discussion Byron's domestic difficulties which have nothing to do with the question at issue. "Harroviensis" brings the supposed blasphemies of *Cain* to the test of Milton. If Byron is charged with expressing his own sentiments through the mouths of his characters, then Milton (and Shakespeare, too) are his abettors. Ten pages of parallels follow between *Cain* and *Paradise Lost. Cain* is considered as a strictly dramatic problem ; the motives of Lucifer and his ways of tempting Cain are scrutinized. The critic finds clear differentiations in character, for Adah, who is firm against Lucifer's lures, presents the moral and religious contrast to her husband. The poetic beauty and imaginative quality of the flight of Cain and Lucifer through the depths of space are praised ; and the gradual undermining of Cain's moral nature is traced.

The train of argument, by which the tempter in *Paradise Lost* prevailed on Eve to eat of the forbidden tree was not dissimilar to the progress of Cain's seduction.

No ground is found to impugn *Cain's* moral tendency. It is urged that the attacks on Byron's infidelity apply in reality only to Lucifer's utterances, and that Byron's own

private religious beliefs have nothing to do with the matter.
In conclusion, the writer describes his pamphlet as "this
endeavour to rescue *Cain* from the grasp of prejudice, and
to secure it a place amongst the admitted sources of instruction and mental gratification."

Byron was pleased with this defence; in April and May,
1822, we find several references to it in his letters.[1] " Who
is my Warburton ? " he inquires of Murray, " for he has
done for me what the Bishop did for the poet against
Crousaz. His reply seems to me conclusive; and if you
understood your own interest, you would print it together
with the poem." Again he writes : " Can you tell me the
author of the defence of *Cain* ? If you understood your
own interest, you would get it circulated as much as you can."
And again : " I recommend to you (when you republish),
to append the defence of *Cain* to that poem. Who is the
author ? He must be a good-natured fellow as well as a
clever one." Murray evidently did not take kindly to
Byron's suggestion, and in reply spoke slightingly of
" Harroviensis," for Byron answers : " The defender of *Cain*
may or may not be, as you term him, ' a tyro in literature ' ;
however, I think both you and I are under great obligations
to him."

But " Harroviensis " stirred up the resentment of lovers
of Milton, and a rejoinder was promptly published : *A
Vindication of the Paradise Lost from the Charge of Exculpating
Cain. By Philo-Milton* (1822). Byron's words are chosen
as a motto : " If *Cain* be blasphemous, *Paradise Lost* is
blasphemous." " Philo-Milton's " object is two-fold : to
avoid self-reproach for *not* defending Milton's aspersed name ;
and to obviate " one particle " of the mischief to society
caused by *Cain*. He does not wish to probe into Byron's
motives ; he knows him only in his works ; the tendency, not
the object, of those works is his concern. Such is the opening,
and continuing, he refers courteously to " Harroviensis "
as " one, who is evidently a scholar, a calm inquirer,
and an advocate for social order," and " a conscientious

[1] LJ, vi, 49, 54, 60 and 76.

advocate " whose purpose was to confront offensive passages
in *Cain* with what he considered parallel passages in *Paradise
Lost*, " and to move an acquittal of the former, from a charge
of impious tendency, on the same grounds upon which it
has been universally granted to the latter." But, " Philo-
Milton " goes on, to find daring impieties in Milton does
not defend *Cain ;* for Milton's object was to " assert eternal
providence," and to do so it was necessary to have it
impugned. " The objectionable argument must be *stated*,
in order to draw out the refutation." *Paradise Lost* everywhere offers the antidote to its own blasphemies. *Cain*
does not in the purity of the female characters, nor in the
resignation of Adam, nor in the humility of Abel. It
is admitted that Milton casts " an unhealthy splendour "
around his ruined archangel ; but " Satan's baser qualities
peep out in succession, and not after long delay " ; throughout the poem Satan falls. Byron invests Lucifer with
qualities which Milton never arrogates to Satan—his
manicheeistic claims, for example, and his insight into
futurity. One by one the parallels set up between the two
poems by " Harroviensis " are examined and set aside. He
confutes Byron's defence that the personages of the drama
are " creatures of the imagination " by exclaiming
emphatically that they are *not ;* they are part of the
Sacred Record. There follows a long critique on *Don
Juan* and its moral degradation, in which the earlier
suavity of the critic's tone disappears. Towards the end
he says :

Who did not shudder when he heard that Lord Byron was
busied upon the subject of *Cain ?* I thought I saw the
germ whence the work should spring in his *Prometheus*, and
poems of that complexion.

Of wider scope is a book most conveniently mentioned
here, though only the latter portion of it applies definitely
to *Cain*. This is : *Revolutionary Causes : with a Brief
Notice of some late Publications* (1822). The introductory
" advertisement " is signed " Britannicus." This book was

prompted by Byron's remark [1] that the writings of Voltaire and Rousseau were not the causes of the French Revolution, but that the burdens of the people had become more than they could bear. " Britannicus " (evidently a bigotted Tory) admits that grievances as to taxation were one cause of the Revolution, but he stresses far more the disordered state of morality, of religion, and of literature. He then applies these considerations to contemporary England. The English nation, he thinks, is at large " replete with piety and virtue," and dangerous men are scarce. Literature, however, " appears to have suffered considerable degradation of late " ; the genius of the age is of a high order but there is evidence of " bad taste, or impious aim in the choice of subjects." Commending the *Quarterly's* review of *Prometheus Unbound*, he admits that he has not read Shelley's drama, but it is evidently—he adds—" downright nonsense."

God forbid [he exclaims] that deluding orators and atheistical poets should continue multiplying upon society, for then would society be seriously in danger !

With Shelley he groups Maturin, the author of *Melmoth the Wanderer*.

But these, after all, are your middle writers with talent enough to weave showy sentences, but without the genius to disguise the pestilence they are meant to propagate. . . . The scope of Lord Byron's mind, his soul is immensely beyond the reach of his followers.

In summing up his case the writer places among the most efficient causes of revolution " publications spreading false notions of religion, of government, of morality." There follows a long " Postscript containing Strictures on *Cain*." Of intentional blasphemy he acquits Byron who has merely imitated the *esprits forts* of the eighteenth century. " The creation and the temptation have withstood all their arrows," he confidently asserts. Byron should re-read *Paradise Lost*, contrasting it with *Cain* :

---

[1] In the Appendix to *The Two Foscari*, in the course of the attack on Southey ; see LJ, vi, 388.

Let him mark this contrast and if he have any heart left, he will shed burning tears of sorrow, that it is no longer in his power to suppress a work insulting to God and pregnant with mischief to mankind.

There are frequent expressions of sheer horror at the play. " Five pages further on," he says, " I was again shocked— shocked ! no, struck with horror ! " So shocked, that it is with reluctance that he quotes Lucifer's speech beginning " Souls that dare look the Everlasting in his face." He offers passages from Milton as " antidotes " to these blasphemies. In conclusion he declares that Byron has " totally mistaken his road . . . Oh, that I could but lead him back to the station which he has deserted ! " A nation would welcome him " to the seat he was born to fill and adorn."

In much the same tone is written an anonymous *Letter of Expostulation to Lord Byron* (1822), in which *Cain* is regarded as a side-issue, the writer's chief concern being not poetry but patriotism.

Poetry may embellish a nation, patriotism preserves it : poetry is a luxury of the few, patriotism a blessing to the many. . . . The object of this address is not so much to remind you of the sins you have committed, in your character as a poet, as to call your attention to the duties you have neglected, as a British senator.

If dissatisfied with England's religious beliefs, Byron might at least help to " purify its political atmosphere." He might be useful at home—" Take that place which the laws of your country have given you." The current Toryism may well provoke a reaction towards radicalism ; Byron's service might be that of a moderator between extremes.

You have [made] your name stand high among wits, . . . make it look glorious among lords, and reputable among patriots. You have done enough for booksellers, do something for history.

Of a more personal interest is a weighty and pretentious discourse, extending to 109 closely printed pages, by Byron's friend the Rev. William Harness : *The Wrath of Cain : A Boyle Lecture* (1822).[1] In his preface Harness says :

In those parts of my Sermon which relate to Lord Byron's poem I have regarded Cain and Lucifer simply as dramatic characters, uttering their appropriate sentiments ; and whenever they are mentioned, it is of Cain and Lucifer only that I speak.

The discourse begins with the statement that the malice of Cain has lately received a vindication. The meeting of Cain with Lucifer is narrated, and their sentiments examined. " Pride is virtue and rebellion duty " is the burden of the " bewildering sophistry " of these sentiments, which are " in hideous uniformity with the malignant spirits and the hollow voices of the apostate angel and the first of murderers." Harness gives warning of the peril of such a publication in a sceptical age ; and turning to the " facts " of the case of Cain, proceeds to " show that those facts bear witness to the benevolence of God." There is a long defence of the literal truth of the narrative in *Genesis ;* it is " a plain relation of events that actually occurred." A special examination of the Fall follows and of the part played by the serpent, and so forth, with long, pompous replies to the objections raised by sceptics to such matters as the creation of Eve from Adam's rib. Harness cites a series of " corroborations " which are to a modern mind amazing. The latter part of the discourse is an attempt to prove that the " facts " bear witness to God's benevolence ; and the preacher considers such problems as the withholding of the tree of knowledge, Cain's lack of awareness of immortality, the wretchedness and punishment of sin, and so on.[2]

[1] The Boyle endowment was for an annual lecture on subjects connected with infidelity. The Lecture by Harness was published, it is worth noting, by Rivington, the firm that had published the attacks on Byron by " Oxoniensis " and " Philo-Milton."

[2] Byron makes no mention in any letter or diary of this discourse by the friend of his youth and young manhood ; but in an article on " Lord Byron," containing reminiscences of a visit to Genoa, a writer in *Blackwood's* (xv, June 1824, 700) says : " I mentioned a late production of a Harrow man

It is with relief that I turn from these examples of a long-since discredited literalism to the poetasters who followed the critics in coming to the defence of affronted orthodoxy. The reader will, I trust, find the remainder of this chapter more curious and interesting than the preceding pages.

I note first an anonymous volume entitled *Uriel, a Poetical Address to Lord Byron* (1822). After some prefatory remarks on infidelity and its prevalence despite " the meridian brightness of well-attested miracles," the author points out that in the poem which follows he uses " the language of expostulation, rather than of anathema." The *Address* is written in 79 stanzas. There is an opening tribute to Byron's mighty mind ; the writer has no wish to " check bright genius on the wing " ; he has often followed Childe Harold on his devious way. But why, Byron, have you failed your country ? Does " your lofty towering mind disdain the beaten path ? " Why do you hide your delinquencies behind " the panoply of Milton's holy mind ? " A long argument follows directed against *Cain* and in praise of " the Christian theme." [1] Byron is bidden to note how the Jews have been outcasts since they rejected Christ.

> Read well the Prophecies, and then compare
> Earth, as it is, with all that they declare.

Hearken to the " dulcet voice " that bids you choose the paths of peace ;

in which *Cain* had been noticed. ' I hope,' said Lord Byron, ' he did not abuse me personally, for that would be too bad, as we were schoolfellows, and very good friends.' " The allusion here to Harness seems to me to be unquestionable.

[1] One stanza will serve as a sample of the style and method :

> From Paradise, if our first Parents fell,
> As Inspiration's Sacred legends tell,
> One test of their obedience, only, given,
> To prove their claims to the applause of heaven—
> Shall man complain ? Had they not power to choose,
> The good to take, the evil to refuse ?
> They ate, and violated His command,
> Who holds the fate of worlds within His hand—
> Just are His judgments—all His will shall stand.

Illume your torch at yon undying flame,
Henceforth a Saviour's wondrous love proclaim.
Byron, farewell ! your spirit I would greet,
Pure from its stains—around the mercy-seat—
When time shall be no longer.

There is a concluding Pæan to the Almighty, ending :

The Star of Bethlem—gilds the upper sky,
The Spirit and the Bride proclaim—Salvation nigh.[1]

Other poetasters, more ambitious, aspired to rewrite the drama from the orthodox point of view. We must examine, among other things, *Another Cain, A Mystery*. By William Battine (1822). This is dedicated to Byron, " for his Lordship's consideration." In a preface Battine says :

Accident put Lord Byron's *Cain* into my hand. . . . Curiosity and Lord Byron's name induced my wish to peruse it ; but the blasphemy in the mouth of Lucifer was so disgusting that I soon laid it aside. . . . The immediate publication of " *Another* Cain " became necessary. . . . I am not disputing the laurels with Lord Byron. His Cain has the merit of poetical talent ; my Cain, the merit of Truth.

An account of this play can best proceed scene by scene.

Act I, Scene i : The apostate angels, in council, urge Satan to suggest to Cain the foul thought of murdering Abel. Scene ii : Adam and Eve offer sacrifice with Abel ; but Cain refuses to ask for redemption since his was not the sin. He offers sacrifice in homage. Mahala, Cain's wife, pleads with him " to lay aside the independent tone and spirit of self-righteousness." He will not.

Act II, Scene i : A colloquy between Satan and Cain. Satan upholds the power of Reason, and urges Cain to

---

[1] After the poem come some prose " Observations on *Cain*," chiefly a protest against the unfairness of appealing to *Paradise Lost* as a support for the doctrines in Byron's Mystery ; for (1) Is Cain's language merely such as would be expected in his unhappy situation ? (2) Are his impieties repelled by sound argument or are they allowed to stand ? (3) Is Byron's genius displayed on the side of infidelity or in the defence of the truth ? The play is examined in the light of these questions and in contrast to *Paradise Lost*.

repudiate God. Were he in Cain's place he'd lay his rival (Abel) dead. Cain asks what death is ; and Satan tells him of his condemnation to death and hell, and of his opportunities of vengeance against God. Scene ii : Satan, *solus,* on the use of human Reason to draw men, especially the wise, into his net. Mahala, meeting Cain, pleads with him to accept his lot cheerfully. Cain tells her of his meeting with Satan. She implores him to avoid that Seraph and to consort with the Cherubim.

Act III, Scene i : A prayer and hymn of praise by Abel at sunrise. An angel whispers to him that God is preparing for him a nearer sight of His glory. Do not ask how : " ignorance is bliss." (The angel quotes Gray verbatim.) Scene ii : Mahala tells Cain of an evil dream of blood and exile ; she begs him to abase his pride ; he should imitate Abel. She departs, and Cain speaks, *solus :*

> Out upon Abel ! He's the string, when touch'd,
> Drives me distracted.

He meditates upon the possibility of murder, but decides first to take further counsel of his " disinterested " friend, Satan. Scene iii : He meets Adam, who warns him of Satan's wiles. Cain replies that he has profited by Adam's sin and will do nothing unsanctioned by Reason. Scene iv : Adam and Eve commune together about their elder son, anxious because of his morose demeanour. Scene v : Satan again tempts Cain.

Act IV, Scene i : The debate between Abel and Cain about the accepted and rejected offering. Their words grow sharper, and at length Abel, whose arguments anticipate Job, calls Cain a blasphemer. Cain strikes him—

> See if brains, when once knock'd out, will prove
> The righteousness of Abel, or God's love.

Abel dies. Cain is horrified at the sight of death. Scene iii : Satan, *solus :*

> The foolish being
> By *sense and reason's* blinded to make war
> With God his maker. . . .
> I'll meet and taunt him with his folly.

Act V, Scene i : Cain is accused by God's Angel ; the curse ; the mark of Cain.[1] Scene ii : Satan taunts Cain. Scene iii : Adam, Eve, and Mahala hear from Thirza (Abel's wife) the story of the murder, she having witnessed it afar off. They all stand aghast and stupefied. Cain enters. He admits the deed, but is not truly penitent :

> 'Twas Eve's, 'twas Adam's fault, or 'twas the fiend's,
> Or *Human Reason's*.   I, deluded, fell.

He and Mahala depart. Scene iv : Adam, *solus*, expresses his submission to the will of God, and prays for Abel's soul and for pardon for Cain.

There follows a short " Address to Lord Byron." Take warning, Battine advises, from Cain ; do not trust human Reason ; do not, like Pharaoh, harden your heart.

> Rochester,
> Brilliant in youth, in talent, and in sin,
> Was not less brilliant in his close of day,
> By worshipping before the Cherubim !
> O may the fire of thy bright genius burn,
> Illum'd by spark celestial, and expel
> The darkness brooding in thy faithless *heart !*
> How great the train of sceptics, whom thou lead'st,
> Would follow thee, and thou, their polar star,
> Shine with effulgence to eternal day !

Of similar title, but not to be confused with Battine's long drama, is a short anonymous non-dramatic poem : *Another Cain* (1822). The preface declares that nothing since Voltaire and Paine has been so subversive of the truths of Christianity as *Cain*. The writer, " though with a female's feeble arm," rises " in the cause of virtue and an

---

[1] This is the angel's speech as he sets the mark upon Cain :

> Hence, to denote thee from the holier race
> Of man, thy colour shall be changed ; of black
> And swarthy countenance, *dark as thy heart*,
> Thy features flat, thy face foreshorten'd ; and
> Instead of hair over thy shoulders flowing,
> In graceful ringlets, shall the curly wool
> Of the sheep's fleece cover thy graceless head.

I commend this interpretation of the mark of Cain to Sir James Frazer. Certainly it is rather hard on the negroes, especially since Battine adds a foot-note on the coloured races, whose differences from the Aryans are, he thinks, too striking to be accounted for by " natural causes."

insulted God " to offer an antidote to it. In the poem
she takes her stand on the ground that " all and every part
[of the Bible] is false, or true." Only profligates raise
doubts. " Manfred's cheerful, social heart " and " Don
Juan's chaste and moral page " may teach the age that
accepts doctrine from profligate guides. She apostrophizes
England, home of the virtues ; and evokes the bards of
other days, Milton and Shakespeare. Of the latter she
inquires :

> What praise can yield thy talents just reward ?
> Kings, queens, and fairies, gentlemen and clown,
> All move with equal credit and renown.

Pious Thomson and Cowper are contrasted with Byron.
Her condemnation of the noble poet is tremendous ; she
cries :

> Instead of *bays*, around his brows to shine,
> The deadly *nightshade* shall with *nettles* twine.

Remember, O Byron, how such wits as Voltaire have died :
" what deep remorse, what anguish and despair." Therefore,

> my countrymen, beware of CAIN,
> And let him hold his poison'd cup in vain ;
> Still live like Christians, and like Christians die
> Though *screech-owls* scream, and *birds* ill-omen'd cry.

Scarcely less hysterical is *A Scourge for Lord Byron*, by
Thomas Adams (1823). This very quaint production is
dedicated to " My King and Countrymen." Adams declares
in his preface that he has abstained from intricate technicalities and abstract reasoning, and has applied " the
chastening rod to him, who attempts to throw in a labyrinth
the minds and morals of his fellow-creatures." He denounces
Byron's meanness in " masking his sentiments, by putting
such a tissue of blasphemy into the mouths of Lucifer and
Cain." He goes on :

I almost regret th⸋ I did not write [the *Scourge*] as a plain
argumentative subject, void of rhyme.

He regrets, too, that some great writer has not answered
Byron ; that would have been better than to have the duty

" half performed by an obscure individual, whose very limited education disqualified him." There follows this amazing diatribe :

I now denounce Lord Byron—a blasphemer of his God, in the face of the universe,—for the feebleness of my mind, nor the deficiency of education, or the very secluded manner the nature of my avocation in life has subjected me to, depriving me of much experimental knowledge, shall never intimidate me from lifting my pen in defence, when the truth is endeavoured to be perverted, and a doctrine promulgated to the world that may be liable to blast the morals of my five infant children.

Such a sentence promises well for the poem, and the poem comes up to one's expectations. It begins :

> What ! Byron's senses gone—they surely are,
> With nature and with reason, now at war.

The man is a madly bold wretch who dares deny the Scriptures :

> Reason is fled from him, however great,
> Who damns the Scriptures—doubts a future state.
> Thy recent pamphlets gain thee no applause,
> They crush all moral and religious laws. . . .
> If written by a humble bard like me,
> An inmate of some gaol, my fate would be.

(which, though awkwardly expressed, was probably true.) Byron must cease to mislead youth with his " impious trash."

> While thus you prowl upon the public peace,
> To flog you with my pen, I'll never cease.

After dealing with *Cain* Adams proceeds to attack Byron's *Vision of Judgment*. He praises George III, who was a pattern to all kings—

> How meanly wicked is thy subtle diction
> To ridicule our monarch's sad affliction !

Perhaps the Italian air—he suggests—warps the mind and renders the heart callous. His conclusion is solemn, if ungrammatical :

May calmness guide me, as I make this charge
Against his lordship, to the world at large.
Byron's the man, I challenge him myself,
As beauty's robber, and a worthless elf ;
What tends the human mind to vitiate,
In like proportion mis'ry will create ;
Will dissipate the fervor which impends
O'er love connubial, or devoted friends,
Will speak [*sic*] the flow of friendly intercourse,
Is virtue's foe, and honesty's divorce,
Will make the virgin mourn, the wife decay—
Such is the merit his two books display ;—
The man who vice pursues becomes a slave,
His ruling passions excavate his grave.[1]

Far more pretentious than the blow from the " female's
feeble arm " or the " scourge " administered by the father
of five infant children is a piece called : *Cain. A Poem,
Intended to be Published in Parts* (though only one part was
published), by Henry Wilkinson (1824). In fanciful moments I like to think that the author was the genuine,
original " Mr. Wilkinson, a clergyman." His preface is
long and curious. He tells us that in early youth, having
read Gessner's *Death of Abel*, he conceived the idea of an
epic poem which should begin at the point where Gessner
stopped, *i.e.* at Cain's departure for the wilderness. He
was discouraged by his father, " who told him that all had
been written that could be written, and that any additional
work of poetry must necessarily be plagiarism." Nevertheless, in 1794 he took up the sacred theme again, but
after writing a good deal, he abandoned his epic, " being

---

[1] Adams seems to have had some private *animus* against Byron, for
he says :

> Kind-hearted Pope did here his friendship show ;
> He took young authors by the leading strings,
> And led them to the pure Castalian springs ;
> And as they wrote, he view'd their works with care,
> Gave them advice, and rais'd them from despair.

Perhaps Byron had ignored some earlier pieces submitted by Adams for
his approval. There is a long passage on the duties of poets towards the
public ; to be moral, lively and sincere ; to point out the " blissful port "
of religion for " all disabled vessels " ; etc.

> We are the pilots, and should bear the blame ;
> Our dutious task gains us immortal fame

Poor Adams !

convinced he was not a Poet." Unfortunately this wise conviction did not endure, for he goes on to tell that lately he was encouraged by two gentlemen to whom he recited some of his verses. By these gentlemen he was told of *Cain*. " Of Lord Byron the Author had heard of course, but he had not read any of his works except the *Farewell* and the *Corsair*." His curiosity was excited. He tried to buy *Cain* ; " but to the credit of the York booksellers not one of them could supply the solitary demand." He procured from Leeds a cheap pirated edition, read it, and determined to refute its sophistries. He turned therefore to his long-neglected epic, filled in various gaps so as to link the fragments together, and supplied arguments directed particularly against Byron.[1]

The poem is in heroic couplets, broken by triplets and alexandrines. A long invocation to the Muse ends :

> Sweet silence reign, while soft effusions flow,
> And, taught by you, I chord the sounds of woe.

What we are to expect of Wilkinson's style is at once apparent, for—

> Dark was the night . . .
> When sin and death in foul conjunction leagu'd,
> Taught hell to triumph o'er man's 'bellious seed.

" 'Bellious seed " is good ; and what are we to think of his description of Satan ? As an epitome of all the faults and falsities that go to make bad poetry I do not know its equal ; it is almost incredible ; and atl east a specimen of it must be quoted. I relegate it, however, to a foot-note.[2]

---

[1] " The notes were added," he says, " from the conviction, that the work, they in part criticize, is not worth a full poetical answer."

> Glore o'er his head fast canopied by fate,
> A paly crown of vap'rous poison sate,
> Wherein a viper bathed, and when he list,
> Filled with the frothy unction of the mist,
> Slured deep into his head and gend'red there,
> The cromious poison of the tortur'd air . . .
> Shrunk from the fearful form, and hover'd round the shade,

and so on. Obviously, there is here ample material for that long looked-for dissertation for the doctorate, *Der Jabberwoch von Ludwig Carroll und seine Quellen*.

Continuing, the poet tells how

> Chill thro' the soul of night
> The voice of death depress'd the sooty flight
> Of the dark night-bird.

The " night-bird " is Satan, who hears Death brooding over the body of Abel. The effect of Death's words is thus described :

> He said, and deeplier gloom'd. The mournful night,
> Far in her ebon caves, shrunk back with wild affright ;
> Sad silence trembl'd as he clasp'd her round,
> And almost shook her terror into sound.

Then comes Satan's flight to Earth, piercing " the vast vacate." His temptation of Eve is told, and a description follows of the Earthly Paradise lost through her transgression. The action of the poem is then suspended and a consideration of Byron's *Cain* is introduced ; from this the following excerpts will indicate how Byron was regarded by the more ruthlessly orthodox of his contemporaries.

> Perhaps, in future time remote, may rise
> Some daring mind, with mighty energies,
> Some human demon,—impious, bold, and vain,
> Stubborn, insatiate, eager to inflame
> Man 'gainst his God, to execrate His name,—
> With native genius, and consummate pride,
> And talents great, but foully misapplied. . . .
> Heedless of others' peace, he'll reckless try,
> To spread the taint of infidelity.
> And now, emerg'd from the mysterious shade,
> With daring front, see Byron stands, display'd—
> The horrid work, detestable, abhorr'd !
> The fiend-sprung fancy of this maudlin lord,
> In bold defiance to the world he flings,
> Tired of his satire on the best of kings. . . .

Wilkinson addresses Byron thus :

> Thy daring preface, foul and falsely writ,
> Shews more thy infidelity than wit ;
> And first thy characters thou dost preserve,
> But this will not the poor evasion serve ;

For shewn, detected, vile in every line,
The words seem *theirs*, the blasphemy is *thine*.
And in the Bible thou dost then relate,
There's no allusion to a future state.
Read Daniel, daring unbeliever, read ;
Leave infidelity, embrace the creed.

Here, as in many other parts of the poem, one follows the general course of the idea through the mazes of ungrammatical and half-articulate excitement. The piece now runs for some time parallel with a series of extracts from *Cain* which are given in foot-notes.[1] It closes with an appeal to Byron to contemplate the starry night ; there surely he will gain a sense of the Author of the Whole and will no longer doubt the soul's divinity.[2]

In sum, Wilkinson's poem is an instructive document. On the satiric side it illustrates the last feeble efforts of the tradition derived from Pope ; regarded as an essay in the metaphysical sublime it offers us the last dregs and degradation of the Miltonic tradition.

An anonymous poem in heroic couplets entitled *A Layman's Epistle to a Certain Nobleman* (1824) is especially concerned with *Cain*. In those of high birth, says the author (a man, evidently, of limited knowledge of the world), we expect perfection ; " 'tis scarce in them a merit to be good." He therefore stands aghast at the productions of " this fall'n peer." Formerly he laughed and blushed by turns at the products of Byron's pen ; but it is " a downward Muse " that makes a jest of God and revels in orgies.

---

[1] Wilkinson's ridicule is expended upon Byron's idea of the pre-Adamites and the monsters of former days, Byron's purpose being, it is claimed, by lowering our estimate of man compared to beings of an earlier world, to make us doubt the validity of man's pretentions to immortality. This is, I think, a fair statement of Byron's intention.

[2] Some thirty pages of prose observations follow the poem, largely taken up with a consideration of the flight of Lucifer and Cain through the abyss of space. I wish it were possible to quote the whole of this matchless specimen of the art of sinking in criticism. Wilkinson claims the right to judge Cain's exploit by the strict rules of physics and astronomy. Cain could not have breathed in the ether, as the experience of climbers in the Andes proves. Nor could he have trodden it. Who fixed on his wings ? How did he jump off the earth ? How could Lucifer " chatter " with him, going at the rate they were ? If the earth had become a small circle in the distance, how could he see the moon at all ? And so forth.

Byron is compared to a " maniac cur," a wasp, and an
" angry adder."

> If, then, my lord ! you would disturb my peace
> With daring blasphemies you send from Greece ;
> If thoughts profane contaminate your page,
> Shall I read on, nor speak my honest rage ?

Byron should re-read the Scriptures. If Reason is not a
safe guide, is not Conscience ? He is upbraided for vilifying
Milton's page.

> " To justify the ways of God to man,"
> If I remember, was his sacred plan ;
> To hold up Lucifer a blameless king,
> Is your intent, or I mistake the thing !

The poem sinks to this matchless anti-climax :

> Why seek perdition, and, perchance, what's worse,
> Call down upon thee a wise nation's curse ?

" The preacher at Kentish Town against *Cain*," whom
Byron mentions in one of his letters,[1] was the Rev. John
Styles,[2] who published his Sermon on *Lord Byron's Works*
just after the poet's death. The text chosen is, " Am I my
brother's keeper ? " Byron, says this charitable clergyman,
" scattered the seeds of a moral pestilence around him."
" What," he exclaims later, " if the impious spirit that has
breathed forth its execrations against God should also
presume to speak disloyally of the king ! " [3] We can only
echo, " What, indeed ! " and suffer this preacher to sink,
none too gently, back to the limbo from which this chapter
has drawn him for a moment.

The next piece of Byroniana that lays sufficient emphasis
on *Cain* to warrant its inclusion in this chapter rather than
elsewhere is " A Dissertation on Lord Byron ; his Moral
Character ; *Don Juan ; Cain*," by James and Edward
Aston.[4] This is on the whole a defence of Byron. It

---

[1] LJ, vi, 9.
[2] On Styles see also my *Dramas of Lord Byron*, p. 5.
[3] Virulent orthodoxy seems to have led naturally to the anti-climax.
[4] This is a sort of appendix to their *Pompeii and other Poems* (1828).

concedes the "dangerous tendency" of some of his later writings, but denies any "malignant attempt at general demoralization." *Cain* is defended whole-heartedly. Adam's resignation; Abel's serenity; Adah's "love-breathing heart"—these are all "refutations of the self-torturing sophist." Further analysis of these charitable but not very profound remarks is unnecessary.

In 1830 there was published an edition of *Cain* unlike any before or since. The editor was Harding Grant. In this stout, handsome, well-printed volume the text of Byron's drama is interrupted every few lines by voluminous notes that extend the book to no less than 448 pages. The notes are too wordy; are thoroughly orthodox; but are often acute, generally not uninteresting, and always quite charitable and tolerant in tone.[1] As it is impossible to give a full account of Grant's editorial methods within any tolerable limits, I subjoin a few specimens of his commentary in a foot-note.[2]

I come now to John Edmund Reade, a somewhat significant person in the history of Byron's After-fame. Reade is the most fulsome and slavish of all imitators of Byron, and if I have called him "significant" it is because the writings of such poetasters as he were responsible for the rapid decline in Byron's prestige between 1830 and 1850. For a while at least Reade enjoyed considerable popularity; reviews of his books were often singularly favourable;

---

[1] A reviewer of this edition in *The Monthly Magazine*, May 1830, says : " He is thoroughly orthodox, but also thoroughly good-humoured. . . . The bane and the antidote are both before us : the evil, if evil there be, is neutralized ; and the good, too, some will perhaps add." See also *Fraser's Magazine*, iii, 285 f., and Kölbing, *Englische Studien*, xvi, 310.

[2] Pp. 40–48 : an examination of Cain's first soliloquy, trying to prove that Cain had no valid grounds to complain of life or to question God's wisdom. P. 48 : " Enter Lucifer." Grant's note begins : " Before we engage with this formidable dramatis persona, we would prefer endeavouring to ascertain, if there are reasonable grounds for believing that such a being *really* exists." P. 75 : Grant answers Lucifer's speech, " Souls who dare use their immortality " point by point. This discussion extends to p. 99. And so forth. . . . A French work of somewhat similar character to Grant's is *Cain, Mystère Dramatique. Traduit en Vers français, et Réfuté dans une suite de Remarques Philosophiques et Critiques ; précédé d'une Lettre addressée à Lord Byron, sur les Motifs et le But de cet Ouvrage.* Par Fabre d'Olivet. (Paris, 1823.) See Estève, p. 145. The copy I have seen is in the library of Trinity College, Cambridge.

and he attained the dignity of a collected edition of his
poems which was more than once reprinted. His first
volume of poems was *The Broken Heart* by " Edmund J.
Reade " (1825). This may be passed over with the remark
that it is filled with Byronic echoes and plagiarisms, including
the line

> Still roll thee on, thou reckless Ocean, roll !

This was followed by *Cain the Wanderer* (1830), the title-
poem in a volume of miscellaneous pieces. It opens with
a prose dialogue between the Author and a Friend. This
is not without some interest. (The punctuation is that of
the original.) The Author says :

If the fairest test of genius were to be tried by the influence
it exerts on cotemporary literature, I hardly know how high
we are to rank the name of BYRON. What a change he has
created, not only in our poetry, but in our dramas, novels,
and almost national literature. . . . Passion, and intensity,
and heaven, and hell, and burning thoughts, and (brains
I may add) have been the rage with all our poets and
novelists. . . . Open shirt-collars, and melancholy features ;
and a certain *dash* of remorse, were as indispensable to
young men, and are so still, as tenderness, and endurance,
and intense feeling of passion among the fair sex. . . .
The only poet we have ever had who thought and felt *out*
of the mode and mould in which our poetry is peculiarly
cast.

Byron, the Author continues, unmasked hypocrisy, moral
and political ; he recognized humanity's ignorance ; he
taught that man's resource is within himself ; he exhibited
the grandeur and abasement of the soul. " It does indeed
sicken one to hear our little poets (God save the mark !)
prate of his failings." Reade then tells his friend of the
inception of his poem. He had made a draft of it at the
age of eighteen ; but when Byron's drama appeared he
threw the manuscript of his poem into the fire.[1] But the

---

[1] This MS, we are asked to believe, contained a scene in the Abyss
of Space.

theme continued to appeal to him, and at length he resumed it, his idea " enlarged and inspired " by Byron's work. He ends modestly :

The height of my ambition is that the critic, when commenting hereafter on his sublime production, may recall another to memory of the same name, which was in some respects intended as a sequel.

It would be a pity not to gratify—for once—this wish.

The play opens with a Prologue in Heaven, where Michael reports the death of Abel to the Almighty. Satan enters, and a colloquy follows between God and him. It is agreed that Cain shall be " the mark of trial " between them. I find it unnecessary to recount the plot scene by scene. Cain, in the desert, leaves his wife and son and wanders forth alone. He expresses, *solus*, his despair. Lucifer appears, and is described in these lines in which imitation of Byron reaches the pitch of pastiche :

> Magnificent spirit !
> Do I look on thee unblasted ?   I see still
> The thunder trenched upon thy regal brow,
> Like the red streak of lightning through the clouds !
> Yet pride is deeper stamped, and scorn of all :
> And the unconquerable will.

The Byronic rhetoric and the Byronic cadence, together with super-Byronic solecisms, are present throughout the play. Cain and Lucifer talk of will and pride and the foreknowledge of death. Despite self-reliance and intellectual freedom there yet remains " the sense of nothingness." Lucifer takes Cain to the Centre of the Earth and shows him the central force and the womb of all things. Then follows a flight through space, where the plagiarisms are amusingly and amazingly bold and bare-faced, as in Cain's exclamation :

> O what a mass of living lights !   O thou
> Bright star-dewed wilderness of ether ! etc.

After many experiences Cain returns to die at his father's

dwelling-place, finding comfort in the universal law of death.[1]

Two decades after the publication of Byron's *Cain* there was still some one ambitious of producing a poetic reply. The last of such refutations that I know of is *Abel : Written, but with great humility, in reply to Lord Byron's Cain.* By Owen Howell (1843). In a foreword Howell throws into antithesis his own and Byron's purposes : Byron's object was to embody " all the emotions of Despair " ; his own, " to personify Hope, and to bring together as many pleasing expectations as possible." Part I. of this piece is a colloquy between Abel and Lucifer, in which Abel rejects the fiend's advances. Part II. is occupied with a voyage in Heaven made by Abel under the conduct of the Archangel Michael. The philosophy (such as it is) of the poem reflects the popular universalism of the period :

> God cannot err,
> And evil is because that he from evil
> Does now or will produce a greater good,
> The fathomless future is the ultimate
> Of his intentions.

[1] In the course of an unsigned review of Reade's *Record of the Pyramids* (*Blackwood's*, lii, July 1842, 119) Walter Savage Landor offers this epigram :

> The reign of justice is return'd again :
> Cain murdered Abel, and Reade murders Cain.

In other poems Reade follows Byron even more closely than in *Cain the Wanderer.* His *Italy* (1838), a large handsome volume, is not utterly contemptible, at least in the judgment of a person whose love of that country makes him blind to defects in a poem that sings her praises. It is the frankest, most ingenuous, and closest imitation of Byron that I have ever seen—and I have seen many. It is written in *Childe-Harold*-ish Spenserians. The author's pen is as facile as are his enthusiasms. The poem opens at Florence and supplies rapturous descriptions of the art treasures of the city : a stanza begins " The Niobe—the majesty of woe ! " The Marble Fawn and the tombs in San Lorenzo follow. Then come meditations on Dante and Galileo ; then Fiesole, the Val d'Arno, Vallombrosa, and so forth. The next canto finds us at Venice, and at the sight of " yon grey palace " a tribute to Byron rises to the poet's lips (six stanzas). In a later canto there is a huge amount of observation of Rome, and Reade does not shrink from juxtaposing the Coliseum, the Laöcoön, the Dying Gladiator, and the Apollo of the Belvedere. Thereafter we follow this sentimental traveller to Naples, Vesuvius, Amalfi, and all along that divine coast, and the poem ends with sunset at Paestum. Reade also wrote *The Deluge* (1839), a poem on the theme of the love of the Sons of God for the Daughters of Men ; but an advertisement declares that the play was written earlier than Byron's *Heaven and Earth* and Moore's *Loves of the Angels.* The names Irad and Astarte are suggestive of Byron's influence, and the whole play is Byronish. This volume contains, among other pieces, a poem on " Prometheus Bound."

We catch here an echo of *Festus*. The thought was to be frequently repeated in Browning's poetry, and it receives its best expression from the mouth of the great Pope in *The Ring and the Book*.

In closing this chapter let me return to Byron himself. He watched the development of the controversy precipitated by *Cain ;* and to his friend Kinnaird he wrote in November 1822 : [1]

As to myself, I shall not be deterred by any outcry ; your present public hate me, but they shall not interrupt the march of my mind, nor prevent me from telling those who are attempting to trample on all thought, that their thrones shall yet be rocked to their foundations.

The heterodoxy of yesterday is the orthodoxy of to-day ; the heresy of to-day is the commonplace of to-morrow. Times change, and thoughts and manners with the times. Though a more refined æstheticism no longer finds pleasure in it as a work of art, and though it seems now but to scratch the surface of the problems it seeks to probe, *Cain* remains a monument of protest against the fetters which a hundred years ago bound freedom of discussion, and with which some people even to-day still seek to bind it.

[1] LJ, vi, 140.

CHAPTER VII

MISCELLANEOUS BYRONIANA : 1816–1824

IN this chapter I shall consider a number of unrelated and unclassifiable estimates and critiques of Byron and a few satires and imitations that were published during the eight years between his departure from England in April 1816 and his death in April 1824. An examination in chronological order of the miscellaneous books and pamphlets of this period will be followed by a survey of a few representative reviews.

The publication of *Manfred* suggested a poetical *Address to Lord Byron*. By F. H. B.[1] (1817). This begins with an appeal to Byron to " mingle with his kind " :

> The spirit of thy loneliness, the strain
> Pervades—'tis seen in Conrad,—and its chill
> Gives Lara deeper horror. Manfred, now,
> Surpasses all ; cold damp surmounts my brow,
> As pond'ring o'er his incantation dread !

Byron is warned that knowledge misapplied and talents abused " shall work eternal woe." He should make God's glory his theme ; if he aims at singularity, then let it be the " singularly good." Of *Manfred* (which a generation later was to provoke Meredith's satire) a note says :

Bad as is the age, we yet dare hope and believe no English audience would endure the daring impiety of many of the scenes. Even in the closet it shocks us to peruse the dialogues between demons, spirits, a star, a witch, and Manfred.[2]

---

[1] Not " T. H. B.," as given in *N. & Q.* 4th Series, i, 167; and in Lowndes' *Bibliography*, i, 340.

[2] Nevertheless *Manfred* has been performed on the stage on various occasions. They may be recorded here. (1) With music by Bishop it was produced as a " choral tragedy in three acts " at Covent Garden Theatre,

Of the " Hymn of the Spirits " a note says : " We forbear to quote the passage, which is dreadfully impious."

One of the numerous offshoots of the *Faust* theme during the period is *The Warning Voice, A Sacred Poem, addressed to Infidel Writers of Poetry*, by the Hon. and Rev. Edward John Turnour (1818). The angels in heaven lament man's fall ; they discuss the progress of infidelity on earth and the popularity of writers who seek to undermine confidence in God. One angel proposes that a man should be incited to write a poem in praise of God and to inspire hope of salvation. This angel is dispatched to earth ; he sees the Pastor assembled with his family at Morning Prayer ; he inspires him with the idea and departs ; and the Pastor's " Warning Voice " begins. It is addressed particularly to Byron :

October 29, 1834, Denvil taking the part of Manfred. The play was received with applause which the free-list *claque* seems somewhat to have overdone. It ran until November 14, with intermissions. See *The Athenæum*, November 2, 1834, p. 811. (2) Phelps revived the piece at Drury Lane, October 10, 1863. This revival occasioned the pamphlet : *Lord Byron's Manfred. At Drury Lane Theatre. By a Dilettante behind the Scenes* (1863) in which the performance is praised and is interpreted as an effort on Phelps's part " to inaugurate a reaction against the too realistic tendencies of the day in matters theatrical " and " to restore some dignity and some elevation to the productions of the English stage." See also Henry Morley's *Journal of a Playgoer* (1866), p. 318 : " *Manfred* crams the pit and fills the theatre. . . . A play with so little dramatic action . . . would not draw for a week, if there were not a high intellectual power in the thoughts and language." (3) Charles Calvert produced the play at Manchester in March, 1867, and (4) again at Liverpool, 1867. In all these productions the music of Sir Henry Bishop seems to have been used. In Lacy's Acting Edition of English Plays, volume lx, there is *Manfred : A Choral Tragedy, in three acts. The Dublin University Magazine*, lxxxiii, April 1874, 502 f., has an article by " the London Hermit " on " *Manfred :* Poem and Drama " which is extravagant in its praise : " I believe that . . . *Manfred* has the highest capabilities of becoming, under favourable circumstances, a magnificent acting drama." This seems to have been Sir Henry Irving's opinion also, for towards the end of his life he planned to revive the play. See *The Academy*, August 11, 1900, p.113. But both Bram Stoker's *Personal Reminiscences of Henry Irving* and Austin Brereton's *Life of Henry Irving* are silent on this matter. At Irving's request, Sir A. C. Mackenzie composed incidental music for *Manfred*, in 1897 ; this was performed in London in 1899. Schumann's *Overture* is well known ; his incidental music and choruses not so well known. (See *Manfred : A Dramatic Poem. By Lord Byron. The Music by Robert Schumann. Opus 115. With connecting text in the form of prologues . . .* by Richard Pohl. Translated from the German and adapted for the use of the N. Y. Philharmonic Society, by J. R. Cornell. New York, Torrey, 1869). Schumann's music was composed in 1850. Tschaikowsky's " Manfred Symphony " was composed in 1885.

> Thou, noble Scribe ! of atheistic mind,
> Pride more than human, and perverted sense !
> Thee, too, I warn ; oh, may I not in vain ! . . .

He throws down his pledge of combat :

> God's Holy Records in the Bible be
> My only shield.

A second canto deals with the attributes of God : Mercy, Forbearance, Judgment ; the consolations of Christianity ; and so forth.

Francis Hodgson, the friend of Byron's youth, was the author of an anonymous satire, *Childe Harold's Monitor* (1818). The subject is literary, not moral or personal, for the most part ; and various poets besides Byron are noticed. Hodgson is loyal to the dying classical school and declares that Byron has followed the false models of " the Gothic band." Byron has even imitated Wordsworth, who

> dares on Keswick's banks to plant
> The verse of Klopstock with the sense of Kant.

All Byron's friends are

> indignant to observe his muse
> Gathering poor scraps, that Coleridge might refuse.

But though he admires the pseudo-classic poets, Hodgson has been touched by the Elizabethan revival, and counsels Byron and his contemporaries to

> Enrich your tongues, ye moderns ! now and then,
> With grave, sweet Massinger, or pithy Ben ;
> Or, balmier yet be sorrow's music pour'd,
> Dipped in the liquid tenderness of Ford.
> But scorn to steal the body of their style—
> Nor drag their glory from its Gothic aisle.

The first signs of Byron's mature satiric manner appeared in *Beppo* (1818).[1] It promptly inspired imitations. *More*

---

[1] I have not seen *A Poetical Epistle from Delia to Lord Byron* (1817) which is announced to appear in a newspaper clipping in the B. M. scrap-book, vol. i. The verse-epistle which William Stewart Rose sent to Byron in the spring of 1818 is reprinted by Prothero (LJ, iv, 212 f.) and need

*News from Venice, By Beppo, Translated from the Original
by Julius,* was published in the same year.   The eighty-one
stanzas of this piece are roughly modelled on Byron's *ottava
rima,* but the rhyme-scheme is irregular and there are
frequent alexandrines.   The satire is dull and rambling.
It opens with the remark that a tale from a great distance
always finds believers, and instances of this fact are given.
Then :

> But to my story.   'Twas some months ago,
> Their number needless to complete the tale,
> A certain Noble—all the world doth know
> (To broach his name were now of no avail,
> But for the sake of ease I must do so,
> Or else my rhyming faculty would fail),
> Came to our goodly state with many a spire on—
> His name, and his forefathers', take it—B***n.

> This is the man, all solemnness and mystery,
> That loves to wander at the noon of night,
> And if the truth is stated in his history,
> He's Pope of Poets by exclusive right.

Byron is described : his travels, his many loves, the loss
of his First Love, his marriage, his separation from Lady
Byron, and so forth.   Beppo thinks he should have been
a Mussulman.   All ladies are advised to keep their distance
from him.

Another offshoot of Byron's Venetian Tale is : *Beppo
in London.   A Metropolitan Story* (1819).   According to
this tale Beppo was not really wrecked ; he travelled over
Europe, sold his cargo well, visited various countries, and
came at length to London where he spent his time in drinking,
wenching, and seeing the sights.   This gives occasion for
much satire on society, politics, literature, the stage, morals,
the new system of lighting by gas, and so forth.   At last

not be quoted here.   And to this foot-note may be consigned reference
to *The Literary Bazaar ; or, Poet's Council,* by " Peter Pepperpot " (1816).
This is an obscure member of the long series of " Sessions of the Poets "
which extends through English Literature from Suckling to Buchanan.   The
poets—Byron, Wordsworth, Southey, Scott and others—come together to
consider means of quelling the booksellers and routing duns.   Canto i. is
a debate as to who should lead the attack on the booksellers ; Canto ii. is
a battle between the poets and the booksellers.   It is all very poor stuff.

Beppo is arrested for debt, and the author leaves him in prison. One stanza will serve as a specimen :

> Imagine Beppo now arriv'd in town,
> In London—famous for its gas and smother—
> Its men of wit—its poets of renown,
> Who laud the pretty stanzas of each other—
> Such as are stitch'd, and sold for half-a-crown,
> Hot press'd by this—and publish'd by another—
> All very fair and pleasing to the vision,
> But sadly wanting grammar and revision.

The last line precisely characterizes this production.
Two lines in *Beppo*—

> But for those children of the " mighty mother's,"
> The would-be wits, and can't-be gentlemen—

occasioned another offshoot of very different character :
A Poetical Epistle from Alma Mater to Lord Byron (1819),
which is a violent onslaught on the poet. The University
of Cambridge is imagined as addressing her " degenerate
Son." Byron's jealousy, hate, discontent, rude rhymes,
want of wit, and failure in satire are all tilted at :

> Come, come, my lord, write ballads and be wise,
> Revile you may—you cannot satirize.

Byron is called the quack of Parnassus, the " Pierian
Charlatan." After a detailed recipe for Byron's " fresh
concocted plagiary hash " come these lines :

> See, of thy proper taste, expos'd for sale,
> Rent marriage bonds, a trifle, or a tale ;
> For want of subject and the sake of pelf,
> Thou trick'st for sale thine own peculiar self,
> Thy morbid heart's distemper'd tale is told,
> And e'en thy griefs, if thou can'st grieve, are sold.

O for some mighty moralist, the satirist exclaims, to drive
off such puny flutterers from the literary stage !

> Then might we clear our intellectual view,
> And every loftier, better sense renew,
> Then might due praises wait on Crabbe or Scott,
> And thine unhallow'd ravings be forgot.

This *Epistle* is signed " Alma." By this time the reader will have observed that when indignant moralists ventured to cross swords with Byron they did so almost invariably from behind the shield of a pseudonym.

The earliest work to introduce Byron in the infernal regions anticipates his death by several years. This is : *Childe Harold in the Shades* (1818). A sufficient idea of this excessively tedious piece may be had from the argument with which it opens, part of which is as follows :

The noble shade commenceth his recital of the Childe's infernal Pilgrimage, by informing his readers how little he regardeth them or their opinions. He affirmeth that his mind continueth a prey to the same morbid dispositions as in life. He proceedeth to describe the various scenes he hath beheld in the lower regions, and beginneth by depicting the Furies. He . . . relateth that he met, first, the shades of those bards who in these degenerate days have discovered some claim to praise, and then of those whom infernal justice hath for their bad verses condemned to a suitable punishment. Among the latter he noteth his friends H—nt and C—le—ge. He seeth the pains inflicted on the race ycleped Dandies, as also on gluttons, and on those who have betrayed the liberties of their country. . . . He beholdeth the condition after death of hypocrites, false friends, venal critics, and others. He also vieweth the shades of Dr. Johnson and Dan Chaucer.

This stupid piece introduces S—th—y, C—bbe, C–mpb–ll, and others ; " the author has killed them by poetic license."

Some thirty lines are devoted to Byron in Sharon Turner's turgid and bombastic poem, *Prolusions on the Present Greatness of Britain* (1819). Turner appeals to him to avoid the tempest of passion, to hearken to the " voice of future times," to warm " our best affections," and to " wither our base stuff." In peculiar contrast to most current criticism his estimate concludes :

> One laurel is thy own. Thy muse of fire
> Has never wallowed in corruption's mire.
> Thy lays have not descended to the vile,
> Nor sung the flush'd bacchante's wanton smile.

Let thy proud lyre for man's best interests sound :
By him with fame ; by heaven, with blessings crown'd.[1]

Into the tedious controversy between Byron and the
Rev. William Bowles on the subject of the merits of Pope's
poetry as compared with the moderns. I do not propose
to enter. It has been often discussed and has no bearing
upon the history of Byron's reputation.[2]

The first lengthy and ambitious biography of Byron—
there had of course been many " sketches " of his life—
appeared anonymously in 1822 : *Memoirs of the Life and
Writings of Lord Byron, with Anecdotes of some of his Con-*

---

[1] Some Byroniana *minima* of these years may be consigned to a note.
There are references to the poet in J. G. Lockhart's *Peter's Letters to his
Kinsfolk* (1819) ; see i, 304 ; ii, 217 ; and especially ii, 220, where Lockhart compares the love-poetry of Byron and Coleridge greatly to the latter's
advantage. To 1820 belong : (1) *Critique from the Edinburgh Review, on
Lord Byron's Poems, which occasioned " English Bards and Scotch Reviewers."*
The republication of Brougham's notorious article is evidence of the interest
taken in all phases of Byron's career. (2) *Despair ; A Vision*, etc. These
two quite close parodies of *Darkness* and *The Giaour* are of political significance only. (3) A lecture delivered in 1820, but not printed till 1824,
(probably just after Byron's death) is *A Discourse on the Comparative
Merits of Scott and Byron.* In the dazzling constellations of contemporary
poets two stars reign supreme, says the lecturer. Byron surpasses Scott
in power and grandeur. Scott's poetry is " external " and has " few marks
of deep thought." Byron is superior also in imagination, power of suggestion, style, and versification. In fact, he leaves " the rivalry of his
own era at a hopeless and immeasurable distance. . . . The Lover, the
Enthusiast, the ardent and the misanthropical, will garner up the burning
and heart-piercing strains of Byron." (4) *A Letter . . . on the Injustice
and Illegality* [of] *representing Lord Byron's Tragedy of Marino Faliero.*
The writer protests against the disregard of Byron's wishes and the unfairness of judging a play by its lack of success on the stage when it was
written for the " closet." (Yet even *Marino Faliero*, dull as much of it is,
attracted interest and made it worth while to publish : *Marino Faliero, or
the Doge of Venice ; Who was Executed for a Conspiracy. . . . An Interesting
Tale.* A folding double-page coloured frontispiece bears the date 1824.
It is a prose account of the story of the play. I have seen the third edition.)
(5) *The Stage : A Poem*, by John Brown. In advising actors not to turn
too suddenly from the grave to gay an illustration is drawn from " that
titl'd bard " who

Now raves at home, now wanders to Aleppo,
Now threatens self-destruction, now writes " Beppo."

[2] Prothero gives a full account in LJ, v, Appendix iii. See my
bibliography under " Bowles " and " Fabius." Maginn published in
" Familiar Letters from the Adjutant " (*Blackwood's*, ix, May 1821, 131 f. ;
reprinted in *The Odoherty Papers*, i, 227 f.) some amusing comments on the
inconsistencies of Byron's theories and poetry. See also *Blackwood's*,
same number, p. 227 f. M. McDirmot's *Letter to the Rev. W. L. Bowles*
(1821) has little reference to Byron.

temporaries. It is by John Watkins.[1] In the main, though there are some concluding extenuations, he is violently hostile to Byron. He accuses the poet of forming a " school of immorality and profaneness," and calls him " the noble president " of " this new academy of blasphemy " in which Shelley and Hunt are professors. A dedicatory letter calls on Gifford to " bring this haughty spirit to a sense of shame and a course of propriety." At the very end the tone changes singularly :

He wants nothing but a noble moral motive to render his works imperishable. . . . Attempts have been made to set up some other living poets, in comparison with Lord Byron, but these are futile.

Byron has eloquence, vigour, imagination, range of thought and subject ; but he wants judgment and has perverted his talents to licentiousness.

The satire which Gifford wrote upon *The Liberal* and then suppressed will be described in my chapter on Byron in Fiction. Another attack on Hunt's unlucky periodical is *A Critique on " The Liberal "* (1822). The anonymous author remarks that adverse criticism is unpleasant to write, but that tendencies towards immorality must be " lashed." He then proceeds :

Though no avowed authors are announced in the title-page, it is to be understood, that there were three contributors to this work ; Lord Byron, Leigh Hunt, Esq., and Percy B. Shelly [*sic*], Esq., lately deceased. The talents of the triumvirate have been long known : the first two, especially, have ranked high in the annals of literature.

---

[1] Richard Edgcumbe (*N. & Q.* 7th Series, i, 265) states that Dean Ireland was the author. This is erroneous. Isaac D'Israeli described the biography as " a bungling trick . . . performed by a hoary garrettier *en chef*, a Dr. Watkins, who is a dead hand at a Life ! " (Letter to Byron, quoted LJ, vi, 86, note). Shelley wrote to Leigh Hunt, June 24, 1822 (published for the first time in *The Nation and the Athenæum*, March 19, 1921, p. 877) : " Lord Byron, I hear, is in a state of supernatural fever about some lying memoirs published of him." Byron himself wrote that he thought of publishing his own " *Memoirs now*, should it be necessary to counteract the fellow " (LJ, vi, 101). There was a favourable review of Watkins' *Memoirs* in *The European Magazine*, September 1822, pp. 255 f.

The *Critique* is mainly devoted to an analysis of Byron's *Vision of Judgment*, which is very adversely viewed. The author concludes :

We have now gone through this poem, which every reader must see to be very poorly written. Waving the blasphemy it contains nothing but abuse. . . . Instead of politics we find railing. . . . And this they call *Liberalism*, the essentials of which are candour and moderation.[1]

Ebenezer Elliott attacks Byron in " The Giaour, A Satirical Poem " (1823).[2] His anti-patriotism, his portrayal of " Nature *versus* Byron's envious hate," his malignancy, his self-portraiture are berated, and Elliott cries :

> Childe ! Giaour ! and Corsair !—names by which men call
> Bad copies of a worse original.

Yet Elliott should have recognized in Byron an ally.

I return now to the year 1816 to review briefly a few characteristic notices of the chief volumes published by Byron in his later years.

Scott's and Jeffrey's reviews of *Childe Harold*, canto iii. will be considered in the next chapter. John Wilson reviewed *Manfred* in *Blackwood's ;* [3] he was impressed by its power and imperfections and devoted most of his notice to an account of the poem. In the following number [4] he threw out the suggestion that Byron was indebted to Marlowe's *Faustus*. This, as we shall see, Jeffrey discussed in his review of *Manfred*. Of the many reviews of *Childe Harold*, canto iv, I postpone the consideration of Scott's, and note here John Wilson's.[5] This opens with a comparison of Byron and Rousseau : each has filled his works with expressions of his own character ; each has been an object of profound interest to the world.

---

[1] For other attacks on *The Liberal*, see LJ, vi, 122.
[2] In *Love. A Poem in Three Parts. To which is added, The Giaour* (1823).
[3] June 1817, pp. 289 f.
[4] July 1817, pp. 388 f., in an article on *Faustus*.
[5] *The Edinburgh Review*, xxx, June 1818, pp. 87 f.

We feel chiefly the influence of such a writer while he lives.
. . . When death removes such a writer [as Rousseau] from
our sight, the magical influence of which we have spoken
gradually fades away ; and a new generation, free from
all personal feelings towards the idol of a former age, may
perhaps be wearied with that perpetual self-reference which
to them seems merely the querulousness or the folly of
unhappy or diseased egoism. . . . It is at least certain, that
by the darkness of death such luminaries are shorn of their
beams. . . . Such must be more or less the fate of all
works of genius, however splendid and powerful, of which
the chief interest is not in universal truth, so much as in
the intensity of individual feeling and the impersonation
of individual character.

Wilson believes that Byron does not stand in this predica-
ment to the same degree as did Rousseau ; but

posterity may make fewer allowances for much in himself
and his writings, than his contemporaries are willing to do ;
nor will they, with the same passionate and imperious
zeal, follow the wild voice that too often leads into a haunted
wilderness of doubt and darkness. To them, as to us,
there will always be something majestic in his misery—
something sublime in his despair.

The accurate forecast of the future change in public taste
makes this one of the most striking judgments to be found
in contemporary criticism of Byron. Continuing, Wilson
says that

there is felt to be between him and the public mind a stronger
personal bond than ever linked its movements to any other
living poet. And we think that this bond will in future
be still more closely rivetted.

Canto iv. is pronounced far better than the earlier instalments of *Childe Harold*.

It is a nobler creature who is before us. The ill-sustained
misanthropy and disdain of the two first Cantos, more
faintly glimmer through the third, and may be said to
disappear wholly from the fourth, which reflects the high
and disturbed visions of earthly glory, as a dark swollen

tide images the splendours of the sky in portentous colouring and broken magnificence.

There follows a discussion of scepticism in modern poetry and an analysis of the canto at great length, with many excerpts and accompanied by high praise.

Of the Poet himself, the completion of this wonderful performance inspires us with lofty and magnificent hopes. It is most assuredly in his power to build up a work that shall endure among the most august fabrics of the genius of England.

The extraordinary interest in Byron during his later years may be illustrated from the amount of material published in two magazines. The Byroniana in *The New Monthly Magazine* during 1819, I consign to a note ; [1] and

[1] In February (pp. 1 f.) : " Observations on Lord Byron's Juvenile Poems, with Specimens " by " X." The extracts and account of Byron's juvenilia are given because of Byron's determination " never to suffer " the book to be reprinted and its consequent extreme scarcity. In April (pp. 193 f.) : " Extract from a Letter from Geneva, with Anecdotes of Lord Byron, &c." Already visitors were coming to the Villa Diodati, where the poet had lived in 1816, to see souvenirs of Byron. " I trod the floors," says the writer, " with the same feelings of awe and respect as we did, together, those of Shakespeare's dwelling." Several anecdotes are told ; the Byron-Shelley-Mary-Claire scandal is positively denied. The ghost-story party is narrated, and " The Vampyre ; a Tale, by Lord Byron " is printed. This attribution was corrected by Polidori in the May number (p. 332). See my chapter on the Byron Apocrypha. In May (pp. 330 f.) J. H. Wiffen contributes a letter " On the Character and Poetry of Lord Byron." He commends the magazine's interest in the subject, as shown by the numerous papers on the poet, and continues : " Him I have ever regarded as a persecuted individual. . . . After reading *Childe Harold* or *The Corsair*, one can do nothing ; it absorbs and unnerves us. A lady once observed to me, ' Moore's *Lalla Rookh* I can take up and lay down ; I can take up a work of theology and read with equal attention ; but I must have a night's sleep after reading *Lara* or *The Corsair*.' " Wiffen warns those who are engaged in attacking Byron : " The men who neglected to alleviate the misfortunes of the *living* Burns, are *raising to the dead statues of stone*. . . . For myself, I cannot refrain from avowing, that I consider it a glory in my life, that I live in the age of Lord Byron." In June (pp. 388 f.) " J. M." (*i.e.* **John** Mitford) contributes an article on " Lord Byron's Travels in Greece." This contains various apocryphal anecdotes met with in early Byroniana : " his favoured fair Berinthia," his long residence at Mitylene, his departure therefrom after the death of his infant son, his humanity, generosity, and so forth. In July (pp. 527 f.) there are " Lines on reading the last canto of *Childe Harold*," in which the anonymous writer hails Byron as " the high priest of Beauty." Finally, in November, this same indefatigable magazine published a " Critique on Lord Byron " which is of little consequence.

pass to *Blackwood's* during 1822. A review of the three plays, *Sardanapalus, The Two Foscari,* and *Cain,* is followed in the January number by a reprint of Southey's letter to *The Courier* which I shall discuss in the next chapter. In February a long letter signed " Siluriensis," pronounces unfavourable judgment upon the plays, both in art and morals, and denounces Byron as, in *Don Juan,* " the armed champion of profligacy." In March the first instalment of the " Rhapsodies over a Punch-Bowl " contains allusions to the Byron-Bowles controversy, Byron's letter to Bowles being called " that prime specimen of humbug." In April there is a verse " Critique on Lord Byron," signed " Palaemon," written by William Maginn, beginning :

> So the Public at length is beginning to tire on
> The torrent of poesy pour'd out by Lord Byron.

A view of Byron's poetical career contains this amusing estimate of his miscellaneous pieces :

> Sad Tasso's Lament—soft occasional verses—
> And levell'd at Elgin stern Pallas's curses ;
> Mazeppa's long race, that intrepid rough-rider,—
> And adieus to a Lady, whose Lord can't abide her.
> Within two blue paste-boards what contraries meet—
> The fragrant, the fetid, the bitter, the sweet :—
> Like a garden neglected these fences enclose
> The violet, the nettle, the nightshade, the rose.

The piece ends :

> 'Twould be wrong, noble Bard, oh ! permit me to tell ye,
> To establish a league with Leigh Hunt and Byshe [*sic*] Shelley ; . . .[1]
> The world cries in chorus, 'tis certainly time
> To close up your flood-gates of blank verse and rhyme.
> Hold ! Hold !—By the public thus sated and cramm'd
> Lest your lays, like yourself, stand a chance to be d——d ![2]

A more good-natured satire is " The Literary Police

---

[1] A note comments upon Byron's praise of Lady Morgan and Shelley, " the Hibernian Lady-errant and the poetico-metaphysical maniac."

[2] A " Letter from Paddy " follows, poking fun at Byron's metaphysicalities and attempted sublimity in *Cain.* A postscript suggests that *Blackwood's* forbid contributors to mention Byron for at least nine months ; " do, for novelty's sake, give us some respite." Indeed, after this, Byron is not discussed in " Maga " for some time.

Office, Bow Street " [1] which depicts the trial of various poets. One charge against Wordsworth is that of impersonating his own grandmother. Byron, " a young person of apparently ferocious habits," is charged with a violent assault on several " literary gentlemen."

A new note sounds in *The London Magazine* of December, 1823, when George Darley writes : [2]

Here is Minor Beddoes, . . . born amidst the very rage and triumph of the Byronian heresy . . . yet what does Minor Beddoes do ? Why write a tragedy himself. . . . He totally rejects . . . the use of prose-poetry. . . . *The Bride's Tragedy* transcends, in the quality of its rhythm and metrical harmony, the Doge of Venice. . . . I am almost tempted to confess after the perusal of our Minor's poem, that I have been premature in pronouncing the decline of English poetry from the Byronian epoch.

The Anti-Byronism that so quickly overtook the poet's posthumous renown is here definitely beginning within his lifetime. Byron was himself conscious of a decline in popularity in 1823 ; indeed, his realization of this adds something to the pathos of his last year in Italy, and may have stimulated him to undertake the expedition to Greece. The death of Shelley had moved him more than he cared to betray ; the failure of the Italian uprising had disappointed him ; he was bored by La Guiccioli. Moreover, the venture of *The Liberal* was an unhappy one. The association of his name with Hunt rendered him restive. His plays had not succeeded on the stage, a contretemps that mortified him notwithstanding his repeated declarations that they were not intended for the theatre. The later cantos of *Don Juan* lacked, he sometimes thought, something of the freshness and ease of the earlier ones.[3]

---

[1] *The London Magazine*, February 1823, pp. 157 f.
[2] Quoted by Ramsay Colles, *Poems of T. L. Beddoes* (London : Routledge, n.d.), pp. 445 f.
[3] We have seen that Maginn's verse-critique more than hints at Byron's waning popularity, and attacks his alliance with Hunt and Shelley. The same theme is touched on in the first number of the *Noctes Ambrosianæ* (*Blackwood's*, xi, March 1822, 363). To Odoherty's remark, " This holy alliance of Pisa will be a queer affair," the Editor replies, " Byron is a

The news that Byron had sailed for Greece changed all this. It thrilled the imagination of Englishmen of whatever political party. It heartened Liberals everywhere. It raised the poet again to the heights of reputation. His death followed swiftly.

prince ; but these dabbling dogglerers destroy every dish they dip in. . . . Imagine Shelly [*sic*], with his spavin, and Hunt, with his stringhalt, going in the same harness wth such a caperer as Byron." The influence of this decline in popularity upon Byron was recognized by some contemporaries. *The London Magazine*, of October 1824 (quoted in *Byron painted by his Compeers*, p. 13) says : " Before he went to Greece, he imagined that he had grown very unpopular and even infamous in England ! when he left Murray, engaged in *The Liberal*, which was unsuccessful, published with the Hunts, he fancied, and doubtless was told so by some of his aristocratic friends, that he had become *low*, that the *better* English thought him out of fashion, and voted him vulgar."

CHAPTER VIII

THE OPINIONS OF GREAT CONTEMPORARIES

THIS chapter, like that which has immediately preceded it, must be an *omnium gatherum*, for I find it more convenient to gather together in one place a record of the views of Byron expressed by great contemporary men of letters than to scatter through various chapters individual allusions in chronological order. As far as possible I have arranged these opinions in logical sequence, beginning with Scott ; passing to Wordsworth, Coleridge, Southey and Landor ; thence to Shelley, Keats and Hunt ; and thence to Lamb, Hazlitt, and Jeffrey. It is not my purpose to write of Byron's personal relations with these men, nor to summarize his opinions of their writings. We are concerned solely with their views of him and his poetry.

Scott [1] protested to Jeffrey against *The Edinburgh Review's* treatment of *Hours of Idleness ;* " I thought they contained passages of noble promise," he said.[2] Of the first two cantos of *Childe Harold* he wrote to Miss Baillie : [3]

A very clever poem but gives no good symptom of the writer's heart or morals. . . . You cannot for your soul avoid concluding that the author, as he gives an account of his travels, is also doing so in his own character. . . . Yet with all this conceit and assurance, there is much poetical merit in the book. . . . Though there is something provoking and insulting to morality and to feeling in his misanthropical ennui, it gives, nevertheless, an odd piquancy to his descriptions and reflections. This is upon the whole a piece of most extraordinary power, and may rank its author with our first poets.

[1] See Margaret Ball's dissertation, *Sir Walter Scott as a Critic of Literature,* pp. 92–6.
[2] Lockhart's *Life of Scott,* iii, 169.   [3] *Ibid.,* iii, 339, 342

Scott's annoyance at the lines satirizing him in *English Bards* was quickly cleared away and a cordial friendship and reciprocal admiration ensued between him and Byron.   His characteristic generosity and lack of jealousy were amply exercised.   To Ballantyne he writes : [1] " Byron hits the mark where I don't even pretend to fledge my arrow."   In May 1816 Scott, watching the scandal, writes : [2]

Lord Byron . . . with high genius and many points of a noble and generous feeling, has Childe Harolded himself, and outlawed himself, into too great a resemblance with the pictures of his imagination.

And in December of the same year : [3]

The third canto of *Childe Harold* is inimitable.   Of the last poems, there are one or two which indicate rather an irregular play of imagination.

The recollections of Byron which Scott furnished to Thomas Moore [4] betray the differences of the two poets on matters of religion and politics.   Scott says that Byron entertained no " very fixed opinions " on either subject. There follows the expression of Scott's belief that had he lived Byron would have become a Roman Catholic.   Again Scott writes :

On politics, he used sometimes to express a high strain of what is now called Liberalism ; but it appeared to me that the pleasure it afforded him as a vehicle of displaying his wit and satire against individuals in office was at the bottom of this habit of thinking, rather than any real conviction of the political principles on which he talked.

The remark indicates the extent to which Scott failed in real insight into Byron's character ; but it must be remembered that his impressions were of the year 1815, and that Byron's political convictions deepened in later years.

A like view of Byron's politics appears in Scott's notice

---

[1] Lockhart's *Life of Scott*, v, 27.   [2] *Ibid.*, v, 127.
[3] *Ibid.*, v, 156.
[4] Reprinted LJ, iii, Appendix iv.

of *Childe Harold*, canto iii.[1] He finds in Byron vigour, originality, spontaneity ; accuracy in description, and a unique ability to vary the interest of his poem " although the most important personage [retains] the same lineaments." But of the stanzas on Waterloo he says : " It is melancholy to see a man of genius duped by the mere cant of words " ; and he declares that Byron's political sentiments are " the sport of whim and singularity " rather than " the expression of any serious or fixed opinion." The review ends on a question : *Why* is Byron unhappy ?

Lord Byron may not have loved the world, but the world has loved him, not perhaps with a wise or discriminating affection, but as well as it is capable of loving any one.

In his notice of the fourth canto [2] Scott reviews the circumstances of Byron's popularity, accounting for it in part because Byron has been the first poet since Cowper to express *himself*, and in part because his powers have been equal to his pretensions.

In spite of bad metaphysics and worse politics, he may yet be a person, whose high talents the wise and virtuous may enjoy. . . . The harmony of verse, and the power of numbers . . . are all so subordinate to the thought and sentiment, as to become comparatively light in the scale.

When Byron died Scott described him [3] as " a man of real goodness of heart, and the kindest and best feelings, miserably thrown away by his foolish contempt of public opinion." His formal article, " The Death of Lord Byron," [4] has been frequently reprinted.[5]

[1] *The Quarterly Review*, xvi, October 1816, 172 f.
[2] *Ibid.*, xix, April 1818, 215 f.
[3] Lockhart, vii, 297.
[4] *Edinburgh Weekly Journal*, 1824 ; part reprinted in *The Pamphleteer*, xxiv, 169 f. ; and in *Miscellaneous Poems* [of Byron], . . . *To which are prefixed Memoirs of the Author, and a Tribute to his Memory by Sir Walter Scott* (1824). This " Character of Lord Byron " is reprinted in the one-volume edition of Byron's Works, Frankfort O.M., 1829, p. xliii f. It, and the two reviews of *Childe Harold*, are in Scott's *Miscellaneous Prose Works* (1841–7), vol. i.
[5] Of Scott's opinions of Byron Miss Ball says (p. 96) : " His views seem perfectly rational now " and (p. 106) : " In regard to Byron Scott expressed a critical estimate that the public is only now getting ready to accept after a long period of depreciating Byron's genius."

Henry Crabb Robinson [1] tells of an episode which must have occurred just about the time that Scott was protesting to Jeffrey against the review of *Hours of Idleness*.   One day he was sitting with Lamb, and Wordsworth, entering with a copy of *The Edinburgh Review* in his hand, looked annoyed, and said : " Here is a young man, a lord, . . . who has published a little volume of verse ; and these fellows attack him, as if no one may write poetry unless he lives in a garret. The young man will do something, if he goes on." It is a pity that Byron never heard of this generous remark.   He called Wordsworth " Wordswords " ; he made other and less innocent puns upon his name ; he satirized him repeatedly in *Don Juan*.   Wordsworth's allusions to Byron, with one exception, occur in his private letters.   During the scandal of 1816 he writes : [2]

Let me say only one word upon Lord Byron.   The man is insane ; and will probably end his career in a mad-house. . . . The verses on his private affairs excite in me less indignation than pity.

He advises that the best way to treat such men is to expose their want of any genuine literary powers and the insubstantial basis upon which their productions rest.   They are, he declares, " in all essentials dunces."   Demonstrate this, and " by abating their pride, you will strip their wickedness of the principal charm in their own eyes."   In 1823 he predicts to Henry Taylor [3] " the severe chastisement which you, or some one else, will undoubtedly one day give him."   (Taylor did one day administer this desiderated chastisement.)   The chief grounds on which Wordsworth complained of Byron to Taylor were that he did not acknowledge his " poetical obligations."   This complaint first appeared in 1817, when he wrote : [4]

---

[1] *Diary, Reminiscences, and Correspondence.*   Selected and edited by Thomas Sadler (1870), ii, 481.   Robinson's Diary contains many allusions to Byron ; see the index to Sadler's edition.

[2] *Letters*, ed. Knight, ii, 83.

[3] *Ibid.*, ii, 212.

[4] *Ibid.*, ii, 104.   The bust doubtless pleased him more than any other new thing he could have seen.

I have not seen . . . Lord Byron's last canto of *Childe
Harold,* where I am told he has been poaching on my manor,
nor any thing new whatever, except a bust of myself.

The grievance was not easily remedied.   In 1820 Wordsworth
paid a visit to Thomas Moore which the latter records in his
journal.[1]   Wordsworth " spoke of Byron's plagiarisms from
him " ; " the feeling for natural objects . . . not caught by
Byron from nature herself, but from him (W.), and spoiled in
the transmission. *Tintern Abbey* the source of it all."   It
was in 1834 that Wordsworth wrote the lines, " Not in the
lucid intervals of life," [2] in which, as he admitted to Miss
Fenwick, he had " Lord Byron's character as a poet " before
him :

> Nor do words,
> Which practised talent readily affords,
> Prove that her hand has touched responsive chords ;
> Nor has her gentle beauty power to move
> With genuine rapture and with fervent love
> The soul of Genius, if he dare to take
> Life's rule from passion craved for passion's sake.

Of *Don Juan* Wordsworth wrote [3] protesting against the
Quarterly because

it leaves that infamous publication . . . unbranded.
I do not mean by a formal critique, for it is not worth
it, . . . but by some decisive words of reprobation, both
as to the damnable tendency of such works, and as to the
despicable quality of the powers requisite for their production. . . . I am persuaded that *Don Juan* will do more
harm to the English character than anything of our time.

Coleridge's earliest reference to Byron is a characteristic
one.   In April 1812 he wrote to his wife [4] that all the world
was talking of *Childe Harold,* adding that he had not yet read
it,

---

[1] Lord John Russell's *Moore,* iii, 161.   Lord John adds a foot-note :
" If he wrote the third canto of *Childe Harold,* it is his best work."
[2] *Poetical Works,* ed. Knight, vii, 402.
[3] *Letters,* ii, 168.
[4] *Letters,* ed. E. H. Coleridge, ii, 583.

but from what I hear it is exactly on the plan that I myself
had not only conceived six years ago, but have the whole
scheme drawn out in one of my old memorandum books.

His personal relations with Byron, especially in the matter
of the stage-production of *Remorse*,[1] do not concern us ; nor
need we inquire into the causes of Byron's fierce attack on
him in *Don Juan*.   He admits the beauty of some of his work,
notably the return of Lambro in *Don Juan* (which he likens,
curiously, to the pictures of Nicholas Poussin) ; [2] but finds
that Byron lamentably neglects the art of versification, and
with Byron in mind, questions the possibility of " connecting
very great intellectual power with utter depravity." [3]   His
championship of Wordsworth led him on various occasions
to contrast the ephemerality of Byron's fame with the slow
and steadfast growth of Wordsworth's renown.[4]

Southey's opinions of Byron cannot be resumed without
some reference to the quarrel between the two poets ; but
that story has been so admirably narrated and documented
by Prothero [5] that the briefest summary is all that is necessary
here.   When Byron and Southey met in September 1813
the lines in *English Bards* were politely forgotten and the
two men exchanged courtesies.   From that time till the
publication of *Don Juan* Southey refers to Byron but three
times in his letters.[6]   Byron, meanwhile, alludes to the
Poet Laureate often, and always with increasing bitterness
and contempt.   His reasons were religious, political, and,
especially, personal, for he believed that Southey had spread
a scandalous report concerning Shelley and himself in 1816.
The Dedication to *Don Juan* was written in November
1818 ; but the poem appeared in July 1819 without it.   It

---

[1] See J. Dykes Campbell's *Coleridge*, pp. 185–188 ; 216–218.
[2] *Coleridge's Literary Criticism*, ed. J. W. Mackail, pp. 156–157.
[3] *Specimens of the Table-Talk of S. T. Coleridge* (1835), December 29,
1822.
[4] See *Table-Talk*, p. 138 ; G. M. Harper's *Wordsworth*, ii, 349 f. ; Gill-
man's *Coleridge*, p. 267.   Henry Nelson Coleridge's introduction to the
Table-Talk shows bitterness against Byron ; he speaks (i, p. xxx. f.) of
Coleridge and Southey as Byron's " invulnerable antagonists."   In a note
(ii, 154) he calls an opinion expressed by Byron " insincere, splenetic trash."
[5] LJ, vi, Appendix i.
[6] *Life and Correspondence of Robert Southey*, iii, 169 ; iv, 73, 105.

contained, however, various irritating allusions to Southey.
Southey heard of the Dedication, and tells a correspondent [1]
that if he finds it necessary to strike Byron he " will leave a
scar." The review of *Don Juan* in *Blackwood's*, August 1819,
prompted Byron's *Reply* which contained a fierce attack on
Southey, but which was not printed till after Byron's death.[2]
The first public attack came from Southey, in the preface to
his *Vision of Judgment* (1821),[3] in which he denounced Byron
as the leader of the " Satanic School." Byron replied,
partly in *Don Juan* [4] but chiefly in a note to the appendix
to *The Two Foscari* (1821). To this scathing onslaught
Southey replied in his equally effective and immoderate
letter to *The Courier*, dated January 5, 1822.[5] This reduced
Byron—in prose—to silence. He replied by a challenge
to a duel, sent through Douglas Kinnaird, who wisely suppressed it. Byron's *Vision of Judgment* appeared in *The
Liberal*, number i, October 1822. Of this satire Southey
took no public notice.[6] There the matter rested till Byron's
death, when Wordsworth writes to Samuel Rogers [7] that
Southey is " not quite so charitably disposed to Don Juan
deceased as you evidently are." When the news of Byron's
death reached England the Poet Laureate wrote to Henry
Taylor a cold-blooded and self-righteous letter from which
I quote but one sentence : [8] " I am sorry for his death,
therefore, because it comes in aid of a pernicious reputation
which was stinking in the snuff." Medwin's account [9] of
how Byron received Southey's first letter to *The Courier*
prompted Southey's second letter to the same newspaper
(December 13, 1824) in which he again assailed Byron. I
quote a sentence from the last paragraph of this priggish and
most ungallant attack upon the defenceless dead :

[1] *Life and Correspondence of Robert Southey*, iv, 352.
[2] See LJ, iv, Appendix ix. Prothero (LJ, vi, pp. 380 f.) published
for the first time a fragment of another intended attack on Southey.
[3] *Poetical Works*, x, 195 f.
[4] Canto iii, stanzas 79–81 ; 93–94.
[5] Reprinted, LJ, vi, 389 f.
[6] But see *Life and Correspondence*, iv, 126.
[7] *Letters*, ed. Knight, ii, 242.
[8] *Life and Correspondence*, v, 178 f.
[9] *Conversations with Lord Byron* (1824), i, 212 f.

It might have been thought that Lord Byron had attained
the last degree of disgrace when his head was set up for a sign
at one of those preparatory schools for the brothel and the
gallows, where obscenity, sedition, and blasphemy are retailed
in drams for the vulgar.[1]

Blackwood's [2] reprinted this " second letter " with the
following introductory comment which is, I think, a fair
verdict :

In Southey, one of the most learned and accomplished
scholars, and pure and virtuous men, that the modern world
has produced, Byron could see nothing but the Tory partisan.
. . . . In Byron, . . . in one of the greatest of the great
poets of England—in a man who never wrote three pages
without pouring out some emanation of a soul beautiful,
lofty, and glorious, if ever such a soul dwelt within a human
bosom,—in this great and godlike Poet of England, Southey
could see nothing else but a " pander-general to youthful
vice," and the founder of " a Satanic school." . . . We
are sure the world will not thank the survivor.

It is with some relief that one turns to Walter Savage
Landor.   At the opening of his quarrel with Byron, in the
preface to *A Vision of Judgment*, Southey referred to Landor
in a foot-note in terms of high esteem.   Byron, in the preface
to his *Vision*, called attention to the fact that this was
the same Landor who in his *Gebir* had put George III in
Hades.   Landor, thus drawn into the fray, preserved his
not over-abundant good nature and described Byron as
" Mr. George Nelly " in a famous and admirable paragraph

---

[1] This gratuitous side-blow occasioned the publication of the following
pamphlet : *A Scourge for the Laureate*. By W. Benbow (1825). Benbow
was the publisher at " Byron's Head." He upbraids Southey for the blasphemy of *A Vision of Judgment ;* for the sedition of *Wat Tyler ;* and for
the obscenity of introducing incest into one of his narrative poems. He
repudiates the charge that he sells drams of sedition and obscenity, de-
claring that his aim is to print cheap books for the poor. Benbow's
language is strong, but it is evidently inspired by genuine and not un-
justified indignation. As a sample of several piratical pamphlets which
printed Southey's tribute to George III. and Byron's satire side by side
I note one which is not recorded in E. H. Coleridge's bibliography : *The
Two Visions ; or Byron v. Southey* (New York, W. Borradaile, 1823).
Note also *The Particulars of the Dispute between the late Lord Byron and
Mr. Southey* (Edinburgh, 1824).

[2] In an article on " Southey and Byron," xvi, December 1824, 711 f.

of the Conversation between " Bishop Burnet and Humphrey Hardcastle." [1]

Mr. George began with satirizing his father's friends, and confounding the better part of them with all the hirelings and nuisances of the age. . . . He soon became reconciled to them, and they raised him upon their shoulders above the heads of the wittiest and the wisest. This served a whole winter. Afterwards, whenever he wrote a bad poem, he supported his sinking fame by some signal act of profligacy, an elegy by a seduction, a heroic by an adultery, a tragedy by a divorce. On the remark of a learned man that irregularity is not indication of genius, he began to lose ground rapidly, when on a sudden he cried out at the Haymarket, *there is no God.* It was then surmised more generally and more gravely that there was something in him, and he stood upon his legs almost to the last. Say what you will, once whispered a friend of mine, there are things in him strong as poison and original as sin.

Two other Conversations in the volumes of 1824 refer to Byron. In that between Southey and Porson,[2] Porson criticizes Byron's grammar and style. Some of Byron's lines are parodied. The tone of the allusions is utterly scornful ; but it must be remembered that Landor's art is dramatic. In the " Abbé Delille and Walter Landor," [3] Landor says :

We have in England, at the present time—many poets far above what was formerly thought mediocrity ; but our national taste begins to require excitement. Our poems must contain *strong things :* . . . we reprove our children for not calling a *rose* a *gul ;* we kick the first shepherd we meet, and shake hands with the first cut-throat.

Scarcely had these Conversations been written when the news of Byron's death reached Landor, and he at once wrote to Southey saying he had been affected, " even deeply affected," by the untimely death of their assailant.[4] Southey, replying, made no reference to the event.

In a much later Conversation, between Archdeacon Hare and Landor,[5] is this interesting passage :

[1] *Imaginary Conversations* (1824), i, 153 f. ; *Works*, 1876, iv, 89. The conclusion is : " Let us hope the best : to wit, that the mercies which have begun with man's forgetfulness will be crowned with God's forgiveness."
[2] *Works*, iv, 44 f.　　　[3] *Ibid.*, iv, 127.　　　[4] *Ibid.*, i, 270.
[5] Parts of this Conversation appeared in *The Examiner,* in 1849 and

Hare : Next in criminality to him who violates the laws of his country is he who violates the language. . . . Byron is among the defaulters. On Napoleon he says, " Like *he* of Babylon." . . . There is a passage in Tacitus on a vain poet, Luterius, remarkably applicable to our lately fashionable one ; " Studia illa, ut plena vecordiae, ita inania et fluxa sunt : nec quidquam grave ac serium ex eo metuas qui, suorum ipse flagitiorum proditor, non virorum animis sed muliercularum adrepit."

Landor : It suits him perfectly. I would, however, pardon him some false grammar, some false sentiment, for his vigorous application of the scourge to the two monsters of dissimilar configuration who degraded and disgraced, at the same period, the two most illustrious nations of the world. . . . Byron had good action, but he tired by fretting, and tossing his head, and rearing.

Landor wrote six poems on Byron, three of which he afterwards suppressed, while one of them he never published.[1] One published poem is the well-known " To Recruits," [2] in which he counsels young poets :

> Asthmatic Wordsworth, Byron piping-hot,
> Leave in the rear, and march with manly Scott.
> Along the coast prevail malignant heats,
> Halt on high ground behind the shade of Keats.

In studying Shelley's opinions of Byron one must bear in mind Shelley's facile, generous, and ill-considered

1850 ; it was first published entire in *The Last Fruit off an Old Tree* (1853), pp. 97 f. ; reprinted in *Works*, v, 111.

[1] The three suppressed pieces I have not seen ; I know of them from references in *A Bibliography of W. S. Landor*, by T. J. Wise and Stephen Wheeler (London : The Bibliographical Society, 1919), pp. 75, 198, 202. The earliest in date is an " Epithalamium " beginning " Weep, Venus," on Byron's marriage (*Gebir, Count Julian and other Poems*. London : Moxon, 1831, p. 326). *The Heroic Idyls, with additional Poems* (London : Newby, 1863) contains "Remonstrance and Advice to Byron" (p. 148) and "Byron," beginning " Like mad-dog in the hottest day " (p. 203). The piece which Landor never published was first printed by Sir Sidney Colvin (*Landor*, 1881, pp. 22–23). It is a curious bit of verse. Though the allusion to Byron is almost certain it is equally applicable to Shelley, and accuses a " youth " of borrowing the name " Ianthe " :

> I went, and planted in a fresh parterre
> Ianthe ; it was blooming, when a youth
> Leapt o'er the hedge, and snatching at the stem
> Broke off the label from my favourite flower
> And stuck it on a sorrier of his own.

[2] First published in *Dry Sticks Fagoted* (1858), p. 71. Cf. *Works*, i, 474.

enthusiasms and his gusty antipathies.[1]   On the personal
relations of the two great poets a volume might be written ; [2]
here all that is possible is a summary in connection with
quotations from Shelley's writings.   The two men first met
in Switzerland in the summer of 1816 ; at that time Shelley
exerted a marked influence upon Byron.[3]   Between 1816
and 1818 occasional letters passed between them, chiefly
about Allegra, Byron's natural daughter.   In 1818 they were
together at Venice, and in August Shelley wrote *Julian and
Maddalo.*   The prose introduction to that poem describes
Count Maddalo (*i.e.* Byron) as

a person of the most consummate genius. . . . His passions
and his powers are incomparably greater than those of other
men, . . . and have mutually lent each other strength. . . .
I say that Maddalo is proud, because I can find no other
word to express the concentrated and impatient feelings
which consume him ; but it is on his own hopes and affections
only that he seems to trample, for in social life no human
being can be more gentle, patient, and unassuming than
Maddalo. He is cheerful, frank, and witty. His most
serious conversation is a sort of intoxication ; men are held
by it as by a spell.

The poem itself is so well known that I need quote only
these five lines :

> [I] argued against despondency, but pride
> Made my companion take the darker side.
> The sense that he was greater than his kind
> Had struck, methinks, his eagle spirit blind
> By gazing on its own exceeding light.

[1] Swinburne, in the preface to *Miscellanies* (p. vii), writes : "When I
am reminded by friends or others that my estimate of Byron is far different
from the opinion professed by a poet whom I should rank among the
greatest of all time, I cannot but avow that my belief in Shelley is not the
belief of a papist in his Pope or a bibliolater in his Bible.   I may, of course,
be wrong in thinking so lightly as I certainly do of his critical or judicial
faculty ; but I cannot consent to overlook or pretend to ignore the significance of the fact that the great poet who bowed down his laurels before
Byron's was also proud to acknowledge his inferiority to Moore, and ex-
uberant in the expression of his humility before the superior genius of
Leigh Hunt."

[2] For an excellent summary see Barnette Miller's *Leigh Hunt's Relations
with Byron, Shelley, and Keats,* pp. 93 f.

[3] See Gillardon's *Shelleys Einwirkung auf Byron* (1898).

From this mood of admiration Shelley reacted suddenly, and on December 22, 1818, he wrote of *Childe Harold*, canto iv : [1]

The spirit in which it is written is, if insane, the most wicked and mischievous insanity that ever was given forth. . . . Nothing can be less sublime than the true sources of these expressions of contempt and desperation. . . . Contemplating in the distorted mirror of his own thoughts the nature and the destiny of man, what can he behold but objects of contempt and despair ?

The question was prompted by knowledge of Byron's degraded life at Venice of which, in the same letter, Shelley gives an account.

Between 1818 and 1820 the two poets were separated, though they were in constant correspondence about Allegra and her mother.   In November of the latter year Shelley writes : [2] " His indecencies . . . sit very awkwardly upon him.   He only affects the libertine."   The period between August 1821 and January 1822 is that of Shelley's greatest admiration of Byron ; we have already seen what he thought of *Don Juan* and *Cain*.   But in July 1822 there came another reaction, caused in large part by a personal revulsion from Byron and Byron's way of life.   He writes : [3]

I detest all society—almost all, at least—and Lord Byron is the nucleus of all that is hateful and tiresome in it. . . . I write little now.   It is impossible to compose except under the strong excitement of an assurance of finding sympathy in what you write. . . . Lord Byron is in this respect fortunate.   He touched a chord to which a million hearts responded, and the coarse music which he produced to please them disciplined him to the perfection to which he now approaches.

Even when repelled personally Shelley is generous.   Court-hope well says : [4] " Shelley viewed Byron in the light of his own idealism."

[1] *Letters*, ed. Ingpen, ii, 650 f.
[2] *Ibid.*, ii, 839.
[3] *Ibid.*, ii, 976 f.
[4] *History of English Poetry*, vi, 246.

In the *Lines written among the Euganean Hills* Shelley says that of Venice there is one remembrance sublimer even than the tattered pall of Time, the memory, namely, that

> A tempest-cleaving Swan
> Of the songs of Albion,
> Driven from his ancestral streams
> By the might of evil dreams,
> Found a nest in thee.

And continuing he declares that as Avon is filled with " divinest Shakespeare's might," even so with the memory of Byron shall be filled the city that gave him refuge. Extravagant praise ; yet who, even of those who are generally indifferent to Byron, does not remember him at Venice ?

Lastly, there is the stanza in *Adonais*, which shall be quoted without comment :

> Thus ceased she : and the mountain shepherds came,
> Their garments sere, their magic mantles rent ;
> The Pilgrim of Eternity, whose fame
> Over his living head like Heaven is bent,
> An early but enduring monument,
> Came, veiling all the lightning of his song
> In sorrow.

Of Keats's two allusions to Byron in his verse, one, the sonnet of 1814, has already been referred to. The other is found in lines 230-247 of *Sleep and Poetry*, for Keats had Byron in mind when he wrote :

> Strength alone though of the Muses born
> Is like a fallen angel. . . .
>   Forgetting the great end
> Of poesy, that it should be a friend
> To soothe the cares, and lift the thoughts of men.

This is of 1816. The few allusions in Keats's letters are uniformly unsympathetic, as how could they fail to be ? In one,[1] writing of the " two distinct tempers of mind in which we judge of things," he places Byron with Buonaparte in " the first place in our Minds " in " the worldly, theatrical

---

[1] *Letters of John Keats*, edited by H. B. Forman, p. 217.

and pantomimical " way, as opposed to " the unearthly, spiritual and ethereal." This is in 1818, as is the following sentence : [1] " We have seen three literary Kings in our Time—Scott—Byron—and then the Scotch novels." He adds, curiously : " All now appear to be dead." In 1819, apropos of Reynolds's skit on *Peter Bell :* [2] " It would be just as well to trounce Lord Byron in the same manner " ; and later in the same year : [3] " *Don Juan* (Lord Byron's last flash poem)." In another letter Keats sums up the contrast between Byron and himself : [4] " There is this great difference between us : he describes what he sees—I describe what I imagine." [5]

The story of Leigh Hunt's connection with Byron's contemporary and posthumous reputation covers many years.[6] His earliest reference to Byron is a commendation of the *Address* delivered at Drury Lane in 1812.[7] The original version of *The Feast of the Poets* [8] did not mention Byron, but in the edition of 1814 several pages of notes are added on his poems. They are of little importance. After various smaller notices and after the dedication to Byron of *The Story of Rimini* (1816) comes a review of *Don Juan*, cantos i and ii,[9] that contains a peremptory denial of the charge of immorality brought against that poem.

[1] *Letters of John Keats,* edited by H. B. Forman, p. 247.

[2] *Ibid.,* p. 308.

[3] *Ibid.,* p. 398.   Elsewhere Keats spoke of the storm and shipwreck in *Don Juan* as " a diabolical outrage on [the reader's] sympathies." (Quoted by H. B. Forman, Keat's *Works,* iv, 107 f.)

[4] *Letters,* p. 405.

[5] John Hamilton Reynolds is so closely associated, with Keats that here may be best introduced a reference to his article, " Literature. *The Quarterly Review*—Mr. Keats," published in *The Alfred, West of England Journal and General Advertiser,* October 6, 1818 (reprinted by Forman, Keat's *Works,* iii, 373 f.).   This defence of Keats contains the following passage on Byron : " Lord Byron is a splendid and noble egotist. . . . It is as if he and the world were the only two things which the air clothed. His lines are majestic vanities. . . . He is liked by most of his readers, because he is a lord.   If a common man were to dare to be as moody, as contemptuous, and as misanthropical, the world would laugh at him. There must be a coronet marked on all his little pieces of poetical insolence, or the world would not countenance them."

[6] See in general Barnette Miller, *op. cit.,* pp. 93 f.

[7] *The Examiner,* October 12, 1812.

[8] First published in *The Reflector,* 1810.

[9] *The Examiner,* October 31, 1819.

The fact is at the bottom of these questions, that many things are made vicious which are not so by nature ; and many things made virtuous, which are only so by calling and agreement.

Similar opinions are expressed in the notice of cantos iii, iv and v,[1] where Hunt attacks " the careless contempt of canting moralists." In 1822, in the course of a series of " Sketches of the Living Poets," [2] there appeared an article on Byron. The praise here is by no means unqualified. Hunt admits Byron's passion, humour, and learning ; but he condemns his narrative poems as " melodramatic, hasty, and vague " ; and, despite the merits of individual passages, he concludes that Byron has no qualifications for the drama. *Don Juan*, Hunt says, is his best work, " the one by which he will stand or fall with readers who see beyond time and toilets." Later favourable reviews of *Don Juan* in *The Examiner* consist chiefly of analyses and extracts.

Hunt's personal relations with Byron were far from happy ; and the ill-success of *The Liberal* helped to embitter him. Four years after the poet's death he published a book which E. H. Coleridge has called [3] " Hunt's revenge for the slights and indignities which he suffered in Byron's service." This is : *Lord Byron and some of his Contemporaries* (1828). The portrait of Byron in this book is elaborately unfavourable ; the testimony adduced of his conceit, arrogance, cant, hypocrisy, and insincerity is so distorted as to be scandalous. In his preface Hunt admits that his " account is coloured, though never with a shadow of untruth, [by] the spleen and indignation, which I experienced as a man who thought himself ill-used." *The Quarterly* [4] published a drastic and thorough-going attack

---

[1] *The Examiner*, August 26, 1821.
[2] *Ibid.*, July 29, 1822.
[3] *Encyclopædia Britannica*, article " Byron," iv, 902 (Eleventh edition).
[4] xxxvii, March 1828, 402 f. The writer availed himself of many unpublished manuscripts in John Murray's possession regarding Hunt's relations with Byron and especially regarding *The Liberal*. The refutation is, so far as documentary evidence goes, nearly complete. What the reviewer did not know about at first hand was the humiliation or fancied

on Hunt. The newly-founded *Athenæum*,[1] on the other hand, defended him. In a new preface to his second edition (also 1828) Hunt turned savagely on the *Quarterly*, but expressed the wish that his book had never been written " as far as the sincerity in it has taken a splenetic turn."

Hunt certainly betrayed ingratitude for many favours ; he helped to prejudice minds against Byron. He aroused John Murray to action, though two years earlier Murray had already begun work with Thomas Moore on the official biography of the poet.[2] Hunt deserved the chastisement which Moore administered in his satire, " The Living Dog and the Dead Lion." A fiercer reproof was uttered many years later by William Ernest Henley : [3]

He wrote this stuff because he wanted money . . . and with a littleness of mind unparalleled in any but a cast mistress or an embittered poetaster, he essayed to present the man on whom he had spunged . . . as a cad of the first magnitude.

Hunt's grudge against Byron waned but slowly. This conversation of many years afterwards is recorded by Lord Houghton : [4]

" Do you really think Byron was never in earnest ? " Hunt

humiliation which Byron had inflicted on Hunt. One passage in the review refutes Hunt's statement that Byron admired Keats. " Our readers have probably forgotten all about *Endymion, a poem*, and the other works of this young man, the all but universal roar of laughter with which they were received some ten or twelve years ago, and the ridiculous story . . . of the author's death being caused by the reviewers " (p. 416). " We hope and trust," says the reviewer, concluding, " that the public reception of this filthy gossip will be such as to discourage any more of these base assaults upon Lord Byron's memory."

[1] In its very first number (January 2, 1828) are excerpts from Hunt's forthcoming book ; and a long review was soon published (January 23 and 30, 1828). The first instalment considers Hunt's portrait of Byron, which is said to be very different from the idea of the poet commonly held, but which is that to which those who judge him only by his poems have come. For his writings exhibit selfishness, waywardness, and affectation. " It is now, indeed, time that we should begin to judge him calmly and fairly ; for the renown and the all but disgrace which alike filled the air . . . have shrunk . . . into a narrow urn." The second instalment deals with " Shelly," who is highly praised, and with Keats, whose " reputation is at present but the shadow of a glory."
[2] See *Dictionary of National Biography*, xxviii, 270.
[3] *Works*, iv, 149.
[4] T. W. Reid, *The Life of Lord Houghton*, ii, 205.

was asked. He thought a moment, and then said slowly, " No ; never." " Not even at Missolonghi ? " " Decidedly not at Missolonghi," responded Leigh Hunt, promptly. " There was no doubt whatever in my mind that Byron was all the time strutting about as on a stage."

But in old age he thought better of his position in 1828 ; and in his *Autobiography* (1850) [1] he goes over again the history of his connection with Byron, and in manly fashion confesses the unfairness of his earlier attack.

I do not mean that I ever wrote any fictions about him. I wrote nothing which I did not feel to be true, or think so. But . . . I was then a young man, and . . . am now advanced in years. . . . I was agitated by grief and anger, and . . . am now free from anger. . . . I was far more alive to other people's defects than to my own. . . . I am now sufficiently sensible of my own to show to others the charity which I need myself.

Hunt glances at the handicaps suffered by Byron in his upbringing, his life, and his temperament ; and then continues :

Should we not wonder that he retained so much of the grand and beautiful in his writings ? that the indestructible tendency of the poetical to the good should have struggled to so much purpose through faults and inconsistencies ? . . . He was never incapable of generosity : he was susceptible of the tenderest emotions. . . . I am sorry that I ever wrote a syllable respecting Lord Byron which might have been spared. I have still to relate my connection with him, but it will be related in a different manner. . . . I had prided myself . . . on not being one of those who talk against others. I went counter to this feeling in a book ; and to crown the absurdity of the contradiction, I was foolish enough to suppose, that the very fact of my so doing would show that I had done it in no other instance.

The account of the Italian sojourn follows, told with moderation and good taste. Leigh Hunt thus lived to make a generous *amende*.

---

[1] Vol. ii, chapter xix, in the Harper edition (1872). This has been superseded by Mr. Ingpen's edition, 1903.

To Charles Lamb Byron's character was naturally antipathetic ; and though there are no such shocking references to him as those in which the " gentle " Elia indulged in regard to Shelley after Shelley's death,[1] the main allusions to Byron in his letters are by no means gentle.   He writes : [2]

I have a thorough aversion to his character, and a very moderate admiration of his genius : he is great in so little a way.   To be a Poet is to be a Man, not a petty portion of occasional low passion worked up in a permanent form of humanity.

And after Byron's death : [3]

So we have lost another Poet. . . . He was to me offensive, and I never can make out his great *power*, which his admirers talk of.   Why, a line of Wordsworth's is a lever to lift the immortal spirit ! Byron can only move the Spleen.   He was at best a Satyrist,—in any other way he was mean enough. I dare say I do him injustice ; but I cannot love him, nor squeeze a tear to his memory.

Hazlitt sympathizes in great measure with Byron's politics ; he distrusts his rank.   The latter feeling is on the whole the more evident.   His notice of *Childe Harold*, canto iv,[4] is generally unfavourable.   Hazlitt animadverts against Byron's planlessness ; his capricious versification ; his offensive attitude towards the public.   He declares that " the judgments pronounced are often more dogmatical than profound "—aptly characterizing many of his own judgments.   And : " Lord Byron's poetry, in its irregular and gloomy magnificence, we fear, antedates its own doom."

---

[1] Only the halo of " gentleness " that surrounds Lamb's memory has kept critics from commenting with severity upon his disgusting letter to Bernard Barton after Shelley's death, with the lines :

> Full fathom five the Atheist lies,
> Of his bones are hell-dice made.

(*Letters*, ed. Ainger, 1888, ii, 47.)
[2] *Ibid.*, ii, 28 f.
[3] *Ibid.*, ii, 106.
[4] Published in *The Yellow Dwarf*, May 2, 1818 ; reprinted in *Works*, ed. Waller and Glover, xi, 420 f.

Three years later Hazlitt reverts to the theme of the uncertainty of Byron's future fame.[1]

Has *he* had only half his fame ? Or does he already feel, with morbid anticipation, the retiring ebb of that over-whelming tide of popularity ? . . . Lord Byron has been twice as much talked of as he would have been, had he not been Lord Byron.

These two articles are Hazlitt's less important pronouncements on Byron, and I dismiss them quickly.

More carefully considered is the estimate in the *Lectures on the English Poets*.[2] " Byron," says Hazlitt,

might be thought to have suffered too much to be a truly great poet. [He] shuts himself up too much in the impenetrable gloom of his own thoughts. . . . A mind preying upon itself, and disgusted with, or indifferent to all other things. There is nothing less poetical than this sort of unaccommodating selfishness. . . . But still there is power ; and power rivets attention and forces admiration. . . . He gives the tumultuous eagerness of action, and the fixed despair of thought. In vigour of style and force of conception, he in one sense surpasses every writer of the present day. . . . Yet he has beauty lurking underneath his strength, tenderness sometimes joined with the phrenzy of despair.

Hazlitt's first tribute to Byron, on hearing of his death, found place in an article on " The Posthumous Poems of Shelley " : [3]

To this band of immortals [4] a third has since been added !— a mightier genius, a haughtier spirit. . . . Greece, Italy, the world, have lost their poet-hero ; and his death has spread a wider gloom, and been recorded with a deeper awe, than has waited on the obsequies of any of the many great who have died in our remembrance. Even detraction has been silenced at his tomb ; and the more generous of his enemies have fallen into the ranks of his mourners. But

[1] " Pope, Lord Byron, and Mr. Bowles," *The London Magazine*, June 1821 ; *Works*, xi, 486 f.
[2] 1818. *Works*, v, 152 f.
[3] *Edinburgh Review*, xl, July 1824, 494 f. ; *Works*, x, 256 f.
[4] *I.e.* Shelley and Keats.

he set like the sun in his glory ; and his orb was greatest and brightest at the last.

The chapter on Byron, save the last paragraph, in *The Spirit of the Age*,[1] was written before the news of Byron's death reached England. It contains such judgments as the following :

Instead of taking his impressions from without . . . he moulds them according to his own temperament. . . . [He] thinks chiefly how he shall display his own power. . . . [He] cares little what it is he says, so that he can say it differently from others. . . . It is not the value of the observation itself he is solicitous about. . . . Self-will, passion, the love of singularity, a disdain of himself and of others. . . . One who obstinately and invariably shuts himself up in the Bastile of his own ruling passions. . . . Lord Byron makes man after his own image, woman after his own heart.[2] . . . The pamperer of . . . prejudices, by seeming to think there is nothing else worth encouraging but the seeds or the full luxuriant growth of dogmatism and self-conceit.

How curiously unaware of the real Byron this last remark shows Hazlitt to have been. Continuing, he praises *Don Juan* save the " flashy passages " ; and declares that Byron's scorn of popular applause is affected and insincere. His summary is as follows :

In a word, we think that poetry moves best within the circle of nature and received opinion : speculative theory and subtle casuistry are forbidden ground to it. . . . His ruling motive is not the love of . . . truth, but of singularity. . . . He may affect the principles of equality, but he resumes his privilege of peerage, upon occasion.

It was at this point that Hazlitt heard of Byron's death ;

---

[1] 1825. *Works*, iv, 253 f.

[2] Compare Mazzini's comment on this oft-quoted sentence : " One very much over-rated critic writes that ' Byron makes man after his own image, and woman after his own heart ; the one is a capricious tyrant, the other a yielding slave.' . . . [He] forgot that while he was quietly writing criticisms, Byron was dying for new-born liberty in Greece " (*Life and Writings*, vi, 64).

and with an impressive change of tone he ends with the magnificent words of Cæsar on Pompey in *The False One :*

> Nothing can cover his high fame, but Heaven ;
> No pyramids set off his memories,
> But the eternal substance of his greatness ;
> To which I leave him.[1]

Finally, from an essay on " Byron and Wordsworth "[2] (1828) I quote this :

His poetry . . . is stately and dazzling, arched like a rainbow, of bright and lovely hues, painted on the cloud of his own gloomy temper—perhaps to disappear as soon !

Jeffrey's earliest critiques of Byron and his review of *Cain* I have mentioned in former chapters. His other pronouncements on Byron remain to be considered. Of these the most noteworthy is the review of *Childe Harold,* canto iii,[3] in which Jeffrey connects Byron with the " Lake School," thus showing a dim realization of the fact that Byron and Wordsworth were alike putting new vitality into poetry. Jeffrey analyses the Byronic hero-type, but offers no explanation of its origin or popularity. He explains Byron's ethics as merely self-will and sees no analogy with the entire spirit of the epoch. He regards Byron's popularity as due entirely to devices of style, and fails to see that the poet voices the sentiments of countless restless minds. Of the more intimate poems, such as *The Dream,* he says that it is impossible to mistake them

for fictitious sorrows, conjured up for the purpose of poetical effect. There is a dreadful tone of sincerity, and an energy

---

[1] In view of this conclusion *Blackwood's* reply to Hazlitt (xvii, February 1825, 131 f.) seems even more harsh and unjust than usual : " If Mr. Hazlitt had seen the living Lion down, he would have rejoiced in kicking him ; he now does his pleasure with the dead. . . . The paltry and contemptible caitiffs, who, while they fain would have derived some skulking benefit from his name, never regarded either the poet or the man, but with all the rancours of despairing imbecility and plebeian spite."

[2] *Works,* xii, 328.

[3] *Edinburgh Review,* xxvii, December 1816, 277 f. ; reprinted in *Contributions to the Edinburgh Review,* 1846, ii, 435 f. The points in this essay to which I direct attention are well indicated by Professor L. E. Gates (*Essays of Jeffrey,* Athenæum Press Series, pp. 198 f.).

that cannot be counterfeited, in the expression of wretchedness and alienation from human kind, which occurs in every page of this publication.

The same critic, though impressed with the power of *Manfred*,[1] thought there was a falling off in the last act, and considered the drama unpleasing and not truly dramatic, for Manfred, despite (or perhaps because of) his superhuman force, is the only figure in the piece.   Contradicting *Blackwood's*, he says :

The style . . . of Marlowe, though elegant and scholarlike, is weak and childish compared with the depth and force of much of what we have quoted from Lord Byron.

" Elegant," " scholarlike," " weak," " childish "—could any four adjectives be less appropriate to the style of Marlowe ?

Finally,[2] there is the familiar passage from a notice of Mrs. Heman's *Records of Women :* [3]

The tuneful quartos of Southey are already little better than lumber :—and the rich melodies of Keats and Shelley—and the fantastical emphasis of Wordsworth—and the plebeian pathos of Crabbe, are melting fast from the field of our view.   The novels of Scott have put out his poetry.   Even the splendid strains of Moore are fading into distance and dimness, . . . and the blazing star of Byron himself is receding from its place of pride.[4]

That Jeffrey was in the main fair-minded, impartial, and just Byron recognized ; and he paid him this tribute,[5] not often vouchsafed by Byron to his reviewers :

> I do not know you, and may never know
> Your face—but you have acted on the whole,
> Most nobly ; and I own it from my soul.

---

[1] *Edinburgh Review*, xxviii, August 1817, 418 f. ; *Contributions*, ii, 128 f.
[2] I leave aside the review of *Beppo* (*Edinburgh*, February 1818) and of *Marino Faliero* (*ibid.*, July 1821 ; *Contributions*, ii, 271 f.).
[3] *Edinburgh Review*, October 1829 ; *Contributions*, ii, 551 f.
[4] Professor Elton (*Survey*, i, 390) comments admirably on this passage and gives an excellent summary of Jeffrey's opinions of Byron.   For another summary, from a critic of very different tastes, see Professor Saintsbury's *Essays in English Literature*, 1780–1860, first series (New York : Scribner, 1891), pp. 131 f.
[5] *Don Juan*, x, 16.

CHAPTER IX

BYRON IN FICTION

BEFORE his death Byron had appeared, thinly disguised under an imaginary name, in four novels. He appears in other later novels, one so recent as 1913, while in 1921 his story was made the subject of a photo-play, " The Prince of Lovers." In this chapter I shall tell of the novels and romances in which his life and personality are set forth ; and I shall add some comments on a few curious pieces of early Byroniana that are most appropriately to be recorded here, together with some other semi-fictitious evocations of his character.[1] Books that are easily accessible I shall consider briefly, according more generous space to such as are difficult of access.

The first novel on my list—it is a bad beginning—is the once notorious *Glenarvon* (1816). Though published anonymously this was immediately known to be by Lady Caroline Lamb. It is still well known by title, but is little read and almost unreadable. In her preface the author states :

This work is not the offspring of calm tranquillity. . . . It was written under the pressure of affliction . . . in the bitterness of a wounded spirit.

The book is indeed the product of hysteria. Lady Caroline goes on to make an express disavowal of any personal application : " Events have no foundation in fact with respect to character." This, I hardly need say, is not true ; for the Glenarvon of the novel is Byron, Calantha is Lady Caroline,

---

[1] For a brief incomplete preliminary check-list see my article, " Byron in Fiction," *N. & Q.* 12th Series, iv, 10.

Avondale is her husband, William Lamb. The scene is laid in Ireland. The secret of Glenarvon's mysterious life is that he had committed murder.[1] Goethe, it will be remembered, half believed some such story of Byron; for this absurd rumour the reading of an autobiographical implication into certain episodes of the Oriental Tales furnished an unstable foundation. Lady Caroline's story is highly rhapsodical, with some occasional imaginative interest but with a total want of art in the composition and of taste in the style. The parting of Glenarvon and Calantha [2] is typical of the melodramatic exaggeration of the book:

" Look not on me, frail, fading flowret," he said, in a hollow mournful tone—" ah look not on me, nor thus waste thy sweets upon a whited sepulchre, full of depravity and death. . . . Let others mock at my agony; . . . but do not you refuse to believe me. Young as I appear, I have made many miserable : but none more so than myself."

The circumstances of its appearance, just after the scandalous separation of Lord and Lady Byron, served to give this rubbish a success that was throughly undeserved. It went through many editions; and was reprinted so lately as 1865 with the title changed to *The Fatal Passion*.[3]

In 1817 there was " printed for the author " an anonymous novel entitled : *Six Weeks at Long's. By A Late Resident.* This is by Eaton Stannard Barrett, novelist and satirist, whom Byron had referred to slightingly in *English Bards* and who had attacked Byron in *The Talents Run Mad* (1816).[4] Long's was of course a famous Bond Street hotel.

---

[1] See volume ii, p. 258.
[2] Volume ii, chapter xxix.
[3] Undated, but of 1865 according to the accession date in the copy in the British Museum.
[4] The article on Barrett in the *Dict. Nat. Biog.* fails to mention this novel, but it is ascribed to him in the catalogue of the British Museum. See also *N. & Q.* 1st Series, viii, 423. In 1807 Barrett, under the pseudonym " Polypus," published a satire, *All the Talents*. This Byron alluded to in *English Bards* (line 745). The piece was one of a numerous batch of ephemeral political *jeux d'esprit* occasioned by the formation of the famous coalition ministry. (For others of this group of satires see E. H. Coleridge,

To it comes a rich North-countryman with his wife and niece. The plot of the book, such as it is, is the old one of the gulling of the wealthy provincial by a crew of urban swindlers and sharpers in high life. Coulter (the wealthy countryman) is rescued from various scrapes by Morland, the hero, who in the end plays a rough practical joke on the rascals who have tried to abduct the niece, Hyppolita, who, the better to observe London society, has feigned idiocy but is in reality very sensible and charming. In the end she and Morland are married. There are scenes of gambling and drinking ; at the opera ; balls ; " literary evenings " ; and so forth. A host of real people are introduced, thinly disguised as fictitious characters. Probably most of the London characters could be identified were it worth while.[1] Tom Moore appears in a minor role as " Little " ; Wordsworth and Southey appear for a moment.[2] Our interest centres, however, in Lord Leander, who appears many times, though he takes no part in the main action, being rather a portion of the satirically sketched background. The jeeringly unsympathetic tone employed towards this character reflects certainly the personal animosity towards Byron which Barrett had expressed in *The Talents Run Mad.*

Leander appears first in a " box " at Long's. His dress (especially the open collar) ; his unamiable habit of turning against old friends ; his pose of magnanimity towards enemies ; his gloom and refusal ever to laugh—these and other traits are sneered at. Presently Leander fights an absurd duel, using a javelin while his adversary uses a bow-and-arrow. The book is full of such crass puerilities, which are like nothing in the world so much as the coarse, violently coloured drawings of Thomas Rowlandson. But Barrett is

Poetry, i, 294.) Barrett introduced a long attack on Byron into a supplementary satire, *The Talents Run Mad ; or, Eighteen Hundred and Sixteen* (1816). I had intended to quote this diatribe ; but it is ill-natured, incoherent, unimportant, and merely personal, and I have decided to leave it where I found it, at pages 23–26 of the satire. A foot-note warns " his Lordship " to " expect no mercies from " Barrett.

[1] Some of these actual people are merely sketched ; at other times there are elaborate character-portraits in the manner, though crudely done, of the seventeenth century.

[2] See volume i, pp. 220, 225, 226.

occasionally rather clever and sharp ; there is a scene in the coffee room at Long's ; [1] Leander is present—

but he was not drinking wine out of the skull of one of his ancestors, nor had he eaten his dinner with a fork carved out of his great great grand uncle's cross bones. These were luxuries in which he never indulged except when he had invited company to his house.

A little later there is a flashy scene in which a "blue-stocking" lionizes Leander in order to receive mention in his next poem, but quickly changes her tactics and abuses him as the best way to gain her ends.   Leander asks her : " Pray, may I beg to know what modern works most excite your admiration ? " " Your own productions, my lord," answered she,

" especially your Epistle to the Governess.[2]   Oh ! how I should like to be an object of your enmity, if I could find no other means of obtaining a niche in your divine verses ! " " There is but one step towards becoming my enemy," answered his lordship, " and that one is by first making yourself my friend."

Here is a speech of Leander's : [3]

" I once had a bear : yes, a sweet bear ! the most interesting and most shaggy animal in existence.   The friends of my soul might be false—the day might be o'ercast with clouds— a stubborn stanza might mock the ingenuity of my brain —but my faithful bear was still the same—still lovelily uncouth, still endearing in its ruggedness.   Oh, ye golden hours of my early adolescence, shall I ? must I ? can I ? "

This bit of satire is gentle and deserved enough ; but Barrett does not always refrain from the scurrilous, as in this episode : [4]

Lord Leander was sitting next to the countess ; and as it was a principle with him that every woman adored him, he in a short time began to make downright love to her.   Now, as it so happened that the countess admired no man who could not dance, and as poor Lord Leander could not dance

---

[1] Vol. ii, pp. 11 f.
[3] Vol. iii, p. 10.

[2] *I.e. A Sketch from Private Life.*
[4] Vol. iii, p. 35.

at all, he found himself to his utter astonishment making but a small progress in her affection. He talked of his tenderness —she was cold. He talked of his honour—she was indifferent. He talked of his villainy—she was disgusted.

Two pages further on there is a long " character " of Leander :

Now it was a caprice of his lordship's always to act towards enemies and friends the very reverse of what they would naturally expect from the common nature of the human heart. But it was his lordship's great delight to seem as if his heart had been turned inside out, or upside down, or backside foremost. Whoever did him a kindness, was sure to receive an injury in return, and whoever did him an injury was certain to be compensated by a kindness. He loved to astonish, to strike, to confound, to be magnificent. He would give a beggar-woman twenty guineas just to make her stare her eyes out ; and he would call this sublime. He would practise whole days before a glass the art of frowning ; and has said that he can never consider himself happy till he can establish an habitual wrinkle between his eye-brows. It was this propensity to excite emotion which induced him to drink out of skulls newly torn from the grave ! And it was the dread, lest, by growing fat, he should lose all appearance of sentiment, pathos, and philosophy, that made him continue, till lately, the practice of running ten miles a-day in seven waistcoats, two of them flannel !

The countess snubs Leander with a candidly adverse opinion of his poetry. He leaves the room in mortification, and the lady, determined to bring down his conceit, tells the company that he has taken poison. They all rush after him, and in a coarse slap-stick scene, redolent of Rowlandson, give him vigorous antidotes, despite his protests. Later [1] there is a masquerade ball at which the fair Hyppolita appears wearing a masque like a skull. Leander makes love to this terrible apparition. His speech is an illuminating example of the brutality of what passed for humour in the days of the Regency ; I quote but one sentence :

Suffer me then, oh, lady of the skull ! to gaze upon thy

---

[1] Volume iii, chapter xvii. The similarity to the skull-headed lady in Polidori's *Vampire* will be noted.

gristle, to compose lines upon thy fleshless cheeks, and to drink delirium from thy eyeless sockets.

The passages that I have cited and some others dimly anticipate a little masterpiece of satiric fiction, but before we come to that masterpiece an imitation of Barrett's book must be noted.

This is : *Three Weeks at Fladong's. By a Late Visitant* (1817). The motto—

> A race of youthful and unhandled colts,
> Fetching mad bounds——

is an appropriate one, for the tale is of clubs, gambling dens, debts and debtors' prisons, watch-houses, brothels, seductions, mistresses, and scandals of all sorts. It is less clever than Barrett's book ; but Byron, who appears as Lord Stanza, is more favourably treated than in *Six Weeks at Long's*. The Honourable Douglas Kincat (*i.e.* Byron's friend, Douglas Kinnaird) and a Scotch girl whom he has seduced are leading characters. The plot has to do with the attempt of Sir Henry Priapus to abduct this girl ; in the end his machinations are thwarted and he is discomfited by Lord Stanza. Thereafter he passes out of the story. Early in the tale there is an account of Stanza's unhappy marriage ; an interesting estimate of his character follows : [1]

With all a poet's fire and fancy, his lordship certainly possessed all a poet's faults. He was wild, enthusiastic, inconsistent : his motive was too frequently the mere impulse of momentary feeling, instead of the result of an union of deep penetration, calm reflection, and an unbiassed judgement. The child of nature, he worshipped even her in her imperfections and her depravities, and scorned to conform either his habits of thinking or acting according to the fashion of the world. His genius was dazzling yet redundant : his muse soared widely and loftily on its first wings, which had received no pluming nor pruning from any fastidious interference of pretended taste. There was an originality of sentiment in most things which he uttered which gave his arguments an

---

[1] Volume i, pp. 186 f.

advantage which they very frequently did not deserve, for they tended to confirm the judgement, even where they failed to convince the understanding. From the general tenor of his writings, Lord Stanza had obtained the epithet of misanthropic ; for he seemed to feel an especial pleasure in dwelling upon all the darker shades of human character, and in shewing man in the most unamiable shape and complexion. His villains were not half begotten, nor half qualified for the objects to which he designed them ; and the few virtues with which he skilfully illuminated their portraits, served only as a foil by which the shadows which surrounded them were rendered more marked and distinct. His poetry was harmonious, comprehensive and energetic ; his powers of discrimination were fully equal to the difficult task of analysing human nature.

As indicative of the higher view of Byron adopted in this novel, it is noteworthy that the mere rakes find no pleasure in Lord Stanza's society. Nor has he any pleasure in empty renown. He is always civil to opponents ; he defends his religious views ; he snubs a debauchee.

That these two novels point in the direction of *Nightmare Abbey* must now be evident to the reader.[1] Peacock had attacked Byron in the clumsily ironic dedication to his satiric ballad of *Sir Proteus* (1815).[2] He regarded Byron, Mr. Van Doren remarks, as " one of the worst offenders against a rational view of life." In June 1818 he wrote to Shelley : [3]

I think it necessary to " make a stand " against the " encroachments " of black bile. The fourth canto of *Childe Harold* is really too bad.

Yet he was not without discernment of Byron's merits, and could write : [4]

Cain is very fine ; *Sardanapalus* I think finer : *Don Juan* is

[1] It was, indeed, Mr. Carl Van Doren's delightful *Life of Thomas Love Peacock* (pp. 94 f.) that guided me to the two forerunners of Peacock's satiric tale.
[2] Quoted by Prothero, LJ, iii, 90 note.
[3] *Letters of T. L. Peacock*, edited by Richard Garnett (1910), p. 64.
[4] *Ibid.*, p. 94.

best of all.   I have read nothing else in recent literature that
I think good for anything.

Before this opinion was formed, however, he had written
Nightmare Abbey (1818) in which Coleridge, Shelley and
Byron are satirically portrayed.

In this famous and witty book Scythrop Glowry, the
leading character, is drawn after Shelley.   With that
portrait we are not here concerned.   In chapter xi Mr.
Cypress, the poet, appears.   He is " on the point of leaving
England."   " Sir," he remarks, " I have quarrelled with
my wife ; and a man who has quarrelled with his wife is
absolved from all duty to his country.   I have written an
ode to tell the people as much."   Many of Mr. Cypress's
remarks are prose paraphrases of passages in *Childe Harold*.
He   and   Mr. Flosky (*i.e.* Coleridge) dispute frequently
together.   Mr. Hilary and the Rev. Mr. Larynx sing the
famous ballad " Seamen Three " (with the fine refrain,
" And our ballast is old wine ") to counteract the effect of
Mr. Cypress's dismal song :

> There is a fever of the spirit,
> The brand of Cain's unresting doom,
> Which in the lone dark souls that bear it
> Glows like the lamp in Tullia's tomb :
> Unlike that lamp, its subtle fire
> Burns, blasts, consumes its cell, the heart,
> Till, one by one, hope, joy, desire,
> Like dreams of shadowy smoke depart.
>
> When hope, love, life itself, are only
> Dust—spectral memories—dead and cold—
> The unfed fire burns bright and lonely,
> Like that undying lamp of old :
> And by that drear illumination,
> Till time its clay-built home has rent,
> Thought broods on feeling's desolation—
> The soul is its own monument.

" Admirable," says Mr. Glowry ; " let us all be unhappy
together."   But another of the company proposes a catch,
and when the ballad is sung, praising the excellent ballast,

the company disperses ; " Mr. Cypress, having his own ballast on board," departs, " to rake the seas and rivers, lakes and canals, for the moon of ideal beauty." [1]

Of a very different nature is a book that is on the border-land between the novel and the biography : *Wanderings of Childe Harold*, by John Harman Bedford (1825). This work, in three volumes and extending to nearly seven hundred pages, is a loose, vulgar and grossly unjust review of Byron's life, with a great many purely fictitious anecdotes and episodes. There is a story of an early love-affair with Mary Styles, the daughter of a neighbouring farmer. This is followed by a much confused account of Byron's first journey to the East. Then comes his marriage to " Miss Wellbank " and the separation, caused by his cruelty and the discovery of a woman in his room. He again leaves England, and there are various fantastic journeys around the Mediterranean with tales of debauched nuns and of many mistresses, among which one finds the oft-repeated story of Byron's residence in the Island of Mitylene. Then the final journey to Greece and the poet's death. The characterization throughout is quite as crude as the summary with which the author dismisses his protagonist : [2] " He was an *honest* man, with very little *moral* virtue—and a truly good Christian, without knowing himself to be so."

Though Professor Dowden long ago indicated [3] the bearing of *Lodore* upon the lives of the Shelleys, Lord Byron and others of Shelley's circle, it is only very recently that

---

[1] See M. R. Mitford's *Letters*, 2nd Series, i, 41, for her recognition of the parodies of Byron and Coleridge. Of Mr. Cypress's song Mr. Van Doren well says (*op. cit.*, p. 122) that it is " all the more admirable a parody because it parodies the Byronic spirit and not any specific poem." To round out the account of Peacock's estimate of Byron it should be added that in 1830 he reviewed the first volume of Moore's biography in *The Westminster Review*. He disliked Moore and had satirized him on more than one occasion previously. Unfortunately he reserved his full estimate of Byron's character for the appearance of Moore's second volume. But meanwhile Murray quarrelled with Bowring (the editor of the *Westminster*) over Peacock's first review, and consequently no notice was taken of volume two in that journal. (See Van Doren, *op. cit.*, pp. 188 f. ; Bowring's *Autobiographical Recollections*, 1877, p. 351.)

[2] Volume iii, p. 235.

[3] Edward Dowden, *The Life of Shelley* (1886), i, 436 f.

Professor W. E. Peck[1] has shown the amount of biography
that is present in all Mary Wollstonecraft Shelley's novels.
Byron figures as Lord Raymond in *The Last Man* (1826).
He is drawn in marked contrast to Adrian who represents
Shelley. He holds Adrian's philanthropic visions in contempt; he is brilliant, cynical, unstable; yet capable of
benevolence and generosity. His eloquence, wit, grace,
wealth, and "powerful and versatile talents" make him
"feared, loved, and hated beyond any other man in
England." Lord Raymond's love of Perdita shadows
forth Byron's liaison with Claire Clairmont; their child
Clara represents Allegra. The connection is not a happy
one.

In *Lodore* (1835) Mrs. Shelley describes in veiled fashion
her privations in London in 1814. With that aspect of the
book we are not, however, here concerned, nor with the
portraits, other than Byron's, which it contains. Lodore,
the father of the heroine of the tale, is modelled on Byron,
the portrait being generous in its emphasis upon the pathos
and romance of his character and career. A graduate of
Eton and Oxford, he is rich, impulsive, passionate, and
generous. In his youth he had had a love-affair with a
Polish countess the offspring of which was a son. Years
later Lodore married, his worldly-minded wife knowing
nothing of this early liaison. The two Poles—mother and
son—come to London and become intimately acquainted
with Lady Lodore. She and the son have a harmless
flirtation which, however, Lodore resents. He strikes his
son and then, rather than run the chance of killing him in
a duel, chooses dishonour and disappears to America with
his baby daughter. Twelve years later he decides to return
to England, but in New York he hears a man speak insult-
ingly of the old Lodore scandal and strikes him. A duel
follows in which Lodore is killed. These events occupied
only the first seventy-odd pages of the novel, the remainder

---

[1] " The Biographical Element in the Novels of Mary Wollstonecraft
Shelley," *Publications of the Modern Language Association of America*,
xxxvii, March 1923, pp. 196 f., especially pp. 209 f.

of which, though it centres in the daughter, has nothing to do with Byron.[1]

Claire Clairmont protested vigorously to Mrs. Shelley against this flattering portrait of Byron, writing : [2]

Good God ! to think a person of your genius . . . should think it is a task befitting its powers, to gild and embellish and pass off as beautiful what was the merest compound of vanity, folly, and every miserable weakness that ever met together in one human being.

I come now to the classic instance of the portrayal of Byron in fiction : Disraeli's *Venetia, or the Poet's Daughter*.[3] From a very early age Disraeli was attracted by the personality of Byron.   The glamour of the East which was shed over the poet's oriental tales appealed strongly to him ; and the *Hebrew Melodies* made their writer, as Richard Garnett has said,[4] " in some sort the laureate of Disraeli's own race."   Moreover, he had special means of information as to Byron and Shelley, through Tita Falcieri, Byron's valet, who after his master's death entered the elder D'Israeli's service.   Trelawny, Lady Blessington, and Leigh Hunt were also within his father's circle of friends.   Isaac D'Israeli had himself been in correspondence with Byron, who had praised his writings.   Father and son were intimately connected with the set of literary men who met frequently at the home of John Murray in Albemarle Street.   Disraeli's close associations with Edward Bulwer-Lytton may have also stimulated his interest in Byron.   W. F. Monypenny says : [5]

Disraeli had grown to manhood in an atmosphere where

[1] For especially Byronic traits see pp. 21, 23, 25, and 26 in the edition published at New York by Wallis and Newell, 1835.   With the cause of Lodore's separation from his wife, compare, of course, *Parisina*, though in Mrs. Shelley's tale there is a mere flirtation, not adultery.

[2] See Mrs. Julian Marshall's *Life of Mary Wollstonecraft Shelley* (1889), ii, 265.

[3] For this and other novels by Disraeli I have used the edition published by the Harvard Publishing Company.

[4] " Shelley and Beaconsfield," a paper read to the Shelley Society in 1887 and reprinted in *Essays of an Ex-Librarian* (1901), pp. 101 f.

[5] *The Life of Benjamin Disraeli, Earl of Beaconsfield*, vol. i (1916), p. 361.

reverence for Byron was almost a religion, and to him, even more than to most of the aspiring youth of the day, Byron had been an inspiration and a model.

A conversation in *Vivian Grey* (1826) is Disraeli's first published estimate of Byron. The hero, Grey, has been sent to Wales to enlist the services of Cleveland, a retired politician, in the formation of a new political party.[1] From the conversation of Grey and Cleveland I quote the following passage : [2]

" We certainly want a master-spirit to set us right, Grey. Scott, our second Shakespeare, we, of course, cannot expect to step forward to direct the public mind. . . . Besides he is not the man for it. He is not a *litterateur*. We want Byron."

" Ah ! there was the man ! [Grey, *i.e.* Disraeli, replies]. And that such a man should be lost to us, at the very moment that he had begun to discover why it had pleased the Omnipotent to have endowed him with such powers ! "

" If one thing [says Cleveland] was more characteristic of Byron's mind than another, it was his strong, shrewd, common sense—his pure, unalloyed sagacity."

" You knew the glorious being, I think, Cleveland ? "

There follows a description by Cleveland of the sad change in Byron's appearance at the time he saw him last. This description is taken almost verbally from Disraeli's journal, November 27, 1822, on which day, at John Murray's, he heard Moore describe the alteration in Byron's appearance.[3]

From Geneva, on August 1, 1826, Disraeli sent his father a long letter telling of conversations with Byron's boatman, Maurice, who told him of Byron's affectations, his exploits in the water, his lack of appetite, and so forth.

There are recognizable Byronic traits in the character of the young Contarini in *Contarini Fleming* (1832), and the higher ideal in this book, as compared with *Vivian Grey*,

---

[1] There are autobiographical allusions here to Disraeli's mission to Scotland for the purpose of trying to interest Lockhart in a projected new periodical. See Monypenny, i, 87.

[2] Book iv, chapter i, p. 119.

[3] Monypenny, i, 97 f.

is evidently inspired by the nobler phases of Byron's character and career.[1]

Then, in 1837, came *Venetia*. In his dedication Disraeli writes of

the feelings with which I had attempted to shadow forth, though as " in a glass darkly," two of the most renowned and refined spirits that have adorned these our latter days.

He had by now become a conservative, but, as Monypenny remarks,[2]

by choosing as his heroes the two greatest revolutionary figures that England had produced he made proclamation in no uncertain tones that as an artist at all events he was determined to retain his freedom.

The same biographer has well analysed [3] the curious assignment of the characteristics of the two poets to the two chief figures in the novel :

The division of parts between the two poets is very curious and complex. The genius and personality of Byron are assigned to Cadurcis ; but the external circumstances of Byron's life are apportioned almost equally between Cadurcis and Herbert. To Cadurcis are given the wilful childhood, the foolish mother, the sudden poetic success, the relations with Lady Caroline Lamb, who appears in the book as Lady Monteagle, and the outburst of popular hostility which closed Byron's career in England ; but his unhappy marriage and subsequent relations to his wife and " Ada, sole daughter of my house and heart," are transferred to Herbert, who has the genius and personality of Shelley. Both poets are involved in a common end—the end, in fact, of Shelley.

The period of the story is set back nearly a generation, to a time shortly after the American revolution. In brief outline the tale is as follows. Cadurcis, a headstrong boy, falls in love with Venetia Herbert, whose mother, Lady

---

[1] Monypenny, i, 182 f., and Garnett, *op. cit.*, p. 105.
[2] *Ibid.*, i, 361.
[3] *Ibid.*, i, 363.

Herbert, is separated from her husband and keeps her
daughter in ignorance of her father. Venetia discovers the
family secret, sees a portrait of her father, and is fascinated
by him. Cadurcis speaks to Venetia in strong condemnation
of Herbert's writings and bids her think only of her mother.
They separate. Cadurcis soon becomes famous in London
society because of the success of a poem he has written.
A little later he is won over to Herbert's school of thought.
This damns him in Lady Herbert's eyes, and she refuses to
consent to his marriage to Venetia. Presently he is involved
in a duel with Lord Monteagle on account of his relations
with that nobleman's wife,[1] and as a result of the duel is
compelled to leave England amid popular fury against him.

The public, without waiting to think or even inquire after
the truth, instantly selected as genuine the most false and
the most flagrant of the fifty libelous narratives that were
circulated. . . . Society had outraged him, and now he
resolved to outrage society. . . . He was anxious about
Venetia. . . . But for the rest of the world, he delivered
them all to the most absolute contempt, disgust, and execra-
tion. . . . His only object now was to quit England.

Cadurcis joins Herbert in Italy. There, somewhat later,
the two poets meet Lady Herbert and Venetia, who are
travelling for the latter's health. There follows a somewhat
unconvincing reconciliation between Herbert and his wife,
and a period of serene happiness comes that is brought to
a tragic conclusion by the drowning of Cadurcis and Herbert.
Venetia marries George Cadurcis, a cousin of the poet.

The portrait of Byron presented in this thin and confused
disguise is very favourable. He is wilful and moody, but
generous and sincere, and endowed with high genius. Disraeli
imagines the poetic gift as coming to him later in life than

[1] This episode is introduced at some length ; Disraeli even uses the
gossip about Lady Caroline Lamb's visit to Byron's rooms disguised as a
page. It is curious to remember that though the unfortunate Caroline
had died long before Disraeli's novel appeared, her husband was still living
and was at that moment the Whig Prime Minister. One should notice
that in the somewhat entangled fictitious reproduction of events Disraeli
takes strongly the side of Byron in the matrimonial quarrel, for Lady
Herbert is represented as cold, aloof, and unsympathetic.

was actually the case. There are no *juvenilia ;* the blaze into great poetry is instantaneous. Towards the end of the book Herbert (*i.e.* Shelley in the main) [1] is depicted as having a more profound intelligence and a rarer genius than Cadurcis.

The Edinburgh Review made the following comment on *Venetia :* [2]

At what distance of time the melancholy incidents in the life of a great but erring man may become the property of the novelist, may be a matter of question ; but few, we think, can doubt that it is still a little too soon to think of weaving three volumes out of the misfortunes of Byron, or the morbid peculiarities and too early fate of Shelley.

The part which Disraeli took in the movement in 1876 to erect a national memorial to Byron will be narrated in a later chapter.

Nearly seventy years passed before Byron's career was again drawn upon as material for English fiction. In 1904 Hallie Erminie Rives (Mrs. Post Wheeler) published *The Castaway.* This book follows the incidents of Byron's life with just sufficient perversion of events and characters and motives to make the perusal of it irritating to any reader acquainted with the details of Byron's career. His character is " whitewashed " and sentimentalized painfully. Everywhere he is depicted as more sinned against than sinning. Lady Byron and Lady Caroline Lamb are both painted in dark colours. Mary Chaworth does not appear. La Guiccioli is the heroine. She and a friar of the Armenian convent near Venice are with Byron when he dies. All the characters are taken from real life except a certain Trevanion who is the villain of the novel. The illustrations, by Howard Chandler Christy, are of a piece with the text.

---

[1] On Shelley see especially book iv, chapter ii.
[2] lxvi, October 1837, 68. In La Guiccioli's *Recollections of Lord Byron* (1869), ii, 433 f. will be found some " Reflections upon Mr. Disraeli's novel *Venetia,*" in the main commendatory. Brandes (*Main Currents*, iv, 258 f.) gives a scene from *Venetia*, condensed and with the real names substituted for the fictitious ones. See also H. B. Hamilton's and Gustav Hahn's dissertations listed in my bibliography.

Mrs. Humphry Ward's *The Marriage of William Ashe* (1905) is based upon the marital troubles of William Lamb and Lady Caroline. The time of the story is about 1865–75. Geoffrey Cliffe, a poet, traveller and adventurer, plays a prominent part in it. Lady Kitty (*i.e.* Lady Caroline) is at one time infatuated with him. He is described as " a kind of modern Byron," " a great ruffling Byronic fellow," " a fantastic Byronic mixture of libertine and cad." Lady Kitty burns Cliffe in effigy because of certain ungallant verses which he sent her. Later on she and Cliffe are actually in Byron's rooms together at Venice, and she compares Cliffe with Byron. Throughout the book there are many allusions to Byron.

In the same year, 1905, F. Frankfort Moore published *He Loved but One.*[1] The tale is based on the love-affair of Byron and Mary Chaworth; the characters appear with their own names. Lady Caroline Lamb figures largely. At the close Byron is about to run away with Mary when an accident to her worthless husband leads her to remain with him and devote herself to nursing him. The title furnishes a hint as to how the poet is portrayed. He is idealized and much bowdlerized.

Maid of Athens, by " Lafayette McLaws "[2] appeared in 1906. This poor novel synthesizes the Thyrza mystery, the Maid of Athens episode, the separation from Lady Byron, Byron's melancholy, and the motive of his final expedition to Greece. The Maid of Athens is at the bottom of all these varied affairs.

Though much better than the last three novels named, Maurice Hewlett's *Bendish : A Study in Prodigality* (1913) is among the least successful of that talented and graceful writer's books. With his usual freedom in dealing with historical material, and this time with absolute unconvincingness, Mr. Hewlett has transferred the character of Byron to the reign of William the Fourth. The anachronism of such

---

[1] The American edition has the title *Love Alone is Lord*.
[2] A pseudonym, according to the catalogue of the Library of Congress, for Emily Lafayette.

poetry as Byron's (and Shelley's) in the eighteen-thirties is disconcerting. The novel is a study of Byron's character and, vaguely, of his career. The scene is laid in London and Italy ; the events centre around the passage of the Reform Bill. Lord Bendish attempts to seduce Mrs. Poore, the wife of the idealistic poet Gervase Poore (who faintly suggests Shelley). Mrs. Poore spurns Bendish, who puts his woes into " The Wanderer," a poem that has an enormous success and is described by Mr. Hewlett as follows :

The Wanderer is very eloquent. His music wells out from him, now gushing forth with gurgitations and breaking spray, now streaming steadily, now a dropping fall of sound ; but never ceasing to flow. It handles the primal emotions in the grand manner ; it is very dignified but persistently despondent ; it deals with women more in sorrow than in anger ; it frequently appeals to Heaven. It borrows largely from Nature in her more terrific moods and manifestations. Chasms and torrents, rainbows and rolling clouds, mountain peaks and venerable towers on the borders of lakes : these and other splendid witnesses assist at the obsequies of the poet's massacred affections. . . . These phenomena . . . reverberating with the sighs of a most unhappy young man of family and rank——

and so on. In this poem Gervase Poore recognizes a slander on his wife. He meets Bendish and horsewhips him ; a duel follows in which Bendish wounds Poore, though not fatally. Other mortifications to Bendish's pride follow swiftly, and he leaves England. The story ends with the promise of more to follow ; but Mr. Hewlett did not keep the promise, though there were signs enough before his death that his opinion of Byron remained unaltered.[1]

In *Bendish* Mr. Hewlett makes a grudging admission of the poet's genius, but only Byron's worst qualities are portrayed and they are exaggerated in the portrayal. We see only his vanity, theatricality, insincerity, selfishness,

---

[1] See " Don Q. on Don Juan," the London *Times*, July 20, 1922. This is an attack on Byron by Mr. Hewlett in a caustic review of Sir Arthur Quiller-Couch's Nottingham lecture on Byron (1918), printed in *Studies in Literature*, 2nd Series, 1922.

heartlessness, and snobbishness. This trait is elaborately exposed, as in this passage :

He might have been the most distinguished peer in England but for his conviction that it was distinction enough to be a peer at all. Other careers attracted him for a time, and he pursued them with a zest that soon tired : poetry, politics, love, philosophy, affairs. He found them and their rewards flimsy stuff beside the solid fact of being a lord among commoners.[1]

Having now described this baker's-dozen of English novels, I turn to other more or less fictitious evocations of Byron's character, whether in dramatic or non-dramatic form, or offered to the public as authentic anecdotes of his life.

Mr. Thomas J. Wise possesses the unique copy, apparently a revise-proof, of a suppressed skit, *The Illiberal! Verse and Prose from the North! Dedicated to My Lord Byron in the South!!* (1823).[2] In a preface the anonymous author evokes the erudite writers of *The Liberal ;* he has written *The Illiberal* to supply the " pleasant and ingenious " matter promised by the writers of *The Liberal* but not found in that publication. The piece is a playlet ; the scene Italy ; the *dramatis personæ,* " Lord B—n ; Mr. H—t ; the Little Aitches, imported from the Land of Cockneys, as Assistant Scribblers to the Liberal ; the Ghost of Percy P. Shelly [*sic*] ; Conge, B—n's valet ; and Pizette, his housekeeper." Each scene is very brief. I shall give an account of this curiosity scene by scene.

---

[1] See further, " Hewlett's Picture of Byron," *Current Opinion*, January 1914, p. 48. In addition to the thirteen novels I have described, the following reference seems to provide some sort of clue, which, however, has led to nothing in my investigations. *Byron Painted by his Compeers* (1869), p. 39, quotes from *The Magic Lantern*, January 1, 1823, this sentence : " His [Sir George W——'s] wife was a *blue stocking*, and had penned a novel, in which Lord Byron was introduced as a repentant husband."

[2] Mr. Wise's privately printed catalogue of *The Ashley Library*, i (1922), 167 f., gives a collation of *The Illiberal*, with a facsimile of the title-page. The sheets were found in Bentley's warehouse on a bill-file. Papers found with them suggested Gifford's authorship, but that is very doubtful. The piece was evidently suppressed before publication. Through Mr. Wise's courtesy I have been able to read the skit and to give a more detailed account of its contents than there was space for in Mr. Wise's catalogue.

Act I, Scene i : B—n at his desk at Pisa. He is composing " Lines on the Past " on the theme of repentance for his sins. H—t enters and insists on reading a " sonnet." B—n pretends to admire it. Exit H—t. B—n exclaims : " Damn the Liberal ! But how get out of the partnership ? " Scene ii : B—n is now interrupted by a Little Aitch who brings an elegy of his own composition on the death of Castlereagh. Another Aitch brings an " Ode on Mamma's Lap-Dog." Both these precious compositions are for the second number of *The Liberal*. B—n exclaims " O Lord ! " and act one closes.

Act II, Scene i : Pisa ; the banks of the Arno. B—n tells H—t of a horrid dream in which the ghost of Shelley appeared to him and led him to the place of the damned, with warnings to avoid it. Scene ii : Conge, the valet, much excited and speaking in broken English, tells Pizette of seeing the ghost of " Monsieur Shelle " in the study. Scene iii : B—n in his study finds a letter from Shelley on his table. He muses : " Possibly he may have escaped a watery grave." Conge speaks : " It vas von Spectre, Milor ! " B—n reads the letter, which describes Shelley's journey to hell and the tortures and howling there. It ends :

> Such is my fate, and will be of that man,
> Who does reject Jehovah's mighty plan.
> And 'tis permitted thus . . . that I to thee,
> A *Warning* and a *Monitor* should be.

B—n declares that the letter is a mere trick, and is about to throw it into the fire when the Ghost of Shelley enters. B—n exclaims, " Shelly ! " and the ghost replies, " Ay, Shelly ! the poor deluded victim of his own conceit. . . . Behold his reward." " He uncloses a kind of shroud and discovers a ghastly form with serpents coiling round it." The ghost bids B—n " be virtuous and walk humbly with thy God." Repent ! It vanishes, and B—n cries " Repent ! I will, I do repent ; . . . but will Heaven forgive so great a sinner ! ! ! " Exit. Finis.

If this wretched trash be indeed by Gifford, a sad decline had come over him since the days of the *Baviad and Mœviad*.

Quite as worthless and almost equally unknown is *Byronna, the Disappointed*, a poem by John Taylor.[1] " My hero," says the author in his preface, " is a poet, disappointed in his first love, and then the victim of capricious passions." Lupeena is one sweetheart's name. Separated from her the " hero " flies to Dalla's charms. There is much about gloom and disappointment. Need more be said ?

Far better is an ambitious piece that is not unworthy of fairly detailed comment : *Harold de Burun. A Semi-dramatic Poem ; in Six Scenes*, by Henry Austin Driver (1835). This long-forgotten poem is by no means con-temptible and is of interest to students of Shelley as well as to students of Byron. It is ingenious and has some power of characterisation. Byron's motives and ideas are under-stood, perhaps superficially, certainly sentimentally—but they are not perverted. The Byronish blank-verse is of course rhetorical, but it is never absolutely bombastic. It has cadence. It is written with care. The characters in the piece are : Harold ; Teresa ; Percy ; a Minstrel ; a Hermit ; Maledicus (Harold's Evil Genius, the personifi-cation of Public Calumny, etc.) ; Patronus (Harold's Better Genius). The time occupied is one day. The scene is the Alps (by which is meant merely some undetermined high mountains near a sea-coast). Each scene opens with a description in heroic couplets.

Scene I. Maledicus and Patronus discuss Harold de Burun ; Maledicus spreading calumny and ill-report, Patronus opposing his influence. Harold enters. Maledicus accosts him with sneers and infamous rumours. Patronus encourages him. The spirits depart ; and Harold observes someone approaching :

> But see !
> There, on the brink of yonder precipice,
> Strays my friend Percy. In his step is sadness :
> His slender form seems drooping 'neath the weight

---

[1] This poem is undated ; it probably belongs to the early eighteen-thirties. There is no copy in the British Museum ; that which I have read is in the Boston Athenæum. On the title-page is " Part I." I believe, and hope, that no further parts were printed.

Of his vast mind ; e'en as the delicate flower
Bends with the load of its luxuriant bloom.
How pale his features ! and his large full eyes,
That wont to flash with an unearthly force,
How deeply shadowed !

Harold and Percy discourse together on immortality, Percy
denying its possibility, Harold upholding the belief. Percy
urges Harold to go sailing with him. Harold refuses ; " I
feel a strange reluctance," he says. They make an appoint-
ment for that night at the hermit's cavern.

Scene II. Teresa and Harold. He makes a vow to go
to the aid of Greece. A love-colloquy follows. Enter
Maledicus, who whispers to Harold : " Where is thy wife ? "
Harold recounts to Teresa the mistake of marrying as he
did. He speaks of the incompatibility of his wife's temperament, but does not seek to justify himself. Maledicus
triumphs over him in this truly prophetic speech :

The crudest phrases of your casual speech—
Thoughts that your judgment would have writ on sand ;
Shall be collected, and with flimsy shreds
Of gossip eked, be patched upon your fame.
Nay—as Mezentius by the dead destroyed
His living subjects—we will disinter
Your still-born fancies ;—your rejected thoughts,
Though dead, shall not be buried ; but the living
Shall bear about with them their cold remains,
Till they are tainted by them.

Maledicus departs, and Harold speaks to Teresa of their
difficulties as unlawful lovers.

Scene III. A serenade by the Minstrel and a band of
singers in honour of Harold. They urge him to put aside
gloom and let joy come again to inspire his lyre. These
singers have come from England. Harold admits that he
has only affected to despise England. There follows a long
talk with the Minstrel on the delusions and emptiness of
the fashionable world. He tells of the bitterness of his
lameness, and of the gossip about his personality which
has been inspired by the supposed self-revelations in the
characters in his poems.

                              If it be ill,
        I am at once the painter and the picture :
        I lift the veil of hypocrites, and lo,
        I stand revealed a hideous manicheist !
        I dream of liberty—I am an anarch ;
        I sing of love—I am a libertine ;
        I talk of wine—I am a loathsome satyr.
        Too darkly faithful, I have wrought at times
        Unlovely images, perhaps unwisely ;
        But, though I quarry in the human breast
        For my materials, heaven forfend that I
        Should find them all within my *own* !

Scene IV.   Harold and Patronus on the way to the
Hermit's cave.   Patronus from the analogy of mountain-
climbing draws the lesson of the need to exert the mind
and spirit.   Harold resolves to live henceforth not for himself alone ; by worthy deeds he may impugn his crudest
musings.   He loathes war, but desires to help Greece.   He
looks forward to the triumph of Reason and Democracy.
He meditates upon the mountains, the symbol of God's
infiniteness and man's littleness.   His foot slips, and to
catch himself he grasps the nearest object ; it is a wayside
cross.   He muses on the Cross, and realizes that his loathing
of the actions of those who claim it for a symbol has made
him mistakenly turn from the Cross itself.

Scene V.   Harold and the Hermit ; a storm is gathering.
There is a long debate on religion, morality, the problem of
evil, and so on.   The Hermit admires Harold's poetry ;
but what has he to offer for the beliefs he desires to take
away ?   Harold tries to analyse himself and his motives :

        I loathe myself for doing what I loathe ;
        So I abhor the coward reticence
        Of sleeker crime, dissembling or concealment.
        I claim no merits that are not my own ;
        I shun no censure that is justly due.
        Whate'er my conduct, I have rather stood
        My own detractor than my vindicator—
        And I have suffered for my candour deeply.

He gives a long account of his life, and the Hermit delivers
an opinion upon Harold's writings :

When I have read
The chequered page, it seemed to me as though
Two Angels, one of darkness, one of light,
Had wrestled which should prompt thee. . . .
A temple hast thou built—a splendid fane !
But with a tessellated floor where Vice
And Virtue are commingled with a skill
So masterly—they look most fair together.

Harold declares that on his tomb should be inscribed :
" Here lies the enemy of Harold." . . . The storm increases ;
peasants report that a skiff has been seen far out at sea.
They all hurry away ; and Maledicus is heard laughing from
the rocks.

Scene VI. The Minstrel reports the death of Percy in
the storm ; and Harold pays this tribute to him :

We were not of one mind : but oft have I
Admired and marvelled where I least approved.
He had a soul that grasped beyond the reach
Of common natures. He beheld, afar,
Things that they saw not ; but so overstrained
His mental vision that he saw them all
Confused in their sublimity. He tried
The trackless heights where inspiration fails.
And, as the mind hath its own atmosphere,
Which grows too thin for its subsistence when
It climbs beyond its density, the end
Hath sometimes been Insanity. His heart
Was, as hearts should be, but as few are found,
Warm, generous, gentle ; the Samaritan
Of other hearts ; and only pained, itself,
That it could do so little.

Harold meditates upon death. He decides to burn Percy's
body on the shore. He bids farewell to the mountains. He
meditates upon his own after-fame.

'Tis now too late to flatter—or deny
That I have gained high honours in my day.
And, in this consciousness, I now may make
My lone self-estimate. Yes ! I now perceive
I have made friendships with my future kind ;
My voice is gone before me ; and my soul
Forehears their welcome. I behold the doors

Of the far chambers of futurity
Unfolding at my name ; and I shall stand
Like a familiar spirit in the midst
Of multitudes of minds to me unknown.
Millions shall know me, when I know not them ;
And pity me, when I shall need no tears ;
And honour me, when I no more shall feel ;
And, haply—may condemn me.   Shades there are
That have obscured my glory.   Time alone,
With its most just arbitrament, will shew,
Which were the sooty volumes that arose
From the black fumes of malice, which the clouds
That were engendered in the fitful sky
Of my own genius :—Time alone will shew !

He departs.   Teresa tells the Minstrel of a dream she had
in which she saw Harold leading armed men up a mountain.
He reeled and, as he fell over a precipice, still pointed
upwards.   Maledicus gloated over his body, but was at
length driven off by Patronus.

I have now to record four anecdotes of Byron's life,
published as authentic but properly to be classed as fiction.

An " Extract from a Letter, containing an Account of
Lord Byron's Residence in the Island of Mitylene " [1] purports to tell how in 1812 " we " (whoever " we " are) visited
Mitylene and found an English nobleman residing there.
His house and surroundings are described, and emphasis
is laid upon his many charities to the inhabitants of the
island.   He was eccentric but philanthropic.   The writer
learned that he was Lord Byron, though not till later did
he become acquainted with Byron's poetry.   This account is
now (1819) made public " in justice to his lordship's good
name, which has been grossly slandered. . . . [His] character
is worthy of his genius.   To do good in secret, and to shun
the world's applause, is the surest testimony of a virtuous
heart and self-approving conscience."

[1] This is included in Polidori's *Vampyre* (1819), pp. 75–84, a book I
shall discuss in the next chapter.   The " Letter " may be a fabrication by
John Mitford ; see *The New Monthly Magazine*, April 1819, pp. 193 f. ;
Hone's Every-day Book, *sub* April 19 (p. 486) ; *The Radical Triumvirate*,
p. 37.   For Byron's repudiation of this fabrication, first published in
Galignani's Messenger, 1819, see LJ, iv, 288.

In 1824 appeared a quaint fabrication entitled a *Narrative of Lord Byron's Voyage to Corsica and Sardinia*.[1] The voyage was made, it is claimed, in 1821 ; the pretended reminiscences of Byron and Shelley abound in absurdities. Byron is lauded throughout and becomes a theatrical sort of prig. He is very devout :

> Lord Byron was certainly neither an irreligious nor a superstitious man !—he kept the Sabbath day holy, and made all his domestics do the same ; on that day he permitted no one to labour, and at all times swearing was his detestation, though, in a moment of passion, he has been betrayed to utter an oath. As to religion—I once heard him remark on board the yacht, when reasoning with Mr. S— on the folly of scepticism, " If there is not a future state, I shall be as well off when dead, as you who would persuade yourself there really is none ; if there is a hereafter, of which I have no doubt, then I have a decided advantage over you, and surely the trouble of believing is less than that of doubting, and more pleasing." [2]

Byron's bravery [3] and generosity [4] are illustrated by various incidents. The most curious part of the book, however, is the amazing sketch of Shelley that it contains.[5] The claim

---

[1] Reprinted at Paris in 1825. I have given a longer account of this book in an article, " A Byron-Shelley Hoax," *The Nation* (N. Y.), cvii, August 24, 1918, pp. 199 f. An inquiry with regard to the authorship was printed in *N. & Q.* 7th Series, ix, 127. See also *The London Literary Gazette*, November 6, 1824, pp. 107 f. for a review that commented upon the number of journals and individuals that had been gulled by this hoax.

[2] By a curious coincidence this is precisely the contrary of what Byron did actually once remark ; see LJ, v, 490.

[3] *E.g.* during a great storm and when the excursion was interrupted by a rencontre with a Turkish man-of-war. On the latter occasion Byron, dressed in oriental finery, including " a linen turban with a gold crescent " (" beard he wore none, but the Marchioness fixed on his upper lip a pair of moustaches made of her own hair "), went aboard the Turkish ship and by his exquisite tact persuaded the pirate to allow the " Mazeppa " to proceed unmolested.

[4] *E.g.* he provides a dowry for a poor Corsican girl ; he is generously indulgent towards Shelley.

[5] During the storm Percy S—— completely lost his nerve, wept like a child, and " in moving accents of serious prayer " called upon the Being whose existence he had formerly denied. When the storm subsided he " recovered from his fits of fear, and came from his cabin like a spectre from the tomb. . . . A glass of rum and water, warm, raised his drooping spirits and in twenty-four hours he was the same free-thinking, thankless dog as ever." But Percy stayed at San Fiorenzo till he could get return

is made that the Narrative is from the journal kept by the commander of the yacht, Captain Benson, R.N.

The rumours current about the destruction of Byron's Memoirs were bound to give rise to prurient and filthy fabrications. Of these one is " A supposed chapter from Byron's own Memoirs " which graced the initial number of *The John Bull Magazine*.[1] The title of this wretched fraud is " My Wedding Night ; the Obnoxious Chapter in Lord Byron's Memoirs." It tells of Lady Byron's coldness ; of Byron's nightmare of a visit to hell ; and of his awakening to find his bride so pale and cold that he scarcely refrained from repeating his dream-words, " Hail, Proserpine ! " [2]

The latest of the faked scraps of Byronic biography is " An Event in the Life of Lord Byron " (1853).[3] It tells how the poet, with La Contessa, her brother, and a French marquis went by gondola to spend the day on an Adriatic isle near Venice. The gondola drifted away, and the party was confronted with the danger of starvation. An attendant

passage in a larger ship than the yacht. " He was an eccentric being, and much attached to his Lordship, who had treated him with great kindness for several years. . . . Poor S——, in doubt and tears, stood upon the pier waving his handkerchief till the wind bore us beyond his sight—at dinner his Lordship remarked, that he could have better spared a better man."

[1] July 1824, pp. 19 f. A foreword says that more than two copies of the " destroyed " Memoirs still exist ; that five hundred people or more have read them ; and that as it is quite impossible for them to remain unpublished " we " expedite the publication by giving this chapter " with due mutilations." The genuineness is vouched for by " one " with the best opportunities for seeing the original.

[2] *Blackwood's*, xvi, July 1824, 115 f., published as No. 16 of the " Letters of Timothy Tickler, Esq. to eminent literary characters " a letter " To the Editor of the John Bull Magazine. On an Article in his first Number." This reproves the Editor for publishing the chapter from the Memoirs, without, however, questioning the genuineness of the thing :

> Byron's *chapter* proclaims him the Worst of the Bad—
> Unless Charity whispers, most wild of the mad.

Was such a publication generous ? Was it just ? *John Bull* (August, 1824, pp. 78 f.) reprinted Tickler's Letter with a reply between each stanza, *e.g.*—

> Byron's Chapter proclaims him to be *what he was*,
> For vexation I own I can't see any cause. . . .
> And *Charity* too ! Well, I may be tar-barrell'd,
> But *that's* the last feeling I'd have for Childe Harold.

See also *John Bull*, November 1824, p. 163.

[3] By " The Author of *The Unholy Wish* " ; *The New Monthly Magazine*, xcix, 138 f.

named Cyclops rigged up a water-cask as a boat, sailed off
in it, and managed to procure help. There is much about
Byron's feelings against his English " traducers " and about
his eternal love for Mary Chaworth.

A recent drama and a recent photo-play complete my
list of English imaginary portrayals of Byron. *The Pilgrim
of Eternity*, by K. K. Ardaschir, was produced at the Duke
of York's Theatre, London, in November 1921. It met
with no favour and was withdrawn after a short run. During
the summer of 1922 an excellent photo-play, *The Prince of
Lovers*, was shown at the Philharmonic Hall, London. This
" British Screencraft " production was adapted by Miss
Alicia Ramsey from her play *Byron*. Mr. Howard Gaye
acted the part of the poet. Interesting Byron relics, lent
by Mr. Murray and by Mrs. Fraser (the present owner of
Newstead Abbey), were used or copied for the film. The
costumes and furnishings were satisfyingly free from
anachronisms. The action centered in the years 1812–1816,
and then, omitting the Italian period, passed to the last
phase in Greece. Liberties are taken with historical facts,
but save for the somewhat sentimentalised conclusion—
Hobhouse appears at the bedside of the dying poet with a
message from the King of England—there was hardly a
note in the performance to jar upon the sensibilities of
a spectator who was well acquainted with the facts of
Byron's life.

To foot-notes may be consigned two biographies of
Byron that are fictitious rather than authentic ; [1] a brief

---

[1] *The Private Life of Lord Byron*, by J. Mitford (n.d., 1836) is a smutty
little book, the contents of which are sufficiently indicated by the enormously long title, for which see my bibliography. There are a number of
vulgar plates in colours (in the copy in the Widener collection at Harvard ;
the copy in the British Museum has but one plate and that not coloured).
A French translation " par M. F. . . ." with the title *Vie Privée et Amours
secrètes de Lord Byron*, is in the " Inferno " of the Bibliothèque Nationale.
For the full title of this version see *L'Enfer de la Bibliothèque Nationale*,
Paris, Bibliothèque des Curieux, 1919, pp. 201 f. The French version is
from the tenth English edition (1837), an indication of the demand for this
sort of thing. A similar publication, equally unauthentic, is *Les Amours
secrètes de Lord Byron. Traduites de l'anglais* (Paris, 1839). Most of the
incidents are faked. It is a shoddy and rather obscene little book. I have
never come across the English original, and in common with Estève (p. 273)
I doubt whether one ever existed.

list of French,[1] Italian,[2] German,[3] and Norse [4] works of
fiction that introduce Byron ; and, by way of contrast, a
brief list of English novels that contain characters drawn
from Shelley.[5]

[1] On Edouard Magnien's *Mortel, ange, ou demon* (1836), a trilogy which
Elze (*Life of Byron*, p. 330) refers to as *Lord Byron : Man, Angel or Devil*,
see Estève, p. 272.   Elze seems to imply that this was translated into
English ; but I have found no trace of such a translation.   I have not seen
Elie Fourès, *Le Premier Amour de Lord Byron, nouvelle inédite* (Paris,
1885) See also Bibliography, *sub* Drouineau.
[2] A curious Italian piece, depicting Byron's penitence and conversion,
is *Il venerdì Santo—Scena della Vita di Lord Byron* (Turin, 1847).   In 1837
Gian Battista Cipro published a drama in four acts entitled *Lord Byron a
Venezia*.   See further, Guido Muoni, *La Fama del Byron e il Byronismo in
Italia*, and especially the same author's *La Leggenda del Byron in Italia*,
pp. 2–9.
[3] A German novel dealing with Byron and La Guiccioli is Alexander
Buchner's *Lord Byron's letzte Liebe. Eine biographische Novelle* (Leipzig,
1862).   Richard Ackermann (*Lord Byron*, p. 168) describes another novel
of the same title by Karl Bleibtreu (1881).   Bleibtreu wrote also *Lord Byron's
letzte Liebe, Drama in funf Akten* (Leipzig, n.d.).   See Bibliography, *sub*
Bleibtreu, Laube, Schmidt, E., Wilkomm and Zitz.
[4] I cannot read a Norse novel by Mathilda Malling that deals with the
Caroline Lamb episode chiefly : *Manden-Hustruen og Lord Byron* (Köben-
havn og Kristiania, 1912).
[5] Peacock introduces Shelley in *Headlong Hall, Melincourt, Nightmare
Abbey* (as we have seen), and *Gryll Grange*.   On Shelley in Mrs Shelley's
novels see Professor Peck's article, previously referred to.   *Venetia* I have
discussed.   The character of Ladislaw in George Eliot's *Middlemarch* was
evidently drawn with Shelley in mind ; Ladislaw is in fact described as
" a sort of Burke with a leaven of Shelley."   Finally, there is Alexander
Harvey's curious book, *Shelley's Elopement*.

CHAPTER X

THE BYRON APOCRYPHA

In addition to some of the spurious continuations of *Don Juan* described in a previous chapter there exists a large number of poems, with some pieces in prose and some pretended translations into French, that have been attributed, whether by error or with fraudulent intent, to Byron. These things I shall now describe, taking up first the several spurious books ; then the various scattered separate poems ; then the French " translations " ; and finally a prose allegory and two collections of letters purporting to be by Byron.[1] I shall indicate in foot-notes the editions of Byron's writings in which each of these hoaxes appears, if in any. Thus the reader will gain an idea of the currency which each fraudulent piece attained.

At the time of Byron's final departure from his native country there was published *Lord Byron's Farewell to*

[1] No full account of these non-canonical Byronic pieces exists, and this chapter is planned to supply that lacuna in Byronic bibliography. In 1887 W. Roberts published in *Walford's Antiquarian* (xii, 101 f.) a description of " Some Poems Attributed to Byron." He gives a list of nine pieces, but some of them are genuine. In many cases he does not trace the poem to its original place of appearance, nor does he give a complete list of the editions in which the various pieces appear. *N. & Q.* has from time to time printed comments on some of these spurious poems ; see especially the index to vol. ii of the seventh series. E. H. Coleridge noted a few pieces in his bibliography (*Poetry*, vol. vii) and in other places in his edition of Byron ; but his list is far from complete and not altogether accurate. Professor Kölbing described several items in *Englische Studien*, xxvi, 67 f., and refers to others in his edition of Byron's *Werke*, ii, 46 f. M. Forster's article " Zur Pseudo-Byron-Litteratur " (*Englische Studien*, xxvi, 463 f.) considers a few short pieces only. Descriptions of a few impostures may be found in works on Byron such as Elze's *Life* and Mayne's *Life*. In *N. & Q.* May and June, 1919 (12th Series, v, 113 f. and 143 f.) I published a tentative list. Upon that list, with corrections and much amplification, this chapter is based.

England : with three other poems (London : J. Johnston, 1816).[1] The title-poem [2] is in fifty-nine quatrains, and begins :

> Oh ! land of my fathers and mine,
> The noblest, the best, and the bravest.

The next poem, in six stanzas of ten lines each, is an *Ode to the Island of St. Helena*,[3] beginning :

> Peace to thee, isle of the ocean !
> Hail to the breezes and billows.

It expresses a sentimental sympathy with the fallen Napoleon. Then follows *To my Daughter, on the Morning of her Birth*,[4] twelve eight-line stanzas ; and finally *To the Lyly of France*,[5] twelve quatrains, of which this is a sample :

> As a bye-word thy blossom shall be,
> A mock and a jest among men,
> The proverb of slaves and the sneer of the free,
> In city and mountain and glen.

This volume had a great success, and, as my notes have indicated, the four pieces were reprinted in many collections, notwithstanding the injunction proceedings brought against Johnston, and Byron's express repudiation of the poems.[6]

---

[1] For Byron's repudiation of this book, see LJ, iii, 337 ; for the injunction proceedings instituted against Johnston, see LJ, iv, 19 f.

[2] This *Farewell* obtained a wide circulation. It is in the collections piratically issued by Thomas, Sheppard, Limbird, Bumpus, Knight and Lacy, Cole, Bembow, Dove, and Jones. It is quoted in full in *The Life, Writings, Opinions, and Times of Lord Byron* (1825), i, 273 f. It is in no Galignani edition of Byron's works (the Galignani editions contained several spurious pieces), but occurs so late as the Bohn edition of 1851.

[3] The *Ode* is reprinted in all the miscellaneous collections mentioned in the last note. It is also in Galignani 1828 and 1831, but was removed from 1835, from which many spurious pieces were weeded out. It is in Bohn, 1851.

[4] Byron remarked : " On the ' Morning of my Daughter's Birth ' I had other things to think of than verses " (LJ, iii, 337). This piece is in all the collections listed above ; in all Galignani editions except 1835 ; in Bohn, 1851 ; and is quoted in part in the *Life, Writings*, etc., i, 288.

[5] " As to the ' Lyly of France,' " wrote Byron (*l.c.*), " I should as soon think of celebrating a turnip." But the poem was reprinted in all the pirated editions I have named ; in all Galignani editions except 1835 ; and in Bohn, 1851.

[6] Some copies of *Poems on his Domestic Circumstances*, by Lord Byron (Bristol : W. Sheppard, 1816) contain at the end a poem entitled, " On Reading Lord Byron's Farewell to England," which begins, " Still my

Another volume that coincided with Byron's departure was *Reflections on Shipboard, by Lord Byron* (London : Kirby and Allason, 1816).[1] This, too, contained four pieces. The title-poem begins :

> Once more the swelling sails are all unfurl'd,
> That waft me, England, from thy parent shore,
> Would that they bore me to some distant world,
> Where memory's shaft could wound this breast no more !

The indignant wave is an emblem of the loved form whose anger pursues him. He indulges in " dreams of unsubstantial bliss," but on waking he feels himself to be a " wretched outcast "—

> Sever'd those ties that bound my heart to life,
> Feebly it beats—and soon, I trust, will cease,
> Then, oh ! severe—but much beloved wife,
> Thy anger will subside to pitying peace.

The second piece is *The Poet Refuses Consolation*, of which the first stanza is :

> Tell me not of Grecian maids,
>   Of Sion's daughters fair,
> Who weave with gems the amorous braids
>   Of their luxuriant hair ;
> Blunted will fall young Cupid's dart
> From such a sear'd and wither'd heart.

" Snowy arms," " classic lore," " music's strains," and so forth have no power over this heart, which only one person can warm to life again. Then follows *The Birth of Hope,* beginning :

> The butterfly, with bright and burnished wing,
> Does from the chrysalis unsightly spring,
> So does this cold and almost blighted breast
> Give birth to *hope*—and prove its living nest.

bosom's indignation." See E. H. Coleridge's bibliography, *Poetry,* vii, 257. The last page of the copy in the British Museum has, however, been torn out, and I have been unable to see another copy.

[1] See Kölbing, *Englische Studien,* xxvi, 76 f. The four poems in this volume obtained, so far as I have been able to discover, no circulation whatsoever. I have therefore described them in more detail than I have those that are accessible in Galignani and other obsolete editions of Byron's works.

And it ends :

> Still then I'll hope—and as I devious stray,
> Will feel like pilgrim sent some vow to pay,
> My beauteous saint, perchance—my penance o'er,
> May softly say—" *Return and sin no more !* "

Lastly, there is *The Poet Moralizes on Waterloo*.   The theme is that the poet, who is starting on a pilgrimage to foreign climes, plans to visit that crimson field, " manur'd by heaps of slain " from which the purple grape and the laurel will rise.

J. Johnston, the publisher of the *Farewell to England*, returned quickly to the profitable trade of issuing spurious volumes by Byron, when he published *Lord Byron's Pilgrimage to the Holy Land. . . . To which is added The Tempest*. Johnston advertised that he had paid Byron five hundred guineas for the exclusive copyright of this volume.   Byron at once wrote to Murray : [1]

Nothing surprises me, or this perhaps *would*, and most things amuse me, or this probably would *not*.   With regard to myself, the man has merely *lied ;* that's natural ; his betters have set him the example.   But with regard to you, his assertion may perhaps injure you in your publications ; and I desire that it may receive the most public and unqualified contradiction.   I do not know that there is any punishment for a thing of this kind ; and if there were, I should not feel disposed to pursue this ingenious mountebank farther than was necessary for his confutation.

Proceedings were instituted November 30, 1816, and an injunction was obtained against Johnston ; hence a second edition (1817) has as its title merely *A Pilgrimage to the Holy Land*.[2]   The promptness with which the injunction was granted prevented the book from obtaining any further circulation as Byron's work ; but an examination of the *Pilgrimage* is worth while for the light it will throw on the literary qualities which Byron's contemporaries considered Byronic.   The poem is in two cantos, in heroic couplets. The Pilgrim's name is Flavius ; he is thus described :

[1] LJ, iv, 19 f.
[2] See *N. & Q*. 4th Series, i, 267.

> His pensive soul no kindred fellow found,
> An intellectual desert reigned around :
> No bosom greeted him—he greeted none—
> The wandering minstrel was, indeed, alone.

He journeys through various countries, moralizing on the past, and occasionally he seizes his harp and relieves himself of very mediocre lyrics, such as this :

> Kindly blow, thou fitful breeze !
> Onward roll, thou briny billow !
> O'er the wide and trackless seas,
> Speed thy course, my gallant *Willow !* [1]

He passes Spain, Morocco, Agrigentum ("no hellish Phalaris" is there now) ; Malta, Crete, and the Ægean. Then comes a section on the degeneracy of modern Greece. Thence on to sultry Egypt, the Nile, and Acre. The Sultan is denounced, and the Pilgrim, finding a conveniently located cliff, sits thereon and pours forth his song, which is a kind of Ode to Contemplation. The second canto describes the wanderings of Flavius in the Holy Land. The degradation of Syria is lamented ; and finally, homeward bound once more, Flavius appeals to Britain to free herself from tyrants. *The Tempest*, which follows, is a fragment in the metre and manner of *The Giaour*. It tells of the escape of a mysterious stranger from a shipwreck. This stranger afterwards dies in the arms of a friendly leech, who hears his dying words and could tell strange tales, an he would. It hits off fairly cleverly the superficial characteristics of Byronic romance.[2]

Of very different kind is *Leon to Annabella. An Epistle after the Manner of Ovid,*[3] which has always been current *sub*

---

[1] " Willow," fortunately for the rhyme's sake, is the name of the ship.

[2] *The Portfolio, Political and Literary,* No. vi, December 7, 1816, pp. 121 f. contains an article on " Literary Frauds " that mentions this *Pilgrimage* and dismisses it as obviously spurious, and then considers *The Prisoner of Chillon,* at length coming to the conclusion that it, too, is an impudent forgery.

[3] The only copy I know of, of the undated, apparently original edition (London : Mac John, Raymur and Company) is in the library of Mr. J. Pierpont Morgan. In 1865 it was reprinted " for the booksellers " by W.

rosa and which has lately been reprinted. Though usually
associated with a similar poem of later date, this piece
belongs, I believe, to 1817 or 1818. An introductory prose
notice tells of the discovery of the manuscript of the poem
near Pisa, in a cottage where an English gentleman " whose
name could not be learned " used to visit. The poem, in
rhymed couplets, tells in the first person of Byron's bad upbringing, his marriage and quarrels with his wife, their
separation and his flight from England. There are guarded
suggestions that the vice of the cities of the plain was the
cause of the separation. The justification offered is that all
human beings are bad. The piece is very coarse and cynical,
and, despite assertions to the contrary, is indisputably not
by Byron.

In the copy that I have used (in the British Museum) of
*Childe Harold's Pilgrimage to the Dead Sea : Death on the
Pale Horse : and Other Poems* (1818) there is no attempt
made to palm the work off as Byron's, for there is a dedication to the author's father and the memory of his mother,
and an introductory poem, " To My Forsaken Harp,"
tells of the death of the author's beloved wife. But some
people evidently believed the book to be by Byron, and
Byron expressly repudiates it : [1]

All the things attributed to me within the last five years—
Pilgrimages to Jerusalem, Deaths upon Pale Horses, Odes to
the Land of the Gaul, Adieus to England, Songs to Madame
La Valette, Odes to St. Helena, Vampires, and what not—of

Dugdale, a publisher of evil repute. It was again reprinted, with the title
The Great Secret Revealed, by Dugdale in 1866. Copies of this reprint are
bound up with separate pagination in the 1866 edition of *Don Leon*. *Leon
to Annabella* was reprinted at Brussels in 1875, and is included in the Paris
edition of *Don Leon* still current. It is also in *Poetica Erotica*, edited by
T. R. Smith, vol. iii, New York, Privately Printed, 1922. The piece is
described by Ashbee in the *Index Librorum Prohibitorum*, pp. 192 f., but
Ashbee did not know the edition earlier than 1865. According to his
account Dugdale bought the manuscript believing it to be authentic and
hoping to get a large amount from Lady Byron for its suppression. " A
gentleman," says Ashbee, proved its fraudulency to Dugdale by pointing
out allusions to events that occurred after Byron's death. It is scarcely
necessary to note that " Leon " is merely " Noel " spelled backwards.

[1] In his " Reply to *Blackwood's Edinburgh Magazine*," LJ, iv, 474 f.

which, God knows, I never composed nor read a syllable beyond their titles in advertisements. . . .

Whether a fraud was intended or not, the protagonist of the title-poem is certainly Byron. The poem displays very clearly the characteristics of Byronism that imitators could fairly easily apprehend. The Pilgrim speaks, by the Dead Sea :

> I sought this land whose barren womb
> Seems of all things the sullen tomb. . . .
> I sped to its shores, too, in hope to find
> Some likeness to a blasted mind. . . .
> I like the dreary and the dead,
> They are a paradise to the eye
> Of him whose writhing heart hath bled
> Beneath the scourge of misery. . . .
> Scarce thirty years have o'er me rolled,
> Yet my bloom is gone—my heart is cold.

The Pilgrim tells how his health and reason fled when his True Love married another. Days of sin and nights of blasphemy followed that loss ; but in purer moments the Muses woo'd his brain. He became a Poet, and was envied and gazed at. But the flowers of his fancy are tainted by sin ; the vulture train feeds on his heart :

> The meanest peasant would reject
> A lot so splendid—and so wrecked.

The mere change of scene is no cure for the mind's distractions ; he has been to Greece and seen many things there (all duly enumerated) that were " types to a fallen mind " of its own decay. At Thermopylæ he found the " perishable wreath of fame." But why sorrow that Leonidas is forgotten there ? In the grave our wild despair becomes a dreamless sleep. The Pilgrim would not grieve though no tears were shed over his bier :—

> And yet—there *is* an eye whose tear
> Should bless a father's dying bed ;
> There *is* a hand, which, kind and dear,
> Should scatter roses o'er the dead.

But his child will never know a father's love. He invokes

Judea, his dreary home. Jerusalem has become the lair of tigers ; her people are enslaved. How easily, he muses, could we bear the ills of this life were we certain of another. Is there no guiding star ? no hand divine ? Harold in despair is about to throw himself into the Dead Sea when a Voice is heard : " Hold, Mortal of the unbelieving heart ! " The day of Judgment draws near ; Death on his Pale Horse will come. Is Harold's name written in the Book of Life ? Repent, repent !

Death on the Pale Horse, a grandiose blank-verse poem in the manner of Byron's *Darkness*, follows. And then an insignificant " fragment " called *The Battle of Waterloo ;* and the last piece in the book is *To the Brave*, an elegy on the dead in battle.

The Vampyre, a Tale (1819) was quickly repudiated by Byron, and Dr. Polidori acknowledged its authorship.[1]

The most curious of all the spurious books is *The Duke of Mantua, A Tragedy. By* —— (1823).[2] On the title-page there is a vignette portrait of Byron, peeping with the left eye from behind a mask which he holds in his right hand. On the leaf following the title is a dedication : " To Lady Byron the following pages are dedicated by ——." A second edition, anonymous and with the vignette portrait, appeared in 1833. The play was again reprinted, without the portrait and without the dedication to Lady Byron, in *The Legendary and Poetical Remains of John Roby*, in 1854. Roby's widow supplies an introductory sketch of his literary life. Roby was born in 1793 and drowned in 1850 in the wreck of the

---

[1] For Byron's repudiation, see LJ, iv, 286. For a detailed account of the publication of *The Vampyre*, with a discussion of the problem whether Polidori was guilty of a deliberate deception or whether the blame attaches to the editor or publisher of *The New Monthly Magazine*, in which the tale first appeared (April 1819), see W. M. Rossetti's introduction to *The Diary of Dr. John William Polidori* (1921), pp. 11 f. The contents of the book are in four sections ; An Extract from a Letter from Geneva ; an Introduction (on vampyres) ; The Tale ; and An Account of Byron's Residence in the Island of Mitylene. For the influence of Polidori's tale in France, see Estève, pp. 76 f. ; see also Bibliography, *sub* Hock.

[2] In the B. M. scrap-book, vol. i, there is a reprint of this title-page with the printed announcement at the top : " Just published." In *N. & Q.* 6th Series, xii, 249, there is a query by W. Nixon as to the authorship of this play, which remained unanswered.

" Orion." Of *The Duke of Mantua* the " sketch " simply says :

It went through three or four editions in a short time, and was pronounced by the critics, " worthy of a place among our best closet plays." It has been long out of print, and is included in the present volume.

Not a word is said of the hoax by which it was first introduced into the world. The play is an instance of the attempts to win success under the protection of Byron's great name ; it is utterly unlike anything which we can imagine him writing. An Italianate tragedy of love, rivalry, and assassination and revenge, it belongs with the many plays of the Elizabethan revival, though in technique it is much inferior to Milman, and judged as poetry it cannot compare with Beddoes's beautiful fragments.

I come now, according to the chronological order that I have tried to establish, to the infamous piece, *Don Leon,* which has generally been regarded as a forgery of the eighteen-sixties but which may in reality date from about 1824–1830. For in *Notes and Queries,* 1853,[1] under the heading " Immoral Works," a writer who signs himself " I.W." gives a brief description of the poem and adds :

Is the writer known ? I am somewhat surprised that not one of Byron's friends has, so far as I know, hinted a denial of the authorship ; for, scarce as the work may be, I suppose some of them must have seen it ; and it is possible that a copy might get into the hands of a desperate creature, who would hope to make a profit, by republishing it with Byron's and Moore's names in the title-page.

" I.W." states that the copy he has seen " was printed abroad many years since." I have found no trace whatsoever of this first continental edition. In 1866 " I.W.'s " prophecy was singularly fulfilled, when *Don Leon* was republished with Byron's and Moore's names on the title-page. To it was added *Leon to Annabella,* a piece I have already

---

[1] First series, vii, 66.

described.[1] No detailed description of *Don Leon* is possible.
It begins :

> Thou ermined judge, pull off that sable cap.

The satirist attacks the puritan cant that seeks to suppress
the facts of passion, and a long story follows of his amours,
including those with Rushton and Eddleston. He tells of
adventures in the East and of researches in classical literature that justify his predilections. The piece, which extends
to 1455 lines, is amazingly coarse ; in dealing with such
offscourings of literature the warning of Virgil to Dante is
applicable :

> Saper d'alcuno è buono :
> Degli altri fia laudabile tacerci.

Those who remember the circumstances in which this warning was uttered may derive therefrom a further hint as to the
subject-matter of *Don Leon*.

We return now from the *banlieus* to the reputable depart-
ments of literature. *Arnaldo ; Gaddo ; and other unacknowledged poems ; by Lord Byron and some of his Contemporaries ;*
collected by Odoardo Volpi (1836), is a handsome, well-
printed volume of three hundred and ten pages.[2] A writer

---

[1] I believe that the book is in the British Museum, but it is not catalogued. I have seen copies in two private collections. In *N. & Q.* 3rd
Series, xi, 477, S. Jackson inquires as to the authenticity of *Don Leon*.
This inquirer later (*ibid.* xii, 137) states that " owing to some interference,
the poem of *Don Leon* has been burked." The piece itself gives no indication of the publisher. According to Messrs. Davis and Orioli's book-
catalogue (No. xxii, 1918) the publisher was John Camden Hotten (who
was quite capable of putting out such a thing). Ashbee, however (*Index
Librorum Prohibitorum*, pp. 189 f.), states that the publisher was W. Dugdale
(who was equally capable !). For a full account of *Don Leon*, with copious
extracts, see Ashbee, *l.c.* That indefatigable bibliophile evidently knew
nothing about the existence of the pre-1853 edition mentioned in my text.
Within the last few years a facsimile reprint of the 1866 edition has been
surreptitiously circulated in and from Paris. Of that issue I have seen
two copies.

[2] The title is ambiguous ; only *Arnaldo* and *Gaddo* are attributed to
Byron. The volume also contains a poetic version from the *Decameron ;*
some imitations of Thomas Hood (" By Thomas Ood ") ; ten cantos of a
translation of the *Inferno ;* and a large number of sonnets. Sonnet x
(p. 242) begins :

> I stood within that chamber, where, amid
> Death's sable pageantry, was Byron's bier.

The writer says that at that hour he felt Death's presence more profoundly
than he could have felt it on a field of battle.

who is anonymous contributes an interesting preface. He tells how he became acquainted at Florence with the late Odoardo Volpi, a man well informed about English poetry, and a student of music and the fine arts. Volpi wrote English verse with facility. He belonged to a group of literary men who used to meet to discuss literature. At one of these meetings Volpi proposed a plan of publishing at Florence an English annual miscellany, in which poetry composed by various authors travelling in Italy should appear. Volpi told the writer of this preface that several eminent English poets promised contributions. Byron gave him two tales, not to be published, however, under his name. Volpi expressed his regret to the Noble Poet that he had stopped writing tales like *The Giaour.* Byron replied : " What ! would you have me replunge into barbarism, after having become a civilized author ? I have had a letter from Murray this very day, asking me to write something in the old style : but the fellow shall not induce me to tickle the ears of the groundlings any more in that way." It was a juvenile production of the old sort that Byron allowed Volpi to have. Later he gave him a comic tale entitled *Giuseppino,* which was published anonymously in England and which re-appeared, it is believed, as by Byron, at Philadelphia in 1822.[1] It is now issued as *Gaddo,* with additional stanzas. Byron would not acknowledge it, for he thought it far inferior to *Beppo.* These facts Volpi communicated to the writer of the preface, and dying suddenly shortly afterwards, left the writer all his literary papers. Volpi enjoined secrecy as to Byron's authorship. Were Byron still living the secret should still be kept, but the writer holds that it is his duty to give to the public all the information that he possesses as to the authorship of the two poems. He does not assert positively, but contents himself with reporting what

[1] I have found no trace of the London edition of *Giuseppino ;* but the British Museum contains *Giuseppino, An Occidental Story* (Philadelphia, Carey and Lea, 1822). In this edition the poem is in 125 stanzas, occupying 68 pages. There is no evidence that any claim was set up for Byron's authorship. The catalogue of the British Museum says that the author was E. V. Shannon. If so, he may have been the perpetrator of the entire hoax.

he heard from the former owner of the manuscripts. Perhaps
Volpi amused himself with passing on a harmless forgery.
So far the preface, which is written with great show of frank-
ness and circumstantiality.

Arnaldo is the longest and most ambitious of all the
pseudo-Byronic poems.[1] A dedication to " the Young,"
an address to Italy, and a denunciation of Tyranny lead to
the narrative. To outline this wild, confused story is difficult.
Arnaldo loved Lorenza and she him ; but his " monkish
foes " falsely told her that he had been killed in battle and
so had persuaded her to enter a convent. He returned from
the wars, and she escaped from the convent to him. For a
time they lived happily in the Italian Alps (which are
described at length), but coming home one evening from the
hunt Arnaldo found that Lorenza had been stolen away.
He raises a neighbouring troop of bandits—" Thine be the
maid, and ours the prey ! "—and rushes to the rescue. But
the raid is unsuccessful. Arnaldo is wounded and escapes
to the mountains. On his recovery he manages, " clad in
palmer's weed," to gain entrance to the abbey where Lorenza
is immured ; but he again fails to find her. The first canto
closes with a description of the wolf-haunted ruin in which
he dwells, meditating upon his lost love, and denouncing
Time ultra-Byronically :

> O Time the Scather ! Time the Slayer !
> Time the Dethroner of all might !
> Twin-vanquisher with Death ! Betrayer
> Of every hope, desire, delight !

and so forth and so on, with much about the Heart's
endurance and Memory's pangs.

The events of the second canto take place some years
later. A grim band of men come to the ancient hall where
dwells the aged Alviano, the uncle of Lorenza, who had shut
her in the convent. Of his six sons five have perished by
violence. There is revelry in the castle, for it is the wedding-
feast of Giulio, the sole remaining son. A stranger shouts

---

[1] It is in three parts and occupies pp. 1–106 of the volume.

that he has tidings for Alviano, tidings from the dead ; that the hall is surrounded by armed men ; and that resistance is useless. This stranger is Arnaldo, and he tells Alviano incoherently that he has come to wreak vengeance for the death of Lorenza (who, it appears, was buried alive for breaking her vows as a nun).[1] Atrocious vengeance falls on Giulio. In the third canto it appears that Arnaldo was the illegitimate child of Alviano. Alviano dies heart-broken, as well he might, and Arnaldo is condemned to be burned alive.

All this is pseudo-Byronic with a vengeance indeed. The rapid, abrupt, disjointed mixture of narrative and highly rhetorical dialogue ; the wide gaps in the sequence of events ; the hints and mysteries and vague suggestions ; the dark passions ; remorse, crime, jealousy, hopeless love, eternal severance ; the fearful punishments ; the bandits and lairs and ruined buildings ; the dungeons and emaciated captives ; the concluding bastardy and hint of incest—all make up a conglomeration for which the Eastern Tales, especially *The Giaour,* afforded many a suggestion. The piece is an instructive imitation of Byron's earlier narrative manner ; but it is without any passages of genuine poetic power (such as relieve the theatrical strutting and heroic rant of Byron's own tales) and without any such sincere foundation of revolutionary fervour as is undoubtedly at the basis of the genuine Byronic poems.

Gaddo, in 144 octave stanzas, is better, because less exaggerated, imitation. " To scribble tales is rational and pleasant," the author declares ; he has no desire for fame. He has browsed in search of incidents through the old romances which Southey has galvanized into life, and he has learned to appreciate mediaevalism and chivalry. Still,

[1] A note to the lines—

A new-made grave . . .
Alive into that nook she went
To be in breathing burial pent—

says : " Well, thank heaven, we have reached the year 1835 ! there is not a monk in Spain ! When will beautiful Italy have as much to say ? Bye and Bye " (p. 105).

modern improvements are pleasant, and he catalogues many such : Vauxhall and country houses, newspapers and reviews, free speech and freedom of belief and disbelief.

> Then, as to Faith : if now a man would travel
>   To Pandemonium, where so many are gone,
> He may go post ; no priest shall dare behave ill,
>   Or damn him with book, candle, bell and jargon,
> Because his sturdy wits cannot unravel
>   The creeds wherewith so many have so far gone.
> The faithful now can never broil ungracious
> Dolts who won't understand St. Athanasius.

The author had thought of composing a mediaeval or oriental lay, but he realizes that " the Beppic has outdone the Epic style " ; and he writes instead

> the history, both sad and funny,
> Of one who fell too much in love with money.

Gaddo was a young man of Leghorn who, to escape his creditors, went to England, sold faked old masters (thus getting " some laughter at the Conoscenti "), moved in high society, and was at length entrapped into marriage with a girl who pretended to be an heiress in such poor health that she was certain to die soon, and who turned out to be no heiress and in blooming health. Gaddo rages and deserts her. Several years pass, and we find Rebecca, the wife, on board ship in the Mediterranean. Pirates attack the vessel and she is captured. The pirate-captain turns out to be Gaddo, now a Mussulman with three wives :

> " I've thirty children, most of whom, my pretty mate,
> Are very little more than illegitimate."

Gaddo takes Rebecca to wife again, and she and the three oriental wives live comfortably with him till at length, getting old, he thought it proper to " set about repenting," for " his faith in infidelity got colder." He became a Catholic again, converted his four wives, put the three oriental ones in a convent, and spent the rest of his life with his English wife.

Not for eighty years was another volume added to the

Byron Apocrypha.   In 1916 *The Bride's Confession,* " poem attributed to Lord Byron," was privately printed at Paris.[1] The jogging anapæsts, the phraseology, and other qualities indicate that this was probably written in Byron's time, or else that it is a good imitation of the now so forlorn and stale erotic sub-literature of the Regency.   It is of course not by Byron.

Having now surveyed the ten spurious books I turn to the various spurious poems that obtained admission to a greater or smaller number of editions of Byron's works. Of such poems there are ten.   By far the most famous is the *Ænigma* (*H*), " 'Twas whispered in heaven, 'twas muttered in hell."   The author was Catherine Maria Fanshawe.[2] Her striking poem was apparently first ascribed to Byron in *Three Poems, not included in the Works of Lord Byron* (London : Effingham Wilson, 1818).[3]   How it came to be attributed to Byron I do not know.   It obtained wider circulation as his than a similar *Ænigma* (*I*).[4]

The authorship of two other pieces is known.   *The Triumph of the Whale,* a very feeble satire on the Prince Regent by Charles Lamb, was ascribed to Byron, probably on political grounds.[5]   *Lines found in Lord Byron's Bible* are by Sir Walter Scott.[6]   They may have actually been copied out by Byron.[7]

[1] The full title (see Bibliography) provides sufficient indication of the contents.   Apparently only *The Bride's Confession* is ascribed to Byron ; it occupies pp. 11-27.

[2] Not " Harriet Fanshawe," as E. H. Coleridge calls her.   A discussion of the authorship of this *Ænigma* on the letter H was carried on in *N. & Q.* 1st Series, vol. v.   See especially pp. 427 and 522.

[3] It is included in W. Clark's edition of *The Waltz,* 1821 ; in Byron's *Works* (Philadelphia, Moses Thomas, 1820) ; and in numerous later piracies.   It was still attributed to Byron as late as the Bohn edition, 1851.

[4] This, too, is by Miss Fanshawe.   It occurs as Byron's in the Galignani edition, 1831, and (which is noteworthy) in Galignani, 1835.   It is not in Bohn, 1851.   For the text of this piece, see *N. & Q.* 1st Series, v, 427.

[5] In Galignani, 1826, 1828, 1831 and 1835 ; in this last edition the title is changed to *To the Prince of Whales.*

[6] *The Monastery,* chapter xii.

[7] They were apparently first ascribed to Byron in the *Life, Writings,* etc. (1825) iii, 414.   They are among the " attributed poems " in Galignani, 1826, but I have found them in no other collection of Byron's works.   That such attributions die hard is shown, however, by the fact that the lines are quoted as by Byron in Nahum Sokolow's *History of Zionism* (Longman, 1919), i, 95, note 1.

The remaining six are of unknown authorship. The *Ode* beginning, " Oh, shame to thee, Land of the Gaul ! " is an invective against the French people for their desertion of Napoleon when fortune no longer attended his arms. It is sufficiently Byronic in rhetoric and sentiment to make it not astonishing that it for so long passed current among his genuine works.[1] *Madame Lavalette* is in praise of the virtue and intelligence of the wife of Count Lavalette who escaped from Paris in January 1816.[2] *Stanzas to her who can best understand them* [3] may be more easily illustrated than described. This is the last of eighteen stanzas :

> But—'tis useless to upbraid thee
> With thy past or present state ;
> What thou wast, my fancy made thee,
> What thou art, I know too late.

The stanzas entitled *To Lady Caroline Lamb*, beginning, "And sayst thou that I have not felt," must not be confused with the genuine poem addressed to the same person, beginning,

---

[1] It was first published, over the signature " Brutus," in *The Morning Chronicle*, July 31, 1815. The piece turned up promptly and persistently in early pirated editions of Byron's poems, notwithstanding the fact that it had been repudiated by Byron in a letter (July 22, 1816) to Murray that deals with several of these fabrications (LJ, iii, 337). It is in the collections pirated by Hone, Edwards, Robertson, Sheppard, Limbird, Bumpus, Fairburn, Knight and Lacy, Bembow, Dove, and Jones. It was in Galignani from 1819 (vi, 121) till 1835, when it was withdrawn. (This 1835 edition was, as I have said, carefully combed through). It is ascribed to Byron in *The Laurel*, a collection of fugitive verse published by Tilt, 1841 ; is in *The Select Works of Lord Byron* (Halifax, William Miller, 1838) ; and is among the " attributed poems " in Bohn, 1851. In John Robertson's edition of " *Fare thee well* " *and other Poems* (Edinburgh, 1816) a note (p. 24) states that the *Ode* " has been ascribed by many to the Author of the *Pleasures of Hope*." But I fail to find it in any edition of Campbell's works. The copy of Edwards's edition of the *Poems on his Domestic Circumstances* (1816) in the New York Public Library contains a manuscript note (p. 27) : " By William Cone—but published under Lord Byron's name." I know of no William Cone ; the annotator may have intended to write William Hone. A query as to the authorship of the *Ode* in *N. & Q.* 2nd Series, ii, 48, remained unanswered.

[2] It was first published, over the initials " B.B.", in *The Examiner*, January 21, 1816. Hone printed it in all his pirated editions of the " domestic " poems. It is in many other such collections. Robertson (*op. cit.*, Edinburgh, 1816, p. 30) apologizes for including it. It is in the Baudry edition of Byron's *Works* (Paris 1825, vii, 349) ; in Galignani, 1826 and 1828 ; in Bohn, 1851. Byron repudiates it, LJ, iii, 337.

[3] In Galignani, 1831 and 1835 ; in the one-volume edition of the *Works* (Hartford, Andrus, 1847) ; and in the reprint thereof, 1851.

" Remember thee." These spurious lines are sentimental, not satiric. Their love is a crime, the poet declares ; he must try to break the chains ; she must help him by exhibiting disdain ; only thus can she avoid shame.[1]

Finally, two pieces are of similar inspiration. *Lines found in the Travellers' Book at Chamouni* contrasts the character, talents, race, and aims of the visitors to that place. What passion moves the present writer ? Who loves him ? What person is faithful to him ? At least he has sufficient wisdom to conceal his name.[2] The piece beginning " All hail, Mont Blanc ! Mont-au-Vert hail ! " sometimes called *Lines found in the Album of the Hotel . . . at Chamouni,* is a meditation in solitude upon Divinity, eternity, and destiny, and upon the high joys and profound sorrows of the poet.[3]

This brief review of the ten spurious short poems being accomplished,[4] I come to my third group, consisting of some pretended translations of poems by Byron into French. The first of these was frequently reprinted ; the rest seem to be almost unknown.[5]

The Bibliothèque Nationale contains more than half a dozen reprints of a *dythyrambe, La Mort de Napoléon,* translated from the English of Lord Byron. Some editions include a notice of Napoleon's life and death by " Sir " Thomas Moore. This fraud appeared of course in 1821. A foreword states that the piece was composed in a single evening and " il nous a été envoyé par sir Arthur Smylders, ami du noble lord." Here are a few lines, as specimens :

[1] This piece is in Galignani, 1826 and 1828 ; in Andrus, 1847 and 1851.
[2] In Galignani, 1826, 1828, 1831, and 1835. In *The Nottingham Magazine,* No. iv, February 15, 1886, pp. 51 f., it is still attributed to Byron.
[3] This appeared first, so far as I know, in the *Life, Writings,* etc. (1825), ii, 384. Of the Galignani editions it occurs only in 1826.
[4] Two other pieces, set down as spurious in my article in *N. & Q.,* are genuine. No. 23, " Lord Byron to his Lady," turns out to be an alternative version of the epigram entitled, " To Penelope " (*Poetry,* vii, 71). No. 28, " To my dear Mary Anne," is pronounced spurious by E. H. Coleridge (*Poetry,* vii, 440) ; but the genuineness of these lines is beyond question and has been admitted by Mr. Murray. See an article by H. B. Forman, in *The Athenæum,* June 11, 1904, where a letter from Mrs. Musters is quoted vouching for the poem. The original manuscript, with this attestation, is now in the possession of Mr. H. C. Roe, of Nottingham.
[5] For Rabbe's *Le poignard du Moyen Age,* see Bibliography.

Le héros est tombé sous la faux des noirs genies. Muses, brisez vos harpes
  glorieuses ; le grand homme n'est plus . . .
Grand dans le revers, comme dans les faveurs de la fortune. . . .
O lâcheté ! honte éternelle ! . . . Napoléon trouva des chaînes sur une
  terre hospitalière.

Le Cri d'Angleterre (1821) is on the death of Queen
Caroline, whose wrongs history will avenge. There are
many slurs on George IV. A foreword states that the original
was first published in *The Sun*, April 10, 1821.

Irner, par Lord Byron (1821) is a romance of the East
in two volumes. It contains much facile Byronism ; for
example : " Un froid scepticisme dessecha son coeur en
ébranlant ses opinions religieuses. A force d'interroger les
cadavres, il crut que la mort etait le secret de la vie." There
is much about " orgueil," loneliness, mystery, and so forth.
There are forests, castles, revenge, the balm afforded by
nature, the hero's unalterable love for one woman, and the
rest of the tattered trappings of romanticism. " Le mystère
dont cet homme était toujours enveloppé cachait peut-être
quelque horrible secrèt." I know of no English original of
this novel.

*Lettre de Lord Byron au Grand Turc. Précédé de la Lettre
de Sa Hautesse au Noble Lord* (1824) is a product of French
interest in Byron's final expedition to Greece. An " avis "
explains that " Milady R*** " permitted the translator to
see a copy of the manuscript that had been current in London
during the past week. An opening letter, " Lord Byron à
Sir Thomas Moore," declares Byron's love for England and
his desire to fight for Greece. Then comes the Sultan's
letter, urging Byron to fight on the side of the prophet ; if he
will not, then death, swift and certain, will come upon him.
Then Byron's reply, repelling the suggestion that he break
faith with the Greeks and defying the Sultan and his armies.

The Four Barbers of Bagdat. An Oriental Allegory,
which is quoted as by Byron in the *Life, Writings,* etc. (1825),
ii, 161 f., is a sort of prose parallel to Moore's *Fables for the
Holy Alliance,* for it is a satire upon the Congress of Vienna.
Each of four barbers shaved his customers in a particular

fashion, so that each class of clients jeered at the other three classes. Quarrels ensued, and each class claimed for its mode divine origin. One man kept aside from the dispute, bantered them all, and was deemed an idiot. At last there was so much bloodshed that all consented to abide by the fool's decision. This was : Let each person follow his own taste and compel the barbers to perform their functions for the public good. This was done, and peace and prosperity followed.

Two important collections of spurious or partly spurious letters by Byron now claim attention. The earlier of these introduces the famous story of the forged Byron-Shelley papers.[1]

In the summer of 1848 a young lady called at Mr. William White's bookshop and told him a story of her life at St. John's Wood with an invalid sister. The sisters needed money and proposed to raise it by selling a number of letters of Byron's which had come to them from their deceased brother, who had been a surgeon and had attended in his last illness Byron's servant Fletcher. Fletcher in gratitude had given the surgeon these letters. The story seemed to White reasonable enough, and he bought some of these letters, presently buying more, and at length purchasing also a large number by Shelley. There seems to be no reason for believing that White was a party to the fraud involved, at least to the original fraud. Before the end of 1848 White became suspicious and insisted on visiting the home at St. John's Wood, where he found no invalid sister and forced from the lady of the letters a confession. She turned out to be the wife of a Colonel Byron.[2] Notwithstanding the cock-and-

---

[1] There is a good account of this picturesque episode in literary history in J. A. Farrer's *Literary Forgeries*, chapter x, pp. 175 f. This account I follow fairly closely with considerable additions of my own.

[2] He is sometimes referred to as " Colonel," sometimes as " Major " Byron. According to some accounts (*e.g. The Westminster Gazette*, December 11, 1905) Icobad George Gordon Byron claimed to be the son of the poet by " the Maid of Athens." This is erroneous. Mr. John Murray possesses a letter from this self-proclaimed bastard, dated Wilkes Barre, Pennsylvania, July 1, 1843, and addressed to John Murray III, in which Byron says : " My poor mother belonged to an old noble Spanish family." In this letter he sketches his adventurous life, tells of his financial losses, and begs Murray for a set of Lord Byron's works and an autograph

bull story of the invalid sister and the deceased surgeon, the
Byron pair insisted on the genuineness of the letters and
wrote out for White an attestation of their authenticity.
What should have confirmed White in his suspicions is that
already, early in 1848, this Colonel Byron has advertised the
forthcoming publication of *The Inedited Works of Lord
Byron*.[1] He had widely circulated a report that much of the
material in this collection came from Mrs. Leigh. Exposures
had begun in *The Athenœum*, March 24, 1848, and Mrs.
Leigh, in the same journal (April 1, 1848) denied that she was
in any way responsible or had supplied any material for the
work. It was shortly after these exposures that White
received his first visit from the young lady. After their confession to White, Colonel Byron went to America, and in 1849
began the publication of his long-contemplated work : *The
Inedited Works of Lord Byron, now first published from his
Letters, Journals, and other Manuscripts, in the possession of his
son, Major Gordon Byron* (1849). The plan was to publish
this work in monthly instalments ; it was to be completed in
four volumes. Parts of the material are authentic ; much
old matter is republished, furbished out with new anecdotes
and some new letters. After the appearance of two parts
the work was discontinued, and the manuscripts in Colonel
Byron's possession passed by purchase to John Murray III.[2]

Meanwhile, on April 28, 1849, William White sold his

of the poet. Another letter in Mr. Murray's possession reads : " I am a
Byron, the bar sinister notwithstanding." He complains again of his
poverty and of ill-treatment by his relatives, in a letter of July 5, 1844.
About 1846 he began to write to many of the poet's surviving relatives
and friends, proposing to write a *Life* of his father. He seems to have
obtained several autograph letters ; these he studied and copied cleverly ;
then returned the originals and sold the forgeries. Concerning this adventurer's origin and life more will be found in a clipping from the St.
Joseph (Mo.) *Herald*, in the Wheildon Byron-Stowe scrap-book in the
Boston Public Library (shelf-mark : 6540.11). Lord Byron, according to
this account, had secretly married a Spanish lady whom he deserted when
he went to Greece. Colonel Byron was their son. It was the discovery
of some letters from this Spanish lady to Byron that led to the separation
of Lord and Lady Byron !

[1] See, for example, *Douglas Jerrold's Weekly Newspaper*, March 11,
1848, where W. S. Orr and Co. announce that they are to publish the work,
and that the authenticity of the material is vouched for by members of
the Byron family.

[2] See LJ, vi, 460.

Byron letters to Murray. Murray, who assuredly knew Byron's handwriting, expressed no doubt as to their genuineness. In August 1850 White sent the Shelley manuscripts, together with some Keats manuscripts also purchased from Colonel Byron, to Sotheby's. They were sold at auction in May 1851.[1] Edward Moxon bought the Shelley letters, persuaded Browning to write his famous introductory essay, and published his collection early in 1852. A copy sent to Tennyson and examined by Francis Palgrave led to suspicions of fraud which were promptly confirmed.[2] Ultimately White repaid Murray the purchase price of the letters, received them back, and presented them to the British Museum.[3]

I do not believe that White was deliberately dishonest; but he was inexcusably lax in his notions of commercial candour. It is, indeed, barely possible that Colonel Byron had himself been taken in by some clever forger, but this is not likely. The resemblance in features between Lord Byron and his son, if he was the poet's son, is said to have been striking, as was the resemblance between the poet's handwriting and Colonel Byron's.[4]

[1] See Sotheby's *Sale Catalogue*, May 1851.

[2] The forgery was denounced in *The Literary Gazette*, February 28, 1852. *The Athenæum*, too, which in its issue of February 21 had reviewed the letters without a suspicion of their genuineness, denounced the book in its issue of March 6, with some caustic remarks against William White. This occasioned White's pamphlet: *The Calumnies of the Athenæum Journal Exposed.* This open letter to Murray, dated March 11, 1852, tells of how White obtained the MSS. and of their subsequent sale to Murray and Moxon. White protests his innocence, and stresses the fact that whereas he had never before seen autographs of Byron and Shelley, Murray and Moxon, who were experts, both believed the MSS. genuine. " It still remains," White goes on, " to be seen what part of the MSS. . . . are forgeries. That all are so, or even the greater portion, I do *not* believe, and the discernment must be left to wiser heads than mine." To this *The Athenæum* replied on March 20, and Murray, in *The Literary Gazette* of the same date, makes the damaging accusation against White that he failed to inform the purchasers of the suspicious fact that the Byrons had for many weeks taken him in with the story of the invalid lady of St. John's Wood.

[3] Additional MSS. 19,377. There are 47 Byron letters and 23 Shelley letters. Those purporting to come from Byron are addressed to Kean, Webster, Mackintosh, Kinnaird, Hoppner, Lord Holland, Hanson, and Shelley, among other minor correspondents. Some of them (*e.g.* that to J. Wedderburn Webster, dated Venice, November 9, 1819 ; that to Douglas Kinnaird, August 23, 1821) are amazingly clever forgeries. It is not necessary to describe the collection in detail.

[4] See plate lxxxi in Sotheby's *Principia Typographica* (1858), ii, opposite p. 114. This work contains (pp. 104 f.) Sotheby's account of the entire episode.

There is a close connection between Colonel Byron's manuscripts and the suppressed volume of 1872 entitled : *The Unpublished Letters of Lord Byron. Edited with a Critical Essay* by H. S. Schultess-Young.   Prothero [1] refused to accept the authority of the volume.   There is, however, matter of much interest in it.   The introductory essay is nearly negligible.   Its thesis is that Byron's philosophy and true opinions are to be found not in his poems but in his private letters.   Schultess-Young indulges in much philosophic vapouring about Plato and pantheism, and so forth.   The latter part of the essay deals with Byron's relations with women and with his private character.

Of the letters themselves twelve to his mother had previously been published in whole or in part by Moore or Dallas, and are reprinted by Prothero.   There is a long series to a woman whom Byron addresses as " My dear L.," " Dearest L.," etc.[2]   He had, it would seem, seduced this girl and now, regretting having done so, he gives her good counsel, for she is having difficulty in keeping " straight."   On page 149 begins a group of " Attributed Letters."   These are taken from the White manuscripts in the British Museum.   The letters to Shelley (April 11 and 24, and May 27, 1822) are typical forgeries ; a few in this group are, it is barely possible, genuine.   Of the authenticity of those to " L." there can, I think, be very little doubt.[3]

---

[1] LJ, vi, 460.   Mr. Murray has a copy and another is in the library of Mr. Thomas J. Wise.   Another copy was offered for sale a few years ago by a London bookseller.   I tried to procure it, but it was already sold.   According to the bookseller's catalogue this copy contained a manuscript note by Alfred Austin, as follows : " Mr. Bentley consulted me concerning them, and at my instance, withdrew the volume."   This is the copy which has, I believe, recently become the property of Mr. Clement K. Shorter.   Mr. Wise's copy contains a letter from Bentley, the publisher, to Dr. Doran, sending the volume for review, but telling him not to review it yet awhile as he is not certain that the book will be published.   This caution was justified, for the book was suppressed by an injunction and all but a very few copies were destroyed.

[2] The series occupies letters xiii–xxix, except xxviii, which is misnumbered xxiii.

[3] *The Athenæum*, November 30, 1901 (p. 726), says : " Evidence internal and external is known to a few persons still living to have stamped much of the mixture as genuine beyond all question. . . . Sooner or later the embargo will have to come off them, unless some of the interested parties succeed in getting hold of the surviving copies of Mr. Schultess-

I shall now close this chapter with some brief notes upon a few miscellaneous pieces that are in one way or another connected with the Byron Apocrypha.

The reader may be surprised to see *The Burial of Sir John Moore* mentioned here ; and it would take me too far afield to tell of the early discussions of the authorship of Wolfe's poem, when several claimants were brought forward. It is necessary to note, however, that Medwin [1] tells that after it had been read in Byron's presence and highly praised by the assembled company, Byron did not deny the authorship. Medwin prints the poem and ascribes it to Byron. Medwin's assertions, unless corroborated, are, however, worthless.[2]

In the *Life, Writings*, etc.[3] there is an allusion to a poem entitled *Hannibal* by Byron, written in a light and sarcastic mood and making Hannibal " the slave of sensuality." It is further stated that the manuscript of the poem is still (1825) in the possession of La Guiccioli. Whether it ever actually existed and, if so, what became of it, I do not know.

Most of the poems that I have described possessed at least some of the externals of Byronism that enabled some of them to pass current among his minor poems in pirated editions of his works. Quite inexplicable as an intentional fraud is a volume entitled *Lord Byron's Tales . . . With all the notes : Hebrew Melodies, and other Poems* (Halifax, 1845). E. H. Coleridge [4] was puzzled by the book. I believe

Young's book." The volume concludes with a letter (pp. 234 f.) to Schultess-Young from John Milne, headed " Recollections of Lord Byron," and dated April 3, 1872. Milne had been in charge of Byron's body on the ship which brought it back from Missolonghi to England. He tells this gruesome anecdote : " The sailors wanted to drink the spirits that his Lordship was preserved in, and it has not seldom happened among drouthy tars, that they would even go the length of broaching the Admiral." Dr. Brown, the ship's surgeon, prevented this by giving out the report that the liquid in which the body was preserved was poisonous. That this hoary tale, which was of course told of Nelson's body after Trafalgar, should here be applied to Byron casts doubt upon the trustworthiness of Milne's whole letter.

[1] *Conversations*, p. 75 (of the Wilder and Campbell edition, New York, 1824).

[2] The only edition I have found of Byron's works that contains Wolfe's poem is that of H. L. Broenner, Frankfort O. M., 1829. See p. 193, *post*.

[3] Vol. iii, 89.

[4] *Poetry*, vii, 156.

that in the slight ambiguity of the title-page lies the explanation of the apparent attribution to Byron of twelve poems, utterly unlike his genuine writings. That is, among the " other poems " a dozen pieces not by Byron and not intended to be taken as his were inserted. I have therefore not considered it necessary to set down the titles of these pieces.[1]

In 1816 James Hogg published *The Poetic Mirror*,[2] the purpose of which book he sets forth in his autobiographical memoir,[3] namely, to write " so completely in the style of each poet, that it should not be known but for his own production." Hogg tells how Ballantyne read aloud the imitation of Byron " with extraordinary effect ; so much so, that I was astonished at the poem myself, and before it was half done, all pronounced it Byron's." The caricature of Wordsworth's poetry hindered the other poems, Hogg thinks, from being accepted as genuine. *The Guerilla* is the title of the Byronic piece ; it is a Spanish tale of love, jealousy, feud and fighting, in halting Spenserians with affected archaisms. It has often been described as a parody,[4] but it is really a serious imitation or pastiche and seems occasionally to have been taken for Byron's own work.

Mrs. Hemans's *Modern Greece*, a poem of the Childe-Haroldish school, was published anonymously by Murray, in 1817. It seems to have been attributed by some people to Byron.[5] *The Count Arezzi*, a tragedy in five acts, published anonymously in 1824, was so widely attributed to Byron that its real author, Robert Eyres Landor, was forced to acknowledge his work. Thomas Hope's *Anastasius, or*

---

[1] For brief descriptions of them see, if curiosity pushes any possible reader so far, my article in *N. & Q.* June 1919, pp. 144–145. See also *N. & Q.* 4th Series, v, 225 f. This Halifax collection was reissued in 1864 as *The Choice Works of Lord Byron*. This volume is not mentioned in Coleridge's bibliography. It contains but ten of the dozen pieces found in the earlier volume.

[2] Reprinted in the *Poetical Works of the Ettrick Shepherd* (1840), iv, 5 f.

[3] *Ibid.*, v, p. lxii.

[4] *E.g.* by *The Quarterly Review* (xv, July 1816, 470) ; by the *Dictionary of National Biography*, in the article on Hogg.

[5] The copy in Mr. H. E. Huntington's library is stamped on the binding " By Lord Byron " and has a like attribution in manuscript on the title-page. I have been unable to find a copy of *Modern Greece*. A *Parody addressed to Lord Byron*, to which I have occasionally run across references.

Memoirs of a Greek (1819) also suffered from this result of anonymity.[1] Lastly, a curious volume entitled *Poems Written by Somebody* (1819) has been occasionally attributed to Byron.[2]

To summarize the non-canonical Byronic writings[3]—the Byron Apocrypha consists of ten separate books; ten shorter poems; one brief prose satire; two collections of letters (parts of which are genuine); and eight miscellaneous items that have been on one slender ground or another at some time or other attributed to him. The bibliographical history of no other modern English poet contains a chapter similar to this. It casts light upon his fame.

[1] *Blackwood's* (x, September 1821, 200 f.) denied that Hope could have written the novel, and adduced many parallels in thought, subject-matter, and mode of treatment as proof that Byron was the author. The review is cleverly done; but it was probably intended merely to " quiz " Hope, who replied in the next number (x, 312) affirming his authorship. *Anastasius* was favourably reviewed in the *Edinburgh* and the *Quarterly*, but without the suggestion of Byron's authorship. Byron himself told Lady Blessington that when he read *Anastasius* he wept for two reasons; that he had not written it and that Hope had. The book has still a sort of pallid renown, but I find its mixture of wild adventure and coarse high spirits insufferably tedious. For a modern estimate more favourable than mine see Elton, *Survey*, i, 375 f. See also Bibliography *sub* Pfeiffer.

[2] For the quaint title in full, see (as usual) my bibliography. A copy sold at Sotheby's in 1919 passed into the collection of Mr. H. C. Roe, of Nottingham, where I have seen it. It was catalogued as a presentation copy from Byron, with this autograph inscription : " Mrs. Lawson from the Author with sincere regard. Feb. 1818." Mr. Roe tells me that the sale produced considerable interest, for though the book had been attributed to Byron no copy had ever come into the market with his inscription. The handwriting certainly resembles Byron's, but I am inclined to think it a resemblance only. I know of no Mrs. Lawson among Byron's acquaintances. The book is ascribed to Byron in Watt's *Bibliotheca Britannica ;* in Cushing's *Initials and Pseudonyms ;* and elsewhere, but nowhere by any unquestioned authority. I cannot believe that Byron had any share in this book. There is in it no allusion whatever to him or his interests or his ideas. The poems are very dull, and nowhere is there any sign that any sort of a hoax was intended.

[3] The melodrama *Illusion* was never, so far as I know, printed. See my bibliography.

ADDENDUM.—Mr. Murray tells me that he possesses a pair of pistols, presented to his grandfather, which were carried by Sir John Moore at Corunna. Two lines from Wolfe's poem are engraved upon each, with an ascription to Byron. See p. 191, *supra*.

CHAPTER XI

THE DEATH OF BYRON

MANY years after the event, Edward Bulwer-Lytton wrote of Byron's death : [1]

Never shall I forget the singular, the stunning sensation, which the intelligence produced. . . . Among the youth of that day a growing diversion from Byron to Shelley and Wordsworth had just commenced—but the moment in which we heard he was no more, united him to us at once, without a rival. . . . So much of us died with him, that the notion of his death had something of the unnatural, of the impossible.

Of the same news Jane Welsh wrote to Thomas Carlyle : [2]

If they had said the sun or the moon was gone out of the heavens, it could not have struck me with the idea of a more awful and dreary blank in the creation than the words, " Byron is dead."

And Carlyle, moved to unwonted generosity of judgment, had replied :

Poor Byron ! alas, poor Byron ! the news of his death came upon my heart like a mass of lead ; and yet, the thought of it sends a painful twinge through all my being, as if I had lost a brother. O God ! that so many souls of mud and clay should fill up their base existence to its utmost bound ; and this the noblest spirit in Europe should sink before half his course was run. Late so full of fire and generous passion and proud purposes ; and now forever dumb and cold. Poor Byron ! and but a young man, still struggling amidst the perplexities and sorrows and aberrations of a mind not

---

[1] *England and the English*, ii, 94.
[2] J. A. Froude, *Carlyle : First Forty Years*, i, 173.

arrived at maturity, or settled in its proper place in life.
Had he been spared to the age of three-score and ten, what
might he not have done ! what might he not have been !
But we shall hear his voice no more. I dreamed of seeing
him and knowing him ; but the curtain of everlasting night
has hid him from our eyes. We shall go to him ; he shall
not return to us. Adieu. There is a blank in your heart
and a blank in mine since this man passed away.

Even more emotional, but, I think, equally sincere was the
tribute of James Hogg, the Ettrick Shepherd : [1]

I canna express what my feelings are as to some things—
but I have them for a' that. . . . I canna bide to think
that Byron's dead. There's a wonderful mind swallowed up
somewhere—Gone ! and gone so young !—and maybe on
the very threshold of his truest glory, baith as a man and as
a poet. It makes me wae, wae, to think o't. Ye'll laugh at me,
Captain Odoherty ; but it's as true as I'm telling ye, I shall
never see a grand blue sky fu' of stars, nor look out upon the
Forest, when all the winds of winter are howling over the
wilderness of dry crashing branches, nor stand beside the sea
to hear the waves roaring upon the rocks, without thinking
that the spirit of Byron is near me. In the hour of awe—
in the hour of gloom—in the hour of sorrow, and in the hour
of death, I shall remember Byron.

The dead poet's closest and most loyal friend, John Cam
Hobhouse, records these sober impressions in his private
diary just after Byron's death : [2]

His power of attaching those about him to his person was
such as no one I ever knew possessed. No human being
could approach him without being sensible of this magical
influence. . . . There was a mildness and yet a decision in
his mode of conversing, and even in his address, which are
seldom united in the same person. . . . He was full of
sensibility, but he did not suffer his feelings to betray him
into absurdities.

The fifteen-year-old Lincolnshire boy who was destined to
succeed Byron in enormous popularity, on hearing the news,

---

[1] *Noctes Ambrosianae*, number xv ; *Blackwood's*, xv, June 1824, 717.
[2] *Recollections of a Long Life*, iii, 41.

went to the wooded hollow not far from Somersby rectory
and wrote upon a stone amid the mosses and ferns, the words :
" Byron is dead." In after years Tennyson said that on
that day " the whole world seemed to be darkened for me." [1]

I find it impossible to record all the elegies and tributes in
verse that were occasioned by Byron's death. The periodicals, especially the newspapers, were full of them.[2] Our
survey must be limited almost entirely to those that appeared
either as separate volumes or in collections of poetry.

William Howitt's *A Poet's Thoughts at the Interment of
Lord Byron* (1824), in twenty-one Spenserian stanzas, is
moralizing and compassionate. Howitt feels more deeply
than he can express the sense of Byron's presence and the
associations with him in the country around Hucknall. He
meditates upon the mingled gloom and glory of his poetry.
" His lays are dashed with evil," says the poet ; but calm
souls should not presume to judge one so impassioned.

> Rest in thy tomb, young heir of glory, rest !
> Rest in thy rustic tomb ! . . .
>   When we are still
> In centuries of sleep, thy fame shall be awake.[3]

---

[1] Annually, on the nineteenth of April, the memorial column of the
London *Times* reminds us that Sir Walter Scott said of Byron's death
that the light of life seemed to have gone out. For the anecdote of Tennyson, see the *Memoir*, i, 4. See also Bibliography, *sub* Tennyson.

[2] *The Mirror*, for example (xc, June 26, 1824), after some " Recollections of Lord Byron," published no less than six poetical tributes, viz.
" Greece—Lord Byron," by Timo ; " From a Poem entitled *Retrospection* "
(anonymous) ; " On the Death of Lord Byron," by C. ; " Lines on Lord
Byron," by R. B. ; " On the Death of Lord Byron," by E. L. ; and " On
the Death of Lord Byron " (anonymous). A special " supplementary
number " (No. xcix.) of the same periodical, after an account of Byron's
last moments, the oration of Spiridion Tricoupi, and the funeral, printed
nine more such tributes. For some years *The Mirror* was indefatigable in
publishing Byroniana. In 1826 (vii, 201) we find " The Death of Byron,"
a poem commemorating the anniversary of his death, signed " Daniels."
In 1828 there are articles on " Byron at Missolonghi " (pp. 245 f.) and
" Byron's Interview with a Monk " (pp. 239 f.). And so on. I take these
few specimens from one periodical to indicate the impossibility of recording
all such elegies and estimates. The B. M. scrap-books of Byroniana contain
many clippings of this kind from periodicals, some of them not now identi-
fiable. For an impressively long list of French elegies on Byron, see
Estève, pp. 533 f. For German elegies see my bibliography.

[3] Howitt lived to take part in the defence of Byron's memory against
Mrs. Stowe ; see his letter to *The Daily News*, September 4, 1869, quoted
by Elze, pp. 191 f. For other estimates of Byron by Howitt, see my
bibliography.

A deeper sense of the tragedy of Byron's death is shown in Thomas Maude's *Monody on the Death of Lord Byron* (1824) : [1]

> His feet were set on ice—and, if he fell,
> What marvel ? . . .
> He had no specious worldly art,
> The eccentric movements of his thought to hide. . . .
> It shall not be forgotten that he gave
> The energies of an unconquered spirit,
> Brave,—yet not poorly, like the hireling's, brave,
> To a great cause of all-unquestioned merit.

J. W. Lake,[2] in *A Poetical Tribute to the Memory of Lord Byron* (Paris, 1824), muses upon the misery of the poet's lot, the emptiness of fame, and the " tainting breath of calumny." But that " reptile vampyre " must " droop his dark eye " when he reads—

> Here sleeps the Poet in his bed of peace,
> BYRON, the friend of liberty and Greece.

W. G. Thompson's *Lines on the Death of Lord Byron* (1824) opens with the conventional questions as to where the departed soul is now. " Vainly questioned ! " The tale of love and song of freedom are over ; the Greek sits " all voiceless on his shore."

> Son of immortal Song ! thy death
> With victory's palm should have been crowned,
> Thou shouldst have yielded forth thy breath,
> In valour, as in song, renowned—
> Yea, on the battlefield expired,
> With thy ancestral glories fired.

---

[1] This is in five stanzas of irregular length. The *Monody* is followed by a reprint of Mavrocordato's proclamation on the death of Byron.

[2] Lake was one of Byron's earliest biographers. In 1826 he published at Paris *The Last Canto of Childe Harold's Pilgrimage, translated from the French of M. De Lamartine.* (There is a good review of this translation, with copious extracts, in *The London Literary Gazette*, December 2, 1826, pp. 754 f.). Another version of Lamartine's poem, with the same title as Lake's, but better done, appeared in 1827. I do not know the translator's name. On Lamartine's *Dernier Chant* see also " Lamartine's Pilgrimage of Harold " in *The Monthly Review*, November 1825. I have not seen another English elegy printed at Paris : *Irregular Ode on the Death of Lord Byron écrite à Paris par un Anglais* (Paris, Didot, 1825). See Estève, p. 534. Two French offshoots of *Childe Harold* not mentioned by Estève may here be recorded : *Childe-Harold aux Ruines de Rome. Imitation du Poème de Lord Byron. Par M. Aristide Carry. Se Vend au Profits des Grecs.* (*Paris, à la Librairie Moderne*, 1826) is a close imitation of Byron's manner and themes ; *Les Pèlerinages d'un Childe Harold Parisien. Par M. D—— J—— C—— Verfèle* (Paris, Ambroise Dupont, 1825) is a parody.

The elegist contrasts the stir in the world caused by Byron's death with the " no name, no fame, no monument " which is the lot of most of us.

There is much about Byron's efforts for Greece and his breaking of " tyrant fetters " in an anonymous *Elegy on the Death of Lord Byron : Intended as an humble but sincere Tribute to the exalted Virtues and brilliant Talents of that much lamented Nobleman : to which is prefixed a Dedicatory Address . . . on Behalf of Suffering Greece* (1824).   The long title is in itself a sufficient indication of the theme of this evidently deeply felt effusion on " Patriot-Byron of the noblest heart."

Notably magnanimous in tone is *Childe Harold's Last Pilgrimage* by W. L. Bowles, with whom Byron had lately been in controversy.[1]   The kindly poet prays that " not one thought unkind " be murmured over Byron's grave, and that Heaven's mercy may rest upon him.

The throng of elegies did not quickly pass.   In 1825 appeared an anonymous piece in twenty-six Spenserian stanzas, entitled *To the Departed.*   After meditating upon Byron's fame and misfortunes, the writer touches on the debt of Greece to him.   Italy, too, is filled with memories of him.   Will England weep for him also ?—

> Thou dost not sleep beneath the Gothic roof
> Where England's favoured sons of fame repose.

Yet no poet since Milton has been Byron's equal.

This is perhaps the best place to describe an exceedingly curious book that includes an elegy on Byron, entitled *The Book of Spirits and Tales of the Dead.*[2]   It is embellished " with plates in gold and colour."   A folding frontispiece shows Byron in a red jacket and striped pantaloons, seated upon a rock overlooking the ocean ; a figure bearing a laurel wreath points out to him a band of poets standing within the portico of temple-shaped clouds above the sea.   The opening piece in this queer collection is " Lord Byron in the Other World," a prose narrative that introduces some

---

[1] W. L. Bowles, *Poetical Works*, ii, 284 f.

[2] Undated (1825 ?).   It is not in the British Museum.   I have seen Mr. H. C. Roe's copy.

quotations from Byron's poems and a number of original copies of verses, and purports to be an account by Byron himself of his experiences after death. The manner is grotesque and comico-horrific. The spirit tells how " from the dark reverberations around me, I found I had just been deposited within the dark barriers of the tomb." He heard the chorus of worms :

> Oho ! brother worms, oho !
>   Who is so happy as we ?
> Who lives like the worm below
>   In his halls of revelry ?
> No sweeter pleasures we crave,
>   No, no, brother worms, no, no,
> Than those which enliven the grave,
>   Oho ! brother worms, oho !

Byron's spirit meets a company of skeletons and is conducted by them to the Hall of Death. He sees there a band of culprits who are, he learns, Edinburgh reviewers. Presently he reposes " upon a rock, by the side of a flashing mass of falling waters," and from thence he has a vision of a gorgeous temple in the skies.

From the splendid portico of the temple there came forth a vast assemblage of persons, clad in the garbs of various ages. The countenances of many of them were familiar to me, and they were lit as if by the mind's purest illuminations. They were indeed spirits of the olden time—bards of every clime and age.

There follows " Lord Byron's Immortality ; or, The Vision of Childe Harold," a sort of poetic apotheosis and interpretation of the frontispiece, beginning :

> The wand'rer, Harold, on a lonely shore,
> Sat musing by a gush of falling waters.

This lucubration is signed " Mr. H. Davenport." It is followed by " The Death of Lord Byron," fifteen stanzas by " Mrs. Henry Rolls." This poem is entirely serious and consorts ill with the odd contents of the book. The writer

muses upon the mingling of guilt and greatness in Byron's
nature ; on his exile ; and on his self-sacrifice for Greece :

> His inmost heart, fair Greece, was thine !
> Be thou its consecrated shrine—
> Round it thy deathless laurels twine,
>   For thou a mighty prize hast won !
> For never, in thy proudest day,
> Arose a sweeter, loftier lay
> Than his, who thus his life could pay,
>   To be regarded as thy Son !

The cadence here is not unworthy of Byron himself.

A somewhat similar oddity, though less macabre, is
Death's Doings (1826), a series of compositions in prose and
verse intended to illustrate twenty-four plates by R. Dagley.
Opposite page 25 is the plate " Death and the Poet," showing Byron at a table, holding a manuscript inscribed " Ode
to Immortality," while Death, a skeleton, stands in the
background.   The accompanying sets of verses, one called
" The Poet " (signed " Alfred ") and the other called " Death
and the Poet " (by the Rev. H. Stebbing), are utterly insignificant.

Four other elegies on Byron appeared in books of 1826.
George Lunt's *The Grave of Byron* is vaguely pastoral,
uncritical and dull ; and extends to eighty-seven Spenserian
stanzas.   A " Monody on the Death of Lord Byron " is
included in J. W. Simmons's *Inquiry*, which will be mentioned
later in this chapter.   It is sad, says the monodist, when
even the humblest dies ; far sadder when a Genius passes
away.   His other reflections are quite as banal.   An " Elegy
on the Death of Lord Byron " is in the *Tales of Chivalry and
Romance*, another book to be discussed later.[1]   In a satire
on government and reform, containing some interesting
references to society and current literature and entitled
*Eighteen Hundred and Twenty-six.   Carmen Seculare.   By
Somebody*, the reader is bidden to " shed a sacred tear " to
Byron's memory.   A tribute to him follows—" 'Twas thine

---

[1] The elegist meditates in trite fashion on fate, death and genius ;
Memory pours a tribute on Byron's tomb ; Greece laments.

to lash the follies of the age." And then an elegy in four octaves :

> Let maudlin moralists affect to blush
> Over thy muse.

And so forth.

If James Hogg occupied three years in composing his " Ode for Music. On the death of Lord Byron," published in *Blackwood's*,[1] the effort was certainly a lamentable waste of time. A prelude tells how by " Dee's winding waters " and " dark Lock-na-Gaur " a wild song of despair is heard,

> As if the sweet seraphs of heaven
> Had mixed with the fiends of the air.

Then comes a Chorus of Demons :

> Sound ! sound
> Your anthem profound,
> Spirits of peril unawed and unbound !

For (they explain) he, the greatest of earthly name, must join this night in their revels. But a Chorus of Angels responds :

> Sing ! Sing !
> Till heaven's arch ring,
> To hail the favour'd of our King. . . .
> The greatest of all the choral throng . .
> Hath fallen at Freedom's holy shrine. . . .
> Then hail to his rest
> This unparallel'd guest,
> With songs that pertain to the land of the blest.

It is a relief to turn from this well-intentioned rubbish to the estimate of Byron which Robert Pollok introduced into the fourth book of *The Course of Time* (1827). The passage contains the only two lines of Pollok that have remained well known. Pollok's analysis of book iv. is as follows :

The unequal distribution of worldly possessions and intellectual gifts, plainly taught that God did not estimate men by outward circumstances only, or by their knowledge, but by their moral worth. Illustrated by the history of the gifted Byron.

[1] xxi, May 1827, 520 f.

This theme is expanded in the poem. Byron's rank, riches, fame ; the flattery poured upon him ; his opportunities for books, travel, nature, love, friendship—" Aught that could rouse, expand, refine the soul "—are chronicled. His poetic fancy " soared untrodden heights."

> Others, tho' great,
> Beneath their arguments seemed struggling, whiles
> He from above descending, stooped to touch
> The loftiest thought. . . .
> With Nature's self
> He seemed an old acquaintance, free to jest
> At will with all her glorious majesty.
> He laid his hand upon " the Ocean's mane,"
> And played familiar with his hoary locks.

Various aspects of Byron's familiarity with Nature are considered ; and Pollok reflects upon his knowledge of all human passions. He is compared to " some fierce comet."

> The nations gazed, and wondered much and praised.
> Critics before him fell in humble plight ;
> Confounded fell ; and made debasing signs
> To catch his eye, and stretched and swelled themselves
> To bursting nigh, to utter bulky words
> Of admiration vast ; and many too,
> Many that aimed to imitate his flight
> With weaker wings, unearthly flutterings made,
> And gave abundant sport to after days.

Yet Byron died wretchedly ; satiated ; all his passions dead save pride :

> A wandering, weary, worn and wretched thing,
> A scorched, and desolate, and blasted soul.

In his end lies the proof

> That not with natural or mental wealth
> Was God delighted.

The remainder of Pollok's moral may be guessed.

And now I come to what is by far the finest of these early poetical tributes—the passage which Samuel Rogers added to the section on " Bologna " in his *Italy*.[1] The " pleasures of memory " are here interwoven with sadness in lines which in dignity and magnanimity reach a higher level than Rogers attains anywhere else in his verse. He tells how one night at Bologna, where he was staying, a traveller arrived ; it was Byron.

> Much had passed
> Since last we parted ; and those five short years—
> Much had they told ! His clustering locks were turn'd
> Grey ; nor did aught recall the Youth that swam
> From Sestos to Abydos. Yet his voice,
> Still it was sweet ; still from his eye the thought
> Flashed lightning-like. . . .
> As in happier days
> He poured his spirit forth. The past forgot,
> All was enjoyment. Not a cloud obscured
> Present or future.

The cynical old banker-poet seems to forget his faded conventionalities of verse, and in the estimate of Byron is as sincere in his metrical harmonies as in his thought.

> He is now at rest ;
> And praise and blame fall on his ear alike,
> Now dull in death. Yes, Byron, thou art gone,
> Gone like a star that thro' the firmament
> Shot and was lost, in its eccentric course
> Dazzling, perplexing. Yet thy heart, methinks,
> Was generous, noble—noble in its scorn
> Of all things low or little ; nothing there
> Sordid or servile. If imagined wrongs
> Pursued thee, urging thee sometimes to do
> Things long regretted, oft, as many know,
> None more than I, thy gratitude would build
> On slight foundations : and, if in thy life
> Not happy, in thy death thou surely wert,
> Thy wish accomplished ; dying in the land
> Where thy young mind had caught ethereal fire,
> Dying for Greece, and in a cause so glorious !

---

[1] P. 97 f. of the famous edition of 1830. Rogers's few allusions to Byron in the *Table-Talk* (ed. Dyce) are not important. He says that Byron " always had the weakness of wishing to be thought much worse than he really was " (p. 237) ; and elsewhere : " There is a great deal of incorrect and hasty writing in Byron's works ; but it is overlooked in this age of hasty readers " (p. 241).

They in thy train—ah, little did they think,
As round we went, that they so soon should sit
Mourning beside thee, while a Nation mourned,
Changing her festal for her funeral song ;
That they so soon should hear the minute-gun,
As morning gleamed on what remained of thee,
Roll o'er the sea, the mountains, numbering
Thy years of joy and sorrow.
                    Thou art gone ;
And he who would assail thee in thy grave,
Oh, let him pause ! For who amongst us all,
Tried as thou wert—even from thine earliest years,
When wandering, yet unspoilt, a highland-boy—
Tried as thou wert, and with thy soul of flame ;
Pleasure, while yet the down was on thy cheek,
Uplifting, pressing, and to lips like thine,
Her charmed cup—ah, who among us all
Could say he had not erred as much, and more ?

With these moving lines I bring to a conclusion this rapid survey of specimens of the verse-tributes to Byron's memory.[1]

[1] I am not minded to spoil Rogers's gentle tribute by quoting any more of these elegies in my text ; but the list might be much extended. Verses are introduced into several prose estimates just after his death. Thus, *The Morning Chronicle* (May 17, 1824), after announcing the death of Byron, " in the flower of his age, in the noblest of causes," publishes some " Verses " signed " A Harrow School-fellow of Lord Byron," beginning :

O ! well Childe Harold has his fame restored—
And well his wayward pilgrimage has clos'd.

The same newspaper on July 15 had some verses on Byron's funeral that contain this fine liberal tribute :

                    I know
That he had evil in him—but to bow
To tyrants—but to fawn upon the foe
Of Freedom—but to proffer up a vow
For aught but man's most sacred interests—No !
This Byron never did.

Blackwood's (*Noctes Ambrosianæ*, xv, xv, June 1824, 706 f.) has this prophecy : " I think Byron . . . will be remembered in the year of grace 1924 ; and I think the name of Byron will then be ranked as the third name of our great era," *i.e.* before everybody else except Scott and Wordsworth. It is in the course of this ambrosian symposium that Hogg's prose tribute, already quoted, is introduced ; and Odoherty (*i.e.* Maginn) closes the discussion with a song to " The Memory of Byron " which is too mediocre to quote (it being easily accessible in *The Odoherty Papers*, i, 319 f.). An elegy on Byron may be found in a pathetic volume entitled *Attempts at Verse, by John Jones, an Old Servant : with some Account of the Writer, written by himself ; and an Introductory Essay on the Lives and Work of our Uneducated Poets, by Robert Southey, Esq., Poet Laureate* (1831). Southey's priggish and patronizing essay extends to 168 pages, from Taylor the Water-Poet to Robert Bloomfield. Poor Jones's stanzas " On the Death of Lord

The investigator of Byron's posthumous fame is confronted with an enormous mass of writings in prose during the years immediately following his death. The problem of arrangement is a difficult one. On the whole it seems best to glance first at the group of books which deal with Byron's connection with the Greek revolution,[1] and then pass on to the books that took the place for a time of the official biography.

Count Pietro Gamba, the brother of La Guiccioli, accompanied Byron to Greece. The two men were intimate friends, and Gamba was present at Byron's death. In 1825 he published *A Narrative of Lord Byron's Last Journey to Greece*. The fact that this book bore Murray's imprint and was dedicated to Hobhouse gave it, so to speak, an official flavour. The portrait of Byron is most sympathetic, and Gamba's narrative is still of value as showing the combination of patience, prudence, intelligence, courage and magnanimity which Byron exerted in dealing with the intriguing factions in Greece.

William Parry was sent out to Greece in 1823 by the Greek Revolutionary Committee in London. He was a specialist in ordnance, but at Missolonghi he was helpless from lack of men and money. Byron was attracted to him and saw much of him ; he nursed Byron in his last illness, and in 1825 published *The Last Days of Lord Byron*. His narrative of the fatal illness has been used by all subsequent biographers. Like Gamba, he gives a very favourable

Byron " (pp. 306 f.) declare that Byron chose bad themes and made a great mistake in leaving England.

> Though reckless of these was thy story,
>   And left to more impotent lays,
> The Corsair shall glow in thy glory,
>   The Wanton shall bask in thy praise. . . .
> The land of thy sires was forsaken,
>   Its worthies thy genius abused,
> No pride in her virgins was taken,
>   Its sons were a tribute refused—

whatever that may mean ! As a final indication of how wide-spread are these ephemeral tributes I note : *Original Poems*, by Charles Hodges (Munich, 1836). The dedicatory poem, " To his Most Gracious Majesty, Lewis I, King of Bavaria " contains (pp. 3 f.) a long tribute to Byron.

[1] These still possess some authority ; upon them in the main Richard Edgcumbe bases the first part of his *Byron : the Last Phase* (1909).

view of the poet. " Knowing him," he declares, " was for me a source of satisfaction unmingled with one regret." [1]

Edward Blaquiere went out to Greece in 1823 to collect information for the London Committee ; he saw Byron at Genoa and was influential in getting him to go to Greece. He then returned to London, and on a second visit to Greece arrived after Byron's death. His account is therefore at second-hand. In 1825 he published *A Narrative of a Second Visit to Greece, including Facts connected with the Last Days of Lord Byron*. Part ii, dealing with Byron, has separate pagination and is in part reprinted from *The Westminster Review*. He praises the fine qualities of character and leadership exhibited by Byron at Missolonghi, saying that the poet " has raised the best monument to his own fame, and has furnished the most conclusive reply to calumny and detraction."

Blaquiere also praises the conduct of Colonel Leicester Stanhope, who had been criticized by Parry for acting in opposition to Byron. Colonel Stanhope replied to Parry's " calumny," as he called it, in *Greece in 1823 and 1824 . . . to which are added, Reminiscences of Lord Byron* (1825). Stanhope denies that he had reflected on Byron's conduct or character ; his strictures were directed solely against his policy. He includes a fine tribute to Byron, and the concluding character sketch is on the whole favourable and pleasant.[2] George Finlay,[3] who met Byron at

---

[1] Professor Elton (*Survey*, i, 446) calls Parry's book " an inflated doubtful production " ; and Elze (*Life*, p. 297, note) says : " Though he professes himself to be the author . . . it is evident that he contributed only the materials for the book." Parry's work is illustrated by three coloured plates in the manner of the time, showing Byron's house at Missolonghi ; Byron and his Suliote Guards ; and Byron on his death-bed.

[2] The significant portions of Stanhope's estimate of Byron are reprinted by Elze (*Life*, Appendix, Note G, pp. 488 f.).

[3] Finlay included " Reminiscences " of Byron in his *History of the Greek Revolution*, 1861 ; they are reprinted in his *History of Greece*, 1877. Portions of the sketch which he wrote for Stanhope are reprinted by Elze (pp. 479 f.). Other reminiscences, drawn from Finlay's memoranda, are quoted by F. B. Sanborn in " Lord Byron and the Greek Revolution," *Scribner's Magazine*, September 1897, pp. 435 f. In addition to Gamba, Parry, Stanhope, Blaquiere, and Finlay, I must mention, though I have not seen, Colonel Leake's *Historical Outline of the Greek Revolution* (*circa* 1825 ?) which Edgcumbe refers to (*N. & Q.* 7th Series, i, 425), and a privately printed pamphlet of forty-eight pages entitled *Byron in Greece* (1825).

Cephalonia, contributed an appreciation of the poet to Stanhope's book. He writes :

I believe that, for some time, he will not be dealt with more fairly than during his life. . . . Time will put an end to all undue admiration and malicious cant. . . . It will then be possible to form a just estimation of the greatness of his genius and his mind, and the real extent of his faults. The ridiculous calumnies which have found a moment's credit will very soon be utterly forgotten. . . . It is information, not scandal, that will be sought for.

It is evident, then, that the testimony of Byron's fellow-workers for the cause of Greek independence was entirely, or almost entirely, favourable to him ; without doubt this group of disinterested witnesses did much to rehabilitate the reputation which the last years in Italy had somewhat tarnished.

But a great injury had been done to that reputation by the suppression and destruction of Byron's " Memoirs " ; it appears to be beyond question that almost the entire manuscript might have been published without giving offence ; at most the judicious suppression of a few indiscretions should have sufficed. The destruction of the document in the fireplace of number 50, Albemarle Street, caused suspicion and gossip and created a mystery.[1] The

---

[1] The destruction was first announced in *The Times*, May 19, 1824. The facts of the oft-told story of the holocaust are sifted and admirably presented by Miss Mayne (*Byron*, ii, 321 f. ; Appendix II). Hobhouse's version may be found in volume iii. cf *Recollections of a Long Life ;* Murray's, in a letter of May 19, 1824, to Wilmot Horton, quoted by Elze (Appendix, Note E, pp. 456 f.), who summarizes the case. In Thomas Moore's *Memoirs, Journals and Correspondence*, edited by Lord John Russell (iv, 186) there may be found Moore's own account, with Lord John's statement (he had read the manuscript) that with the exception of three or four indecent pages, the " Memoirs " were harmless enough, but with little trace of Byron's genius and no interesting details of his life. " On the whole," says Lord John, " the world is no loser by the sacrifice." *The Quarterly Review* (xciii, June 1853, 239 f.) in the course of a long review of the *Memoirs,* etc. of Moore, relates, in no very impartial manner, the story of the burning, and reveals Moore's injustices to Murray, his inaccuracies, and the general sordidness of the affair. J. C. Jeaffreson, Lord Lovelace, and, in fact, all biographers of Byron, have written about it. I need not resume the whole case. It is sufficient to say that though Moore afterwards posed as having sacrificed his own interests in the matter, he had in fact no property claim upon the manuscript whatsoever. It belonged to Murray. It was Hobhouse who most of all insisted upon the destruction. His influence won

rumour was widespread that one or more copies were still in existence,[1] and before long spurious fragments of autobiographical reminiscences appeared that professed to be the original of the " Memoirs." [2] The most authentic and best-documented account of the burning of the Memoirs is recorded by the fourth John Murray, in *Lord Byron and his Detractors*, privately issued in 1906.

The destruction of the " Memoirs " and the lack of an official biography were invitations to journeymen of letters to satisfy public curiosity and supply the demand. These biographies of 1824–26 were divided by Leigh Hunt [3] into five classes. Hunt writes :

Mrs. Leigh to support him. Lady Byron was represented at the destruction, but she refused to give any opinion as to whether the work should be destroyed or published. The proper course to have taken was, as Lord Lovelace has said, to seal the document for a term of years, at the expiry of which term it could have been edited with such deletions as should have seemed wise to a judicious and responsible editor. Murray, though the " Memoirs " became his property absolutely by Byron's death, accepted back the two thousand guineas which he had paid Moore for them. There was some talk of Lady Byron and Mrs. Leigh reimbursing Moore, but it came to nothing. Moore was repaid by being commissioned by Murray to write the official *Life*.

[1] *The Attic Miscellany*, for example (i, October 1824, pp. 26 f.), says : " Lord Byron's death once ascertained . . . the whole interest of society seemed centred in his *Memoirs*. Curiosity swallowed up grief." It refers to the belief that at least one copy is still in existence. In the *Noctes Ambrosianæ* xv (*Blackwood's*, xv, June 1824, 709) Tickler urges Odoherty to " patch up " the missing Memoirs. Tickler goes on to describe the manuscript (which John Wilson may have seen), and says that a copy made by a Florentine lady is now owned by Galignani and is to be published by that firm. *Blackwood's* later (xvi, November 1824, 530 f.) denounced the destruction and especially Moore's responsibility for it. This was unjust.

[2] I have already described the " Suppressed Chapter " published by *John Bull*, 1824. *The Life, Writings, Opinions and Times of Lord Byron* (1825) claims on the title-page that it contains " copious recollections of the lately destroyed manuscript." E. H. Coleridge (article " Byron," *Encyclopædia Britannica*, 11th edition, iv, 902) thinks that external evidence (especially ii, 278 f.) shows that the writer may have had an opportunity to read the " Memoirs." In *The Living and the Dead. By a Country Curate* (1827), a book which contains much gossip about Byron and an account of the destruction of the manuscript, it is stated on the authority of " Mrs. Ibbottson " that " copious and authentic extracts " are still extant. A further specimen of the efforts to make money out of the mystery is : *Poems by the Right Honourable Lord Byron ; with his Memoirs* (London : Jones and Co., 1825). The worthless memoirs here reprinted (pp. 3–4) reach only to the separation and are a mere reprint of the biographical sketch found in later issues of Hone's pirated *Poems on His Domestic Circumstances*.

[3] *Lord Byron*, i, 159.

Those which really contain something both true and new respecting him ; those that contain two or three old truths vamped up . . . ; thirdly, criticisms upon his genius, written with more or less good faith ; fourthly, compilations containing all that could be scraped together respecting him, true or false ; and fifthly, pure impudent fictions.

I shall consider first those in which the emphasis is biographical rather than critical and literary.

That Byron knew that R. C. Dallas [1] was writing a book about him and was aware of Dallas's animus against him is seen in a letter of 1819 [2] in which he remarks that Dallas is writing " what he calls a posthumous work about me," adding that the cause of Dallas's feeling that he has been ill-used is that he (Byron) will not send him another hundred pounds. The book was compiled in 1819. Immediately after Byron's death, Dallas set about printing it ; but its publication was stopped by a decree obtained by Byron's executors in the Court of Chancery.[3] For among his materials were letters written to him by Byron in early life, as well as letters from Byron to his mother. In a measure he got around the injunction by using the letters in his possession as a basis for his recollections.[4] His original plan had been to write a book to be published, say, about 1860 ; Byron's premature death, followed so shortly by Dallas's death (November 20, 1824), put the responsibility for revision and publication upon Dallas's son, the Rev. A. R. C. Dallas. The result was *Recollections*

---

[1] For an account of his connection with Byron see LJ, i, 168.

[2] LJ, iv, 414.

[3] August 23, 1824. Hobhouse and Hanson obtained the injunction not because they really objected to the publication of these letters but because they and Mrs. Leigh were fearful lest other sections of his correspondence, not so harmless, should see the light ; and they therefore wished to establish the precedent and principle of executors' control. Hobhouse would have accepted as a compromise a statement on the title-page : " Published by permission of the executors " ; but to this Dallas would not consent. The original sheets of the book, printed before the injunction was obtained, are now in the possession of Mr. H. C. Roe, where I have seen them. They amount to 168 pages.

[4] Beyond the reach of the Chancellor's injunction Galignani published in three volumes *Lord Byron's Correspondence with a Friend* (1825) ; and in Philadelphia there appeared *Correspondence of Lord Byron with a Friend* (1825). See my bibliography, *sub* Dallas.

of the Life of Lord Byron from the Year 1808 *to the end of* 1814 (1824). A preliminary statement of the injunction proceedings leads to a defence of the publication of the entire work in France. The tone of the whole book is unfortunate, in the main hostile, pietistic, and heavily weighed down by personal spite. Hunt says [1] that Dallas " was a sort of lay-priest " who " errs from being half-witted. . . . The wild poet ran against him and scattered his faculties." *Blackwood's* [2] recognizes the value of the information as to Byron's early life, but calls the book " utterly feeble and drivelling . . . more about old Dallas than young Byron." These strictures are really not too harsh. The truth is that the man had bored Byron beyond endurance. The disagreeable effect of the book is enhanced by the concluding pages added by the son. He dates Byron's degeneracy from the publication of *Childe Harold*.[3]

Never was there a more sudden transition from the doubtings of a mind to which Divine Light was yet accessible, to the unhesitating abandonment to the blindness of vice. . . . As long as Lord Byron continued to resist his temptations to evil, and to refrain from exposing publicly his tendency to infidelity, so long he valued the friendship of the author.

There are many other remarks in like vein. The only permanent value the book has is that it is the source for

---

[1] *Lord Byron*, i, 161.

[2] Vol. xvii, February 1825, 146. This article (pp. 131 f.) is an important review of Byron's character and achievement, with notices of recent books. It was written by John Wilson (as he admits, *Noctes Ambrosianæ*, xix ; *Blackwood's*, xvii, March 1825, 376). He attacks current mean, ungenerous criticism, and denies that " sensual profligacy " could have been a principal trait in " a man who, dying at six-and-thirty, bequeathed a collection of works such as Byron's to the world." There is fine succinct charity in the phrase : " The deep and passionate struggles with the inferior elements in his nature (and ours) "—and Wilson continues : " There is no possibility that a man should, without the highest genius, exert over the mind of his contemporaries that sort of influence which Byron has exerted, without deserving to do so, and without continuing to exert a mighty influence over the mind of all future time." The following month (p. 376) Wilson adds : " I believe at this moment, that Byron is thought of, as a man, with an almost universal feeling of pity, forgiveness, admiration, and love. I do not think it would be safe, in the most popular preacher, to abuse Byron now."

[3] I put together here passages from pp. 331 and 339.

the text of some of Byron's letters of which the original manuscripts have been lost.

Thomas Medwin's *Journal of the Conversations of Lord Byron at Pisa* (1824) has remained better known than it deserves to be. It is a trumpery affair, giving a fairly amiable impression of Byron, but full of errors and frivolities,[1] and, briefly put, the whole of the testimony of Medwin, unless corroborated by reliable persons elsewhere, is worthless. Medwin profited greatly from the destruction of the " Memoirs," and his book (which was at once reprinted in America) appeared in both octavo and in handsome quarto on heavy paper with broad margins. Murray was much offended by Byron's remarks on him recorded by Medwin, and thought of bringing suit for libel ; but contented himself with a privately printed reply in pamphlet form : *Notes on Captain Medwin's Conversations of Lord Byron.*[2] With a liberal use of the " deadly parallel " he contrasts Byron's remarks to Medwin with the testimony afforded by Byron's letters to Murray. Hobhouse also wrote a reply to Medwin (incorporating also an answer to Dallas). He intended this for the *Quarterly*, but Murray himself held it up, telling Hobhouse " that he and Mr. Gifford had much difficulty in preventing an article defamatory of Byron from being put into the *Quarterly*." [3] The substance of Hobhouse's article appeared in *The Westminster Review.*[4]

---

[1] W. M. Rossetti (*Præraphaelite Diaries and Letters.* London, Hurst and Blackett, 1900, p. 239) has recorded that Tennyson told him that the poem " To —— after reading a Life and Letters " (which has been thought to refer to R. M. Milnes's *Keats*) was written " in a fit of intense disgust " after reading Medwin's *Conversations.* Lounsbury, however (*Life and Times of Tennyson.* Yale University Press, 1916, p. 9) questions the accuracy of Rossetti's report of Tennyson's remark. Sharon Turner wrote to John Murray : " The whole book tends to undo much of the *prestige* with which Lord Byron's character has been artificially surrounded " (Samuel Smiles, *A Publisher and his Friends*, i, 450).

[2] Though printed anonymously, these *Notes* were by Murray himself. They were reprinted in the four-volume edition of Byron's *Works*, 1829 (iv, 401 f.) ; also in the one-volume edition, 1837 (pp. 809 f.).

[3] Lord Broughton, *Recollections*, iii, 83 f.

[4] Vol. iii, January 1825, 1 f. It was from the *Westminster* (July 1824) that Medwin had reprinted Fletcher's account of Byron's last illness. Fletcher's letter to Mrs. Leigh, which was sent in a covering letter to Murray, and is dated April 20, 1824, is now in the possession of Mr. H. C. Roe, who printed it for private circulation : *Lord Byron's Illness and Death*

Two other attacks on Medwin appeared in *Blackwood's*.[1]
Leigh Hunt,[2] on the other hand, though he found some faults,
in the main defends Medwin against Hobhouse. And a
writer using the pseudonym " Vindex " issued a pamphlet
entitled *Captain Medwin vindicated from the Calumnies of
the Reviewers* (1825).[3] Reading a century later the trite
anecdotes and jejune comments that make up Medwin's
book, one has difficulty in comprehending the need for
all this excitement.

How to deal briefly with the enormously long work
entitled *The Life, Writings, Opinions, and Times of Lord
Byron*, published anonymously [4] in three volumes in 1825,
puzzles me. Hunt [5] calls it " a jovial farrago in four [*sic*]
volumes, written by as unparticular a fellow as one should
wish to see with a pair of scissors in his hand." [6] The
work is a compilation from many sources, trustworthy and
otherwise, put together in an ingenuously disorderly fashion.

as described in a Letter from William Fletcher (*His Lordship's Valet and
Confidential Servant*) *to the Honourable Augusta Leigh* (Nottingham, 1920).

[1] Vol. xvi, November 1824, 530 f. I quote two sentences : " It contains
nothing new ; but only repeats scandals that have been long before the
public, and many of which have been refuted. The very falsehood is not
original." In the same issue (pp. 536 f.) is a letter signed " Harroviensis "
attacking Medwin and intimating that his only reason for publishing his
book was to satisfy the morbid curiosity disappointed by the destruction
of the " Memoirs."

[2] *Lord Byron*, i, 164 f.

[3] It is just possible that this is by Medwin himself, though the writer
insists that he knows Medwin only in his book. According to Galt (*Life
of Byron*, p. vi), Medwin himself replied to Hobhouse in a pamphlet which
he later suppressed. (See also *The Gentleman's Magazine*, November
1824.) In 1917 Messrs. Maggs offered for sale (book-catalogue, no. 356)
a copy of Medwin's *Conversations* which had formerly been in the possession
of R. B. Haydon and contained copious remarks and criticisms in his
handwriting, confuting Medwin on various points. From the generous
extracts printed by Maggs (pp. 29–30 of the catalogue) these notes appear
to be of considerable interest. I do not know who is the present owner of
this copy. Medwin's *Angler in Wales* (1824) contains some anecdotes of
Byron.

[4] An inscription on the title-page of the copy in the Peabody Institute,
Baltimore, ascribes it to Matthew Iley, the publisher of the work. J. C.
Roe (*Some Obscure and Disputed Points in Byron Biography*, p. v) makes
the same ascription. According to Mr. Francis Edwards's book-catalogue
(no. 375, item 152) it is by " Dr. J. M. Millingen." Leigh Hunt (*Lord
Byron*, i, 172) calls the book " a curiosity, if it were only for its title."
For the excessively long title see my bibliography.

[5] See Hunt's long commentary on the book, *Lord Byron*, i, 159 f.

[6] The " fellow " describes himself on the title-page as " an English
Gentleman, in the Greek military service, and Comrade of his Lordship."

As criticism it is quite negligible ; the writer reprints (as we have already seen) the spurious *Farewell to England* and prints (for the first and, I believe, the only time) the prose satire on the Congress of Vienna. If the " Recollections of the lately destroyed Manuscripts " [1] are authentic, the loss is not greatly to be deplored, for they are very dull. There are many apocryphal anecdotes, such as one of a journey taken by Byron and La Guiccioli to Corfu and Ithaca. The fantastic story of the separation having been due to an innocent visit from Mrs. Mardyn, the actress, is accepted and repeated unquestioningly. The writer's view of Byron is extremely favourable. " Few and short-lived," he says, " were the errors of Lord Byron, and he made a noble atonement for them." He is liberal in abuse of writers whose estimate of Byron is less enthusiastic than his own. John Styles, Dallas, and Sir Samuel Egerton Brydges are criticized ; but his worst (and most deserved) strictures are reserved for Southey.[2]

Such a farrago of nonsense, scurrility, and grotesque malignity never, perhaps, issued from any other pen than that of Dr. Southey. . . . For one line of inconsistency, falsehood, infidelity, blasphemy, impiety, and obscenity, written by Lord Byron, Dr. Southey has published ten.

The statement is, to say the least, exaggerated ; but if the *tu quoque* is to be resorted to, it is not unpleasant to see it for once applied so whole-heartedly. In closing, the writer applies to Byron Sir Ector's eulogy of Sir Launcelot— the enthusiasm for Byron (whom the writer frequently refers to as " this much-lamented nobleman ") being as unrestrained as is the scorn of his enemies.

Dallas, Medwin, and the author of the *Life, Writings*, etc. are still of some use to the student of Byron. I am now

---

[1] These " Recollections " begin at ii, 227, with a separate title-page, and run to ii, 296.

[2] Vol. iii, 379 f. See also i, 366, where a reply to Southey's letter to *The Courier* is reprinted from *The Morning Chronicle*, where it first appeared over the signature " A Lover of Consistency." On Mrs. Mardyn see i, 253 ; on the visit to Corfu, i, 404 f. ; on Styles, ii, 71 ; on Dallas, ii, 191 ; on Brydges, iii, 334. At iii, 328, there is an unusually favourable appreciation of Shelley.

going to pass in rapid review a group of purely ephemeral biographies. *Full Particulars of the Much Lamented Death of Lord Byron* (1824), a hasty eight-page pamphlet, contains a sketch of his career, a reprint of Mavrocordato's proclamation, and quotations from the principal daily journals, " as specimens of the sensation " the news excited. One of the earliest biographies to appear [1] after the news of the poet's death reached England was *The Life and Genius of Lord Byron*, by Sir Cosmo Gordon.[2] Considering the haste with which it must have been composed, it is quite judicious and is not over-burdened with inaccuracies. Its sane estimate of the poet probably did service against the strong current of morbid curiosity. George Clinton's *Memoirs of the Life and Writings of Lord Byron* (1825) is remarkable chiefly for its length [3] and for the dedication (apparently with no humorous or impudent intention) to " Anne Isabella, the Dowager Lady Byron with sympathy for the irreparable loss she has sustained." The author avows his purpose " to supply the deficiency occasioned by the loss of the Memoirs." The work may be characterized as uncritical eulogy based on very little information, and that little at second hand, and swollen to its monstrous proportions by tireless padding. There are many excerpts from Byron's poems, and many wood-cut illustrations. The fact that these are by George Cruikshank has kept Clinton's book in remembrance. Some of the illustrations, *e.g.* " Don Juan saving a child from the Cossacques," are worthy of Thackeray's burlesques.

Another huge compilation is *Anecdotes of Lord Byron, from Authentic Sources* (1825).[4] The motto on the title-

---

[1] It is announced as published in *Blackwood's*, June 1824.

[2] I suspect a *nom de plume*, but am not certain. This work appeared also in *The Pamphleteer*, xxiv, 175 f. It is republished in the final volume of Baudry's twelve-volume edition of Byron's *Works* (Paris, 1824). Leigh Hunt (*Lord Byron*, i, 160) describes it as " a quick, little, good-humoured supply for the market, remarkable for the conscientiousness of its material." Roe, on the other hand (*Obscure and Disputed Points*, p. vi.) says, " it is full of absurdities."

[3] It extends to 756 pages. It was reprinted in 1826, 1828, and 1832.

[4] This is anonymous. but is ascribed in the catalogue of the British Museum to Alexander Kilgour. The writer denounces Medwin as a spy in Byron's house ; but commends Dallas.

page is " Dead scandals form good subjects for dissection " ; but the charitable tone of the book does not accord with this keynote. Hundreds of anecdotes of Byron, most of them in fairly accurate form, are here gathered together. The book was used by Thomas Moore in the preparation of his biography of Byron.[1]

Lastly, bare mention of J. W. Lake's perfunctory *Life of Byron* (1826) will suffice.[2]

Of the early estimates of Byron that are primarily critical rather than biographical [3] the most thoughtful is the series of *Letters on the Character and Poetical Genius*

---

[1] See *Prose and Verse* by Thomas Moore, ed. Shepherd, p. 410.

[2] Roe (p. vi) describes this as " a kind of vest-pocket edition of Byron's Life." We have met with Lake as an eulogist of Byron in verse and as a translator of Lamartine's *Dernier Chant*. In 1822 he had supplied a brief sketch of Byron's life for the Galignani edition of that year. This was reprinted in later Galignani editions, and elsewhere (*e.g.*, so late as Byron's *Works*, Philadelphia, Lippincott, 1853). In 1829 Lake published at Paris an anthology entitled *The Beauties of Byron*. Mme. Louise Swanton Belloc's *Lord Byron* may be mentioned as the most important early French biography (Paris : Renouard, 1824). She was the translator of Moore's *Byron* into French. She is now chiefly memorable as the friend of Stendhal, with whom she corresponded on Byron and other matters.

[3] The most exacting bibliographer will hardly expect me to note all the estimates of Byron's genius and achievement that appeared in the periodicals. Of the many I have read I content myself with calling attention to two. *The Morning Chronicle*, July 30, 1824, said that Byron " created a new era " in poetry ; he had " a perfect conception of the beautiful and grand in nature " ; above all, he showed " the workings of passion on the mind itself . . . with a power of moral scrutiny and exposure, that if it were ever excelled," has been so only by Shakespeare. The writer urges that Byron be tried by his best work : " he will stand, in all that constitutes genuine poetry, among the first men of any age or nation, and among those of his own day superior and alone." (The political prepossessions of the *Chronicle* must be remembered.) A writer in *The London Magazine*, October 2, 1824, is more guarded in his praise. Here are a few of his opinions. " He avoided the timid driveller, and generally chose his companions among the lovers and practisers of sincerity and candour." " He had grown weary of being known only as a writer." His imagination being stronger than his reason, he might possibly have become a religious fanatic, perhaps even a Methodist. There was some ground for the fear entertained by some people that he would go mad. The only practical good he did for Greece was the *éclat* he gave the cause. " Lord Byron was a Lord of very powerful intellect and strong passions ; these are almost sufficient *data* for a moral geometer to construct the whole figure." And finally, this excellent sentence : " All that men have in general, he had in more than ordinary force ; some of the qualities which men rarely have, he possessed to a splendid degree of perfection." For other such estimates see *The Gentleman's Magazine*, June 1824 ; *The Universal Review*, November 1824–January 1825 ; *The Monthly Repository*, January 1825 ; *The Christian Observer*, February–April 1825 ; *The North American Review*, January 1825.

of Lord Byron, by Sir Samuel Egerton Brydges (1824).[1]
In this book the general discussions of poetical principles,
of imagination, fancy, invention, judgment, and so forth,
suggest that Brydges had studied the *Biographia Literaria*
and Wordsworth's Preface of 1815 with care. Here are
some of his opinions of Byron. Byron failed to " chastise
his first impressions " ; in him the reason was inferior to
the imagination, and he made less use of the imagination
than of the fancy. He exhibits license in thought and theme ;
the fiercer passions prevailed exclusively in his mind ; he
was reckless of all public opinion ; his ancestry explains
many of his errors ; his immorality was a revolt from hypocrisy ; he possesses earnestness, directness, emotion, but
lacks moral truth and wisdom. An interesting discussion,
which anticipates Ruskin, follows on Byron's " intense
sensation of pleasure in looking on nature." The " acuteness
of observation " in his poetry is valuable to encourage a lively
sense of natural beauties ; and Byron's hostility to society
is a positive aid to this excellence as a poet of nature. His
" intense susceptibility " extends to inward sensations as well
as outward images. Equally Ruskinian is Brydges's opinion
of Byron's morality. Even at his worst there is no veiling
of the grossly sensual under " a flowery disguise of delicate
sensibility." Brydges thinks it strange that the intellectual
and emotional excitement in which Byron lived " should
never have proceeded to mental derangement." Returning
to the problem of morality, Brydges says (and again he
anticipates the tone of Ruskin) : " Daring and open crime
always brings with it its own antidote ; but concealed
rottenness works underground." [2] He holds that Byron's
personal hatreds, growing out of political antipathies, are
morally the worst part of his character. His general conclusion is : " If Lord Byron be of all modern poets he whom
we can least spare, that alone is surely magnificent praise." [3]

[1] Announced as preparing in *Blackwood's*, July 1824 ; published
September 1824.
[2] See especially Letter xxiii, pp. 222 f.
[3] For a long notice of Brydges's book see *Blackwood's*, xvii, February
1825, 137 f.

Brydges returned to the subject in : *An Impartial Portrait of Lord Byron, as a Poet and a Man* (1825). There is little in this book that does not appear more fully in the larger work just considered. Brydges analyzes the causes of Byron's gloom and the characteristics of his poetry ; he comments upon the difficulty of stemming the tide of sentiment which is now running strong against the poet. He returns yet again to Byron in his *Note on the Suppression of Memoirs* (1825).[1] He here defends Byron " not as a poet, but as a practical patriot." Parry's book had made Brydges regard the poet " with still less qualified admiration," for Byron's last months show him to have been " a practical, sensible, matter-of-fact man," generous of his fortune and time and energy, led on by pure zeal " for the independence and happiness of a suffering people." He refuses to believe in Byron's " viciousness of heart " and contends that his reputation as a rake was due more to his defiance of public opinion than to vanity. The attacks following his death Brydges attributes to an appeal to mob prejudice against an aristocrat (a singular judgment). Brydges rightly declares that not till 1816 did Byron's mind become fully developed. " He drew a great deal from the fountain of Wordsworth's poetry." And Brydges adds :

Shelley is evidence of the fact. At this time Shelley had gained a strange influence over Lord Byron's mind. Shelley has written two or three short things (posthumous), which have a delicate beauty : on the whole his poetry is fantastic, corrupt, and forced.

A decade later, in his *Autobiography* (1834), the same writer again champions Byron, saying [2]—

There are many who will ask whether all the intense feelings expressed by Byron . . . were not factitious extravagances in which he was not sincere, and which his life belied ? I say, sternly, no ! it is a mean and stupid mind which

---

[1] Not, be it noted, Byron's Memoirs, but Brydges's. These curious rambling notes contain many interesting " strictures on contemporary public characters."

[2] Vol. i, 257. *The Athenæum*, June 14, 1834, p. 443, comments on this passage.

can suspect so : no one can feign such intensities as Byron expresses : when he wrote, he was sincere, but his feelings were capricious, and not always the same. If it can be contended that inconsistency destroys merit, woe be to human frailty.

He contrasts Shelley's and Byron's poetry : [1]

Shelley was more theoretical and abstract ; Byron, however imaginative, had it always mixed up with humanity ;— human passions and human forms. Shelley had gleams of poetry ; Byron was always poetical ; Shelley never put a master's hand upon his subject ; he could not mould it to his will.

It remains within this chapter to glance at a few other early appreciations of Byron. *A Sermon on the Death of Lord Byron. By a Layman* (1824) is a comparatively moderate and just estimate. It falls into four parts : the certainty of death ; man's reluctance to face this certainty ; the fall of a man of mighty mind " whose sudden death created a chilling sensation through the frame of civilized society " ; and the duties and responsibilities of those in elevated station.

A dully philosophic effort with a tendency to condone and to moralize is James W. Simmons's [2] *Inquiry into the Moral Character of Lord Byron* (1824). A sentence from the *Inquiry* itself sums it up aptly : " It is the supreme consolation of Dulness to volunteer its strictures upon Genius." No more need be said.[3]

Much more lively and still readable is *Byroniana Bozzies and Piozzies* (1825) in which, after a " Dissertation on Poetry," there comes, in separate sections, a series of critiques on all Byron's chief poems. A number of Byron's conversations are reported ; the author says that they " must, in their

---

[1] Vol. i, 329. At ii, 369, one notes : " The melancholy excitement awakened by Shelley's fate in a sea-storm has drawn a notice and popularity upon him."

[2] Lowndes, i, 340, gives the author's name as " Simmonds."

[3] See the review in *The Literary Chronicle*, April 29, 1826. (Simmons's book appeared in New York in 1824, and was republished in London in 1826.)

own sterling worth, authenticate themselves. We are not permitted to say from whence we received them." There is no gossip or scandal ; the material is chiefly literary.

After appearing in *The Atlantic Monthly*, October 1825, an article by Andrews Norton [1] was reprinted as *A Review of the Character and Writings of Lord Byron* in London (1826). A preface to the new edition explains the book as an answer to

the ingenious and elaborate apologies which have been offered for his aberrations, and the specious glosses which have been drawn over his sentiments. . . . The tendency of his writings is to evil. . . . The poetical career of Byron is here traced by the hand of a master.

As the point of view of this estimate is sufficiently clear from this preface, and as American criticism is in general beyond our set limits of inquiry, I shall say no more about this *Review*.[2]

[1] The *Review* is anonymous. On the title-page of the copy at Harvard the name Andrews Norton is written in. But on the copy at Yale one finds " By W. Phillips."

[2] An anonymous volume, *Tales of Chivalry and Romance* (1826), contains (pp. 291 f.) an essay on Byron. The writer finds that " the greatest shade " in his character " was his want of nationality."

CHAPTER XII

THE DECLINE OF BYRONISM

WHEN, in 1846, Thackeray bitterly assailed Byron's reputation, he felt constrained to add : " Woe be to the man who denies the public gods." Even in the middle of the century Byron was still one of " the public gods." The decline in his vogue and in the vogue of Byronism was rapid among critics of literature, and though a crowd of poetasters continued for two decades or more to imitate him he did not influence the rising generation of true poets when once, as in the case of Tennyson, they had shaken off the impressions of adolescence. But there was until the eighteen-fifties a constant demand for new editions of his poetry ; and if the critics assailed him and if the poets refused to follow him, at least they did not ignore him. Still, as in his lifetime, he came before them in a " questionable shape." He was attacked and derided ; he was defended and, by a few, still admired. But he was not, and he has never been, among those whom the world willingly lets die.

In attempting a survey of the Byroniana of the quarter of a century following his death I find it necessary to abandon any approximation to chronological order, and I shall proceed according to this scheme. After a brief account of the movement for the erection of a monument to Byron in Westminster Abbey, I shall take up Moore's biography and the controversies and criticisms that it inspired. Then the other biographical and reminiscential works of the early eighteen-thirties ; then two curious belated poems on Byron ; and then the evidences of continuing admiration of the poet as shown in Ruskin and the Brownings, with a side-glance at current American criticism and a word on Mazzini's outspoken defence. I shall then turn to the phenomena of anti-Byronism as exhibited by Beddoes, Carlyle, the brothers Hare, Newman, and Taylor (among others) ; to Bulwer's middle-of-the-road position ; to the rise in fame of Shelley and Keats, and the growing influence of Wordsworth ; and to the emergence of Tennyson. The latter part of this survey will involve some consideration of the practisers of Byronism, for the decline in Byron's popularity cannot be understood without taking into account the harm done to his reputation by the herd of imitators. In this connection it will be necessary to define once more the qualities of Byronism as distinct from Byron's own achievement.

With this word of explanation I turn to my first subject —the proposed monument. At the time of Byron's funeral it was understood that burial in Westminster Abbey was out of the question. It was not until 1828 that a committee for a national memorial was formed ; [1] on June 7 of that year this committee met at John Murray's. Subscriptions were opened with London bankers, and also with bankers in Edinburgh and Dublin and in France and Italy. Soon after the invitation for subscriptions was issued the report became current that the authorities of the Abbey would refuse to admit any monument. This report prompted a large amount of discussion.[2] Nevertheless on May 22, 1829, Hobhouse, for the committee, wrote to Thorwaldsen, the

---

[1] For a list of the committee, with the executive sub-committee and officers, together with the amounts given by the more important subscribers, see an article by E. Walford in *N. & Q.*, 7th Series, ii, 244 f. For the correspondence with Thorwaldsen and later correspondence on the same subject see R. Sinker's article, " The Statue of Byron in the Library of Trinity College, Cambridge," *N. & Q.*, 6th Series, iv, 421 f. Richard Edgcumbe in his *History of the Byron Memorial* (1883) sums up the whole matter. See also Lord Broughton's *Recollections*, iii, 277 f.

[2] Six letters that had appeared in *The Courier* were reprinted in *Sidney's Letter to the King ; and other Correspondence connected with the Reported Exclusion of Lord Byron's Monument from Westminster Abbey* (1828). *The Athenæum* of September 24 and October 1, 1828 (pp. 751 f. and 767 f.), has two articles on " Lord Byron's Monument." The argument for admission to the Abbey is that Byron is an essential link in the chain in Poet's Corner. " No other poet but Byron can fill the chain. Wordsworth and Coleridge belong to the coming ages, and we need not fear that any honour which those ages can pay them will be withheld ; but Byron is ours : he has lived for us, he has written for us ; . . . let us show that we are not ashamed of the influence he has exerted over us." Many years later

sculptor, offering him fifteen hundred pounds for a monument. Two days later he wrote again, stating that the memorial was for Westminster Abbey. In 1831 Thorwaldsen modelled the statue at Rome. It was shipped to England and lay for a long while in the vaults of the customs house. In 1834 it was offered to the Abbey and was refused. Another proffer was made in 1838 and again refused. This occasioned Henry Austen Driver's pamphlet, *Byron and the Abbey. A few Remarks elicited by the Rejection of his Statue* (1838). Driver defends Byron's religion, morality, powers, talents and influence in an unrestrained and unphilosophic fashion. He urges that tribute should be paid to the genius without concern for the faults of the man. He admits the inappropriateness of the Abbey as a place for the monument, and suggests the erection of a new national memorial for great men, a sort of Hall of Fame. Driver concludes : " Peace to his manes ! . . . Let the willow of our Compassion hang over the grave of his Errors "—a sentiment more appropriate to Alfred de Musset than to Byron.

Meanwhile Thorwaldsen's statue still lay in the Customs house. In March 1840, a Mr. De la Prynne suggested to George Peacock (senior tutor at Trinity College, Cambridge) that Trinity would be a fitting place for it. Peacock agreed, but did not dare broach the matter to Doctor Wordsworth, the Master of Trinity. In April 1843, Dean Ireland having died, the statue was once more offered to the Abbey with the hope that the new Dean would accept it ; but it was again refused. Finally, in the same year, William Whewell, who had succeeded Wordsworth, accepted it for Trinity. It stands to-day at the far end of the central aisle of the library.[1]

Within a few months of Byron's death, rumours were current that arrangements were being made that Thomas

Dean Stanley briefly defended the authorities of the Abbey, while admitting their inconsistency, for " if Byron was turned from our doors, many a one as questionable as Byron has been admitted " (A. P. Stanley, *Historical Memorials of Westminster Abbey*, 1887, ii, 151 f. and 199).

[1] Hobhouse's " Remarks on the Exclusion of Lord Byron's Monument " were included in his privately printed tribute to Byron of 1843, which, in turn, he republished as an appendix to his *Travels in Albania*, 1855 (i, 522 f.), itself a reprint in the main of his *Journey through Albania and other Provinces of Turkey*, 1813.

Moore should write an official " Life and Letters " of the poet. In February 1825, *Blackwood's* [1] protested against the choice of Moore as " the formal and complete historian of Byron's life," and urged that duty upon Hobhouse.[2] Murray, however, seems always to have considered Moore the fittest person for the task, both because of his intimacy with Byron and because the engagement to write the biography would be in the nature of a compensation for the loss occasioned to Moore through the destruction of the " Memoirs." In 1826,[3] Murray and Moore began to collect materials in a leisurely way, but it was not until the publication of Leigh Hunt's *Recollections of Lord Byron and some of his Contemporaries* (1828) that Murray was really stirred to action. He then wrote Moore that " in consequence of Hunt's infamous publication " he " felt it a duty no longer to withhold the means which I think I possess of doing justice to Lord Byron's character." Materials were derived from Hanson, Bowring, Scott, Scrope Davies,[4] Mrs. Shelley, Fletcher (Byron's valet), and many other persons.[5] The first volume of the *Letters, Journals, and other Prose Writings of Lord Byron, with Notices of his Life* appeared on January 1, 1830.[6]

---

[1] Vol. xvii, 146.

[2] Hobhouse himself had as few illusions about Moore's book as about Moore. In his *Recollections* he records : " Moore owned very frankly to me that he would make a book to get the money he wanted, but not a book of real merit as a Life of Lord Byron " (iii, 134). Again : " As I felt that Byron certainly intended a benefit to Moore, I cannot but assist him in some degree to gain his two thousand pounds out of Lord Byron's memory. That is his motive ; he has no other " (iii, 315). When the biography appeared Hobhouse wrote : " That the letters and journals raise Lord Byron in public estimation as a man of talent, no one will be foolish enough to assert. What, then, has this publication achieved ? It has put £3,500 at least into the pocket of T. Moore " (iv, 81). Hobhouse, despite his essential honesty, was prejudiced.

[3] For the letters and negotiations between Murray and Moore see Smiles, ii, 306 f. There seems to have been at first some thought of publishing the letters and journals separately from the biography.

[4] Moore feared that Davies's cleverness and the materials he possessed might make him a " formidable competitor " and urged Murray to negotiate with him for his documents (Smiles, ii, 309).

[5] There was indeed an embarrassing superfluity of material. A rumour to that effect being current, Moore actually received a letter offering " to take the refuse off our hands at a guinea per line " ! (Smiles, ii, 313).

[6] The copy of Moore's book in the Widener collection at Harvard is a most interesting one. It is the two-volume quarto edition of 1830, extended

The book was immediately reprinted at Paris and New York, and smuggled copies were sent to England for sale. Surreptitious copies were also printed at Dublin and Glasgow ; and Murray had some difficulty in suppressing this illegal competition. The general effect of Moore's work was a distinct heightening of the estimation in which Byron was held ; and the biography of course centred attention on the poet once more.

The shallowness of Moore's nature is shown in the entry in his journal on the day of Byron's funeral. I quote a few sentences : [1]

Saw a lady crying in a barouche as we turned out of George Street. . . . There were, however, few respectable persons among the crowd ; and the whole ceremony was anything but what it ought to have been. Left the hearse as soon as it was off the stones, and returned home to get rid of my black clothes, and try to forget, as much as possible, the wretched feelings I had experienced. . . . Went . . . to call upon the Morgans. Found Lady Morgan half-dressed, and had the felicity of seeing the completion of her toilette ; looking, however, much more at her handmaid than at herself. From thence went to Mrs. Story's, and supped with her. I and the girls went to Vauxhall : a most delicious night.

While Moore was having his " delicious night " with the girls at Vauxhall, the devoted Hobhouse, alone of Byron's intimate friends, was accompanying the body to Hucknall.

Moore's task was to link together with narrative the abundant documentary material. He was hampered by the need to be discreet. Moreover, though shallow, he was loyal and felt the need to make the work a defence of Byron's character. His sympathies are rather with the earlier romantic Byron than with the later satiric and metaphysical Byron. There were depths in the poet's nature beyond

to six volumes by the insertion of sixty prints (" being an almost complete collection of portraits of Lord Byron, many of them extremely rare "), 634 other engraved portraits, and 115 views.

[1] *Memoirs, Journal and Correspondence of Thomas Moore*, iv, 214 f.

Moore's ability to sound, and there were qualities (not necessarily the worst) that he disliked. Moore makes the error of from time to time abandoning his true function as a compiler and joiner of the materials committed to him and of introducing lengthy passages of a moralizing kind. His perpetual quasi-apologizing, accompanied by innuendo, is disagreeable. The portrait produced is feeble and unconvincing. There are, however, few positive inaccuracies, and the book is complete to the extent possible with the materials at Moore's command and within the limits laid upon his discretion. The lasting merit of the book and the reason why its general effect upon Byron's reputation was favourable is this : that it gave to the public the great mass of Byron's correspondence and journals. But it is not a great biography.[1]

Moore's account of Byron's marriage and separation at once precipitated a controversy. A fifteen-page pamphlet appeared entitled : *Remarks occasioned by Mr. Moore's Notices of Lord Byron's Life.*[2] This was signed by Lady Byron, but seems to have been written by Thomas Campbell.[3] At all events it was reprinted in Campbell's article, " Lady

---

[1] Greville's opinion of the book is a fair specimen of that of the " average reader " of the day. He did not like the plan of stringing letters together with little essays on Byron's character and with hints that various details were too indecent to be told. He disliked the liberal use of initials, half veiling contemporary personages and carrying with them unpleasant implications. (See *The Greville Memoirs*, by C. C. F. Greville. Edited by Henry Reeve. London : Longmans, 1874, i, 272 f. ; entry of February 3, 1830.) On the other hand, Mrs. Shelley, who had no reason to be an encomiast of Byron, wrote to Murray : " The great charm of the work to me . . . is that the *our* Lord Byron I find there is *our* Lord Byron—the fascinating, faulty, philosophical being " (Smiles, ii, 319). Mrs. Shelley was evidently writing rather of the letters and journals themselves than of Moore's own interspersed contributions to the work. Miss Mayne (*Byron*, ii, 256) speaks of " Moore's quasi-caricature " ; for other modern estimates, more judicious and on the whole more favourable, see Stephen Gwynn, *Thomas Moore* (1905), p. 127 ; and Elton's *Survey*, ii, 278.

[2] Another edition of the same year, apparently pirated, has the title : *A Letter to Thomas Moore, Esq., occasioned by his Notices of the Life of the late Lord Byron.* Still another form, an undated octavo reprinted from *The Northern Whig*, is called : *The Living and the Dead ; or Lady Byron's Remarks addressed to Mr. Moore, respecting her Separation from her Husband.*

[3] Harriet Martineau (*Biographical Sketches*, p. 320), speaking of the " sort of disclosure, offered in the name of Lady Byron," declares that " the whole transaction was one of poor Campbell's freaks " and that Lady Byron, refusing to admit the right of the public to know anything about her private affairs, kept silence.

Byron and Thomas Moore." This is a warm defence of
Lady Byron. Campbell refuses to examine Moore's " mis-
conceptions " in detail, for, he says, " the subject would lead
me insensibly into hateful disclosures against poor Lord
Byron." There are other such innuendoes.[1] Madden [2]
writes :

Campbell's feelings in relation to the fame of a brother bard,
who had only recently been a living rival, were . . . something more than merely cold and unkind—they were passion-
ately inimical. . . . Campbell with avidity seized an
opportunity of rushing into print to wound the reputation of
a brother bard whose fame during his lifetime he might not
with impunity have assailed.

Madden goes on to quote *The Literary Gazette* in sturdy
protest against Campbell's

most odious imputations upon the character of Lord Byron
which can possibly be left to the worst imaginations to
conceive. . . Of what monstrous crime was he guilty ? . . .
His accusers are bound by every moral and sacred tie to be
definite in their charge : . . . there can be no shield against
the horribly vague denunciation which has been . . .
hurled at the unprotected and unanswering dead.

[1] In *The Life and Letters of Thomas Campbell* (iii, 64) there is a letter
from Campbell to his sister in which he remarks, à propos of his defence
of Lady Byron : " What I have now to say, I don't give you in absolute
confidence ; but as it *will* be out one day, I give it to repeat with discretion."
A row of asterisks follows. Naturally Campbell's insinuations were brought
to light again at the time of the Stowe controversy. They are reprinted
in *The True Story of Lady Byron*. John Paget, however, stated
categorically (" Recollections of Lord Byron," *Blackwood's*, July 1869 ;
reprinted in *Paradoxes and Puzzles*, 1874) : " It is but justice to state that
the writer of this article knows that Campbell disavowed any intention to
convey the imputation commonly understood to have been implied by his
observations, and expressed surprise that such a construction should have
been put upon them." With Campbell's base insinuating attack upon the
dead poet one may profitably compare the tone of a letter to Byron in
earlier years, asking a favour (*Life and Letters*, ii, 301), and of another letter
in which he speaks of " the kindly feeling I have towards him, in consequence of his always having dealt kindly by me " (*ibid.*, ii, 423). Moore
notes (*Memoirs*, etc., iv, 214) that at Byron's funeral " Campbell's conversation [was] in very bad taste." It has been suggested that Campbell's
rancour may have been caused by the resemblances between his poem,
The Last Man, and Byron's *Darkness*. Such an explanation certainly
does not heighten Campbell in one's estimation.

[2] *Memoir of Lady Blessington*, i, 78.

Hobhouse consulted Lord Holland and other friends, and decided to make no public refutation of the charges which Campbell, by implication, had brought against Byron.[1]

Of the almost innumerable reviews of Moore's biography [2] the most important are those by Lockhart and Macaulay. These I have therefore selected for examination. Lockhart,[3] who had read parts of Moore's book in manuscript and had sent him messages of encouragement as well from Scott as from himself and his wife, roundly asserts :

If . . . any man qualified to understand and enjoy the higher productions of Lord Byron could ever have doubted that [his] . . . real nature was a noble one, this book will put an end to his scepticism ;

---

[1] Lord Broughton, *Recollections*, iv. 17.

[2] *The Athenæum* devoted three notices (over thirty-three columns in all) to the book (December 25, 1830 ; January 1 and 8, 1831). It well sums up the general impression made by Moore : " The effect . . . will be . . . to raise Lord Byron in the esteem, or, at least, in the liking of those who are most inclined to condemn him. . . . We had long ceased to regard him as great ; but we are now persuaded that he was not altogether bad." *The British Critic* of April 1831 contained a review of Moore and Galt that was republished in book-form as a *Review of the Life and Character of Lord Byron* (1833). The catalogue of the British Museum gives C. W. Le Bas as the author's name. The republication is explained on the ground that as the readers of *The British Critic* were chiefly clergymen, the review deserved wider circulation. It is one of the most virulent attacks on Byron that I have read. It opens with bitter denunciations of Moore's motives in publishing his book. The writer declares himself sick of all this talk of Byron. Byron is an evil influence upon youth ; he was an infidel, a scoffer, a libertine. His liberalism was sheer cant. He was the monstrous combination of a peer and a radical. Le Bas believes that Byron talked to Dr. Kennedy on religion in order to get material for a new canto of *Don Juan.* Moore's book is said to be like honey used to embalm a festering carcass ; Moore has tried " to sweeten the memory of dissoluteness and impiety." Le Bas ends : " Let [people] think of the sickening, jaded, and shattered sensualist in the Capreæ of his Italian exile—rebel against God and slanderer of God's creatures— infesting the world with the outpourings of blasphemy and vice, and courting immortal infamy in the cantos of *Don Juan.*" This notice casts light, if not on Byron, at least upon the clerical subscribers to *The British Critic.* Of American reviews of Moore the most interesting and thoughtful are two by Hugh Swinton Legaré in *The Southern Review.* See my bibliography. For other notices see *The Mirror*, No. 411 ; *The Monthly Depository*, December 1830 ; *The Monthly Review*, April 1830 ; *Blackwood's*, February and March, 1830 ; *Fraser's Magazine*, March 1831. W. L. Bowles's *Letter to Lord Holland* (1830) has nothing to do with the history of Byron's fame.

[3] Lockhart noticed Moore and Millingen together in *The Quarterly Review*, xliv, January 1831, pp. 168 f.

and continuing, he speaks of

the sincerity with which, though capable of wasting his talents, . . . Lord Byron appealed, in the works for which posterity will honour his name, to the purest and loftiest feelings of his kind.

He of course attacks Byron's political opinions, and laments

the scandalous insults . . . offered to the late king [which] were . . . designed and . . . calculated to please certain *liberal* circles in those days. . . . They excited, however, proportional disgust. . . . Byron had . . . degraded himself as a man.

To this disgust with Byron's politics Lockhart attributes (rightly) part of the animus in the attacks on Byron in 1816. The decline in the poet's genius, the reviewer continues, was due to debauchery and strong drink, from the heights of *Manfred* and *Sardanapalus* to " such flimsy lucubrations as occupy fifteen out of every twenty stanzas in the later cantos of *Don Juan.*" Lockhart deplores Moore's narration of the details of Byron's Venetian life.[1]

Macaulay's review of Moore [2] is a classic in its way ; not, however, a very admirable way. The estimate of Byron, while not positively hostile, is in the main unsympathetic and mistaken. For long it was influential. Macaulay begins with a survey of Byron's career ; and first, his bad upbring-ing as " a spoiled child " of parent, nature, fortune, fame, and society. Thence to the injustice of the violent reaction from popularity ; and the critic introduces his famous digression on the periodic fits of British morality that demands a scapegoat. This reaction was in part also due to the waning popularity of his writings ; the novelty was wearing off. But after leaving England " his complaints were read

---

[1] Lockhart bitterly attacks Leigh Hunt's " coxcombical libel," remarking that " it is possible to possess, in the almost total absence of every other talent, a potent one for producing deep and permanent disgust. This is Mr. Hunt's forte." Towards the end of his review Lockhart con-siders Byron's views on religion, taking the stand that the poet's emotional reverence is no proper substitute for subscription to definite dogma. Here he quotes much from Millingen's book.

[2] *The Edinburgh Review*, liii, June 1831, 544 f. ; reprinted in *Critical and Miscellaneous Essays* (1841), i, 328 f., and in various other places.

with tears by . . . tens of thousands who had never seen his face." His reckless Venetian life, despite the comparative betterment of the later years with La Guiccioli, were " the ruin of his fine intellect. His verse lost much of the energy and condensation which had distinguished it." Then the unfortunate effort of *The Liberal* and the final expedition to Greece. After this résumé Macaulay turns to general considerations. " Lord Byron," he says (and though he was not the first to say it, his dogmatic assertion fastened the dictum upon literary criticism as the conventional thing to say about Byron), " never wrote without some reference, direct or indirect, to himself." And again : " He was himself the beginning, the middle, and the end of all his own poetry, the hero of every tale, the chief object in every landscape." Only a future age can judge his poems fairly ; " at present they are not books but relics ; to us he is still a man, young, noble, and unhappy." A long digression on the contrasts between classic and romantic poetry leads to the recognition that " Byron was . . . the mediator between two generations, between two hostile poetical sects." Macaulay is the first prominent critic to observe this, though it had been apparent to Byron himself, who remarks on the contradiction between his principles and his practices in poetry. After noting Byron's lack of dramatic talent, his inability to depict different sorts of men and women, the rudeness and carelessness of the structure of his narrative poems, and his excellence in description and meditation, Macaulay turns to Byron's misanthropy. How much was this morbid feeling due to disease of mind, to real misfortune, to fancy, to affectation ?

We are far . . . from thinking that his sadness was altogether feigned. . . . How far the character in which he exhibited himself was genuine, and how far theatrical, it would probably have puzzled himself to say. . . . Men who affect in their compositions qualities and feelings which they have not, impose . . . much more easily on their contemporaries than on posterity. . . . There was not a single note of human anguish of which he was not the master.

And so Macaulay comes to the question of Byron's evil influence, and with characteristic rhetorical exaggeration speaks of the

pernicious association between intellectual power and moral depravity, . . . a system of ethics, compounded of misanthropy and voluptuousness, a system in which the two great commandments were, to hate your neighbour, and to love your neighbour's wife.

But the critic closes on a more generous note : " A few more years will destroy whatever yet remains of that magical potency which once belonged to the name of Byron." Then he must be judged solely by his works. There will be severe sifting ; but much that is imperishable will remain.[1] . . . On the whole the review is as fair an estimate as could be expected from one who represented so much that was antithetical to Byron ; who had so little of the continental outlook ; who opposed the principles of the French Revolution ; who was proud of the commercial greatness of England; who so well embodied what was best in the great middle class that was being swept into power by the Reform Bill and that was itself thoroughly anti-Byronic.[2]

John Galt's *Life of Lord Byron* (1830) was avowedly written to supplement Moore's biography. In his preface Galt says that Moore was over-anxious

to set out the best qualities of his friend ; . . . the spirit of the times ran strong against Lord Byron, as a man ; and it was natural, that Mr. Moore should attempt to stem the tide.

Galt's object is to portray Byron's intellectual character, not to recount the details of his private life. To this task Galt brought the novelist's training in observation and interpretation of character ; but when he attempts to philosophize and

---

[1] One notes with interest how often early critics prophesy the disappearance of the fascination of Byron's personality—the very phase of Byron's appeal that is far stronger in the twentieth century than is that of his poetry.

[2] See G. O. Trevelyan, *Life and Letters of Lord Macaulay* (1877), i, 199 and 227, for Macaulay's other impressions of Byron.

to draw general conclusions he is feeble in the extreme. Yet
on the whole, and despite the fact that the *Life* is a piece of
hackwork, Galt turned his literary craftsmanship to good
account and produced a more human book than Moore's.
There is a disproportionate emphasis on the poet's early life,
for Galt had met Byron at Gibraltar in 1809, travelled with
him for a time, and later saw something of him at Athens in
1811.[1] Galt is partly responsible for the underestimation
(against which Morley long afterwards protested) of Byron's
motives in going to Greece.[2] But even to-day interesting
and picturesque matter may be found in the book,[3] and it
has " lived " better than any other early biography of
Byron.[4]

To touch Byron's life has always been to risk a plunge
into controversy ; and Galt's experience was no exception
to this rule. Hobhouse was much offended by Galt's
references to him,[5] and several unsatisfactory letters passed
between the two men, the upshot of which was that Galt
published the acrimonious correspondence in *Fraser's
Magazine*.[6] Reviews of this *Life* were to a greater degree

[1] *The Athenæum* (September 4, 1830, p. 552), in the course of a harsh
review, remarked that " a steam-boat acquaintance " is not a qualification
for writing a man's biography. *Fraser's Magazine* (October 1830, p. 347 f.)
reproved *The Athenæum* for its strictures and noticed Galt's book
favourably, while not agreeing with his estimate of Byron. " The question
is, had Byron that inappreciable gift which we denominate genius ? We
think, undoubtedly not." Moore's feelings on reading Galt may be
gathered from this entry in his journal (*Memoirs*, etc., vi, 146) : " Amused
myself . . . by composing a squib against Galt's *Life of Byron*, which
that wretched thing richly deserves."
[2] " He was aware that the bright round of his fame was ovalling from
the full. . . . He was, moreover, tired of the Guiccioli " (p. 274).
[3] Miss Mayne introduces many excerpts from it into her biography of
Byron. J. C. Roe (*Obscure and Disputed Points*, p. v) considers it valuable
" as the first attempt at a relation of the history of the Byron family."
Roe evidently did not know of the nine pages devoted to that subject,
quite accurately set forth, by the Rev. J. Nightingale in 1816.
[4] Galt's *Life* was prefixed to a Paris edition of Byron's *Works* in 1837.
It has frequently been reprinted separately, the latest edition being of
1908.
[5] See Lord Broughton's *Recollections*, iv, 47 f. and 53.
[6] " Pot *versus* Kettle," *Fraser's Magazine*, ii, December 1830, 533 f.
From this I quote Hobhouse's remark : " You have fallen into many
errors . . . chiefly . . . from having relied too implicitly on the catch-
penny compilations of your predecessors. . . . Byron . . . was not the
mean tricky creature you have represented him." These charges Galt
denies.

even than usual mixed up with political prejudices, the
notice in the *Edinburgh* [1] being chiefly Whiggery.

We have now to glance at *Conversations on Religion, with
Lord Byron and others* (1830), by James Kennedy. Kennedy
died before his book appeared, and his work, already un-
scholarly, suffered much from ignorant editing. If it
had any influence at all, it may have been favourable to
Byron's reputation among the orthodox. But Byron was
almost certainly quizzing Kennedy. Richard Edgcumbe [2]
speaks of the " worthless tittle-tattle " of the book and adds
that a sense of humour would have deterred Kennedy " from
recording Byron's idle banter as his serious and settled
opinion." Byron's attitude, in a word, as reported by
Kennedy, is that of a sceptic who wishes to believe and who
seeks information on religious subjects. A writer in *The
London Magazine* [3] suggests that " the real reason for his
holding so many conferences with Dr. Kennedy in Cephalonia,
was, that he might master the slang of a religious sect, in
order to hit off the character with more verisimilitude."
This is quite possibly true.[4]

[1] Vol. lii, October 1830, 230 f.
[2] *The Athenæum*, December 14, 1901, p. 814.   According to J. C. Roe
(p. ix) the very worst description of Byron is that of " the psalm-singing
and ignorant Kennedy."   *Fraser's Magazine* (ii, October 1830, 347) calls
Kennedy " a weak-headed Evangelical though a well-intentioned twaddler."
See also *The Monthly Review*, August 1830.
[3] October 1824.
[4] An article on " Lord Byron's Theology," *The Monthly Repository*,
January 1830, should be compared with Kennedy's book.   Other minor
Byroniana of 1830 are : (1) " Lord Byron in Italy," *The Court Journal*,
April 10, 1830, pp. 226 f.   This claims to be specially translated from the
memoirs of " a celebrated French woman."   I have not been able to
identify the original.   It is gossip of La Guiccioli, Byron's lameness, his
friends, his opinions, etc.   (2) " Reminiscences of Lord Byron in Italy,"
The Mirror, 1830, pp. 266 f. and 278 f.   This is a version of Stendhal's
article, " Lord Byron en Italie et en France," *Revue de Paris*, March 1830.
(3) " The Ghost of Byron," *Devizes Gazette*, September 30, 1830.   This
tells of an apparition or " striking hallucination " that came to a person
who had been reading one of the new books on Byron.   (4) *Personal
Memoirs* by Pryse Lockhart Gordon.   This is of some biographical interest.
Gordon met Byron at Brussels in August 1816, and found him cordial and
courteous.   Gordon visited the field of Waterloo with Byron and pointed
out to him the specially important spots.   It was in Mrs. Gordon's scrap-
book that Byron first set down two stanzas on the battle which afterwards,
elaborated, appeared in *Childe Harold*.   It was Gordon who first introduced Byron to Casti's *Novelle Amorose*, thus setting him in the way towards
Don Juan.   Anecdotes of the poet's childhood are included, for Gordon
had known Byron's mother.   This picture of Byron is very pleasant.

In 1823 a physician named Julius Millingen went out to Greece to offer his services in a professional capacity to the revolutionary government. His plan came to nothing, and he opened a dispensary at Missolonghi. There he attended Byron in his last illness; and in 1831 published *Memoirs of the Affairs of Greece with Anecdotes relating to Lord Byron and an account of his last Illness and Death.* Though he testifies to Byron's many good qualities and pronounces himself " incapable of enumerating the faults of one, from whom I received so many marks of kindness," Millingen's book contains no new information.[1] It occasioned a rancorous attack on Millingen and Bruno (Byron's other physician at Missolonghi) from E. J. Trelawny.[2]

After serial publication during 1832, *The Conversations of Lord Byron with the Countess of Blessington* appeared in book-form in 1834.[3] Miss Mayne's judgment [4] of the *Conversations* is:

There is no comparison between this book, so far as it goes, and any other except Galt's for the early days. Taking these together, we get a convincing impression which the longer biographies scarcely do more than impair. This impression is not wholly favourable.

To my mind, the Countess's impressions of Byron, though not altogether intentionally on her part, are distinctly favourable. The evidence which she gives of Byron's lack

---

[1] Edgcumbe (*The Athenæum*, December 14, 1901, p. 814) calls it " as dead as a doornail."

[2] *The London Literary Gazette*, February 12, 1831. Trelawny here prints extracts from an unpublished diary. He tells how every one was suffering from fever on Missolonghi and how he cursed Millingen and Bruno for not having given warning of the danger of remaining there. When Byron was stricken, the fatal outcome proved the ignorance of these " boyish charlatans." Trelawny says that the dying Byron ordered the two doctors out of his room. After Byron's death Millingen came down with fever and Trelawny found him whimpering; but he recovered. Later, says Trelawny, Millingen deserted the Greeks and went over to the Turks. Trelawny is equally bitter against Mavrocordato, from whose possession he extracted with difficulty Byron's money chest after the poet's death. So violent are Trelawny's expressions that the editor of the *Gazette* is constrained to substitute asterisks for some of his sentences.

[3] First published in *Colburn's New Monthly Magazine*, 1832.

[4] *Byron*, ii, 256.

of refinement, vulgar tastes, flippancy, and pride in rank
is partly offset by the obvious signs of pique, disappointment and annoyance that appear in the journal, for (to
use the familiar expression) Byron did not " fall for " her
Ladyship.   Yet to Landor Lady Blessington wrote : [1]

I am glad . . . the *Conversations* . . . give you a better
opinion of Byron. . . . He was arrived at that period
in human life when he saw the fallacy of the past without
having grasped the wisdom of the future.[2]

Lady Blessington's book closes my account of the biographical studies of Byron of this period.   I turn now to
two poems of the same period.

Lord Byron with Remarks on his Genius and Character,
by Edward Bagnall (1831) contains a long prose introduction
on Byron's love of fame, waywardness, passion, intellectual
greatness, and the "sympathizing energy of his work."
There follows the poem in 127 octaves [3] ; it is in the main
a meditation upon the heavy doom under which Byron
lived, leaving friends and country, separated from his family,
and branded by hatred with the epithet " Satanic."   But
the rage of bigots cannot obscure the services of " martyr'd
Byron," to Greece, and " Harold's monument " is in the
mind of man.[4]

In 1836 appeared *An Apology for Lord Byron,* by Stephen
Prentis.   The preface begins : " In submitting this—the
mere sample, as it were, of what, with encouragement, may
ultimately prove a long—poem," the author disavows
" even the slightest covert design against the sacred cause
of religion and morality."   But Byron's shortcomings

---

[1] Madden, ii, 106.

[2] Lady Blessington's *Idler in Italy* (1839) contains many miscellaneous
remarks on Byron and Shelley, but nothing of importance.   In her later
book, *The Lottery of Life* (1842), one finds " Thoughts on Lord Byron,
suggested by a picture representing his contemplation of the Coliseum."
She discusses the beneficial influence of Rome on Byron, but adds really
nothing to the material of the *Conversations.   The Gentleman's Magazine,*
April and May, 1834, and *The Monthly Review,* April 1834, contain the best
reviews of the *Conversations* that I have seen.   See also M. Blümel's dissertation in my bibliography.

[3] With the variant of an alexandrine last line.

[4] See *The Athenæum,* 1831, p. 200.

admit of palliation and call for pity. Prentis calls his first instalment a " mere feeler." It is mainly a queer diatribe against flirts and jilts whom the author holds responsible for turning men of passionate temperament to " Cyprus." Byron, though but a tyro in debauchery, aped the graceless follies of other men and turned to the market. Such action was moral suicide ; but in Byron's case there was another aspect of this lava-flow : poetry. " The choicest chaplet of a bard was twin'd " around Byron's brows. He won fame and flattery, but not happiness, and he felt " the prickly berry of a poet's bays." To shield himself from memories of the past he chose the most ineffectual screen possible, " an uncongenial wife." Here the first part ends ; the author was evidently not encouraged to proceed—which is not surprising.[1]

From poeticules and minor critics I now turn abruptly to the great John Ruskin, who was destined in later years to be influential in the revival of interest in Byron, and who in *Praeterita* tells of his early love and admiration for the poet. Writing of his fifteenth year he says : [2]

I never got the slightest harm from Byron ; what harm came to me was from the facts of life, and from books of a baser kind. . . . The thing wholly new and precious to me in Byron was his measured and living *truth*. . . . Here at last I had found a man who spoke only of what he had seen and known ; and spoke without exaggeration, without mystery, without enmity, and without mercy. . . . In this narrow, but sure, truth, to Byron, as already to me, it appeared that Love was a transient thing, and Death a dreadful one. He did not attempt to console me. . . . He did not tell me that war was a just price for the glory of captains, or that the National command of murder diminished its guilt. Of all things within the range of human thought he felt the facts, and discerned the natures with accurate justice. . . . He sympathized with me in reverent love

---

[1] It is perhaps worth mentioning, as a comment upon literary aspirations, that the leaves of the copy of Prentis's *Apology* in the British Museum remained unopened until I cut them in November 1921.

[2] *Praeterita ; The Works of John Ruskin*, Library Edition, xxxv, 143, 148, 151.

of beauty, and indignant recoil from ugliness. . . . Even Shakespeare's Venice was visionary ; and Portia as impossible as Miranda. But Byron told me of, and reanimated for me, the real people whose feet had worn the marble I trod on.

Already in 1836 Ruskin had fixed upon those noble qualities in Byron which as an old man he was to discuss so eloquently in *Fiction Fair and Foul*. In the precocious *Essay on Literature*, written when he was but seventeen, he remarks that at the mention of *The Bride of Abydos* there is bound to be " a murmur of indignation " from the critics (whom he calls " the multitudes of crawling things "). But he dares to praise that poem ; and then continues : [1]

We have known minds, and great ones too, which were filled with such a horror of Byron's occasional immorality, as to be unable to separate his wheat from his chaff—unable to bask themselves in the light of his glory without fearing to be scorched by his sin. These we have pitied, and they have deserved pity, for they are debarred from one of the noblest feasts that ever fed the human intellect. . . There is not, there cannot be, a human being " of soul so dead " as not to feel that he is a better man, that his ideas are higher, his heart purer, his feelings nobler, his spirit less bound by his body, after feeding on such poetry. . . . There *are* animals who neither have felt this inspiration themselves nor believe that others can feel it. They talk about Byron's immorality as if he were altogether immoral, and they actually appear to imagine that they ! they ! ! yes, they ! ! ! will be able to wipe away his memory from the earth.

In this quotation I have omitted a passage of characteristic generous exaggeration in which the youthful Ruskin declares that Byron, with the exception of Shakespeare only, was the greatest poet that ever lived—and proceeds to cite chapter and verse in proof of the assertion. In after years Ruskin's views on Byron changed from time to time ; in this as in other matters he was above mere consistency. His mature opinions will be considered in a later chapter.

[1] *Works*, i, 373 f.

The extent to which the appeal of Byron's personality was outlasting the attraction of his poetry to thoughtful minds is evident in allusions in the correspondence of the Brownings. In 1842 Elizabeth Barrett writes : [1]

Wordsworth is a philosophical and Christian poet, with depths in his soul to which poor Byron could never reach.

But in her next letter, to some remarks of her correspondent she replies :

I liberal in commending Byron ! Take out my heart and try it ! . . . Why, I am always reproached for my love to Byron. Why, people say to me, " *You*, who overpraise Byron."

Four years later Robert Browning writes to her [2] :

Lord Byron is altogether in my affection again.[3] . . . I . . . am quite sure of the great qualities which the last ten or fifteen years had partially obscured. Only a little longer life and all would have been gloriously right again. . . . I have always retained my first feeling for Byron in many respects [3] . . . the interest in the places he had visited, in relics of him. I would at any time have gone to Finchley to see a curl of his hair or one of his gloves, I am sure—while Heaven knows that I could not get up enthusiasm enough to cross the room if at the other end of it all Wordsworth, Coleridge, and Southey were condensed into the little China bottle yonder—they seem to " have their reward " and want nobody's love or faith.

In this last striking phrase Browning admirably sounds the depth of Byron's appeal to many minds.

That Byronism lasted for a longer time in America than in England might be abundantly shown were not trans-Atlantic criticism beyond the boundaries that I have set to this inquiry.[4] As it is, I must content myself with some brief

---

[1] *Letters of E. B. Browning*, i, 114 f.
[2] *Letters of Robert Browning and Elizabeth Barrett Browning, 1845–1846*, ii, 455 f.
[3] The omissions at these two points are in the published letters.
[4] See, of course, Professor W. E. Leonard's *Byron and Byronism in America*.

comments in a foot-note [1] and pass in another direction
beyond the strict limits of English criticism so as to include
a remarkable protest against anti-Byronism from the pen
of Joseph Mazzini, who, because of his long periods of
residence in England and his intimacy with many English
men of letters, exercised an influence in the land that sheltered
him as an exile. Mazzini's essay on Byron was originally
written in Italian, but a translation appeared in 1839.[2]
His subject is the English reaction against Byron—" I
do not speak of that mixture of cant and stupidity which

---

[1] With no attempt at completeness I note these few items that appear
to me significant: (1) The first of a series of " Stars that have set in the
Nineteenth Century," in *The Democratic Review*, is an article on Byron, by
L. F. T. (n.s., x, 1842, 225 f.) The title is misleading, for the essay is
wholly laudatory. (2) " Byron " by Edwin P. Whipple (*North American
Review*, January 1845 ; reprinted in *Essays and Reviews*, 1848, i, 254 f.).
This essay is notable for its understanding of Byron's function as the voice
of social unrest : " He gave voice not only to the political discontents of
his time, but to the inward misery, the sceptical distrust of goodness and
religion, the diseased sensibility, the half-formed opinions and mad impulses,
which characterized the excitable spirits of his age." (3) " The Moral
Philosophy of Byron's Life," in *Lectures and Essays* by Henry Giles (1850),
i, 93 f. and 136 f. This is frankly not an estimate of Byron's genius and
achievement, but an attempt to establish the moral of his life and genius.
It is severely hostile. I quote one sentence : " The head must be grievously
confused by false reasoning, and the heart deeply imbruted by false
morality, before we can believe that a poet has fountains of inspiration
in petulance, profligacy, and self-infliction." But the moralist adds in
conclusion : " If our opinion must be severe, we should not, in forming it,
forget that he has deprecated nothing by concealment, and that caution
might easily have secured him a better name, though it would not have
made him a better man." (4) " Byron," in *Thoughts on the Poets* by
Henry T. Tuckerman (1858), pp. 165 f. This is very favourable. It
attacks the cant about his " moral perversity." It declares that his verse
reveals " an infinite necessity for love, an eternal tendency to progress."
(5) " Byron," in *Lectures on the British Poets* by Henry Reed (1859), vol. ii.
(The manuscript of Reed's lectures is in the Library of the University of
Pennsylvania, shelf-mark, 820.91. A 253.)

[2] This translation, in *The Monthly Chronicle*, 1839, was later said to be
very incorrect. A somewhat better version—" Byron and Goethe "—was
made in 1870 (*Life and Writings*, 1891, vi, 61 f.). The translator was then
asked by Mazzini to say that " the twenty years [actually over thirty] of
study and experience which have passed over his head since those pages
were written have only tended to increase rather than diminish the
sympathy and admiration with which he has always regarded [Byron]. He
would gladly hope that . . . the article may awaken . . . a new interest
in this very important subject, and lead to a more impartial and serious
study of Lord Byron's life and works than Englishmen have been
accustomed to bestow upon them." Of Mazzini's essay Swinburne said :
" It seems to me that Mazzini alone has hit the mark which should be
aimed at by all who undertake the apology or attempt the panegyric of
Byron " (" Wordsworth and Byron," *Miscellanies*, p. 74).

denies the poet his place in Westminster Abbey, but of literary reaction "—which, says Mazzini, has shown itself still more unreasoning than the German reaction against Goethe. He holds that the mistake has been made of trying to set up an absolute standard of poetic beauty " without regard to the state of social relations as they were or are." It is *with* regard to the state of social relations that Byron becomes significant.

[He] appears at the close of one epoch, and before the dawn of another ; in the midst of a community based upon an aristocracy which has outlived the vigour of its prime.

Byron portrays a hero-type modelled upon " those privileged by strength, beauty, and individual power." His song is " the epitaph of the aristocratic idea." But

the day will come when Democracy will remember all that it owes to Byron. England, too, will, I hope, one day remember the mission—so entirely English, yet hitherto overlooked by her—which Byron fulfilled on the Continent.

If a transition is needed from the group of writers who continued to admire Byron to those who were leaders in the movement away from his influence, it can be furnished by a few words on John Murray's pious and profitable task of a definitive edition of the poet's works. In 1827 Murray wrote to a friend : [1] " The public are absolutely indignant at not being able to obtain a complete edition of Lord Byron's works in his country." He adds that 15,000 sets, printed in France, have been smuggled into England and sold. Murray had before now expressed regret at the foolish " half and half prudery " (as Byron called it) which had resulted in the severance of poet and publisher. About three years after Byron's death he opened negotiations with the brothers Hunt for the purchase of the copyrights of those later works of Lord Byron which they had published. The arrangements were not quickly agreed to, and at length the copyright of all works by Byron not already

---

[1] Smiles, ii, 305 f.

in Murray's possession was put up at auction and bought by Murray for £ 3885. Murray then placed John Wright in charge as editor of the complete collected edition, including the letters, journals, miscellaneous prose writings, and Moore's " Notices." This appeared in 1832–33, in seventeen volumes. Its wealth of new editorial material stimulated comment and interest, and for long it remained the handiest, pleasantest, and most distinguished edition of Byron's works. Even to-day its delightful appearance, its convenient format, and the modesty, sobriety, and restraint of its lovely line engravings make it a charming possession. More than twenty thousand copies were sold by the time the final volume appeared.[1]

For a long while yet Byron was far more widely read than the other great poets, still alive or but lately dead, whose fame was gradually encroaching upon his own ; and the number of imitations of his poetry, the amount of false, shoddy, derivative Byronism that poured from the press testifies to the continued popularity of the mood and manner of his verse. His imitators, however, were engaged in undermining his prestige by wearying people with echoes of his more obvious cadences and by apeing insincerely his more easily reproduced characteristics. In his preface to The Siamese Twins (1831) [2] Bulwer urges that the time

[1] For the collation of this important edition see E. H. Coleridge's bibliography (Poetry, vii, 114 f.).

[2] Bulwer says that Byron's genius " so long taught the public to consider stimulants as a legitimate diet, that while, on the one hand, no succeeding poet could surpass the excitation which he maintained ; so, on the other hand, any simpler—I was about to say any more natural—school of poetry might reasonably be expected to appear commonplace and insipid. . . . Thus it may be no paradox to say that a new poet has of late incurred condemnation on two grounds, . . . one for being unlike Lord Byron, the other for being like him." Some of the ideas set forth in The Siamese Twins Bulwer had already expressed in a Socratic dialogue called " Conversation with an Ambitious Student in ill health " (The New Monthly Magazine, December 1830 ; reprinted in Critical and Miscellaneous Writings, i, 89 f.). Of the Byronists Bulwer here says : " Nothing seems to me more singular in the history of imitations than the extraordinary misconception which all Lord Byron's imitators have incurred with respect to the strain they have attempted to echo. The great characteristics of Lord Byron are vigour, nerve—the addressing at once the common feelings and earthly passions—never growing mawkish, never girlishly sentimental —never, despite all his digressions, encouraging the foliage to the prejudice of the fruit. What are the characteristics of the imitators ? They are

has come for a new school of poetry to arise ; new feelings
require new forms of expression. In the satire itself
Bulwer refers repeatedly to the fact that he is not imitating
Byron.   He describes himself [1] as

> Too glad if thou wilt not despise
> A tale that boasts no charming Giaours ;

and declares : [2]

> My Muse, although no syren
> Is honest, nor purloins from Byron.

Another passage [3] ridicules poetic melancholy, with special
allusion to Byron and Moore ; and in still another [4] he
satirizes the Corsair-like gloom and mystery with which
Chang, one of the persons in the tale, leaves England.
Among the minor pieces in the same volume is a squib
" On the Imitators of Byron." [5]   This tells how the black
Swan hymned mournful music ; the rooks, black also,
tried to sing as mournfully :

> In vain we cry—" the secret you mistook,
> And grief is damned discordant in a rook."

To Bulwer I shall return ; but at this point a digression
is essential in order that we may understand how these
imitators damaged Byron's fame. I have ventured far
into the rank jungle of Byronic pastiche, and from it I have
brought back a few specimens of what grew there. It was
of one of Bulwer's " rooks " that *The Athenæum* wrote : [6]

This is one of the poems which the Laras, the Conrads, the
Alps, and the Mazeppas of Byron have to answer for. . . .
It is much easier to imitate his weakness than his strength.
We have in the works of his imitators, imposing attitudes,

weak—they whine—they address *no* common passion—they heap up
gorgeous words—they make pyramids of flowers—they abjure vigour—
they talk of appealing ' to the few congenial minds '—they are proud of
wearying you, and consider the want of interest the proof of a sublime
genius."

[1] *The Siamese Twins*, Introduction to book ii, p. 70.
[2] *Ibid.*, book ii, chapter i, p. 74.
[3] *Ibid.*, book iii, chapter iii, pp. 177 f.
[4] *Ibid.*, book iv, chapter iii, p. 247
[5] P. 298.
[6] December 31, 1831, p. 846.

fierce chiefs, turbaned hordes, banished princes, wandering
dervishes, strolling virgins, descriptions of rocks and isles,
and ruined temples—plenty of love and abundance of
bloodshed ; but none of that scorching sarcasm, fiery
sentiment, whirlwind passion, and wit withering as the
glance of Beelzebub, which marked the moody Lord.

The name of the imitators is legion. We have seen them
attempting to carry on *Don Juan* or writing would-be
original poems in the manner of Byron's masterpiece.
We have seen their imitations of *Beppo*. We have seen
them foisting upon the public spurious poems as Byron's
work. The accumulated dust of a century rests upon their
productions.

They began betimes. The opening of an anonymous
poem entitled *Rothley Temple* [1] (1815) illustrates the mingling
of elements from Scott and Byron :

> December's eve is dark and still :
> The winds are slumbering on the hill.
> The stars are faint : a crescent low
> Is all the infant moon can show. . . .
> By Rothley brook the strangers come,
> Three shadowy forms, with martial pace,
> Like Phantoms of heroic race.
> The clanking step, the armour's gleam,
> Sounds on the margin, lights the stream.
> The otter, couching on the stump,
> Sinks in the pool with sullen plump.

Here are night and mystery, three shadowy forms, and the
conventional trappings of romance. Of another anonymous
poem, professedly imitated from Byron, the title—*The
Recluse of the Pyrenees* [2]—and the opening lines will sufficiently indicate the manner :

> Helpless he lies, upon his bloody lair,
> No comrade's watchful eye to guard him there.[3]

[1] *Rothley Temple. A Poem. In Three Cantos* (London : Cadell and
Davies, 1815). (As these imitations are not included in my bibliography, I
shall supply in foot-notes the publisher's name.)
[2] London : Longman, 1818.
[3] A reviewer of this piece remarked : " The popularity of a great
poet may . . . be lessened for a time by the botching crew of imitators
which his genius may draw after him " (unidentified newspaper clipping
in the B. M. scrapbook).

Oswald. A Tale, by a writer with the euphonious name of
T. G. Veal,[1] is very definitely in the manner of Byron's
oriental narrative poems.   Another tale so exactly in the
earlier Byronic mood as to be pastiche is *Tancred*.[2] The hero,
a slave, languishes on a foreign coast.   There is a description of sunset on a wild and solitary shore.   The castaway indulges in memories of his Lost Love.   Complications
begin, and, as the tale progresses, increase, with poison,
vengeance, castled halls, and escape " grappling upon the
mountain precipice."   Then follows (according to the usual
recipe for a " Byronic " poem) a description of the simple
life of nature and an encounter with a " beauteous stranger "
who turns out to be the Lost Love.   Tancred's stormy
passions are hushed for a time and he is supremely blessed.
But his tale of course ends tragically.   The Byronic cadences
and the superficialities of the Byronic outlook on life are
combined in an anonymous poem in five cantos entitled
Almegro.[3] The scene is laid in Spanish Morocco.   There
is a castle in which midnight meetings take place.   A
mysterious stranger occupies a large share in the tale.   This
is the opening :

> Slow rose the morn—the eastern sky, array'd
> In soften'd tints, a splendid view displayed. . . .
> Almegro, now the last of all his race,
> Travers'd the dewy lawn with pensive pace,
> His rolling eye was cast upon the green,
> And seem'd to contemplate some distant scene.

He had been " cast early on the theatre of life " ; his " mien "
had altered since former days—

> For still the elements that form'd his mind
> Discordant jarr'd like chaos—scarce confin'd.

The View, by Chandos Leigh,[4] a good example of the

---

[1] London : Longman, 1818.
[2] *Tancred, a Tale ; and other Poems. By the Author of Conrad, a Tragedy.* (London : B. M'Millan, 1819.)
[3] London : H. Hodson, 1819.
[4] London : William Sams, 1819. This piece is written in Spenserians. The volume also contains a brief ranting satire on " Poesy," beginning :

> Who can be silent now ? do thou inspire
> My verse with Gifford's spirit, Byron's fire,
> Great Nemesis !

many imitations of *Childe Harold*, canto iii, deserves
slightly fuller notice, for it is of some interest as showing
English concern for Italy. Beginning in Switzerland, the
writer describes Mont Blanc and other parts of the Alps.
He muses upon " Nature's Deity " and upon Calvin, Mme.
de Staël, and other great personages associated with Lake
Leman. If one had no other duties, he exclaims, in
yonder vale might " a second Paradise " be found. But
he looks towards Italy (as Byron had done at the close
of his canto), and presently he goes there, commenting
upon the country's misery, her need of unity, and her
many puny masters. He longs to find " those happy
Isles " where Nature " gives Byron's muse a deathless
wreath."

Another offspring of *Childe Harold*, but sprung from the
first cantos, is *Childe Albert* (1819).[1] Albert leaves England,
sails the seas, sings execrable songs, and approaching Italy
greets her with—

> Then hail soft Italia !   Hail land of the Graces !
> Hail land of the sweet-flowing river !
> Hail land of the vine !   Hail land of the myrtle !
> Hail land of luxuriance for ever !

Here is the conclusion :

> Out upon gloom !   What need have I
> To mourn—to mourn in Italy,
>   That land of love ?
> But 'tis no use—in vain I fly,
>   In vain I rove
> From clime to clime, from shore to shore,
> Recollection clings to me, and no more
> Will leave me than th' unerring tide
> Its changes stay—yon streamlet cease to glide
> Along its course—Would it were the river
> That history feigns, of forgetfulness for ever !

In Byron's time the Mediterranean was simply infested with
these recollection-haunted vagabonds !

[1] A list of imitations of *Childe Harold* is in Reschke's *Die Spenserstanze*,
pp. 108 f.

I have to note *Misplaced Love*, by S. R. Jackson.[1] This begins :

> Saw ye the spot, where weeping willows wave
> Their spreading branches o'er a lowly grave ;
> Saw ye the spot, where early wild flowers shed
> Their blushing sweetness o'er the silent dead ;
> Mark well the place, for where these willows rise,
> Bernado ! hapless child of sorrow lies.

For Bernado, loving Adelaide, for her sake gave up his relatives rather than renounce her ; and was cast off by his father only to find the faithless Adelaide in the arms of another lover. He slays her ; scorns to slay her paramour ; and kills himself on the spot where formerly he and she had parted with mutual pledges. The piece shows how easily and pointlessly the externals of Byronism could be imitated. Another excessively Byronic volume is *Viatoria*.[2] This tells of travels in the Alps and Italy, with allusions to Waterloo, Cintra, liberty, the fate of empires, and so forth. In the same volume is a " Fragment " in the form of *The Giaour*. Another imitation of *The Giaour* (the fragmentary disjointed narrative made it an easy mark for imitators) is *The Lilian Bride*, by Barton Wilford.[3] In theme, metre, and manner the resemblance is very close.

Before long we find echoes of Byron's Venetian poems. They are very audible in *Estafelle*, by J. D. Newman.[4] The poem opens :

> O Venice, thou proud consort of the sea,
> Thou city of the waters !—not a wave
> Flows by thy palaces but casts at thee
> The sneer of foul reproach. The nobly brave
> Shun thy fallen grandeur, as though lording there
> Were death and desolation and despair.

[1] *The Lament of Napoleon, Misplaced Love, and Minor Poems* (London : Printed for the Author, 1819). The first piece is a rather interesting bit of dramatic monologue, spoken by Napoleon at St. Helena.
[2] *Viatoria, with a Fragment and Other Poems* (London : E. G. Triquet, 1820).
[3] London : Sherwood, Neely, and Jones, 1821. Among the minor poems in this book are stanzas " On Seeing a Lady Weep " which are redolent of Byron.
[4] *Estafelle. The Wreck : A Fisherman's Tale* (London : Printed for the Author, 1824).

The tale is of a wealthy girl who loves a poor gondolier. They attempt to elope, but he is killed and she is taken off by her dead lover's " minion " across the sea. This minion ravishes her; and then falls asleep. The poor Estafelle topples him overboard. He awakes and tries to climb into the gondola again; but she grasps an oar and—

> Full on his forehead fell the deadly stroke,
> The brain was driven from its wonted place.

Later the gondola is wrecked, and her beautiful corpse washed ashore.[1]

Ianthe, by John W. Dalby,[2] is another offshoot of *The Giaour*. Ianthe (note the name) is slain by her father on account of a love affair of which he does not approve.

The Italianizing fashion of the eighteen-twenties is visible in *Ugolino; or the Tower of Famine*, by Edward Wilmot.[3] In a foreword the author admits the resemblance, so far as the tale is of prisoners in a dungeon, to Byron's *Prisoner of Chillon*, and adds, with engaging frankness:

If any faint resemblance in metre should be discoverable, so far from wishing to deny the charge, the Author has only to regret that the resemblance should be *so* faint.

The opening lines will indicate the similarity:

> Tho' Arno's wave be calm and clear,
>   Yet like the guile
>   Of Fortune's smile
> Its flow of peace is not sincere.

---

[1] J. W. Dalby, in the volume next to be named, dedicates some stanzas " To the Author of *Estafelle*," congratulating him on having " fully established " a claim " to a Bardic name." Alas for literary aspirations !

[2] *The Death of Aguirre ; Ianthe, a Tale ; Bodian Castle ; Battle Abbey ; and Other Poems* (London : Leathwick, 1825). The volume is compounded of many influences, chief among them Byron, with Scott a close second, especially in *The Death of Aguirre*. More remarkable are the many echoes of Wordsworth. And interesting because of their early date are some " Lines written after viewing a Bust of the late John Keats." These lines begin :

> My spirit bows before thee, gentle Bust !
> In thee I trace the features of a Bard,
> Once full of fire and feeling—now all dust.

[3] London : William Sams, 1828.

The Traveller's Lay, by Thomas Maude,[1] is a bare-faced imitation of *Childe Harold*. Two stanzas are dedicated to Byron's memory among the other meditations which Lake Leman inspires. Here are a few lines :

> And here I tread where trod the lord of song,
> 'Mid the dwarf orchard where his towering mind
> Reposed a while from the world's fame and wrong. . . .
>   The wondrous Alps behind
> Sleep, as he slept when from their heights he drew
> Meet inspiration. . . .
> Yes ! Jura speaks of *him*—and the blue wave
> Whispers of him. . . .
> *His* shadow fills the scene.

The Last of the Sophis, by C. F. Henningham, A Minor,[2] is a tale of oriental love and war and crime, with interruptions of the narrative and a confession to a priest, in the manner of *The Giaour*. Notice the designation of the author as " A Minor." Lastly, one finds the oriental tradition of bulbuls and guls and rolling eyes so late as 1842 in *The Arab Bride, a Tale*, by S. W. Barber.[3] It begins with the abruptness which was part of the Byronic tradition :

> Far o'er the troubled deep a lurid gleam
> Bursts thro' yon cloud, from the sun's latest beam,
> And lights for a moment, with warning ray,
> A bark who still plougheth her onward way
> Thro' the grey mass of water.

Enough ! Having selected these sixteen specimens of degenerate Byronism I replace them on the shelves where another century's dust will fall unmolested upon them.[4] From George Brandes I draw the appropriate commentary :[5]

---

[1] London : Longman, 1830.
[2] London : Longman, 1831.
[3] London : Edward Bull.
[4] In *The Galaxy Miscellany* (June 1868, pp. 777 f.), W. E. McCann, in an article entitled " Byronism," while showing admiration for Byron, ridicules the absurd extremes of what may be called social, as distinct from literary, Byronism : " Mr. Moore's biography, when it came forth, . . . was eagerly seized upon as a sort of authority upon the Art of Being Byronic. . . . Nobody could be Byronic, without being dissipated and a gross libertine, so the gentlemen of England plunged into the wildest excesses. . . . In 1824 and the years that followed . . . by reference to various prints published at that time, it will be discovered that an astonishing number of persons who became Byronic, lost their wits entirely."
[5] *Main Currents*, iv, 253 f.

A whole succession of Byron's admirers and imitators have forced themselves in between him and us, obscuring the figure, and confusing our impression, of the great departed. Their qualities have been imputed to him, and he has been blamed for their faults.   When the literary reaction set in against those who had understood him half and wrongly— against the broken-hearted, the *blasés*, the enigmatical, writers—his great name suffered along with theirs, it was swept aside along with the lesser ones.   It had deserved better of fate.

To the evidence of this " literary reaction " we now come.[1]

Carlyle never fully made up his mind about Byron.   Two facts stand out when one examines his allusions to the subject : first, he differentiated between Byron and Byronism ; and second, his views gradually became more adverse.   He thus illustrates the change that took place between 1825 and 1840, as Byron's personal fascination temporarily receded into the past.   I have already quoted his eloquent lament on hearing of the poet's death.   In January 1825, writing to Miss Welsh,[2] he says, commenting upon the effect of modern life upon men of letters, that " they become discontented and despicable, or wretched and dangerous. Byron and all strong souls go the latter way ; Campbell and all weak souls the former."   In 1826 he writes : [3] " Our own noble and hapless Byron perished from among us at the instant when his deliverance seemed at hand."   He is still charitably inclined in an allusion of 1827 : [4]

Our Byron was in his youth but what Schiller and Goethe had been in theirs. . . .   With longer life, all things were to have been hoped for from Byron : for he loved truth in his inmost heart, and would have discovered at the last that his Corsairs and Harolds were not true.

---

[1] On March 25, 1825, Thomas Lovell Beddoes wrote to his friend Thomas Kelsall (*Letters*, p. 58) : " We ought too to look back with late repentance and remorse on our intoxicated praise, now cooling, of Lord Byron—such a man to be spoken of when the world possessed Goethe, Schiller, Shelley ! " And on July 19, 1830, he asked the same correspondent (*ibid.*, p 186) : " Do people read Lord Byron still as they used to—or is Montgomery really his successor ? "

[2] J. A. Froude, *Thomas Carlyle : First Forty Years*, i, 221.

[3] " German Romances," *Critical and Miscellaneous Essays*, i, 258.

[4] " The State of German Literature," *ibid.*, i, 69.

The famous essay on Burns (1828) has several notable and in the main still sympathetic references [1] to Byron, who is called "no common man." Having asked the question whether Byron's Harolds and Giaours are "real men . . . poetically consistent and conceivable men," he replies that they exhibit "no natural or possible mode of being, but something intended to look much grander than nature ; . . . more like the brawling of a player in some paltry tragedy."

Perhaps *Don Juan,* especially the latter parts of it,[2] is the only thing approaching to a *sincere* work, he ever wrote. . . . In him we can trace no such adjustment, no such moral manhood [as in Burns] ; but at best, and only a little before his end, the beginning of what seemed such. . . . His life is falsely arranged : the fire that is in him is not a strong, still, central fire, warming into beauty the products of a world ; but it is the mad fire of a volcano ; and now—we look sadly into the ashes of a crater, which ere long will fill itself with snow.

Up to this time, then, Carlyle seems to regard Byron as a Goethe who did not survive the period of storm and stress ; he judges his career as incomplete. Had Byron lived, Carlyle implies, he would have worked out his destiny to triumph. These favourable opinions change as Byronism takes the place of Byron. In 1828, studying the Helena episode of the second part of *Faust,* Carlyle questions the appropriateness of the tremendous allegorical tribute which suggests that Lord Byron is Euphorion, child of Faust and Helen, of the Middle Ages and Classical Antiquity. Reading between the lines of Carlyle's note one sees indications of contempt.[3] In the same year, speaking of *Werther,* he writes : [4]

Byron was our English Sentimentalist and Power-man ; the strongest of his kind in Europe ; the wildest, the gloomiest, and it may be hoped the last. . . . Why should we quarrel with our existence, here as it lies before

[1] "Burns," *Critical and Miscellaneous Essays,* i, 269, 293, 316.
[2] Note Carlyle's sympathy with Byron's attacks on British society.
[3] "Goethe's Helena," *Critical and Miscellaneous Essays,* i, 193.
[4] "Goethe," *ibid.,* i, 218.

us, our field and inheritance, to make or to mar, for better or
for worse ?

In 1830 he notes in his journal : [1] " Byron we call ' a dandy
of sorrows and acquainted with grief.' " In the same year
he asked Napier to allow him to review for the *Edinburgh*
Moore's biography ; Napier, however, fearing Carlyle's
extremes of statement, assigned the task to Macaulay.
Carlyle wrote Napier : [2]

His fame has been very great, but I do not see how it is to
endure ; neither does that make *him* great. No genuine
productive thought was ever revealed by him to mankind ;
indeed, no clear undistorted vision into anything ; . . .
but all had a certain falsehood, a brawling, theatrical,
insincere character.

In an eloquent passage in " Characteristics," [3] Carlyle,
discoursing on the theme of heroes which was now taking
shape in his mind, writes :

The Godlike has vanished from the world ; and they, by the
strong cry of their soul's agony, like true wonder-workers,
must again evoke its presence. This miracle is their
appointed task, which they must accomplish, or die
wretchedly ; this miracle has been accomplished by such ;
but not in our land ; our land yet knows not of it. Behold
a Byron, in melodious tones, " cursing his day " : he mistakes
earthborn passionate Desire for heaven-inspired Freewill ;
without heavenly loadstar, rushes madly into the dance of
meteoric lights that hover on the mad Mahlstrom ; and goes
down among its eddies. Hear a Shelley filling the earth
with inarticulate wail ; like the infinite, inarticulate grief
and weeping of forsaken infants.

This passage leads immediately on to the famous imperious
command in *Sartor* : [4]

Foolish soul ! What Act of Legislature was there that *thou*
shouldst be Happy ? A little while ago thou hadst no right

---

[1] Froude, ii, 75.
[2] Quoted by F. W. Roe, *Carlyle as a Critic of Literature*, p. 82.
[3] *Critical and Miscellaneous Essays*, iii, 31.
[4] Book ii, chapter ix.

to *be* at all.   What if thou wert born and predestined not to
be Happy, but to be Unhappy !   Art thou nothing other than
a Vulture, then, that fliest through the Universe seeking after
somewhat to *eat ;* and shrieking dolefully because carrion
enough is not given thee ?   Close thy *Byron ;* open thy
Goethe.

Carlyle's later references to Byron are uniformly hostile.
In 1832 he compares [1] Cervantes, " a genuine strong man,"
with Byron :

A strong man of recent time, fights little for any good cause
anywhere ;   works weakly as an English lord ;   weakly
delivers himself from such working ; with weak despondency
endures the cackling of plucked geese at St. James's ;   and,
sitting in sunny Italy, in his coach-and-four, at a distance
of two thousand miles from them, writes, over many reams
of paper, the following sentence, with variations : *Saw ever
the world one greater or unhappier ?*   This was a sham strong
man.   Choose ye.

That Byron the personality had been absorbed in Carlyle's
mind in Byronism the literary phenomenon is well seen,
finally, in two passages from the essay on Sir Walter Scott : [2]

In the sickliest of recorded ages, when British Literature lay
all puking and sprawling in Werterism, Byronism, and other
Sentimentalism tearful or spasmodic (fruit of internal *wind*),
. . . British Werterism, in the shape of those Byron Poems,
so potent and so poignant, produced on the languid appetite
of men a mighty effect. . . . The " languid age without
either faith or scepticism " turned towards Byronism with
an interest altogether peculiar : here, if no cure for its
miserable paralysis and languor, was at least an indignant
statement of the misery.[3]

The once famous *Guesses at Truth* by Augustus and Julius
Charles Hare (1827) is representative of the views of many

[1] " Goethe's Works," *Critical and Miscellaneous Essays,* ii, 436.
[2] *Ibid.,* iv, 39 and 59.
[3] Morley says : " As a negative renovation Mr. Carlyle's doctrine was
perfect.   It effectually put an end to the mood of Byronism " (" Carlyle,"
Critical Miscellanies, i, 156).   Miss Mathilde Blind's interesting comments
on Carlyle's later views on Byron will be discussed in a later chapter.   See
also F. W. Roe, *op. cit.,* p. 82 f.

thoughtful men of the younger generation. Byron, the brothers declare,[1]

is eminently the prince of egotists ; and, instead of representing characters, he describes them by versifying his own reflections and meditations about them. . . . No poet . . . was more unfitted by the character of his mind for genuine dramatic composition. He can however write fine, sounding lines in abundance, where self-exaltation assumes the language of self-reproach, and a man magnifies himself by speaking with bitter scorn of all things.

In illustration of this, Manfred's opening soliloquy and his conversation with the Abbot are cited, with this comment :

Now if in these lines *he* and *his* be substituted for *I* and *my*, and they be read as a description of some third person, they may perhaps be grand, as the author meant that they should be. But at present they are altogether false and therefore unpoetical. Indeed it may be laid down as an axiom, that, whenever the personal pronouns can be interchanged in any passage without injury to the poetry, the poetry must be spurious. For no human being ever thought or spoke of himself, as a third person would describe him.

This is not very profound criticism ; nor is the view of Byron profound which John Henry Newman expresses in his essay on Poetry.[2] Of *Childe Harold* he says : " There is much bad taste, at present, in the judgment passed on compositions of this kind. It is the fault of the day to mistake mere eloquence for poetry." Byron " had very little versatility or elasticity of genius." Newman finds in him, as in Gibbon and Hume, " the connection between want of the religious principle and want of poetic feeling."

The most representative enunciation of anti-Byronism is, I think, the Preface to Sir Henry Taylor's *Philip van Artevelde* (1834). In the *Autobiography* written in his old age, Taylor

---

[1] I have used the Ticknor and Fields edition, 1851 ; pp. 404 f.

[2] " Poetry, with reference to Aristotle's Poetics," *The London Review,* vol. i (1829) ; reprinted in *Essays, Critical and Historical,* i, 12, 17 f.

tells of the reception of this play [1] and has this to say of the popular taste of the time : [2]

For about ten years before its publication the popular appetite for poetry had not been of a craving character.   The enthusiasm for Lord Byron's impassioned but often rather empty moroseness and despair, though it may not have suffered a general collapse, had passed away from some of the more cultivated classes, and found, perhaps, its surest retreat in the schoolboy's study and in the back shop.   And thither also had retired the sympathy which, when it is accompanied by anything dazzling in personal attributes or circumstances, intensity of self-love can sometimes excite in the popular mind.   The more just admiration felt for his brilliancy and wit and his general poetic power remained in large measure ; but even this, perhaps, drooped more or less from being entangled with the dead body of the other enthusiasm.   For myself, I have never been able to rekindle my youthful infatuation (as it seems to me now) for Lord Byron's poetry, and I rather think I am not a competent judge of it.   It is not easy for a passion to pass into a reasonably warm regard.

Bearing in mind this admission of incompetence, we turn to the famous Preface.

It opens with a discussion of the " highly coloured " poetry which appeals to very young readers.   Such an appeal cannot be permanent, for, though there is a profusion of imagery and an easy and adroit versification, there is a " want of adequate appreciation " of the intellectual part of poetry.   Taylor reveals his discipleship to Wordsworth in the remark that that poetry is defective which is not concerned with common life and " with what is rational or wise." Byron is the best representative of the poetry " over which the passionate reason of Man does not preside."   He lacks reasoning power ; his " observations upon life and manners "

---

[1] Taylor writes (*Autobiography*, i, 162) : " Notices, more or less, slight or elaborate, swarmed in every direction ; and one of my reviewers applied to me what had been said formerly of some one else (I forget of whom) that I had ' awakened one morning and found myself famous.' " This is certainly disingenuous ; it is unbelievable that he had forgotten of whom this had been said !

[2] *Autobiography*, i, 155.

are merely such as " any acute man of the world might collect
upon his travels." His energy was uninformed, and he had
no proper subject for his powers until it was too late for him
to adapt himself to it. There follows a superficial estimate
of *Don Juan*. Taylor then declares that Byron's
misanthropy, like his tenderness, was " assumed for purposes
of effect." His characters are not composite or complex,
but " exhibit passions personified." To " these puerile
creations " he gives a " romantic colouring." His decline
in popular esteem Taylor attributes rather to " satiated
appetite " than to better taste. There follows a briefer
discussion of Shelley and his school :

They would transfer the domicile of poetry to regions where
reason, far from having any supremacy or rule, is all but
unknown, an alien and an outcast,—to seats of anarchy and
abstraction, where imagination exercises the shadow of an
authority, over a people of phantoms, in a land of dreams.[1]

The notice of *Philip van Artevelde* in *The Athenæum* [2]
is a striking example of perverse anti-Byronism, for, after
dwelling on the fact that art should be considered as a mission,
not as a mere source of gain and reputation, and after declar-
ing that Byron had no glimpse of his high mission as a
poet, but was " a lord who condescended to be a poet "

---

[1] Of Taylor's Preface, Tennyson wrote (*Memoir*, i, 141) : " I close with
him in most that he says of modern poetry, tho' it may be that he does not
take sufficiently into consideration the peculiar strength evolved by such
writers as Byron and Shelley, who, however mistaken they may be, did
yet give the world another heart and new pulses, and so are we kept going.
Blessed be those that grease the wheels of the old world, insomuch as to
move on is better than to stand still." On Byron's influence on Tennyson's
early verse see Arthur Waugh, *Tennyson*, pp. 17 f. Professor Lounsbury
(*Life and Times of Tennyson*, p. 38) writes : " There was a period in
Tennyson's life when he indulged in that cheapest of cheap criticism which
styled the poetry of Byron rhetoric. . . . At a later period Tennyson
took a somewhat different view. He believed that Byron's reputation
would rise." In 1869 Tennyson, talking to Frederick Locker, said :
" Byron's merits are on the surface. This is not the case with Wordsworth. . . . As a boy I was an enormous admirer of Byron, so much so
that I got a surfeit of him, and now I cannot read him as I should like to
do " (*Memoir*, ii, 69). In 1883 he said : " Byron is not an artist or a
thinker, or a creator in the higher sense, but a strong personality : he is
endlessly clever, and is now unduly depreciated " (*ibid.*, ii, 287).
[2] June 28 and July 19, 1834 ; see especially pp. 484 f.

and who " treated the muse like a mistress," the reviewer
continues :

He . . . knew well to what ridicule a man must expose himself
who worships any other gods than those which the coarse
materialism and the servile conventionality of the country
have set up ; and he had not the strength to build up his
own altar and keep his eyes stedfastly fixed on its sacred
flame.

Some Wordsworthian wrote that ; no other critic could have
accused Byron of worshipping the gods set up by the
materialism and conventionality of his country !

The London and Westminster Review,[1] on the other hand,
noticing the play, protests against Taylor's estimate of Byron
and Shelley :

The manner in which [they] are characterized in this preface
is far, we think, from a correct verdict upon them. . . . The
heroes of Lord Byron are not indebted, for the degree of
admiration they still excite, to what is contemptible in
them, but to their really possessing some elements of character [that are admirable] : . . . a strong and predominant
purpose, an unconquerable will, and a self-control so far as
respects all subordinate feelings. . . . Lord Byron's powers
are on the eve of being depreciated as much as at one time
they were over-estimated.[2]

Anti-Byronism reaches it climax in Thackeray's famous
fierce attack.   This belongs to 1846, but already in an essay
called *Memorials of Gormandizing* (1841) [3] this passage is
found :

Ah, what a poet Byron would have made had he taken his
meals properly, and allowed himself to grow fat . . . and
not have physicked his intellect with wretched opium pills,
and turned his feelings sour ! If that man had respected
his dinner, he would never have written *Don Juan*.

---

[1] April 1836, pp. 169 f.
[2] The reviewer adds that Byron established the vogue of too many
misanthropes, and that " the tide has turned in favour of good-nature."
[3] *Fraser's Magazine*, xxiii, June 1841, 710 f. ; reprinted in *Ballads and
Miscellanies*, Biographical edition, p. 577.

This anticipates the very tone of the oft-cited paragraph in *Notes of a Journey from Cornhill to Grand Cairo*, chapter five, where Thackeray compares English girls and oriental beauties : [1]

They may talk about beauty, but would you wear a flower that had been dropped in a grease-pot ? No ; give me a fresh, dewy, healthy rose out of Somersetshire ; not one of those superb, tawdry, unwholesome exotics, which are good only to make poems about. Lord Byron wrote more cant of this sort than any poet I know of. Think of " the peasant girls with dark-blue eyes " of the Rhine—the brown-faced, flat-nosed, thick-lipped, dirty wenches ! Think of " filling high a cup of Samian wine " ; small beer is nectar compared to it, and Byron himself always drank gin. That man *never* wrote from his heart. He got up rapture and enthusiasm with an eye to the public ; but this is dangerous ground, even more dangerous than to look Athens full in the face, and say that your eyes are not dazzled by its beauty. The Great Public admires Greece and Byron : the public knows best. Murray's " Guide-book " calls the latter " our native bard." Our native bard ! *Mon Dieu !* He Shakespeare's, Milton's, Keats's, Scott's native bard ! Well, woe be to the man who denies the public gods !

I return now to Bulwer, for a remark of his of the year 1838 will serve to connect what has gone before with what still remains to be said in this chapter. In that year he wrote : [2]

Byron died—and poetry, like the mistress of some eastern king whose career of despotism and pomp had closed, seemed sacrificed at his tomb. When the multitude ceased to speak of Lord Byron, they ceased to talk about poetry itself. . . . At present we confess that we can recognize no clear and definite symptoms of a second spring in poetry. We fear that we are only amidst the decay of autumn. . . . The eyes of our rising generation are yet too dazzled by the lustre of their immediate predecessors.

---

[1] *Works*, Biographical edition, v, 624 f.

[2] " The Present State of Poetry " (a review of R. M. Milnes's *Poems of Many Years*), *Monthly Chronicle*, 1838 ; reprinted in *Critical and Miscellaneous Writings*, i, 334 f. Bulwer here repeats, in part word for word, the views expressed in *The Siamese Twins*.

Scott, Bulwer says, is no longer imitated ;

Byron, on the other hand, still retains a strong hold over the rising generation ; and we may hear the murmur of his deep tide of melody and solemn thought in almost every shell we pick up by the shores of song. But yet more apparent, haunting, and oppressive, appears the influence of Wordsworth and of Shelley. Perhaps of their imitation of Byron our new minstrels are unconscious ; nor is there any accusation they will resent more loudly. But of the two last, they scarcely affect to conceal the influence.

Bulwer goes on to show that Shelley is a far more dangerous model than Byron, for in the latter's work, unlike the former's, " it is easy, after some experience of the world, and some careful and studious discipline of the intellect, to separate the faults to be shunned from the merits to be conned."

The citation of views and reviews of Byron and Byronism of the fourth and fifth decades of the century might easily be multiplied indefinitely ; but I have given enough of this kind of evidence and must turn to some brief general considerations of the causes of the decline in Byron's fame.[1]

---

[1] This foot-note shall serve as an *omnium gatherum* of the minor Byroniana of the period. For many items a bare reference to their places in my bibliography will suffice ; on a few I give here brief comments. See the bibliography, *sub* ı Cunningham, A. ; Cunningham, W. ; Best, J. R. ; Browne, J. H. ; Chorley, H. F. ; " D " ; *Dames de Byron, Les ;* Finden ; Frazer, W. ; French, B. F. ; Halleck ; Reveil ; and " Z." I. Nathan's *Fugitive Pieces and Reminiscences* (1829) contains, besides a new edition of the *Hebrew Melodies* with an elaborate commentary, many recollections of Byron (pp. 82 f.) on such varied subjects as his connection with Drury Lane and his opinions of John Knox, the Empress Catherine, the Papacy, the French Revolution, etc. Some quite worthless " Poetical Effusions " by Lady Caroline Lamb are included. (For a review of Nathan's book, see *The Mirror*, 1829, pp. 382 f.) " Byron and Napoleon ; or, They Met in Heaven," by Ebenezer Elliott (*The New Monthly Magazine*, 1831) is a quaint piece. Napoleon upbraids Byron for joining in the " yell of millions o'er the prostrate one." Byron bows his head, sobbing. At the close of his harangue Napoleon gazes severely on Milton ; smiles on Byron ; and goes " to laugh with Cæsar tasking Hannibal." Mrs. Chaworth-Musters's death in February 1832 occasioned an *Elegy on the Death of Lord Byron's Mary*, by Thomas Miller (1833). This begins :

> " Well ! thou art happy," and thy race
> On Earth's dark thorny path is run ;
> Thou wert but distanc'd in the chase,
> But now the goal is safely won. . . .
> Rest, angel, rest ! "

A variety of forces militated against Byron's renown.   It

The elegist turns to Byron, " the bird of song " who—

> bore black thunder in his beak,
> And 'mid dark tumult flapp'd his wings. . . .
> Rest, poet, rest !

and so on for forty stanzas.   With this may be compared some anonymous lines on " The Lady of Annesley " (*Tait's Edinburgh Magazine*, 1836) picturing the mournful figure of Mary Chaworth reading over, long after his death, the poems which Byron had addressed to her.   " The Celebrated but Hitherto Unpublished Poem of Lord Byron on Mr. Rogers " (*Fraser's Magazine*, vii, January 1833, pp. 81 f.) contains copious and amusing notes. *Fraser's* (vii, March 1833, pp. 303 f.) published " Critical Illustrations of Lord Byron's Poetry," a valuable review of the seventeen-volume edition of the *Works*.   R. R. Madden's *The Infirmities of Genius* (1833) contains a long discussion of Byron (vol. ii, chapters ix–xvii, pp. 73 f.) that anticipates in an old-fashioned way the studies of Byron's sanity made recently. *Byroniana . . . with the Parish Clerk's Album kept at Hucknall Torkard* (1834) contains many tributes, often touching in their inadequacy, inscribed by visitors to Byron's grave.   None are worth quoting.   On the Album and its subsequent disappearance see Sir John Bowring's *Autobiographical Recollections*, pp. 344 f. (which contains also an estimate of Byron).   See, too, an article by Bowring, who had presented the album, in *N. & Q.*, 3rd Ser., xii, 241.   As late as 1880 *N. & Q.* (6th Series, ii, 125) urged that this *Album*, which had long been out of print, should be re-published.   I do not think that is necessary.   A " Life of Byron " by Henry Lytton Bulwer, prefixed to the 1835 Galignani edition of Byron's *Works*, is a piece of journeyman work intended " for a foreign people in a foreign land."   Noteworthy is the writer's view that on moral grounds *Don Juan* is " the least assailable " of Byron's poems, " being one of the best and most useful satires on a vicious state of society which ever proceeded from human wit." " Christopher among the Mountains," by John Wilson (*Blackwood's*, xliv, September 1838, 285 f.), contains a comparison of Byron and Words- worth.   Compare Wilson's query in *ibid.*, xliii, May 1838, 698 : " Who are the best of our rising or risen Poets, since the burst-out of Byron ? " Very grandiloquent is Sir Archibald Alison's speech on " Scott, Campbell, and Byron " at the Burns festival, 1844 (*Miscellaneous Essays*, pp. 160 f.) in which he declares that these three poets, with Burns, " shine in unapproachable splendour " and " to the end of time, they will maintain their exalted station," etc.   J. L. Armstrong's *Life of Lord Byron* (1846) is in the chap-book class.   There are crude sensational woodcuts ; one of " Lord Byron in the Cave of Ulysses " picturing the poet reclining on his elbow and talking to a friend in a high silk hat.   J. C. Roe (p. vi) characterizes this *Life* as " worthless for purposes of critical research." More important than any of the preceding is the fourth edition, revised (1818), of Isaac D'Israeli's *The Literary Character*.   In a new preface D'Israeli tells of Byron's commendation of the earlier editions of his work ; speaks of his own relations with Byron ; prints a letter to him from the poet (June 10, 1822) ; and attempts a brief estimate of Byron's character. He insists that Byron must be judged as one who had " run but an unfinished course."   Towards the close of his life there were signs of increased profundity of thought.   Byron needed active intercourse with his fellow-men.   I close this long note with two items from the theatre. *Sardanapalus* was produced, for the first time, at Drury Lane, April 10, 1834.   See Macready's *Reminiscences*, i, 414.   Cf. Charles Kean's adap- tation of *Sardanapalus* in Lacy's plays, vol. xi. (n. d.).   On April 7, 18, and 25, 1838, Macready produced *The Two Foscari* at Drury Lane ; see *Reminiscences*, ii, 106.

would be unphilosophical to dismiss this phenomenon of decline as due to a "reaction" against an inordinate popularity ; but that there was a reaction, brought on in part by the satiety induced rather by the Byronists than by Byron himself, is as certain as it is that a similar reaction, caused in part at least by the "Tennysonians," especially Sir Edwin Arnold and Sir Lewis Morris, followed the death of Tennyson.   But for other and more potent causes we must search deeper.   Had Byron continued to express the sentiments of the time there would have been no reaction from his influence.   But in the eighteen-twenties there was a notable decline in revolutionary thought and fervour, when, in place of repressive measures such as followed the close of the Napoleonic Wars, the Tory government adopted the policy of remedial legislation and wide-ranging social reform. This period marks the coming into power of the middle classes, an event that culminated in the passing of the Reform Bill in 1832.   The middle classes, with their commercial ambitions, their pride in prosperity, their acceptance of *laissez aller, laissez faire*, their support of a policy of splendid isolation from continental disturbances and distresses, their gradual evolution of what Mr. Chesterton has called " the Victorian Compromise "—the middle classes were essentially anti-Byronic.   A marked religious revival accompanied this development ; and Methodism, Tractarianism, and the Broad Church Movement were all alike opposed to Byronism though from Byronism had come part of their power.   With these changes there went a marked heightening in standards of morality ; the rough, hard-drinking, fast-living Regency code disappeared and gave place to Victorianism, with its surface of domestic tranquillity veneering, in sections of high society, hidden viciousness.   Such a society was uncomfortable in the glare of Byron's outspoken, unsanctimonious satire.   It could ignore the allegory of the *Idylls of the King ;* but the plain meaning of *Don Juan* disturbed its complacency. Moreover, Byron's ideals in no way overlapped the cloudy German mysticism which Carlyle and Coleridge brought into England ; and they were almost equally remote from the new grand ambitions of the scientists. And in addition to all these considerations—the decline in revolutionary sentiment ; the acceptance of the Restoration ; the rise of the middle classes ; the religious revival ; the heightened moral standard ; the prevalence of mysticism ; and the growth of the scientific spirit—there was the change in literary taste.

In November 1829 a debate took place at the Cambridge Union on the comparative merits of Byron and Wordsworth. Byron triumphed by a large majority ; but at least the question was regarded as debatable.[1] In the following month a debating team, consisting of Arthur Henry Hallam, Richard M. Milnes, and Thomas Sunderland visited Oxford, where they defended the merits of Shelley against the Oxford upholders of Byron. No one, it is said, at Oxford had ever heard of Shelley (which seems hardly possible) ; Shelley received thirty-three votes to Byron's ninety. One present at the debate wrote to R. C. Trench [2] that the Cambridge men had succeeded in making some converts and had

spread the knowledge of the poet, so that some *illuminati* of the sister university, who at first took him for Shenstone, and then " for the man who drives the black ponies in Hyde Park," at last went away with the belief " that he was a man whom Lord Byron *patronized*, and who was drowned a few years ago."

Byron triumphed on both occasions ; but it is significant that there were men to support the superior claims of Wordsworth and Shelley. Referring to this period, Lord Houghton wrote many years later : [3]

There was something . . . in the moral spirit of Wordsworth, as well as of Shelley, which touched the hearts of the Cambridge youth of that period, and led them to revolt against the worship of Byron, which was then almost supreme in the literary world.

[1] See Lounsbury, *Life and Times of Tennyson*, p. 68.
[2] *Letters and Memorials of Richard C. Trench*, i, 50. On this debate see also Frances M. Brookfield, *The Cambridge Apostles*, pp. 128 f. ; Lord Houghton, *Life, Letters and Friendships*, ii, 163.
[3] *Op. cit.*, i, 74.

It was in 1829 that Arthur Hallam and other young enthusiasts had *Adonais* reprinted, thus entwining the growing fame of Shelley with that of Keats. It would take me too far afield to attempt to trace in detail the growth of the posthumous renown of these two poets ; [1] but I must note that Shelley, who had by no means been entirely neglected in his lifetime nor by all critics despitefully used, gathered around his early posthumous fame a small loyal band of followers [2] whose efforts to celebrate his genius might have been more quickly brought to the fruition of public and general recognition of his greatness had not Sir Timothy Shelley, by bringing financial pressure upon his daughter-in-law, prevented for a long time the publication of an adequate and definitive edition of his son's writings. The efforts of the father were to stamp out the memory of the son. This act of suppression undoubtedly retarded the growth of Shelley's fame.

Keats's reputation was held back by his association with the " Cockney School " and by the tradition, unwittingly fostered by both Byron and Shelley, that he had died from the effects of a review, that he was, in a word, a weakling. Elsewhere I have traced the course of these malign associations with his fame.

By 1830 both poets were beginning to come into their own,

[1] On Keats's posthumous renown see Sir Sidney Colvin, *John Keats* (New York : Scribner, 1917), chapter xvii ; and my own article, " Keats After a Hundred Years," *The New Republic*, March 9, 1921, pp. 49 f. On Shelley's early fame there is much important material in Roger Ingpen, *Shelley in England* (Boston : Houghton Mifflin Co., 1917), chapter xviii.

[2] Led by Mrs. Shelley, Hogg, Beddoes, and Trelawny. The *Elegy on the Death of Percy Bysshe Shelley* by Arthur Brooke (pseudonym for John Chalk Claris), published by Ollier in 1822, shows not only strong feeling but the influence of Shelley in thought, turns of phrase, and style. The elegist mourns not only for the dead poet's friends and family, but for the oppressed world, which has lost a champion. This elegy occasioned a bitter attack on Shelley—" This Tyro of the Juan school, that pre-eminent academy of Infidels, Blasphemers, Seducers, and Wantons "— in *The Gentleman's Magazine* (see Ingpen, *op. cit.*, ii, 559). A reply of another kind came from the Quaker poet, Bernard Barton : *Verses on the Death of Percy Bysshe Shelley* (London : Baldwin, Cradock and Joy, 1822), in which pity is bestowed on Shelley's memory while the " dangerous counterfeits " who, still alive, make the dead man the champion of their sceptical creed are denounced. It was à propos of Barton's *Verses* that Charles Lamb composed the disgusting parody of Ariel's song which I have quoted in an earlier chapter.

Shelley more rapidly than Keats. And side by side with the growth of their posthumous renown the fame of Wordsworth spread. From this time on Byron had to contend with the richer melodiousness, more sensitive colouring, more patient art of Keats; with the more impassioned and visionary lyricism of Shelley; and with the more placid depths and more obviously philosophic import of Wordsworth. In contrast to these stars Byron's fire began to pale and seemed to many eyes ineffectual; and the complete emergence of Tennyson in 1842 cast a deeper shade over his memory and made him appear more than ever a figure of the past.[1]

---

[1] There were, as I have shown, those who protested against this effacement; and Byron was never un-read. But I am trying to express the general average opinion of the time. From about 1850 onward there are many comparisons of the rival merits of Byron and Tennyson. On the publication of the *Idylls of the King* Bulwer wrote (*What Will He do with It*, 1859, iii, 133; quoted by Lounsbury, p. 529) : " I could keep up with our age as far as Byron; but after him I was thrown out. However, Arthur was declared by the critics to be a great improvement on Byron ! —more ' poetical in form '—more ' æsthetically artistic '—more ' objective ' or ' subjective ' (I am sure I forget which . . .) in his views of man and nature." Bulwer was of course prompted as much by spite against Tennyson as by admiration for Byron. But this bit of satire, though of 1859, applies to 1842. Note that *The Quarterly Review* (lxx, 1842, 392), in the course of its notice of Tennyson's two volumes, contrasts him with Byron, on the whole to Byron's advantage. This review is by the Rev. J. R. Sterling.

CHAPTER XIII

THE REVIVAL

THE history of Byron's reputation from about 1850, when his fame was at its lowest ebb, to 1880, when a marked revival of interest in him had come about, may be divided into three fairly well defined periods. Between 1850 and 1865 adverse criticism is still expressed by writers of influence, and even Ruskin was dominated for a time by it. Trelawny put the weight of his reminiscences into the scale against the poet's prestige. But the melancholy and disillusioned generation of the fifties, as represented especially by Arnold, turned on the whole with sympathy to this titanic figure of protest against the settlement of 1815 and the compromise which followed in all spheres of life. The reviving revolutionary spirit on the Continent ; the renewed interest in Italy and Italian aspirations ; the liberal sentiment in favour of inter- vention on the Continent—had not Byron been the pro- tagonist of these ardours and endurances ? In the positivistic spirit, which was gaining ground in England, there was something not antipathetic to Byronism, just as there was in it something that led to the beginnings of admiration of the poetry of Blake in the early sixties. This first period, then, though due account must be taken of contrary judgments, is marked, on the whole, by a decided elevation in Byron's fame. Then followed the Stowe " revelations " with their preludes and accompanying con- troversy. Again there must be qualifications, but, generally speaking, Englishmen rallied to the side of Byron, and " when the excitement dwindled to a calm " indignation against his

accuser and loyalty to the defenceless dead had combined
to raise his reputation higher still. This is the second
division of these three decades. Finally, in the seventies
there is an extraordinary increase in the poet's posthumous
renown, marked by Elze's *Life* and other biographies, by the
movement for a Byron memorial, and by numerous critical
estimates, among which that by John Morley stands out as,
I think, the finest study of Byron that has ever been written.
In this chapter I shall survey the Byroniana of these three
decades, following the general course indicated in this
paragraph.

Walter Bagehot, who represents the continuance of anti-
Byronism, dismisses the poet in a single harsh sentence in his
essay on Shelley (1856) : [1] " It was the instinct of Byron to
give in glaring words the gross phenomena of evident objects."
He considers Byron more carefully, though no more
sympathetically, in a later essay [2] :

The poems of Lord Byron were received with an avidity that
resembles our present avidity for sensation novels. . . .
That stimulating poetry is now little read. A stray school-
boy may still be detected in a wild admiration for the *Giaour*
or the *Corsair* (and it is suitable to his age, and he should
not be reproached for it), but the *real* posterity—the quiet
students of a past literature—never read them or think of
them. A line or two linger in the memory ; . . . but this
is all. As wholes, these exaggerated stories are worthless ;
they taught nothing, and, therefore, they are forgotten. . . .
Doubtless there is much in Byron besides his dismal exaggeration, but it was that exaggeration which . . . gave him a
wild moment of dangerous name. As so often happens,
the cause of his momentary fashion is the cause also of his
lasting oblivion.[3]

[1] *Literary Studies*, i, 111.
[2] " Wordsworth, Tennyson, and Browning " (1864), *Literary Studies*,
ii, 305 f.
[3] Other adverse criticism of this period may be found in George
Gilfillan's *Second Gallery of Literary Portraits*, 1850, pp. 39 f. ; in William
Russell's *Extraordinary Men : Their Boyhood and Early Life*, 1853, pp. 211
f. ; and in the perfunctory article which T. H. Lister contributed to the
Encyclopædia Britannica, eighth edition, 1854, vi, 37 f. There is a harsh
attack on Byron in *Rigmarole, a Poem, By Dunstan Dormouse*, 1856, pp. 12 f.
D. M. Moir (the " Delta " of *Blackwood's*) refers to him more moderately

In this there is of course much truth, but Bagehot shows no awareness of the fact that not by the immature oriental tales has Byron been held in remembrance.

Edward John Trelawny's relations with Byron have been a good deal discussed.[1] His *Letters* [2] illustrate in various ways how his attitude was one of growing antagonism and how unscrupulously he invented picturesque stories about his illustrious friends.[3] And his untrustworthiness as a witness against Byron is evident from the following excerpts from his letters, which might, were it necessary, be made texts for cynical comment :

April 28, 1824 : The world has lost its greatest man, I my best friend.[4]

April 29, 1824 : I am sick at heart that I have lost the friend and companion of many years.[5]

in his *Lectures on the Poetical Literature of the Past Half Century*, 1851. For insignificant biographies of this time see my bibliography, *sub* Anderson, W. and Leighton, A. Byron was of course bowdlerized; an edition of 1857 (Edinburgh : Gall and Inglis) bears on the title-page the announcement that " objectionable pieces have been excluded."

[1] See the admirable summary, LJ, vi, 103 f. The evidence there gathered of Trelawny's fickleness and untrustworthiness is challenged by Richard Edgcumbe (*The Athenæum*, December 14, 1901, p. 814) who says that the estimate Trelawny formed in later life of Byron " was, on the whole, favourable to him as a man, and intensely sympathetic as a poet." It cannot be said that Mr. Edgcumbe substantiates this assertion completely.

[2] In addition to those edited by Buxton Forman in 1910 the student must know the two pamphlets privately printed by Mr. Wise which are listed in my bibliography, *sub* Trelawny. In a letter to Jane Clairmont of April 3, 1870 (*The Relations of Shelley with his Two Wives*, p. 9) Trelawny writes : " You have so long nourished your hatred of Byron, that you cannot judge him fairly. . . . As to Lady Byron, she was a rabid fanatic ; remorseless, revengeful as all bigots are." And in another letter to the same correspondent (*The Relations of Lord Byron and Augusta Leigh*) he compares Byron and Shelley, greatly to the latter's advantage, but protests against Jane Clairmont's unreasoning hatred of Byron.

[3] Forman (Trelawny's *Letters*, p. xvii) remarks that Trelawny's motto was " Nor be too slavishly exact." As an example of his inventiveness it may be noted that the famous story of how Byron desired to preserve Shelley's skull in order to turn it into a drinking-cup and of how Trelawny prevented him has no foundation in Trelawny's contemporary account of the burning of Shelley's body (*Letters*, p. 12) except the statement that " Lord Byron wished much to have the skull if possible—which I endeavoured to preserve—but before any part of the flesh was consumed on it, on attempting to remove it—it broke to pieces." No word here about Byron's " profanation " !

[3] *Letters*, p. 76.

[4] *Ibid.*, p. 80.

April 30, 1824 : I am sick at heart with losing my friend —for still I call him so, you know ; with all his weakness, you know I loved him. I cannot live with men for years without feeling—it is weak ; it is want of judgment, of philosophy.[1]

August 1824 : By the gods ! the lies that are said in his praise urge one to speak the truth. It is well for his name, and better for Greece, that he is dead. . . . I now feel my face burn with shame that so weak and ignoble a soul could so long have influenced me. It is a degrading reflection, and ever will be. I wish he had lived a little longer, that he might have witnessed how I would have soared above him here, how I would have triumphed over his mean spirit.[2]

In July 1831 Trelawny writes [3] that his " double object " is " the doing justice to Shelley's memory " and " to dissipate the cant and humbug about Byron." And after the publication of his *Recollections* in 1858 Trelawny writes [4] :

The book . . . has elevated Shelley and shown Byron as he was. . . . The few that knew Shelley and have written have deified him—Byron's friends (if he *had any*) have bedevilled him.[5]

Although the documentary testimony just cited shows an amazing change of opinion within four months of Byron's death, nevertheless in his *Recollections of the Last Days of Shelley and Byron* (1858) a certain sympathy is expressed towards Byron which is almost completely expunged from the later *Records of Shelley, Byron, and the Author* (1878), an expanded form of the *Recollections*. In the *Records* the tendency, seen already in Trelawny's correspondence, to

---

[1] *Letters*, p. 82.
[2] *Ibid.*, pp. 85 f.
[3] *Ibid.*, p. 168.
[4] *Ibid.*, pp. 216 f.
[5] There are various allusions to Byron in *Shelley Memorials*, edited by Lady Shelley (1859) ; see especially chapter xi, " Shelley and Byron at Pisa," where the statement is made that between the two poets " a perfect cordiality seemed never to exist. . . . Shelley . . . in the presence of Byron, felt somewhat oppressed by the weight of what he conceived to be his Lordship's superior poetical powers, though on this point the world is rapidly reversing contemporary judgment."

exalt Shelley at the expense of Byron is very obvious. To do this Trelawny emphasizes Byron's worldliness, cynicism, insincerity, and vanity. The picture presented is a disagreeable one, but it is one of the most vivid of all portraits of Byron drawn from personal acquaintance. Consequently the *Recollections* is a classic in its way. Trelawny's prejudice was in part due to his friendship with Jane (Claire) Clairmont.[1]

About this time Ruskin came under the influence of anti-Byronism, and in the *Lectures on Architecture and Painting* [2] he groups Byron with Voltaire and Schopenhauer among " the powerful and popular writers in the cause of error " who have " wrought most harm to their race." Ruskin is, however, unusually fantastic and whimsical here, for he adds Cervantes as the worst of all such offenders, since " he cast scorn upon the holiest principles of humanity." Again, in the third volume of *Modern Painters* [3] (1856) he chooses Scott rather than Byron to represent the modern attitude towards landscape. " The greatest thing a human soul ever does," he declares, " is to *see* something, and tell what it saw in a plain way." This he considers a greater function than interpretation.

The mass of sentimental literature . . . headed by the poetry of Byron, is altogether of lower rank than the literature which merely describes what it saw.

Ruskin then develops at length the thesis that it is much easier to describe an emotion than to tell a tale, for to narrate properly it is necessary " to grasp the entire mind of every personage," while to describe emotion " it is only needed that one should feel it oneself."

In 1857, in his *Notes* on the Turner bequest,[4] Ruskin emerges from this phase of anti-Byronism. Some comment

---

[1] See the notice of Trelawny's book in *The Westminster Review*, April 1858, pp. 350 f., an article which turns (pp. 357–69) into an estimate of Byron, on the whole favourable but exhibiting no such enthusiasm as for Shelley. The same periodical contains (January 1858, pp. 97 f.) an appreciation of Shelley, who is placed among the " World's Master-spirits."

[2] Delivered 1853 ; published 1854 (*Works*, Library edition, xii, 55).

[3] Part iv, chapter xiv, §§ 8–29 ; *Works*, v, 333 f.

[4] *Works*, xiii, 144.

on Turner's illustrations of Byron introduces the following passage on the poet :

His deep sympathy with justice, kindness, and courage ; his intense reach of pity, never failing, however far he had to stoop to lay his hand on a human heart, have all been lost sight of, either in too fond admiration of his slighter gifts, or in narrow judgment of the errors which burst into all the more flagrant manifestation, just because they were inconsistent with half his soul, and could never become incarnate, accepted, silent sin, but had still to fight for their hold on him.

Like Ruskin, though in very different fashion, George Borrow illustrates the mid-century hesitation in coming to a decision regarding Byron's character and achievement. Every reader of Borrow remembers how Lavengro meets the funeral of Byron in the streets of London : [1]

" An illustrious poet, was he ? " said I. " Beyond all criticism," said the dapper man ; " all we of the rising generation are under incalculable obligation to Byron. . . ." This man, this Byron, had for many years past been the demigod of England . . . and now that he was dead he was followed by worshipping crowds, and the very sun seemed to come out on purpose to grace his funeral. . . . Unhappy ? yes I had heard that he had been unhappy ; that he had roamed about a fevered, distempered man, taking pleasure in nothing. . . . But was it true ? . . . was not this unhappiness assumed, with the view of increasing the interest which the world took in him ? and yet who could say ? He might have been unhappy, and with reason. Was he a real poet, after all ? might he not doubt himself ? might he not have a lurking consciousness that he was undeserving of the homage which he was receiving ? that it could not last ? that he was rather at the top of fashion than of fame ? He was a lordling, a glittering, gorgeous lordling : and he might have had a consciousness that he owed much of his celebrity to being so. . . . A time will come, and that speedily, when he will be no longer in the fashion. . . . This lordling— a time will come when he will be out of fashion and forgotten.

[1] *Lavengro* (1851), chapter xxxix (pp. 229 f. of the Definitive edition, John Murray).

And yet¦ I don't know ; didn't he write *Childe Harold*
and that ode ? Yes, he wrote *Childe Harold* and that ode.
Then a time will scarcely come when he will be forgotten. . . .
He was a poet, after all, and he must have known it.

The pendant to this passage is found in *The Romany Rye* [1]
(1857) where, after the incident of the gentleman asleep in a
field with a volume of poetry beside him—which was, one
gathers from the description, by Wordsworth—Lavengro is
invited to a literary tea-party.

The discourse turning upon poetry, I, in order to show that
I was not more ignorant than my neighbours, began to talk
about Byron. . . . At first I received no answer to what I
said—the company merely surveying me with a kind of
sleepy stare. At length a lady . . . observed . . . " that she
had not read Byron—at least since her girlhood—and then
only a few passages ; but the impression on her mind was,
that his writings were of a highly objectionable character."

A gentleman of the company remarked that Byron " raised
emotion," and proceeded—

" Now emotion is what I dislike. . . . There is only one poet
for me—the divine——" and then he mentioned a name
which I had only once heard, and afterwards quite forgotten ;
the name mentioned by the snorer in the field. . . . So,
poor Byron, with his fire and emotion—to say nothing of
his mouthings and coxcombry—was dethroned, as I had
prophesied he would be, more than twenty years before,
on the day of his funeral, though I had little idea that his
humiliation would have been brought about by one whose
sole strength consists in setting people to sleep. . . . I will
venture to prophesy that people will become a little more
awake . . . and poor Byron be once more reinstated upon
his throne.

I come now to a third representative writer of the
eighteen-fifties, to Matthew Arnold, in whose early verse
there are three significant allusions to Byron. In the
Memorial Verses, *April* 1850, in which Arnold compares

---

[1] Chapter xxii, pp. 140 f.

Goethe, Byron, and Wordsworth, one notes the misunderstanding of Byron's essentially intellectual rebellion, which Arnold imputes to passion only :

> He taught us nothing ; but our soul
> Has *felt* him like the thunder's roll.
> With shivering heart the strife we saw
> Of passion with eternal law ;
> And yet with reverential awe
> We watched the fount of fiery life
> Which served for that Titanic strife.

In *Haworth Churchyard* certain qualities of Emily Brontë are singled out as typically Byronic ; Arnold writes of her

> whose soul
> Knew no fellow for might,
> Passion, vehemence, grief,
> Daring, since Byron died,
> That world-famed son of fire.

And in the later famous lines in the *Stanzas from the Grande Chartreuse* Arnold asks :

> What helps it now that Byron bore,
> With haughty scorn that mock'd the smart,
> Through Europe to the Ætolian shore
> The pageant of his bleeding heart ?
> That thousands counted every groan,
> And Europe made his woe her own ?

Arnold thus finds in Byron the voice of the Time-Spirit ; and he elaborates this view in the essay on Heinrich Heine : [1]

In the literary movement of the beginning of the nineteenth century the signal attempt made to apply freely the modern spirit was made in England by two members of the aristocratic class, Byron and Shelley. . . . But Byron and Shelley did not succeed in their attempt. . . . The resistance to baffle them, the want of intelligent sympathy to guide and uphold them, were too great. . . . Their literary creation is a failure

---

[1] *Essays in Criticism, First Series*, pp. 176 f. ; pp. 192 f. Note, in the essay on " The Function of Criticism," these sentences : " The creation of a modern poet . . . implies a great critical effort behind it. This is why Byron's poetry has so little endurance in it. . . . The English poetry of the first quarter of this century . . . did not know enough. This makes Byron so empty of matter " (*Ibid.*, pp. 6 f.).

(comparatively). . . . Wordsworth, Scott, and Keats have left admirable works ; far more solid and complete works than those which Byron and Shelley have left. But their works have this defect—they do not belong to that which is the main current of the literature of modern epochs, they do not apply modern ideas to life. . . . Byron and Shelley will long be remembered, long after the inadequacy of their actual work is clearly recognized, for their passionate, their Titanic effort to flow in the main stream of modern literature ; their names will be greater than their writings.

Look at Byron, that Byron whom the present generation of Englishmen are forgetting ; Byron, the greatest natural force, the greatest elementary power, I cannot but think, that has appeared in our literature since Shakespeare. And what became of this wonderful production of nature ? He shattered himself, he inevitably shattered himself to pieces against the huge, black, cloud-topped, interminable precipice of British Philistinism. But Byron, it may be said, was eminent only by his genius, only by his inborn force and fire ; he had not the intellectual equipment of a supreme modern poet ; except for his genius he was an ordinary nineteenth-century Englishman, with little culture and with no ideas.

In his " Thoughts on Shelley and Byron " [1] Charles Kingsley presents a most interesting estimate of Byron which at once illustrates the decline in his popularity and a new sense of his greatness. Grouping Wordsworth, Southey, Keats, Shelley and Byron together, Kingsley says :

We have a right to look for some false principle in a school which has had so little enduring vitality, which seems now to be able to perpetrate nothing of itself but its vices.

He finds that Shelley's influence is outliving the influence of his compeers and he believes that it

will grow and spread for years to come, as long as the present great unrest [continues], till the hollow settlement of 1815 is burst asunder anew . . . and . . . this long thirty years' prologue to the reconstruction of rotten Europe is played out at last. . . . It is Shelley's form of fever, rather than Byron's, which has been of late years the prevailing epidemic.

---

[1] *Fraser's Magazine*, November 1853 ; reprinted in *New Miscellanies* (1860), pp. 106 f., and in *Works* (1880), xx, 35 f.

. . . Byron's fiercer wine has lost favour. . . . Byron's Corsairs and Laras have been, on the whole, impossible during the thirty years' peace.

To ladies and gentlemen, says Kingsley, Shelley

is a fallen angel, while Byron is a satyr and a devil. . . . We boldly deny the verdict. . . . If Byron sinned more desperately . . . it was done under [greater] temptations. . . . And, at all events, Byron never set to work to consecrate his own sin into a religion, and proclaim the worship of uncleanness the last and highest ethical development of "pure" humanity. . . . What has put Byron out of favour with the public of late, is not his faults, but his excellencies. His artistic good taste, his classical polish, his sound shrewd sense, his hatred of cant, his insight into humbug, above all, his shallow, pitiable habit of being always intelligible : these are the sins which condemn him in the eyes of a mesmerizing, table-turning, spirit-rapping, Spiritualizing, Romanizing generation, which read Shelley in secret, and delight in his bad taste, mysticism, extravagance, and vague and pompous sentimentalism.

Kingsley then develops at length the theme that " Byron has the most intense and awful sense of moral law—of law external to himself. Shelley has little or none." And, finally, he contrasts the influence of the two poets ; from reading Shelley, he says, there

arose a spasmodic, vague, extravagant, effeminate school of poetry, which has been too often hastily and unfairly fathered upon Byron. . . . Byron is admired and imitated for that which Byron is trying to tear out of his own heart, and trample underfoot . . . something which is not Byron's self, but Byron's house-fiend, and tyrant, and shame.[1]

By the early sixties the flood of imitations of Tennyson

[1] A more fervent but less well-balanced estimate of Byron's greatness is J. C. Ferguson's *Lecture on the Writings and Genius of Byron* (1856). Ferguson declares that Byron had " all combined characteristics of a great poet more than almost any, excepting perhaps Milton and Shakespeare." He studies *Childe Harold*, *The Giaour*, and *The Corsair* in detail, holding that the last is " the noble bard's masterpiece " (a curious opinion). He makes no allusions to *Don Juan* or the other later poems. The value of Ferguson's opinions may be gauged by the fact that he roundly asserts :

was beginning to harm Tennyson's fame just as thirty years before imitations of Byron had harmed Byron's. *The Athenæum* remarked : [1]

The art of imitating Tennyson . . . is the fatal facility of our time. . . . It is something to be grateful for, that his song is so pure, his influence so free from harm. It is something to rejoice over, that he has taken the place of Byron with our verse-writers.

But George Meredith saw more clearly, and in 1864 wrote : [2]

More of Byron !—He's abused, so I take to him ; and I'm a little sick of Tennysonian green Tea. I don't think Byron wholesome—exactly, but a drop or so—Eh ? And he doesn't give limp, lackadaisical fishermen, and pander to the depraved sentimentalism of our drawing-rooms.

In the following year there appeared the most eloquent of all appreciations of Byron—Swinburne's Preface to his *Selection from the Works of Lord Byron*.[3] On reprinting this estimate in 1875 Swinburne added a foreword that included these admirably succinct judgments : " Byron, who rarely wrote anything either worthless or faultless, can only be judged or appreciated in the mass " ; and : " The greatest of his works were his whole work taken together." And of this Preface he wrote at a still later date : [4]

In the year 1865, when the reputation of Byron among lovers of poetry was perhaps not far from its lowest ebb, and the reputation of the illustrious poet who in early youth had been placed by the verdict of his admirers in the seat once occupied

" I know of only one writer who approaches Byron in the masterly and eloquent style of his composition, and that is Bulwer." From Lord John Russell's preface to the *Memoirs*, etc. of Thomas Moore (1853) I cull this estimate : " Two of Moore's cotemporaries must be placed before him in any fair estimate of the authors of the first part of the nineteenth century. Byron rose as a poet above all his rivals. The strength of passion, the command of nervous expression, the power of searching the heart, the philosophy of life, are wonderful. In the last of these attributes only Wordsworth has equalled or surpassed him. In all the rest he has no equal. . . . Scott is the other wonder of this age " (*Memoirs*, i, xxvi f.). The publication of this work of course gave occasion for new comments on Byron ; see, *e.g.*, J. W. Croker's notice in *The Quarterly Review*, xciii, June 1853, 239 f.

[1] April 24, 1861, p. 241.
[2] *Letters*, i, 164 f.
[3] Reprinted in *Essays and Studies*, 1875.   [4] *Miscellanies*, p. 80.

by the author of *Don Juan* was perhaps not far from its highest point of well-deserved popularity, a writer who stood up to speak a modest word in praise of Byron was not ungratified by the assurance . . . that his championship of a " discredited " name had given great satisfaction to Byron's oldest surviving friend.

Five points stand out in Swinburne's essay of 1865 : Byron's sincerity ; his firm grasp upon Nature ; his lack of dramatic power ; the fact that " his openness to beauty and care for it were always inferior in keenness and in hold on him to his sense of human interest " ; and the need to know all Byron's work, his achievement being not of the kind that can be represented in mere selection.   In more detail one may note Swinburne's statement that Byron has been eclipsed by three of his contemporaries and by Tennyson ; that his excellence was that " of sincerity and strength " ; that he had " glorious courage " and " excellent contempt for things contemptible, and hatred of hateful men."   Confronted with Nature, Byron and Shelley showed profounder feeling than any other poets of their age ; " these two at least were not content to play with her skirts and paddle in her shallows."   But Swinburne continues : " No poet of equal or inferior rank ever had so bad an ear."   Of *Childe Harold* he says that " much of the poem is written throughout in falsetto ; there is a savour in many places as of something false and histrionic."   Nor is there much of value in the eastern tales.   In all this early work Byron exhibits " a fretful and petulant appetite for applause."   A change comes over him with his realization of his comic powers ; " the instincts of opposition " roused him.   There follows Swinburne's superb praise of the metrics of *Don Juan ;* and the essay rises to Swinburne's highest flight of eloquence in the concluding paragraph, which is, however, so well known that I need not quote it here.[1]

---

[1] Minor Byroniana of this period may be briefly surveyed in this note. *Thirty Illustrations of Childe Harold* (1855) is a handsome quarto produced under the auspices of the Art-Union of London.   " On Sir Archibald Alison's Views of Lord Byron," *Fraser's Magazine*, August 1856, pp. 159 f., is as unimportant as Sir Archibald's views.   *Brum : A Parody, by Old Sarbot* (no publisher, place, or date given ; the catalogue of the British

We are now on the threshold of the " Byron scandal."
A determining factor in Mrs. Stowe's decision to reveal what
she had heard of Byron's private life was the circumstance

Museum says " 1860 ? "), is a dreary parody of *Childe Harold*, though more
in the tone of *Don Juan*, filled with local allusions to Birmingham.
" Coleridge as a Poet," *The Quarterly Review*, cxxv, July 1868, pp. 78 f.,
has an interesting passage on the importance of Byron as a political poet :
" He had little sympathy with man as man ; . . . but he had profound
sympathy with nations. For liberty . . . he had an enthusiasm neither
fanatical nor theoretical ; . . . but the enthusiasm of a man who knew
something of the breadth of the world, who was not deficient in common
sense, and yet had abundant store of feeling " (p. 105). This article
is by the Rev. J. B. Mozley. In *The Athenæum*, May 22, 1869, p. 702,
R. B. Hoppner writes of Byron's Venetian life, correcting La Guiccioli
on some minor points. A curious pamphlet of 1869 is *Byron ; a
Poem*, by S. R. St. Clair Massiah (no place or publisher given). A
foreword says : " The purity of the style of Dr. Massiah's writings is
such that they may be studied with pleasure by lady readers of whatever age or condition." There can be no doubt of the " purity," but
there is a lack of other saving qualities. Byron is bidden to refrain
from prying into the secrets of Nature ; to " kiss repentantly the chain
you'd rend " ; and to trust in revelation. This is a convenient place to
gather together a list of the books, etc. that deal with Newstead Abbey,
for most of them appeared during the middle decades of the century.
(1) *The Mirror*, January 24, 1824 ; October 25, 1825 ; February 25,
1837. (2) *The Life-Book of a Labourer, by a Working Clergyman* [the
Rev. Erskine Neale], 1839 ; republished with the author's name, 1850.
There is a section on " The Grave of Byron " (pp. 36 f.). It tells of the
pilgrims who visit Hucknall. It ends : " Forgetting for a moment that
I belonged to another and purer communion, humbly and earnestly did
an ejaculation escape me for the rescue and repose of his soul." (3) *A
Visit to Sherwood Forest, including the Abbey of Newstead*, etc., 1850.
(4) Eliza Cook's *Journal*, under date May 1, 1851. (5) *Newstead Abbey :
Its Present Owner, with Reminiscences of Lord Byron* (n. d., between 1852
and 1858. (6) *Hand-Book to Newstead Abbey*, by Thomas Bailey, 1855.
(7) *The Home and Grave of Byron*, anonymous, but by Arthur Ashpitel,
1855. (8) *Newstead Abbey : Lord Byron ; Colonel Wildman. A Reminiscence*, 1856. This is rather more than a guide-book ; it deals with the
origin of Newstead and with the Byron family. (9) " The Home and
Grave of Byron," *Once a Week*, July 2, 1860. (10) *Newstead Abbey and
the Relics of Byron* (n. d.). (11) *Allen's Popular Hand-Book to Newstead
Abbey*, 1872. (12) *A Guide to Newstead Abbey and Gardens*, by A. J.
Lloyd (n. d. ; preface dated 1916). Some notes on Byron in the theatres
at this time may be added here. *Mazeppa, or, the Wild Horse of Tartary*,
first performed at the Royal Amphitheatre, in 1831, was revived, with
Adah Isaacs Menken as Mazeppa, October 3, 1864. This " romantic
drama " is in volume 96 of Lacy's plays, and in French's *Standard Drama*,
No. 134. Another dramatic offshoot of *Mazeppa* is : *Mazeppa, An
Equestrian Burlesque*. By C. White (n. d., later than 1856). This
wretched parody, which transposes the theme of the ride to the American
negroes, is No. iii. in " Brady's Ethiopian Drama." (A very odd bud from
the same poem is *The Knight's Tour*, by H. Eschwege, 1896. This is a
chess " stunt." By following Knight's moves through 48 boards Mazeppa
can be read. The thing is offered to " the World of Chess.") *Sardanapalus*,
which Macready had produced in 1834, was revived by Charles Kean,
June 13–September 2, 1853. (Charles Calvert adapted it and revived it
again at Manchester and Liverpool in 1877.) See also *The Athenæum*,
December 22, 1866, p. 847.

that Byron's poems had gone out of copyright and that consequently a number of unauthorized editions were widening the circle of his readers to proportions not far short of those of forty years before. It was to combat this new competition that John Murray (the third) issued in 1857 " the Pearl Edition " of Byron's poetry, which included a sufficient amount of new material to preserve the copyright. This edition was modelled on the " Globe " Shakespeare. Murray denounced in advertisements the encroachment of " various editions . . . purporting to be Byron's works. None," he declared, " are complete except those bearing the imprint [of Murray], who retains the copyright of pieces which no one else has the right to reprint." This edition, based on new collations of the manuscripts whereby numerous errors were expunged, was very successful ; it was reissued in 1867 ; and, after further revision, in 1873.

A second impulse was given to Harriet Beecher Stowe by the appearance in 1868 of *Lord Byron jugé par les témoins de sa vie*, by the Marquise de Boissy, formerly the Countess Guiccioli. This book was promptly translated into English by H. E. H. Jerningham under the title *My Recollections of Lord Byron and those of Eye-witnesses of his life*.[1] The foolish infatuated extravagance of this book may be guessed from its chapter-headings, such as " Lord Byron considered as a Father, as a Brother, and as a Son " ; " Qualities of Lord Byron's Heart " ; " His Benevolence and Kindness " ; " Qualities and Virtues of Soul " ; " Constancy " ; " His Modesty " ; and so forth. There are several chapters on such " faults " as " Irritability," " Pride," " Vanity," and the like.[2] This absurd hero-worship, combined with La Guiccioli's attacks on the memory of Lady Byron,[3] was the

---

[1] Trelawny calls it " a shallow foolish book " (*Letters*, p. 219), and Pember says (*Lord Byron and his Detractors*, p. 10) that it is " silly and altogether negligible." These judgments are not too harsh. Brandes, however (*Main Currents*, iv, 340 f.), speaks of its " touching evidence of the strength and depth of the Countess's love."

[2] An American reprint, in flaring yellow paper covers, has the title *Memoirs of Lord Byron by his Mistress*.

[3] Mrs. Norton, writing anonymously in *The Times*, February 13, 1869 (see *Astarte*, 1905, p. 38), says : " Lady Byron is maligned with a persistent rancour so excessive that astonishment almost supersedes indignation as

immediate cause of Mrs. Stowe's " revelations " in the following year. Otherwise the book in no way affected Byron's fame ; it was too obviously merely a piece of emotional adoration of which the injudiciousness quite obscured the pathos.[1]

What has been well described as " a prelude to Stowe " appeared early in 1869, namely, *Biographical Sketches*, by Harriet Martineau. One of these sketches is devoted to Lady Byron.[2] The important statement in this article is that the evidence submitted to Lushington and Romilly made them unhesitatingly decide that Lady Byron must not see her husband again. Miss Martineau tells of Lady Byron's dignified silence, her continuing love for her husband, and her labours and sacrifices for her grand-children.

Another " prelude," though of date too late to influence

we read." On the other hand, John Paget's review of La Guiccioli's book (*Blackwood's*, July 1869 ; reprinted in *Paradoxes and Puzzles*, pp. 264 f.) places the blame for the separation and the consequent scandal on Lady Byron. He speaks of the " poisonous miasma in which she enveloped the character of her husband." An immediate answer to Paget was " The Character of Lady Byron " (*Blackwood's*, October 1869 ; republished anonymously in the *Vindication of Lady Byron*, 1871, pp. 69 f.). The *Athenæum's* review of La Guiccioli (May 16, 1868, pp. 687 f.) is noteworthy, for this journal had been, as we have seen, consistently hostile to Byron since its foundation ; and now it treats the Countess with respect and ends (p. 689) : " [Byron] paid a terrible penalty, under which he has well-nigh made utter shipwreck. But the vessel of his fame has righted herself, and his countrymen can afford to forgive him his errors of life and of writings." See also " Byron and the Countess Guiccioli," by W. Stigand, *Belgravia*, vii, February 1869, pp. 491 f.

[1] On La Guiccioli's late years see further H. E. H. Jerningham's *Reminiscences of an Attaché*, 1886. She died at Florence, March 1873 ; see the obituary notice in *The Athenæum*, April 5, 1873, p. 439. J. C. Roe (p. 29), citing the *Victoria Magazine*, November 1873, p. 23, says that part of Byron's correspondence with La Guiccioli is to be published fifty years after her death, *i.e.* in 1923. This I have already referred to, but shall here add some details. *The Pall Mall Gazette*, April 30, 1873, prints a statement of Mr. Karl Hillebrand, of Florence, that he has seen La Guiccioli's manuscripts, including a work, " Byron's Stay in Italy," full of unpublished letters, various autograph MSS. of Byron's, and " an extensive correspondence dating from 1820 to 1823, which, however, is hardly adapted for publication." Maxime Du Camp, in his " Souvenirs littéraires, huitième partie " (*Revue des Deux Mondes*, January 15, 1882, p. 301), tells of having known General Morandi, who had been at Missolonghi and had known Byron. Morandi, after Byron's death, had in his possession the correspondence of Byron and La Guiccioli ; but once, retreating before the Austrians, he had left the correspondence at Ancona and never recovered it. (I give this story for what it is worth, which is not much.)

[2] Pp. 316 f.

Mrs. Stowe, is a series of "Letters, &c. of Lord Byron " which appeared in *Sharpe's London Magazine* in July and August, 1869.[1] These letters seem to be all genuine. All are addressed to Mrs. Leigh, though the name of the addressee is suppressed. I do not know the history of these letters. It is probable that the family of Mrs. Leigh furnished them to the editor of the magazine, possibly to forestall Mrs. Stowe's charges by evidence of the normal affectionate relationship existing between Byron and Augusta, though there is no other evidence that her family were informed in advance that the " revelations " were to appear.

Mrs. Stowe " thought that by blasting [Byron's] memory she might weaken the evil influence of his writings, and shorten his expiation in another world." [2] In September 1869 she published " The True Story of Lady Byron's Married Life." [3] It is needless to repeat here her charges against Byron and Mrs. Leigh.[4] Messrs. Wharton and Fords, the solicitors for Lady Byron's family, at once denied [5] that Mrs. Stowe's story was complete or authentic ; they did not deny the charge itself. Lord Wentworth, Byron's grandson (afterwards the Earl of Lovelace) wrote : [6] " I, for one, can allow that Mrs. Stowe's statement is substantially correct."

---

[1] New Series, xxxv, 14 f. ; 70 f.

[2] Leslie Stephen, in the *Dictionary of National Biography*, viii, 142.

[3] *Macmillan's Magazine*, September 1869, pp. 377 f. The accusation, though hitherto unknown to the general public, was not a new one. There had been rumours of it at the time of the separation. Lord Lovelace (*Astarte*, 1905, p. 19) states that in Browning's youth he had heard many such rumours from Nathan and others who knew Byron, and that in the eighteen-sixties Browning used to discuss the matter of Byron's relations with his half-sister with John Murray III. Lovelace invented this story; Murray did not meet Browning till the eighties. J. A. Symonds (*Letters and Papers*, New York : Scribner, 1923, p. 36) states that his father, Dr. Symonds, knew the story years before Mrs. Stowe made it public. On February 9, 1870, Trelawny wrote to Jane Clairmont (*The Relations of Lord Byron and Augusta Leigh*, pp. 5 f.) : " Mary did not tell me about Mrs. Leigh—it leaked out through Mrs. Trevanion. I knew Mrs. Leigh and Mrs. Trevanion, and her husband and Medora. The book published about her is true—they are all dead. . . . Shelley solved the mystery." Trelawny adds that the attacks on Mrs. Stowe are efforts by Southern sympathizers to break up the Union !

[4] See Mayne's *Byron*, Appendix II (ii, 317 f.).

[5] *The Times*, September 2, 1869.

[6] In reply to a note in the *Pall Mall Gazette*, September 3, 1869 The letter is quoted in full in Elze, p. 166, note.

But his letter is curiously ambiguous and indirect, even if not intended positively to deceive. The effect of the revelations was greatly to increase the sale of Byron's poems, in England and America. When it appeared that Mrs. Stowe had received money for her article opinion turned strongly against her.[1]

Many books and pamphlets appeared, which, for the sake of bibliographical exhaustiveness, must be surveyed briefly. *In the Matter of the Stowe Scandal : Lord Byron's Defence* (1869) is in verse.[2] The title-page has a vignette showing a

---

[1] On September 7 Lord Lindsay published a letter in *The Times* with extracts from Lady Anne Barnard's private family memoirs (written in 1818). Lady Anne was intimate with Lady Byron, yet makes no reference to the Stowe accusation. There are notes on the case in *The Athenæum*, September 4 (p. 305), 11 (p. 336), and 18 (p. 370). On page 373 is a letter from America commenting on the enormous increase in the sale of Byron's works. On October 9 (p. 465) the same journal says : " Lord Byron's complete works for nine pence are selling at the book-stalls like herrings in a plentiful season, . . . another consequence of the detestable scandal." It would be easy, but utterly unprofitable, to review the entire immense amount of newspaper discussion. In the collection of Mr. H. C. Roe there is a huge folio of newspaper clippings. A similar scrap-book is in the Boston Public Library ; and I have seen others. Mr. Roe owns the rare issues of the journal called *The Tomahawk* with the coloured cartoons entitled, " Stowe It ! " and " Look on this picture and on this "—the latter an idealized portrait of Byron side by side with a gross caricature of Mrs. Stowe (September 11 and 18, 1869). Other cartoons appeared in *Fun*, September 18, 1869, and in *The Period*, October 30, 1869. From the hundreds of references which, with zeal worthy of a better cause, I have examined, I select the following more important contributions to the discussion. The list will at least serve to give some idea of the amount of interest the charges aroused. I have added some articles only faintly related to the subject, as indication that a general new interest in Byron was aroused. Preceding Mrs. Stowe are : " Last Records of Byron," *Chambers' Journal*, March 27, 1869 ; " An Incident in the Life of Lord Byron," *The Argosy*, April 1869 ; " Lord Byron's Married Life," *ibid.*, June, 1869. Typical of newspaper discussion are : *The Daily News*, August 23, 1869, September 3 and 8 (the last signed T. Arnold) ; *The Morning Post*, August 30, September 3 and 16 (the last signed A. Austin) ; *The Standard*, September 4, 9, 16 (which is signed R. B. Hoppner) and 17 (signed " The Writer of *The Vindication of Lord Byron* ") ; *The Telegraph*, August 30 and September 6 ; about September 18 (undated clipping) this paper printed " Lady Byron's Answer " ; *ibid.*, October 1 ; *The Morning Herald*, September 9 ; *The Manchester Examiner*, September 14. In the magazines I note, among other things, " Lord and Lady Byron," *The Argosy*, October 1869 ; " Lord Byron's Daughter," *ibid.*, November 1869 ; " The Character of Lord Byron," *Temple Bar*, October 1869 ; " Byron at Work," *Chambers' Journal*, October 9, 1869 ; " Byron's Letter on the Separation," *The Academy*, October 9, 1870 ; " Glimpses of Fashionable Life in the Time of Byron," *Tinsley's Magazine*, October 1870 ; " Byron and Shelley," *Temple Bar*, December 1871. See also " Recollections of Lord Byron," *Blackwood's*, July 1869.

[2] The catalogue of the British Museum gives the author's name as

medallion portrait of Byron half concealing a very unflattering portrait of Mrs. Stowe. Byron speaks from Hades. He admits that he was bad ; but even his wife, who believed much of him, would not have imagined the slander that Mrs. Stowe has invented. " This lewd, loquacious, literary antic " has perpetrated a base, prurient, salacious libel. The concluding stanza runs as follows :

> Enough. I leave to all men's scorn the lie,
> This insult to the living and the dead :
> 'Twas a proud task for woman's hands to try
> To heap defilement on a woman's head.
> The Stowe had scarcely dared to prate, had I
> Been living, but where'er her words are read
> Deep execration must her name environ
> Who dares to meddle with me,
>   Crede,
> Hades, mdccclxix.   BYRON.

" The True Story " of Mrs. Stowe, by Outis [1] contends that Mrs. Stowe's article is ironical and not to be taken seriously.

Byron Painted by his Compeers (1869) [2] is a collection of notices of Byron, chiefly about his marriage, separation and death, from contemporary journals. The argument advanced is that, though journalists of the period were not squeamish, these articles never " disclose, infer, or bear any reference to the one infamous and disgusting charge of this lady writer. . . . God forgive the writer her wickedness ! " Somewhat similar in plan and purpose is The True Story of Lord and Lady Byron, as told by Lord Macaulay, Thomas Moore, Leigh Hunt [etc.], and by the Poet Himself.[3] This, as the title indicates, is made up of excerpts from previously published books and articles. More shabby and sensational

H. S. Clarke. In an unidentified newspaper clipping in a scrap-book of Byroniana in the possession of Mr. H. C. Roe is a poem by Alfred B. Richards entitled Ad Byronis Animam, which expresses charity and love towards Byron and hatred of the " ghoul and vampire " that seeks to destroy his fame.

[1] Undated, but of 1869.

[2] According to the catalogue of the Harvard Library this book was compiled by its publisher, Samuel Palmer.

[3] The catalogue of the British Museum gives " J.M." as the editor. It is undated, but of 1869.

is a *Life of Lady Byron*, . . . *To which is appended a Vindication of Lord Byron.*[1] And the depths of pruriency are reached in : *Light at last. The Byron Mystery.*[2]

Another aspect of the case was brought forward in *Medora Leigh : A History and an Autobiography*, edited by Charles Mackay (1869).[3] Medora Leigh was the daughter, apparently illegitimate, of Mrs. Leigh. She had a sad and bad life. An examination of her autobiography led Mackay to affirm that Mrs. Stowe's charges were untrue, though the attempt has been made to prove that she was Byron's daughter.[4]

Samuel Lucas, the editor of *Once a Week*, compiled *The Stowe-Byron Controversy : A Complete Résumé* (1869). Alfred Austin's *Vindication of Lord Byron* (1869) contributes little that is new, and attacks *The Spectator* and *The Saturday Review* (which had supported Mrs. Stowe in a series of articles contributed anonymously by Mrs. Lynn Linton). Austin contends that the charge was an hallucination which developed in Lady Byron's mind after the separation.[5] From Australia came *Byron : His Biographers and Critics*, a lecture by J. S. Moore which cites the evidence of Byron's letters of 1814 that a moral regeneration had begun in him and that he was beginning to despise the dissipations of high life. In *The True Story of Mrs. Shakespeare's Life* [6] Mrs. Stowe is parodied ; Shakespeare, it appears, was addicted to " secret criminal homicide."

Mrs. Stowe was not deterred by these and other attacks (to some of which I shall return), and in 1870 she published an amplification of her charges, with corrections, new evidence,

---

[1] Undated, but of 1869.

[2] The price of this was a penny. It contains a woodcut " portrait " of Mrs. Leigh which, as a writer of the time noted, had already served as a portrait of Manon Lescaut and Lola Montes !

[3] Also New York, 1870. The story of Medora Leigh is lucidly summarized in Mayne's *Byron*, Appendix III (ii, 327 f.). Pember (*Lord Byron and his Detractors*, p. 10) calls the book " an ill-grown and noxious weed."

[4] Mackay thought (p. 213) that the charge of incest was revived by Georgiana Trevanion, the eldest daughter of Mrs. Leigh. The circumstances of the birth and parentage of Medora are the central point of Mr. Edgcumbe's " solution " of the " mystery."

[5] See also Austin's *Autobiography* (1911), ii, 4 f., for an account of the affair.

[6] Undated, but of 1869 ; this is a bit of American facetiousness.

and replies to her critics, in *Lady Byron Vindicated*. Byron's surviving executor and closest friend, Lord Broughton, now printed for private circulation a *Contemporary Account of the Separation of Lord and Lady Byron* (1870).[1] The most important part of this long book (239 pages) is the definite statement that Hobhouse brought pressure to bear upon Byron to " make a clean breast of it," and that after his interview Hobhouse continued to support his friend unwaveringly.

Light or Darkness ? A Poem (1870) has little in it about the controversy ; its theme is the progress of education ; there is a reference to " genius-hating Stowe " which serves as an excuse for a long " retrospective glance " in prose at the controversy ; but nothing novel is adduced. Another poem, *The Shade of Byron* (1871), a continuation of *Don Juan* with a " repudiation " of the Stowe charges, I have described in an earlier chapter. Finally, in 1871 appeared *A Vindication of Lady Byron*, which, alone among the books called forth by the controversy, supports Mrs. Stowe.[2]

There remain three magazine articles to be mentioned. Abraham Hayward, who was furnished with documents by John Murray, published two articles in *The Quarterly Review* [3] which, reduced to their essentials, amount to the argument that Hobhouse had " racked his imagination " for crimes and vices, and in a list presented to Sir R. Wilmot Horton, Lady Byron's legal agent, specifically included incest ; and had received the reply that the cause of the separation was " none

---

[1] Hobhouse wrote this in 1830 but withheld it from publication on the advice of Lord Holland. It did not become generally known until the publication of Lord Broughton's *Recollections of a Long Life* (1909–1911), when it was reprinted as an appendix to volume ii. See *The Edinburgh Review*, April 1871, p. 298.

[2] This anonymous volume contains five papers on various aspects of the affair, reprinted from *Temple Bar*. The position taken is that Byron and Mrs. Leigh were guilty, between 1812 and 1815 ; that Byron confessed to Miss Milbanke (partly in the original version of *The Bride of Abydos*) ; that she forgave both parties ; and that after his marriage Byron tried to renew relations with Augusta, and was repulsed by her. Hence the separation ; the good terms on which Lady Byron remained with Mrs. Leigh ; and Dr. Lushington's denial that incest was the cause of the separation.

[3] " The Byron Mystery," cxxvii, October 1869, 400 f. ; " The Byron Mystery : Mrs. Stowe's Vindication," cxxviii, January 1870, 218 f.

of these things." John Paget, writing in *Blackwood's*,[1] was without such data as Murray made available for the *Quarterly* writer. He makes the points that Mrs. Stowe's " evidence " rested on Lady Byron's word only ; that that word was unreliable through prejudice ; and that there is much testimony indicating a contrary solution.

The only clear result of Mrs. Stowe's article and book was that the American novelist was lampooned as a " ghoul," discredited, and repudiated, while Englishmen almost unanimously regarded Byron as the victim of posthumous slander. And an increased interest was taken in his poetry. Save for sporadic allusions to it, the matter rested until the year 1905.

With relief I turn from this disagreeable subject, which, at the risk of dryness, I have treated with the utmost brevity, to the important series of essays and books on Byron which appeared between 1870 and the publication of Arnold's famous critique in 1881.

We have first to examine an impudent, sprightly, cock-sure little book, *The Poetry of the Period*, by Alfred Austin (1870).[2] The eighteen-seventies were years of literary controversies, and of them this volume is part of the history. It contains much truth, partially and exaggeratedly expressed. Austin attacks Tennyson, Browning, and Swinburne, denying on various grounds the claims of each to poetic greatness ; and he more violently attacks " The Poetry of the Future," by which he means the writings of Walt Whitman. In general he blames not the poets themselves but the age in which they live for the mediocrity of their verse ; so unsettled a period, he holds, is incapable of great poetry. With amusing lack of logic (considering the " unsettled " conditions of Byron's time) he everywhere holds up the practice of Byron as an example to contemporary poets.

---

[1] " Lord Byron and his Calumniators," *Blackwood's*, January 1870 ; reprinted in *Paradoxes and Puzzles*, pp. 283 f.

[2] Reprinted from a series of articles in *Temple Bar*. Because of the criticism of Tennyson, Austin, on the advice of friends, withdrew the book from circulation in 1873. See his *Autobiography*, ii, 4. The volume is now consequently quite rare.

Shelley, too, though in less degree, is made an exemplar. Thus, he declares that in Tennyson one finds no sublime expression of sublime thoughts, whereas " in really great poets—in Shakespeare, Byron, Shelley—such thoughts crowd upon us." Again, he contends that Tennyson's complaint that " all may grow the flowers " now that he has supplied the seed is a confession of mediocrity, for " who has grown Shakespeare's flowers of poesy—flowers such as Byron's ? " And then, of Tennyson's delight in gardens :

But Shakespeare, Byron, Shelley, have nothing to do with gardens and gardening. Their concern is with the eternal aspects of Nature.

In Tennyson Austin finds next to nothing of " the ever-lasting puzzle of the sympathy, and yet conflict, of Humanity with Nature " ; while in Byron " we have Man, Nature, and the Perpetual Mystery face to face ; no shrinking on any side, and the poet giving adequate voice and expression to all." Turning to Swinburne, Austin's criticism becomes harsher. Byron, he says, " never shirked dealing with sexual passion or sentiment." But he was not forever harping upon it. Of Swinburne's *Song of Italy* he says : " Let him turn to Byron's *Prophecy of Dante* . . . and there see how Italy can be sung "—advice that betrays Austin's limitations as a judge of poetry. He continues :

Mr. Swinburne is very wroth with Mr. Matthew Arnold for making the admirable distinction . . . that Shelley too often only tried to render what he has got to say, whereas Byron invariably renders it. The remark is obviously true.

And when Swinburne says that Byron was " a singer who could not sing " he means, says Austin,—

a singer who did not and would not screech, as poor Shelley now and then unfortunately did ; and who positively *could not* indulge in those falsetto notes which appear to compose most of Mr. Swinburne's emasculated poetical voice.

Austin's immoderate attack on Browning contains little
direct comparison with Byron, and in the section on Arnold
one finds only the remark that " even in the misanthropical
splendours of Byron's strains there is hope " (in contrast
with Arnold's despair).   The final chapter is a direct
challenge and contrast : Byron *versus* the Poetry of the
Period.   The stanzas from *Childe Harold* describing night
and storm in the Alps are quoted, with this comment :

This is not the Poetry of the Period.   Not much holy-
water and laurel-shrubs there. . . . The mountains have
found a tongue, and so has the poet, but not yet one that
contents him.   Mr. Tennyson. . . . says without difficulty
or deficiency what he has got to say ; and no wonder.   But
the greater voice, when it has said immeasurably more,
still feels that it has not said a millionth part enough. . . .
Nothing could more forcibly illustrate the abyss that lies
between poetry that is beautiful and poetry that is great,
and between the periods that give birth to each respectively.[1]

Of Swinburne's reply to Austin, in *Under the Microscope*,
I need not speak ; but the attack on Browning seems to have
produced the curious result of turning Browning, who had,
as we have seen, been in earlier life an admirer of Byron,
against him.[2]   In *Fifine at the Fair* (1872) Browning heaps
scornful and cacophanous ridicule upon " the childish
childe " who—

> outcast, " howls "—at rods ?—
> If " sent in playful spray a-shivering to his gods."

Browning declares that " Man makes thereby no bad
exchange," for when the altitude of the gods is gained,

> Evil proves good, wrong right, obscurity explained,
> And " howling " childishness.[3]

[1] *The Athenæum* (March 19, 1870, p. 386), reviewing Austin's book,
says : " He is only the spokesman of a reaction that is now setting in, a
reaction that has of necessity followed the extreme popularity that Mr.
Tennyson has enjoyed.   Lord Byron . . . underwent the same fate. . . .
Mr. Austin is not the only person who now recognizes the mighty genius
of Byron."

[2] See " Robert Browning and Alfred Austin," by W. L. Phelps, *Yale
Review*, vii, April 1917, pp. 580 f.

[3] " It may be," remarks Lionel Johnson (*The Academy*, May 7, 1898,
p. 490), " that [Byron's] most celebrated passage will be remembered only

In *The Inn Album* (1875) Browning returned to the assault on Byron.[1] Here are the lines :

> But whence and why did you take umbrage, Sir ?
> Because your master, having made you know
> Somewhat of men, was minded to advance,
> Expound you women, still a mystery !
> My pupil pottered with a cloud on brow,
> A clod in breast : had loved, and vainly loved :
> Whence blight and blackness, just for all the world
> As Byron used to teach us boys.   Thought I—
> *" Quick rid him of that rubbish !   Clear the cloud,*
> *And set the heart a-pulsing ! "*

" Rubbish " here, I think, refers not to Byron in particular but to sentimentality in general.   Browning seems to have thought a good deal, and adversely, of Byron while composing the poems gathered together in *Pacchiarotto* (1876).[2]   He has Byron in mind in *At the Mermaid* where he puts into the mouth of Shakespeare his own objection to reading the character of a poet into the character of his poems ; and denies that the public has the right to consider a poet great because his poetry is great ; and, continuing, attacks the poet who reveals himself and his griefs, who has " poohed and pished " instead of living and loving.

> Have you found your life distasteful ?
> My life did and does smack sweet.
> Was your youth of pleasure wasteful ?
> Mine I saved and hold complete.
> Do your joys with age diminish ?
> When mine fail me, I'll complain.
> Must in death your daylight finish ?
> My sun sets to rise again.

by the scornful ridicule of Browning."   Perhaps ; but is not *Fifine* already no longer read by any but the most dauntless student—and is it not less likely to be read in the future than *Childe Harold* ?

[1] Part vi, lines 60 and 61, and context.

[2] Austin, it appears, had been again (but I do not know where) " flea-biting" Browning, as Browning himself put it ; and in stanza xxvii of *Pacchiarotto* he replies coarsely :

> While as for Quilp-Hop-o'-my-Thumb there,
> Banjo-Byron that twangs the strum-strum there—
> He'll think as the pickle he curses,
> I've discharged on his head his own verses,

and so forth, the concluding asterisks disguising faintly the rhyme " sauced in—Austin."

What, like you, he proved—your Pilgrim—
This our world a wilderness,
Earth still gray and heaven still grim,
Not a hand that his might press,
Not a heart his own might throb to,
Men all rogues and women—say,
Dolls which boys' heads duck and bob to,
Grown folk drop or throw away ?
Doubtless I am pushed and shoved by
Rogues and fools enough : the more
Good luck mine, I love, am loved by
Some few honest to the core.[1]

In the *Epilogue* to the same volume occur these lines : [2]

From grape of the ground, I made or marred
My vintage ; easy the task or hard,
Who set it—his praise be my reward !
Earth's yield ! Who yearn for the Dark Blue Sea's,
Let them " lay, bray, spray,"—the addle-pates ! [3]

From this digression on Browning's later allusions to Byron, into which we were led by Alfred Austin's attack on contemporary poets and praise of Byron, I return to consider John Morley's masterly essay on Byron.[4] The critic is less concerned with æsthetic problems than with the place of Byron in the history of thought ; what he gives is an admirable estimate of Byron as the heir of

[1] Stanzas 10, 11, and part of 13. Browning cheerfully disregards the anachronism of putting into Shakespeare's mouth the allusion to the " Pilgrim."

[2] Stanza 20. One result of Browning's repeated ridicule of " there let him lay " was, I imagine, the large number of letters discussing this famous solecism which appeared about this time in the columns of *The Times*. I have seen at Mr. Murray's a set of proofs of *Childe Harold*, canto iv, in which Gifford has questioned, on the margin, this use of " lay " for " lie " ; and in reply to the query Byron admits his own doubts but, through laziness and preoccupations, declines to take the trouble to alter the line. Mr. Murray called attention to these proofs in the *Times Literary Supplement* in 1921.

[3] In stanza 23 Browning scornfully asks, " What is a man beside a mount ? " upon which question Mr. Arthur Symons has made the essential comment : " ' What is a man beside a mount ? ' writes Browning, mocking Byron; but precisely what Byron did was to show the insignificance of the mountains in the presence of man. He could write of the Alps, and fill the imagination of Europe with the mere fact of his presence there " (*The Romantic Movement in English Poetry*, p. 250).

[4] " Byron and the French Revolution," *The Fortnightly Review*, December 1870 ; reprinted as " Byron," *Critical Miscellanies*, i, 203 f.

revolutionary thought, the popularizer and propagator
of revolutionary sentiment, and the embodiment of the
revolutionary principle.[1] Morley regards the poet not
from the insular but from the continental point of view.
Noting that the mere appearance of such a man in England
was an extraordinary phenomenon, he goes on to say that
it is not surprising that his work had comparatively little
permanent influence in his own country. But with the
development of the "historic sense" Englishmen have
come to realize the historic importance of Byron. The
force of the poet's genius becomes the more apparent when
one recognizes the unlikelihood of high poetry emerging
from such elements as doubt, denial, antagonism, and
weariness, for "the idealisation of revolt" does not easily
furnish matter to nourish future generations. But because
Byron cannot be to the later nineteenth century what he
was to the first years of that century is not a reason for
passing him by.

There may . . . be something peculiarly valuable in the
noble freedom and genuine modernism of his poetic spirit,
to an age that is apparently only forsaking the clerical idyll
of one school, for the reactionary mediævalism or paganism,
intrinsically meaningless and issueless, of another.

Morley finds in Byron

a quality of poetical *worldliness* in its enlarged and generous
sense of energetic interest in real transactions, and a capacity
of being moved and raised by them into those lofty moods
of emotion which in more spiritual natures are only kindled
by contemplation of the vast infinitudes that compass the
human soul round about.

Shelley, though a greater poet, is not so stirred by the
course of events as is Byron ; "his muse seeks the vague

---

[1] In his earlier essay on "Carlyle" Morley had said : "In England,
the greatest literary organ of the Revolution was unquestionably Byron"
(*Critical Miscellanies*, i, 161) ; and in the same essay (p. 162) : "Carlylism
. . . is Byronism with . . . shaggy bosom." Minto (in his article on
Byron, *Encyclopædia Britannica*, ninth edition, iv, 607) describes Morley's
essay as one "which ought to be read by everybody who wishes to form
a clear idea of Byron's poetry as a revolutionary force in itself and an index
to the movement of the time."

translucent spaces "; Byron, on the other hand, never forgets man.

Even his misanthropy is only an inverted form of social solicitude. His practical zeal for good and noble causes might teach us this.

And even in the mood when Nature touches his imagination his mind returns

like the fabled dove from the desolate void of waters to the ark of mortal stress and human passion. Nature, in her most dazzling aspects or stupendous parts, is but the background and theatre of the tragedy of man.

In Byron's " glorification of revolutionary commonplace " the poet remains clearsighted ; " sanity and balance . . . marked the foundations of his character." He mastered the tremendous conflict of revolutionary forces and rendered in verse the amazing scene of that conflict. He was the enemy of a society " which only remembered that man had property, and forgot that he had a spirit." Byron was penetrated " with the distinctively modern scorn and aversion for the military spirit, and the distinctively modern conviction of its being the most deadly of anachronisms." " It is no hyperbole to say that he was himself the most enormous force of his time." Though fundamentally " one of the most rational of men," he bore the revolutionary mark of the predominance of passion over reflection.

The higher part of him was consciously dragged down by the degrading reminiscence of the brutishness of his youth and its connections and associations ; they hung like a miasma over his spirit. He could not rise to that sublimest height of moral fervour, when a man intrepidly chases from his memory past evil done, suppresses the recollection of old corruptions, declares that he no longer belongs to them nor they to him, and is not frightened by the past from a firm and lofty respect for present dignity and worth. It is a good thing thus to overthrow the tyranny of memory, and to cast out the body of our dead selves.

But Byron " fills men with thoughts that shake down the unlovely temple of comfort." Above the idea of domestic

calm he placed " the idea of a country and a public cause."
Detractors have tried to pare down the merit of his final
act of self-renunciation ; but in it we gave " an estimate
of the value and purpose of a human life, which our Age
of Comfort may fruitfully ponder." Morley closes his
essay with the sentence which I have placed as a motto
on my title-page.[1]

In 1871 appeared *The Literary Life of the Rev. William
Harness*, by the Rev. A. G. L'Estrange. This pleasant
biography of one of Byron's most attractive friends bore
testimony to the poet's finer qualities, especially his
generosity and fidelity in friendship. Harness thus bears
loyal witness : [2]

Except this love of an ill-name—this tendency to malign
himself—this hypocrisy reversed, I have no personal
knowledge whatever of any evil act or evil disposition of
Lord Byron.

Disregarding chronology I shall associate with this book
another biography which, as a reviewer said at the time,
added much " of a healthy nature to our knowledge of
Byron," namely, *Memoirs of the Rev. Francis Hodgson*,
by his son, J. T. Hodgson (1878). This biography reveals
the manliness, gentleness and charity of Hodgson's relations
with the poet. Towards him Byron showed always his
best and most serious side ; and Hodgson is emphatic
in his testimony to Byron's basic sincerity. The book contained a good deal of new material, including many letters
and some verse. But J. C. Jeaffreson's later publication
in entirety of letters of which scamped versions appeared
in these *Memoirs* did away with much of the importance
of the biography. It should be added that it is difficult
to reconcile the letters addressed by Mrs. Leigh to Hodgson

---

[1] Of this essay Meredith wrote to Morley (*Letters*, i, 233) : " Your
article on Byron admirable : nothing so good yet written on him and from
the highest view. . . . If I could write like that I would write more prose."

[2] Pp. 33 f. The substance of these recollections of Byron is reproduced
in *Personal Recollections of Barham, Harness, and Hodder*, edited by R. H.
Stoddard, 1875, pp. 179 f. See also Elze, Appendix, Note G, pp. 467 f.

with the idea of her guilt ; and indisputably their publication removed further from the sphere of the credible the charges advanced against her.

Karl Elze's Life of Byron appeared in Berlin in 1870 ; and with the author's sanction was translated in 1872 as *Lord Byron. A Biography. With a Critical Essay on his Place in Literature.* In a preface the translator notes that

various signs may be discerned which seem to point to a revival of the old interest . . . in a more chastened and intelligent fashion, which will lead us, after all abatements are made, to see in Byron the most vigorous, the most original, poetical genius which England has produced since Milton.

Elze's book is dull, heavy, conscientious, unilluminating, unimaginative, documented, and thoroughly Teutonic.[1] In an appendix that is still valuable he collects together various estimates of the poet. He deals fully with Mrs. Stowe's charges and believes that the effect of them has been to vindicate Byron. He dwells perhaps too much on the less admirable motives of Byron's final expedition to Greece, and holds that the poet's early death was no great loss to literature, as he had evidently reached the summit of his powers.

Elze's biography inspired Roden Noel's admirable essay, " Lord Byron and his Times." [2] Following Morley, Noel stresses the revolutionary side of Byron, and he finds in the poet's death a symbol of " the holy alliance of poetry with the cause of the people." Of Byron's democratic sentiments and of the *Weltschmertz* in his verse he has much to say. As one would expect from so sensitive a practiser of verse as Roden Noel, he offers detailed comments

---

[1] J. C. Roe describes the biography (p. vi. f.) as " a catalogue of all manner of facts and nonsense, collected with admirable industry, . . . and thrown together with little or no discrimination."

[2] *St. Paul's Magazine*, November and December, 1873, xiii, 555 f. and 619 f. Another interesting notice of Elze is " Byron and Tennyson," by Abraham Hayward, *The Quarterly Review*, cxxxi, October 1871, pp. 534 f., the object of which is " to reclaim a befitting and appropriate pedestal for Byron without disturbing Mr. Tennyson or his School."

upon Byron's prosody and upon his art in lyric, dramatic, narrative, and satiric verse.[1]

The " Byronic revival " is further illustrated in *A Comparative Estimate of Modern British Poets*, by J. Devey (1873). This over-systematic critic divides the entire nineteenth century into " schools " ; thus, for example, Swinburne belongs to the " Androtheist School." Byron, with Scott and Moore as his followers, is the leader of the " Romantic School." His province was to lay bare " the intricate mazes of the feelings." This remark introduces a long comparison of Byron and Wordsworth ; the former represents his age ; the latter " could never represent anything out of himself." An analysis of *Don Juan* follows, which Devey, with amusing ambiguity, puts " on the topmost shelf of English literature." The spiritually empty, money-loving age reflected in this poem shows that *Don Juan* was by no means purposeless and that beneath its " erratic surface " lay a grand significance. In conclusion Devey compares Byron with the Victorian poets. Meaner spirits, he says, have grasped the sceptre over men's thoughts and affections, " though in truth they have not possessed one tithe of his contemplative depth, or his ideal splendour." [2]

Another phase of the revival is the renewal of imitations of Byron. In *The Footprints of Albé* (1874) [3] the anonymous author declares that he frankly follows

the good example of the greatest poet England has ever known. . . . The scenes are those the great master did

[1] Noel comments on the " strange fury " of Browning's recent attacks on Byron. He quotes Morley's remark that Carlyle was Byron " with a shaggy breast " and adds (rather unfortunately, in view of Froude's subsequent biographical revelations) that " one feels . . . less of disordered digestion " in Carlyle than in Byron ! But he defends Byron against Carlyle's famous attack upon him as " a sham strong man."

[2] A " reaction " against the vogue and prestige of contemporary poets is one of the traits of Byronic criticism in the seventies. We have seen several instances of it. It is still more marked in an article, " The Morality of *Don Juan*," by " The London Hermit," in *The Dublin University Magazine*, lxxxv, May 1875, pp. 630 f. This writer bitterly attacks Swinburne and Rossetti ; he declares : " Far more than Byron at his worst, are they not only apologists, but upholders of vice. . . . Such a poem as Rossetti's [*sic*] *Jenney* is infinitely more depraved than anything in *Don Juan*."

[3] Part I. No more was published.

not deign to describe in his incomparable poem, and the thoughts, commonplace though they may be, are all mine own.

In the poem (which is written in heroic couplets with occasional lyrics) the writer tells how he left England and came to Florence. The art-treasures of the city and the beautiful places in the neighbourhood are described. He then proceeds to Rome, where a similar review is pedestrianly versified.[1]

In another poem the new appetite for Byron rises to a climax of extravagantly injudicious laudation. This is : *Lord Byron Vindicated ; or, Rome and her Pilgrim. By " Manfred "* (1876).[2] The preface opens with St. John's Gospel, xv, 13 ; and the poet states solemnly :

I have willingly laid down my life for the noble Spirit whom I devotedly love. It is true I live to pen these lines, but the vitality, the strong principle of physical life has been lost, perhaps forever, in this cause.

Other remarks in the preface make still more clear what we are to expect from the poem. Byron stands as a poet " perhaps second only to Shakespeare " ; of La Guiccioli's *Recollections* he says that " no juster nor more critical analysis of the character of Byron has yet appeared." And so forth. He blends the theme of Byron with that of the Eternal City. He dedicates his poem to the memory of Byron's daughter, Ada. The poem, in tedious Spenserians, is on Rome, Greece, Napoleon, and many other topics, the whole leading up to a passage of hysterical praise of Byron :

I loved him from my Childhood . . .
. . . Thank God ! 'twas no pretense !
Each day it fonder grew—my lone lot's recompense ! [3]

---

[1] Following the title-poem are some " Lines written in the Churchyard at Harrow " in which the writer laments that " where Byron rear'd his fame no marble doth retain his name."

[2] According to the catalogue of the Harvard library the author's name was E. W. Preston.

[3] There follow several stanzas against Mrs. Stowe, intended to be excoriating. The poem is illustrated by a multitude of passages from Byron—142 in all. (The computation is the author's ; "for God's sake reader, take it not for mine ! ")

In 1875 Mr. Richard Edgcumbe, a young admirer and student of Byron's poetry, organized a movement for the erection of a national memorial to the poet.[1] He enlisted the enthusiastic support of Disraeli, then Prime Minister ; and other men who consented to serve on his committee were Alfred Austin, Trelawny, and Swinburne.[2] Subscriptions were opened, and various newspapers and magazines lent their support to the project. There was an immense amount of newspaper discussion, for and against the proposal, which I do not think it is necessary to record. Among the most sympathetic articles was one in *The Dublin University Magazine* [3] which spoke of Byron as " an element in the world's intellectual life which, having once possessed, it could not dispense with." On July 16, 1875, a meeting was held at Willis's rooms at which Disraeli urged the national duty of erecting a monument to Byron. The Prime Minister emphasized the practical results of the appeal of Byron's fire and energy to men's love of freedom, and said :

When half a century has elapsed, private character is scarcely an element in the estimate of literary genius. . . . We are met here, then, to-day, at last to do justice to one of the greatest of England's sons.

Earl Stanhope and George Augustus Sala also spoke.[4]
Edgcumbe wrote to Dean Stanley inquiring as to the

---

[1] See Edgcumbe's *History of the Byron Memorial*, 1883.

[2] Swinburne was at first disinclined to serve, but was persuaded to do so by Trelawny ; see Swinburne's *Letters*, edited by Gosse and Wise, i, 138.

[3] Vol. lxxxvi, December 1875, 727 f.

[4] See the reports of the meeting in *The Times* and *The Morning Post*, July 17, 1875. See also the poem " Crede Byron " in *Punch*, lxix, July 24, 1875, 34. Compare " Shall Byron have a statue ? " (text and drawing), *Punch*, lxxi, November 18, 1876, 212 f. " The Proposed Byron Memorial," *Fraser's Magazine*, n.s. xiii, February 1876, 246 f., is violently hostile. The writer ridicules Disraeli's speech ; declares that Moore's biography was " cunningly manipulated " ; attributes Byron's expedition to Greece to mere weariness and ennui ; and attacks *Don Juan* not only on moral but literary grounds. He says further : " We deeply regret that this Byron question has been brought forward again. . . . Byron, in spite of his brilliant abilities, is not one of those to whom a National Monument . . . . ought to be raised. . . . He neglected his inherited duties as Englishman, as landed proprietor, and as peer of the realm." I have not seen " Lines on the Byron Memorial," fifteen stanzas, dated November 1876.

possibility of receiving the proposed monument in Westminster Abbey. The Dean replied that had he been in Dean Ireland's place half a century before, he would have accepted the Thorwaldsen statue; but that then, especially in the existing circumstances,[1] he could not accept the monument. He therefore requested that no official petition should be laid before him, even for the erection of a tablet to Byron's memory. The original plan of the committee had been to purchase Newstead Abbey, and install therein a collection of Byron relics. But the funds collected fell far short of the necessary amount, and a statue was decided upon instead. Various attractive sites were looked at, but were refused by the authorities, and finally the poor site in Hamilton Gardens was procured. A number of sculptors competed, but the exhibition of their designs was so disappointing that another competition was necessary. A second exhibition, still so poor that one critic [2] described it as " a gallery of the commonplace," was held at the Albert Hall at the end of May 1877. From the twenty-one designs submitted, that by R. C. Belt was chosen. According to Edgcumbe, Belt had talent, but spoiled his work by condescending to the popular taste. The monument, of bronze, on a base of rosso antico marble presented by the Greek government, was unveiled by Lord Houghton, May 24, 1880.[3]

I return now to literary criticism.[4] William Minto's

[1] Dean Stanley refers to the discussion then raging over the reception of a memorial to the Prince Imperial in the Abbey.

[2] *The Observer*, June 1, 1877.

[3] That literary societies were the vogue in the seventies is well known ; and inevitably a " Byron Club " was formed. It met for the first time on January 22, 1876, in temporary quarters at the Temple Club. The chancellor of the Greek Consulate presided, and a " Mr. Morris " (query : Lewis Morris ?—surely not William Morris) was vice-chairman. There were " appropriate recitations and toasts." See *The Standard*, January 25, 1876. Of the later fortunes of this club I know nothing.

[4] The excessively romantic, lyrical, ecstatic *Life of Lord Byron* by Emilio Castelar was published at Madrid in 1873 ; in 1875 the English versions by Mrs. Arthur Arnold appeared, obviously to meet the demand for new books on Byron. The work is of no critical value. Equally unimportant is the " critical memoir " by W. M. Rossetti prefixed to Moxon's edition of Byron's *Poetical Works* (1870). William Bell Scott's introduction to Routledge's edition of Byron (1874) is also negligible. In 1875 a new, revised edition of Thomas Moore's biography appeared—

article on Byron (1876) in the ninth edition of the *Ency-
clopaedia Britannica* [1] is of course mainly biographical,
but in it is visible the same tendency that we have noted
elsewhere to contrast Byron favourably with Victorian
poets. Minto believes that the low opinion of Byron
entertained by the present generation is due to the fact
that poets are now tried by more strictly artistic standards.
The charge of insincerity is by implication brought against
contemporary poets when Minto says that Byron " felt
too deeply to be a poet of the very first rank," for his emotions
would not " leave his hands free for triumphs of execution."
Byron's " passionate sympathy with his own time " was
the secret of his power, and neglect of him in modern England
is due to the fact that " such stormful and melancholy
poetry " as his must always be at the height of its popularity
in times of conflict. At the end of his article Minto remarks
that the fascinating problem of Byron's personality will
draw students to him longer than his verse.[2]

another sign of reviving interest. *Prose and Verse . . . By Thomas
Moore. With suppressed passages from the Memoirs of Lord Byron*, edited
by R. H. Shepherd (1878) is disappointing. The ambiguity of the title
is hardly accidental ; the *Memoirs* referred to are not Byron's, but Moore's
of Byron. The editor, a notorious literary " ghoul " who bothered Tennyson on several occasions, promises that these original notes for Moore's
book will throw light on obscure points in Byron's history, but the notes
are not striking. James Hadley's *Essays Philological and Critical* (1873)
contains (pp. 346 f.) a very hostile estimate of Byron. There is Byronic
material in *The Life and Letters of George Ticknor* (1876), and in W. M.
Torrens's *Memoirs of* [Lord] *Melbourne* (1878) ; see especially i, 102 f.
These *Memoirs* inspired new discussions of Byron's relations with the
Lambs ; see, *e.g.* " Lord Melbourne," by Abraham Hayward, *Quarterly
Review*, January 1878 ; " Lady Caroline Lamb," *Temple Bar*, June 1878.
" The Last Years of Lord Byron," *The Academy*, January 24, 1877, is
not interesting. Thomas S. Perry's " Recent Criticism of Byron," *The
International Review*, vii, 1879, 282 f., is disappointing, for it refers to no
recent criticism specifically or in detail.

[1] Vol. iv, 604 f. Following a favourable review in *The Athenæum*,
Minto published there (September 2, 1876, pp. 306 f.) an attempt to identify
Thyrza (the object of the mysterious elegiac tribute in *Childe Harold*, ii)
with Astarte in *Manfred*. On this problem see also the same journal,
July 5, 1884 ; J. C. Roe's *Obscure and Disputed Points*, p. 1 f. ; Edgcumbe's
Byron, the Last Phase ; etc.

[2] To 1876 belongs *Lord Byron at the Armenian Convent*, by George
Eric Mackay (Venice : Office of the " Poliglotta "). This was written to
stir up interest in the project of the monks of S. Lazzaro to gather funds
for the erection of a memorial to Byron at their convent. In a slovenly
manner Mackay tells of Byron's connection with the monks ; gives snatches
of Armenian history and of the traditions of the convent ; reprints Byron's

Morley had approached Byron from the point of view of revolutionary thought; Edward Dowden now [1] (1877) approached the revolution from the point of view of the English poets. In this survey Byron looms up large;

In its political results the Revolution seemed to him a huge failure; yet it impressed his imagination as so wonderful a phenomenon, a manifestation of popular power so striking and so new, that all promises for the future became through it credible. . . . Byron at once believed and doubted the gospel of the Revolution. What he absolutely disbelieved was the gospel of the Holy Alliance.

Political speculation gave unity to " the mixed and otherwise incoherent elements in Byron."

His nobler self protested and uttered defiance; his baser self answered with ironical laughter. . . . Byron did much to free, arouse, dilate the emotional life of the nineteenth century.

Dowden then institutes a comparison between Byron and Shelley:

Perhaps one may discover something more heroic in Byron's sacrifice of self on behalf of a people from whom he expected no miracle of virtue, and of patriots whom he half despised, than in Shelley's preparedness for surrender for the whole

preface to the proposed English-Armenian Grammar, his translations from the Armenian *Corinthians*, and his Will made at Venice; etc. In chapter vi. he records " The Blind Friar's Confessions " which had been heralded at the beginning of his book as " a new chapter in the romance of Byron's life." Our expectations are disappointed, for all the aged friar remembered was that Byron was " beautiful but very yellow " and gave him a knife. The friar was confident that Byron's soul is in heaven. That is all! Mackay states (p. 102) that a second work, *Lord Byron in Venice*, is in the press; but I have been unable to discover a copy. In an article " Byroniana " (section i), *Modern Language Notes*, xxxiii, May 1918, 305 f., I have given further details of Mackay's book and have traced the connection of it with Father Paschal Augher's *Grammar Armenian and English* (1819; second edition, to which are added " some translations of Lord Byron from the Armenian into English," 1832); *Beauties of English Poetry* (Venice, 1852); and *Lord Byron's Armenian Exercises and Poetry*, 1870. For a rumour that Byron's correspondence with these monks had been discovered see *The Athenæum*, May 16, 1868.

[1] " The French Revolution and English Literature "; reprinted in *Studies in Literature*, 1889, pp. 1 f. On Byron, pp. 23 f.

human race about to be suddenly enfranchised and transfigured, and it is true that there is an absence of sanity and adult force in Shelley's revolutionary propagandism ; but Byron's sacrifice was not unmingled with motives of egoism, and the life he offered up was one worn with excess and weary through satiety.

These views are elaborated in Dowden's later work, *The French Revolution and English Literature* (1897), in which again Byron occupies a large place.[1] Though of date later than the limit set to this chapter, it may be considered here. In summarizing Byron's career Dowden stresses the contradictions in his character, between his aristocratic sentiments and democratic theories ; between his classic tastes and romantic practice ; and so forth. " He had lost faith in what was old, and had not gained a new faith." In all his work there is a mingling of genius and rubbish ; hence selections cannot represent him. Dowden finds in Byron an inability to believe in noble things for long at a time ;

he turns with bitter mockery to revenge himself on the society of worldings and of hypocrites which has helped to make him a mocker and a sceptic. . . . What is best lives in what is worst. Byron's cynicism is his testimony to the truth that man must live by faith. . . . At the last moment his nobler self revolted against the baseness not only around him but within him.

The year 1880 [2] is an important one in the history of the rehabilitation of Byron's reputation ; John Ruskin, John Nichol, Sir Richard Jebb, and John Addington Symonds all published estimates of the poet.

Ruskin's finest contribution to Byron-criticism is contained in the series of four articles called " Fiction, Fair and

---

[1] On Byron pp. 259 f.

[2] To this foot-note I consign reference to the long passage on Byron in Oscar Wilde's rhetorical prize-poem, *Ravenna* (1878). The praise of Byron is extreme, but it rings hollow (*Poems*, Ravenna edition, pp. 311 f.). Another poem of this time is " The Fame of Byron," by " F.R.S." in *The Dublin University Magazine*, n.s. v, February 1880, 224 f. This, too, is highly laudatory. In both pieces " slander " is attacked and Byron *is* declared to be beyond the reach of detraction.

Foul," published in *The Nineteenth Century* and devoted chiefly to Byron and Scott. The third instalment (September 1880) contains these eloquent sentences : [1]

He was the first great Englishman who felt the cruelty of war, and, in its cruelty, the shame. . . . It was his fate to come to town, . . . and modern London (and Venice) are answerable for the state of their drains, not Byron. . . . [He had a] profound conviction that about ninety-nine hundredths of whatever at present is, is wrong. . . . In Byron the indignation, the sorrow, and the effort are joined to the death : and they are the parts of his nature . . . which the selfishly comfortable public have, literally, no conception of whatever ; and from which the piously sentimental public, offering up daily the pure oblation of divine tranquility, shrink from with anathema not unembittered by alarm. . . . To the end of his life, he had a school-boy's love of getting into mischief . . . which extends up even as far as the Commandments themselves. But he never either recommends you to break them, or equivocates in the smallest degree to himself about what they are.

To this phase of Byron's morality Ruskin returns in *Fors Clavigera*, Letter xcii (1883),[2] where he declares :

Nor does Byron in his most defiant and mocking moods, ever utter a syllable that defames virtue or disguises sin. . . . [He never wavers in his estimate] of what is fit and honest, or harmful and base.

Undoubtedly these ringing words of Ruskin influenced later critics who have dwelt upon the " wholesomeness " of the Byronic revival and upon the rightness of Byron's ethics.

Richard C. Jebb, in his essay " Byron in Greece," [3] takes issue with those who hold that Byron's " philhellenism " was a sham and that in the last episode of the poet's career

[1] *Works*, Library edition, xxxiv, 328 f. The last two sentences in the passage quoted are not in the original version, but are supplied from Ruskin's manuscript in the Library edition.
[2] *Works*, xxix, 464.
[3] *Modern Greece*, 1880, pp. 143 f.

nothing " was genuine or sincere, except the aversion which he entertained for the Greeks." On the contrary, Jebb declares that

a generous cause was always more fascinating to him if it was unfriended. . . . With all this there was mixed up, at first, a good deal of mere vanity ; but when he had once fairly engaged in the work there was no more nonsense. . . . No sympathy could have been more genuine, more resolute, or more practical, than that which Byron finally consecrated to the deliverance of Greece.

Jebb's review of the facts of this debated question remained the most authoritative until the publication of Mr. Edgcumbe's *Byron : the Last Phase* (1909).

The not altogether sympathetic essay on Byron which John Addington Symonds contributed to Ward's *English Poets* (1880) [1] is noteworthy for its analysis of the causes of current depreciation of Byron's genius. Symonds, like Swinburne, holds that Byron's best poetry does not admit of selection ; " we must admire him for the sweep and strength of his genius, or not at all." This is a cause of his comparative neglect ; he suffers by the very magnitude of his achievement, his masterpieces being long and having to be known completely. Moreover the quality of his work is very unequal, and indiscriminate contemporary applause injured him with posterity " by stirring up a reaction against claims so obviously ill-founded."

A current of taste inimical to Byron set in soon after his death : Wordsworth, Coleridge, Shelley, Keats, Landor. Hence love of more careful versification, more studied delineation of natural beauty, more reserved passion, more sober artistic aims.

Tennyson and Browning

represent as sheer a departure from Byronic precedent as it is possible to take in literature. The very greatness of Byron has unfitted him for an audience educated in

[1] Vol. iv, 244 f.

this different school of poetry. . . . He wounds our sympathies ; he violates our canons of correctness ; he fails to satisfy our subtlest sense of art.

Like almost all modern critics Symonds considers *Don Juan* Byron's masterpiece ; with it he ranks *Beppo*, a strange judgment due, perhaps, to the critic's interest in the Venetian theme. Of Byron's character he says :

His misfortune [was] to be well-born but ill-bred, combining the pride of a peer with the self-consciousness of a *parvenu*.

What I have to say on John Nichol's *Byron* (1880) in the " English Men of Letters " series may be introduced by some hitherto unpublished excerpts from letters from Nichol to Swinburne.[1] Nichol and Swinburne were close friends from college days, and the former consulted the latter while preparing his biography of Byron. Nichol distrusted Trelawny, trusted Lady Blessington, and relied much on Stanhope in his narrative of Byron's last days. On the first of these points Swinburne disagreed with Nichol, but agreed with him on the other two. On September 27, 1879, Nichol wrote to Swinburne :

. . . For the rest all I can ask is that you do not quarrel with me when you read my book, if indeed Morley accepts it. One thing is certain—about a dozen high-minded English gentlemen who lived more or less on terms of intimacy with Byron have recorded their opinion of him and it is quite different from yours, so is that of Count Gamba, whom even the caddish Leigh Hunt—who with the taste of a poet had the soul of a sub-editor—admits to have been thoroughly reliable. Trelawny sets up Shelley in contrast to the man whose name at an earlier date he made use of as an advertisement, to sell an earlier book. Shelley's opinion of Byron and Scott's is much nearer Goethe's than yours—in fact Landor is the only great man of his age (Wordsworth was a great poet, but a more *selfish* man than Byron) of whom this cannot be said : and I regard Landor as perfectly infatuated on the subject of

[1] Printed, with the kind permission of Mr. H. C. Roe, from the originals in his possession at Nottingham.

that blameless and rancorous prig Southey. Mazzini through Madame Venturi would never admit that I ranked Byron high enough. Castelar writes of him almost in the over-blown style of Guiccioli, and absurd and tiresome, indeed unreadable (it is the only one I have absolutely [illegible]) as her book is, I don't believe that the cur you describe could inspire affection in a mistress that would outlast his death. The desire for notoriety will not explain the evident sincerity of her admiration. . . . Talk of Byronic fever, there is an Anti-Byronic fever just as bad. I found you in it at Oxford, and when I read your admirable notes to Moxon's selections thought you quite cured. I trust the present is only a temporary relapse.

On October 6, 1879, Nichol wrote :

I have just re-read your notes on Byron with every comma of which I concur (in fact I must claim to have said the same thing in a very inferior way in 1860) except in your putting *Parisina* so low among the inferior works and in your comparative estimate of 19th century poets. I am quite satisfied to appeal to that—I mean of course your admirable estimate against what seems to me some of your recent invective.

From these letters it is apparent that Swinburne was already verging towards his later devastating view of Byron. Nevertheless he considered Nichol's biography " the most brilliant and searching estimate ever given of Byron's character, his work, and his career." [1]

From the point of view of literary criticism Nichol adds little to our knowledge of Byron. He is clear-sighted in his understanding of the relation of Byron's early work to the fashions and tastes of the age. He recognizes the deficiencies in the dramatic experiments. He lays weight upon Byron's eloquence, satiric power, and sincerity. He

---

[1] *Miscellanies*, p. 80. In a letter to Mr. Gosse (*Letters*, ii, 80) Swinburne calls it one of the four " thoroughly good books " in Morley's series. J. C. Roe's judgment (p. vii) of Nichol's work is that it is " an immense improvement on Elze's book in its generally impartial attitude towards Byron as a man, and more intelligent comprehension of his character." See, further, *The Athenæum*, August 28, 1880 ; *Harper's Magazine*, December, 1880.

notes his influence on the growth of democratic sentiment throughout Europe. He regards the dissipations of Byron's private life almost as venal faults, not to be set in the balance against his energy, generosity, love of liberty, titanic force, and elevated thought. He states fairly, but in no exaggerated fashion, the technical shortcomings of his poetry. Nichol's biography still remains the best brief summary of Byron's life and achievement.

CHAPTER XIV

THE CLOSE OF THE CENTURY

THE successive phases of Byron's reputation become now more difficult to determine, but a fairly well-defined period may be marked off between the publication of Matthew Arnold's famous essay in 1881 and the appearance of *Astarte* in 1905. Within the period 1881–1904, however, there is a great mass of heterogeneous matter which yields only after a good deal of meditation to orderly arrangement. The mere chronological order becomes more than ever impossible ; and after testing various classifications I have adopted the following plan. The material may be grouped in six divisions, only one of which (the third) is a gathering together of miscellaneous unrelated things. First, there is Matthew Arnold's critique, with the estimates by Henley, Austin, William Hale White, Swinburne, and Saintsbury which it called forth. This division includes also a long digression on " Mark Rutherford's " novel, *The Revolution in Tanner's Lane*, and a brief reference to Andrew Lang's " Letter " to Lord Byron. Secondly, there is Jeaffreson's biography of the poet, with an examination of the reviews by J. A. Froude, Abraham Hayward, and others. Within this section I shall note the minor Byroniana of the years 1881–1886. Thirdly, there is a miscellaneous section which includes three important estimates published in 1886 ; a brief reference to the centenary of Byron's birth (1888) ; an account of Roden Noel's biography and of Lombroso's examination of the problem of Byron's sanity ; a notice of the manner in which the Greco-Turkish War of 1897 drew new attention to the poet ; and some remarks on various matters of minor importance. Fourthly, a division is devoted to Henley's thwarted plan to edit the works of Byron, with an examination of the reviews of his opening (and solitary) volume of Byron's *Letters*. Fifthly, the definitive edition of Byron's *Works*, published by John Murray the fourth and edited by Ernest Hartley Coleridge and Rowland E. Prothero (now Lord Ernle), occupies our attention. This edition prompted many essays in Byronic criticism, by (among other writers) Lionel Johnson, Stephen Phillips, Sir Alfred Lyall, and J. Churton Collins. Here I shall, without apology, pass beyond the limits set to this book in order to include some remarks upon two fine American estimates of the poet—by Professor W. P. Trent and Mr. Paul Elmer More. Lastly, the most important critiques of the first years of this century are grouped together. With the guidance furnished in this paragraph the reader should be able to thread his way through the multitudinous unavoidable details of this chapter. Throughout, at convenient halting-places, I shall gather in foot-notes, with scanty comment, the less significant allusions to Byron.

First, then, of Arnold's preface [1] to the *Poems of Byron* in " The Golden Treasury Series " (1881). Arnold found in Byron an ally in his struggle against the " Philistines " and the comfortable complacency and conformity which the nickname connotes. He found in him, too, a check and antidote to the prevalent insularity against which Arnold fought unceasingly. Unlike Swinburne and some other critics whose writings I have reviewed in previous chapters, Arnold believed that Byron could best be represented in selections, since in " his happier moments " he is " far more free from faults," and since he lacked the " great artist's . . . skill in combining an action or in developing a character " and was better in " bursts of incident, bursts of sentiment "

---

[1] Reprinted in *Essays in Criticism, Second Series*, 1888. According to an anecdote in *The London Mercury* (iii, March 1921, pp. 420 f.), the Earl of Beaconsfield persuaded Arnold to undertake the Byron anthology and the preface. This final act of loyalty to the inspirer of his youthful writings is of special interest, for Lord Beaconsfield died two months after the dinner at Lady Airlie's at which, by arrangement, he met Arnold to discuss the proposed anthology.

than in his " weakly conceived and loosely combined wholes."
Admitting his many failures and but half successes on the
formal side of poetry, and his faults of vulgarity and affectation, Arnold nevertheless adopts Swinburne's phrase, " the
splendid and imperishable excellence of sincerity and
strength," as expressing perfectly the secret of Byron's
power and appeal. Byron revolted from " a system of
established facts and dominant ideas." While other aristo-
crats scorned and yet flattered bourgeois cant, in Byron the
state of society during the first years of restoration and
reaction roused " irreconcilable revolt and battle."

The old order, as after 1815 it stood victorious, with its ignorance and misery below, its cant, selfishness, and cynicism
above, was at home and abroad equally hateful to him.

That dual personality, as it were, which so many critics have
noted in Byron, Arnold reveals with satisfying lucidity :

There is the Byron who posed, there is the Byron with his
affections and silliness. . . . But when this theatrical . . .
personage betook himself to poetry ; . . . then he became
another man ; . . . then at last came forth into light that
true and puissant personality, with its direct strokes, its
ever-welling force, its satire, its energy, and its agony.

Arnold finds in Byron no constructive criticism of society.

The way out of this false state of things which enraged him
he did not see,—the slow and laborious way upward ;—he
had not the patience, knowledge, self-discipline, virtue,
requisite for seeing it.

Towards the close of his essay Arnold dwells, like Ruskin,
upon Byron's " sense for what is beautiful in nature, and
. . . in human action and suffering." In his penultimate
paragraph Arnold reaches a climax into which he puts an
unwonted enthusiasm and passion :

His own aristocratic class, whose cynical make-believe drove
him into fury ; the great middle-class on whose impregnable
Philistinism he shattered himself to pieces,—how little have

either of these felt Byron's vital influence ! As the inevitable break-up of the old order comes, as the English middle-class slowly awakens from its intellectual sleep of two centuries, as our actual present world, to which this sleep has condemned us, shows itself more clearly,—our world of an aristocracy materialised and null, a middle-class purblind and hideous, a lower class crude and brutal,—we shall turn our eyes again, and to more purpose, upon this passionate and dauntless soldier of a forlorn hope, who, ignorant of the future and unconsoled by its promises, nevertheless waged against the conservation of the old impossible world so fiery battle ; waged it till he fell,—waged it with such splendid and imperishable excellence of sincerity and strength.

And the essay closes with the famous highly controversial and oft-debated paragraph in which Arnold, seeking to evaluate the several greater poets of the Romantic Era, places Wordsworth on the whole above Byron, though in certain respects greatly Byron's inferior ; and these two poets above Keats, who died too soon to rival them in accomplishment ; and above Coleridge, " poet and philosopher wrecked in a mist of opium " ; and above Shelley, " beautiful and ineffectual angel."

Wordsworth and Byron stand out by themselves. When the year 1900 is turned, and our nation comes to recount her poetic glories in the century which has then just ended, the first names with her will be these.

Arnold's critique inspired a number of essays and reviews.[1]

William Ernest Henley noticed Arnold's anthology and preface in *The Athenæum*.[2] Beginning with the remark that the inevitable reaction from undue depreciation of Byron has " set in strongly," he adduces, as signs of this change, Swinburne's introduction to the Moxon volume ; Ruskin's " extremely pertinent and just comparison between Byron and Wordsworth " ; Symonds's essay ; and now Arnold's

[1] Professor H. J. C. Grierson, in his admirable lecture, *Lord Byron : Arnold and Swinburne* (p. 3), is incorrect in saying that " only Henley " refused to take part in the " pogrom " against Byron that ensued upon Arnold's preface.

[2] June 25, 1881, p. 839 ; reprinted in *Views and Reviews*, pp. 56 f.

anthology. Henley's criticism of Arnold is severe. He says that he " approaches his subject with too much deprecation." And he attacks Arnold's favourite method of judgment by " touch-stones." He rightly considers Arnold's selection inadequate to represent Byron.

The poet of Haidee and Lucifer has been toned down to the level of Mr. Arnold's enemies the Philistines. In his new guise Byron appears as a very pleasing poet, often capable of short flights of passion and excellent at the composition of *vers de société*.

Another notice is by Alfred Austin,[1] who does not dispute Arnold's judgment that Byron and Wordsworth are the greatest poets of the century, but declares that this " relieves Byron out of danger of rivalry." Austin contends that Arnold's method of selection helps Wordsworth while it harms Byron, for Byron succeeds just where Wordsworth fails, namely, in the composition of long sustained poems, especially the third and fourth cantos of *Childe Harold*. If, says Austin, the qualities which Arnold finds in Wordsworth's best work put him above Byron, then they put him also above all other poets who ever lived, for no other poet has these qualities in equal degree. But Austin denies that Wordsworth's finest merits are those of the highest poetry ; and in contrast to them he exalts Byron's power in Action and Invention and Situation.[2]

William Hale White (" Mark Rutherford ") reproves Arnold[3] for injustice to Byron in that he garbles some of

---

[1] " Byron and Wordsworth," *The Quarterly Review*, cliv, July 1882, pp. 53 f. ; reprinted in *The Bridling of Pegasus*, pp. 78 f.

[2] In a later essay, " The Essentials of Great Poetry " (*The Bridling of Pegasus*, pp. 1 f.), Austin returns to Byron, who is, he declares (somewhat too confidently) the only poet whom the nineteenth century placed among the great poets of the world. He considers " The Isles of Greece " one of the two supreme lyrics in the English language. He classes the last two cantos of *Childe Harold* with *The Iliad*, *Paradise Lost*, the *Divine Comedy*, and *Hamlet* as the world's greatest masterpieces. For it is in epic and dramatic verse that " the essentials of great poetry " are found. Austin's extravagant praise should be considered in connection with the evident influence of Byron on his own very mediocre verse.

[3] " Byron, Goethe, and Mr. Matthew Arnold," *The Contemporary Review*, August 1881 ; reprinted in *Pages from a Journal, with other Papers by Mark Rutherford*, pp. 133 f.

Goethe's remarks on Byron and passes over many others in silence. And White, like other critics, expresses doubts as to the wisdom of attempting to present Byron in mere selection ; he prefers " the whole of him, in all what is called his weakness as well as in all what is called his strength."

The mention of " Mark Rutherford " leads me to digress from the critics of Arnold's preface to the powerful novel *The Revolution in Tanner's Lane* (1887), which so admirably shows the influence of Byron's poetry upon thoughtful people in the lower walks of life in the poet's own generation. The story is of the fortunes of a Calvinistic printer, Zachariah Coleman, who works with political agitators during the terrible years following Napoleon's overthrow. He is at length imprisoned. Later in life, as an old man, he is interested in the Corn Law Repeal agitation and is the friend of a dour Free Trader with whose fortunes the latter half of the book is concerned. The pictures of provincial English nonconformity and of the gradual incursions of liberal ideas are excellently done. Byron is often referred to as one of the great stirrers-up of opinion, one of the guides towards liberalism ; the chief force in revolutionary literature because of his appeal to the average man.

Zachariah found in the *Corsair* exactly what answered to his own inmost self, down to its very depths. The lofty style, the scorn of what is mean and base, the courage— root of all virtue—that dares and evermore dares in the very last extremity, the love of the illimitable, of freedom, and the cadences like the fall of waves on a sea-shore were attractive to him beyond measure. More than this, there was Love. . . . It was not love for a person ; perhaps it was hardly love so much as the capacity for love. . . . It will manifest itself in suppressed force, seeking for exit in a thousand directions. . . . It will give energy to expression, vitality to his admiration of the beautiful, devotion to his worship, enthusiasm to his zeal for freedom. More than that, it will *not* make his private life unbearable by contrast ; rather the reverse. The vision of Medora will intensify the shadow over Rosoman Street, Clerkenwell, but will soften it.

Later in the story occurs this passage :

The revolutionary literature of the time, and more particularly Byron, increasingly interested him. The very wildness and remoteness of Byron's romance was just what suited him. It is all very well for the happy and well-to-do to talk scornfully of poetic sentimentality. Those to whom a natural outlet for their affection is denied know better. They instinctively turn to books which are the farthest removed from commonplace and are in a sense unreal. Not to the prosperous man, a dweller in beautiful scenery, . . . is Byron precious, but to the poor wretch, say some City clerk, with an aspiration beyond his desk, who has two rooms in Camberwell, . . . but who is able to turn to that island in a summer sea where dwells Kaled, his mistress—Kaled, the Dark Page disguised as a man, who watches her beloved dying.

There are other such tributes to Byron, of which I shall quote but one more :

Of the influence of Byron no more need be said here, because so much has been said before. It may seem strange that the deacon of a Dissenting chapel and his wife could read him, . . . but I am only stating a fact.

I return to " Mark Rutherford's " comment on Arnold to cite this final passage :

The root of his excellence is the immense elemental force which dwells in him. . . . He was a mass of living energy, and it is this which makes him so perpetually attractive and sanative too. For energy, power, is the one thing after which we pine, especially in a sickly age. We do not want carefully-constructed poems of mosaic, self-possessed and self-conscious. Force is what we need and what will heal us. . . . Therefore he is infinitely precious. . . . The Byron " vogue " will never pass so long as men and women are men and women. Mr. Arnold and the critics may remind us of his imperfections of form, but they are nothing more than the flaws of a mountain, and Goethe will be right after all, for not since Shakespeare have we had any one *der ihm zu vergleichen wäre.*

From such praise the transition is violent to Swinburne's second estimate of Byron. As late as October 10, 1879, Swinburne had written to Edmund Gosse : [1]

On Byron I have not another word to say in public ; finding nothing to add or recant, and little if anything to modify, on reconsideration of my early essay.

Yet in 1884 he published the amazing onslaught called " Wordsworth and Byron," [2] the real animus of which was that Arnold had dared to rank Byron higher among poets than Coleridge and Shelley.[3] We are not concerned with Swinburne's judgment of Wordsworth ; the portion of the diatribe dealing with Byron begins with the remark that Byron's influence " is already in the main spent, exhausted, insignificant henceforward for better or for worse." A claim to some other merit than that of writing poetry must be devised for Byron if " place among memorable men is to be reserved for him." For he lacks the essential qualities of poetry—imagination and harmony. Swinburne admits his supremacy " in a province outside the proper domain of absolute poetry "—the Bernesque ; and he acknowledges Byron's good sense in being himself often aware of this limitation. He dismisses the question of Goethe's views by noting how often Goethe indulges in absurdities in his criticism of modern poets. He shows more respect for Mazzini's opinion, and qualifies Thackeray's dictum that " that man never wrote from his heart " by noting its injustice on one point, namely that when writing of politics his sympathy was perfectly sincere. Beyond this Swinburne has literally nothing but ill to say of Byron : his wretched blank verse is parodied ; the " two squeaking and disjointed puppets " which are his solitary masculine and feminine characters are sneered at ; and phrases such as " grandiose meanness " and " impotent malignity " are scattered

[1] *Letters*, ii, 42.
[2] *The Nineteenth Century*, April and May, 1884 ; reprinted in *Miscellanies*, pp. 63 f.
[3] Swinburne may also have been offended by Arnold's opening implication that before his volume there had been no satisfactory selection from Byron's poems published.

thickly through the pages. On various grounds Swinburne ranks Crabbe, Scott, and Southey higher among poets than Byron. I forbear further comment upon this fierce, frenzied, and foolish essay.

Indeed, the best comment upon it is found in Andrew Lang's *Letters to Dead Authors*, xx : " To Lord Byron." In these graceful and witty octaves Lang alludes to the controversy stirred up by Arnold :

> There be some that for your credit stickle,
> As—glorious Mat,—and not inglorious Nichol.

Lang thus paraphrases Swinburne's description of Byron's " Pegasus " :

> A gasping, ranting, broken-winded brute,
> That any judge of Pegasi would shoot ;

and comments : " O'er the Eagle thus the Bantam crows." He admits that it is useless to quarrel with the reigning taste ; but Byron has true lovers yet :

> The Germans, too, those men of blood and iron,
> Of all our poets chiefly swear by Byron.

And this is the admirable conclusion of the " Letter " :

> Farewell, thou Titan fairer than the gods !
> Farewell, farewell, thou swift and lovely spirit,
> Thou splendid warrior with the world at odds,
> Unpraised, unpraisable, beyond thy merit ;
> Chased, like Orestes, by the furies' rods,
> Like him at length thy peace thou dost inherit ;
> Beholding whom, men think how fairer far
> Than all the steadfast stars the wandering star.[1]

---

[1] But when Henley in 1896 announced his forthcoming edition of Byron, Lang expressed the opinion that the poet was " forgotten." See *Scribner's Magazine*, September 1896, pp. 385 f. ; *The Bookman*, v, 63. Lang's estimate of Byron in his *History of English Literature* (1912), pp. 519 f., is guardedly hostile. I quote some excerpts : " It is impossible to conjecture what the reaction to the poetry of Byron will be in each reader's case. He was revolutionary ; Matthew Arnold was not ; but it was the placid Arnold who hails Byron as 'the greatest force' in the English literature of the nineteenth century ; and it is the revolutionary Swinburne whose copious vocabulary is overtasked in the effort to find epithets of disdain and disgust. . . . There is at this hour no complete and critical life of the poet : many letters and other documents remain unpublished. But if ever a biography . . . is produced, the discredit thrown on English hypocrisy because of English treatment of the poet will probably be seen to be based on ignorance and sentiment."

It was at the time of Swinburne's essay that Professor George Saintsbury first began to express that " curious rancour " (as Professor Grierson calls it) with which he has ever since pursued Byron, down to his latest critiques of literature. I do not find it necessary to record all Mr. Saintsbury's remarks ; the fullest statement of his impressions of Byron ("impressions" never "corrected") is in his *History of Nineteenth Century Literature* (1896).[1] He believes that Byron is of lower rank than Scott whom he imitates in narrative. Byron's poetry is " much . . . sunk in critical estimation " and the signs of its recovery are slight. He is fluent, facile, faulty, monotonous, theatrical and insincere. " The appearance of intensity " helped an appeal that was based also in part on the use of the unfamiliar scenery, vocabulary and manners of the Levant. The Byronic hero is at once " a sort of fancy portrait " of Byron and also the " old romantic villain-hero," costumed and placed more effectively and " managed with infinitely greater genius." But Byron's Romanticism is " bastard and second-hand " ; and he is not " a poet-star of the first magnitude."

A poet distinctly of the second class, and not even of the best kind of second, inasmuch as his greatness is chiefly derived from a sort of parody, a sort of imitation, of the qualities of the first. His verse is to the greatest poetry what melodrama is to tragedy.

Saintsbury does not think that Byron was an impostor ; he finds in him a genuine feeling for beauty and a sense of the unsatisfactoriness of life. But he thinks it " perfectly fatal " to read Byron in juxtaposition with any great poet.

The light . . . is that which is habitually just in front of the stage : the roses are rouged, the cries of passion even sometimes (not always) ring false.

So much for the numerous offshoots from Arnold's essay. We come now to J. C. Jeaffreson's *The Real Lord*

[1] Pp. 75 f. See also *Macmillan's Magazine*, March 1881.

Byron : New Views of the Poet's Life (1883). This long ambitious work Professor Elton [1] calls a " coarse and candid inquiry " and Miss Mayne [2] calls a " hard, unpleasant photograph." These opinions Jeaffreson himself confirms in his " Parting Note " :

His passions and pettinesses, his follies and foibles, his sins against himself and others, have been recorded. The evil of him has been told in every particular, told with emphasis ; no ugly fact has been glossed ; each dark matter has been brought out to the light of heaven. And this has been done, so that on closing these volumes the reader may be confident that he knows all the worst, though by no means all the good, of the poet's cruelly misrepresented life.

Despite this candour, few writers have more cruelly misrepresented Byron than has Jeaffreson. The endeavour to be fair and open-minded led him to pass rapidly over the poet's excellences and to paint in dark colours his defects. Yet his intention, hinted at in the somewhat arrogant title, was to shed light on " the Byron mystery " that would clear him forever of the worst charges against him. He had found in the Alfred Morrison collection of manuscripts papers which he thought exculpated Mrs. Leigh. These he planned to publish in *The Athenæum*,[3] but the editor was constrained to desist from the proposed publication by the threat of Chancery proceedings. Hence Jeaffreson's book, in which the facts contained in the manuscripts were given without revelation of the sources of the new information.[4]

In the biography Byron's character becomes singularly commonplace ; he is portrayed as neither heroic nor satanic. The attachment to Mary Chaworth is said to be " a fiction of his own concoction." Jeaffreson declares that the " solution of the mystery that has perplexed the world " is discoverable in the affair with Jane Clairmont which began

---

[1] *Survey*, ii, 417.
[2] *Byron*, ii, 256.
[3] See *The Athenæum*, July 8, 1882, p. 49.
[4] See Jeaffreson's *Book of Recollections* (1894), ii, 142 f.

in the midst of the separation and was a new affront to Lady Byron.[1] The jaunty way in which these Gordian knots are cut is an indication of Jeaffreson's qualifications for dealing with the complexities and obscurities of Byron's life. As a critic of Byron's poetry Jeaffreson is worthless. Nevertheless many of the reviews were highly favourable.[2] One review, however, was very hostile. This is Abraham Hayward's notice in *The Quarterly Review*.[3] Hayward indicates many errors of fact (*e.g.*, with regard to the Broughton papers), of inference (*e.g.*, with regard to Jane Clairmont), and of good taste. He writes :

If Mr. Jeaffreson . . . really thought that he was about to elevate the character of Lord Byron, he must have a singularly constituted mind, or have changed his intention before he reached the second volume, throughout which the noble poet is bitterly assailed and the worst possible construction put upon all his words and actions.

[1] Here may be mentioned two articles by William Graham : " Chats with Jane Clairmont " (*The Nineteenth Century*, November 1893–January 1894) and " The Secret of the Byron Separation " (1895) which were reprinted as *Last Links with Byron, Shelley, and Keats* (1898). Graham knew Miss Clairmont in Florence in 1878 ; she gave him information to be published under certain conditions and not till a specified time had elapsed after her death. Her reminiscences of Byron are, as might be expected, very unfavourable. She adored Shelley. Her explanation of the separation is that advanced by Jeaffreson, namely, that Lady Byron became aware of her liaison with Byron after she left her husband's house, and that this caused her determination never to return. Her statements, however, have never been accepted as authentic ; see LJ, iii, Appendix vii, p. 427, for facts that conclusively disprove what she said to Graham. Readers of Henry James may like to be reminded that the origin of his famous story *The Aspern Papers* was his being informed that Jane Clairmont was still alive.

[2] For notices more or less laudatory see *The Saturday Review*, June 16, 1883 ; *The Guardian*, August 15, 1883 ; *The Academy*, March 26, 1883 ; *The British Quarterly*, No. 155, 1883 ; *The Fortnightly Review*, April 1883 ; *The Athenæum* May 12, 1883. Supplementary to his biography Jeaffreson published in *The Athenæum*, September 19, 1884, pp. 369 f., twenty-four letters from Mrs. Leigh. H. Buxton Forman (*ibid.*, September 26, p. 401) noted that with trifling omissions these letters had already appeared in Hodgson's *Memoir*. In reply to Forman, Jeaffreson insisted (*ibid.* October 3, p. 436) that a collation showed many important variants from the Hodgson versions. *The Athenæum*, August 4 and 18, 1883, pp. 206 f. published a series of " Byron Letters " dealing largely with the separation. More letters, dealing with the destruction of Byron's " Memoirs," appeared in the same journal, May 24, 1884, pp. 662 f.

[3] Vol. clvi, July 1883, 90 f. Jeaffreson answered Hayward in *The Athenæum*, August 4 (pp. 143 f.) and 18 (pp. 204 f.).

In *The Nineteenth Century* [1] James Anthony Froude published " A Leaf from the Real Life of Lord Byron," in which he at once disclaimed any intention of reviewing Jeaffreson's book, which he described as resembling " a description of Vesuvius written by some one who did not know that Vesuvius was a volcano." Froude's purpose is to call attention to the most damaging evidence ever discovered against Byron's character, namely, his supposed suppression of Shelley's letter to R. B. Hoppner denying the accusations made by Elise Foggi against Shelley and Jane Clairmont. Into this disagreeable matter I need not enter, for Mr. Edgcumbe has lately done Byron's memory the good service of convincingly ridding him of this odious charge.[2] I must note, however, that Edward Dowden's *Life of Shelley* (1886) [3] and Mrs. Julian Marshall's *Life and Letters of Mary Wollstonecraft Shelley* (1889) [4] repeated the accusation and gave wide currency to it.[5]

[1] Vol. xiv, August 1883, 228 f. Jeaffreson's answer is in *The Athenæum*, September 1 and 22, 1883 (pp. 273 f. and p. 366).

[2] See *Lord Byron's Correspondence*, edited by John Murray, vol. ii, chapter xi. In a hitherto unpublished letter to Watts-Dunton, in the possession of Mr. H. C. Roe, Swinburne crows shrilly over Froude's article : " Ill as I have always invariably thought of Byron I never imagined him such a hound as he is now shown to have been, by irrefragable evidence, in his conduct towards the Shelleys—liar, slanderer, thief, intercepter and suppressor of evidence, intrusted to his honour—*his* honour forsooth ! (I call a man who intercepts letters addressed to another in vindication of a friend's character from hideous calumnies the blackest thief unwhipped and unhung.) Nichol will have to give up one of his two dog-idols (the two worst B's on record, Bonaparte and Byron) now and for ever as far as manhood of character is concerned. I did *not* think any man of any genius could be quite such a cur." Maurois' *Ariel* (1923) repeats the story.

[3] Vol. ii, 423 f.

[4] Mrs. Marshall's book contains many new letters of Shelley and Byron. The letters from Miss Clairmont to Mrs. Shelley are very hostile to Byron, *e.g.*, " I might say that never was there a nature more profoundly corrupt than his became, or more radically vulgar than his was from the very outset " (ii, 266). Again, she speaks (ii, 265) of " the beastly character of Lord Byron."

[5] I shall here collect together brief notes of the minor Byroniana of 1882–1886. Mrs. Oliphant's *Literary History of England* (1882) gives an estimate of Byron and Shelley, considered together and contrasted unfavourably with the Lake poets (chapters iii–v). E. S. Nadal's *Essays at Home and Abroad* (1882) contains (pp. 42 f.) a fair but undistinguished article on Byron. Cesare Cantù's lecture on Byron (1833) was translated in 1883 by A. Kinlock with additional matter : *Lord Byron and His Works*. This is made up of extravagant and valueless praise. T. Hall Caine's *Cobwebs of Criticism* (1883) tells (pp. 91 f.) of the early reception of Byron's poems. The point of view is very hostile. *Childe Chappie's Pilgrimage*

Three important estimates of Byron appeared in 1886. Leslie Stephen's article in *The Dictionary of National Biography* [1] is a plain statement of the facts of the poet's life with very little literary criticism. In view of Stephen's later support of the Earl of Lovelace it is interesting to note that he pronounces Mrs. Stowe's "hideous story" "absolutely incredible."

Byron Re-studied in his Dramas, by William Gerard,[2] is described on the title-page as "a contribution towards a definite estimate of his genius." The writer notes three phases in a poet's fame : first, contemporary praise and blame, alike uncritical ; second, cold reflection producing by reaction an unduly low estimate : third, the calm judgment of posterity. Of the attacks on Byron during the mid-century he says :

Uncritical as were these attacks, they were at least useful in stripping the tinsel from what was a lay-figure.

Lately the real Byron has begun to emerge :

A man Byron, deeply erring but human and noble ; a poet Byron, with terrible faults but of great if dubitable genius.

(1883) is a dull anonymous parody satirizing a "cheap sport." *The Gentleman's Magazine*, December 1883, contains "Lord Byron and his Critics" and "Lady Caroline Lamb." *The Pall Mall Gazette*, May 29, 1884, contains "A Letter from Byron to Teresa." The "Life of Byron" by Alexander Leighton, prefixed to Crowell's edition of the *Works*, 1884, is negligible. *Letters written by Lord Byron during his residence at Missolonghi to Mr. Samuel Barff* is a privately printed volume of 1884. Barff and Hancock were Byron's bankers during his last visit to Greece. *The Weekly Scotsman*, June 21, 1884, contains "A Psychological Study of Byron," on Karl Bliebtreu. *Byron*, by Henry Jowett (1884) is a paper read before a debating society. Jowett was a protégé of Ruskin. W. J. Courthope's "The Revival of Romance" (*The National Review*, v, April 1885, 220 f.) contains an estimate of Byron, reprinted in *The Liberal Movement in English Poetry*. As Courthope expresses the same opinions at greater length in his *History of English Poetry* I postpone for the present consideration of these views. A tentative and still valuable bibliography of Byroniana by Richard Edgcumbe ran through many numbers of *N. & Q.* during 1886 (7th Series, vol. ii). *Gems from Byron* (1886) contains an introduction by the Rev. H. R. Haweis. Roden Noel's *Songs of the Heights and Deeps* (1885) contains the fine poem "Byron's Grave," which is reprinted as an appendix to his *Life of Lord Byron* (1890).

[1] Vol. viii, 132 f.

[2] A pseudonym for W. Gerard Smith. I take this opportunity to make a belated *amende* for my hasty juvenile dismissal of this admirable little book in the preface to my *Dramas of Lord Byron, a Critical Study* (1915).

. . . He has been allowed . . . to take his place among the immortal poets, . . . but only as it were on sufferance. His fame does not rest assured on both a critical and popular basis.

Gerard's object is not to discover new facts but to lay emphasis on things hitherto ignored or too lightly touched on, especially the dramas. He dwells on the sympathetic grasp of Byron's genius, reaching from the noblest empire to the most oppressed of the poet's fellow-men. The spectacle of evil in humanity causes Byron's terrible satire and turns him towards Nature to gain the harmony which he fails to find in man.

To the fastidious and discriminating criticism of to-day the head and front of Byron's offending is his style. . . . If there is no higher unity that embraces the art of Tennyson and the energy of Byron, criticism must retrace its steps to find it.

He admits the lack of " magic " in this style, saying that Byron flings out his thoughts haughtily and at random. His explanation of the weakness of character-drawing in Byron's narrative poems and dramas is that Byron's interest in general humanity obscured for him the qualities of the individual ; and the lack of action in the plays is due to emphasis on motive. There follows a detailed examination of each of the plays in turn. Then, dealing once more with general matters, Gerard bases Byron's claim to rank with the " few sovereign poets " on his universality : " He is the universal poet whose sympathy with human feeling is most searching, most far reaching and profound," inferior in degree but like in kind to Shakespeare ; but, unlike Shakespeare, not veiling his own personality.

The dramatic end is with Byron secondary to the ethical end ; . . . he never palliates or excuses—never tries to make untruth seem truth.

He was, Gerard declares,

no monstrous prodigy who stumbled on greatness by mistake, but a sane poet. working by principle and law. . . . This absolute attainment of the best and highest, so rarely and so hardly reached amid repeated failings, is the mainspring of Byron's power.

Gerard places Byron, when set " in his due relation," above Shelley, Coleridge, and Keats, all three of whom were only " potentialities," though had they lived to attain " full flight " Byron would have been " outsoared." Wordsworth alone is his " peer and co-equal." To Arnold's dictum that Byron " had no light " and lacked culture, Gerard replies : " He had the insight, more priceless than culture, that is eagerly assimilative of new truths." He is filled with " humanism—the yearning to living, actual men ; the yearning to truth ; to active endeavour."

Few women figure in the history of Byron criticism ; of these few the most important is Mathilde Blind, who in 1886 edited a selection of Byron's poems for the " Canterbury Poets." Miss Blind had been editor of the Tauchnitz *Shelley* (1872), whose introduction is a landmark of Shelley criticism. She now applied her keen critical faculty and her knowledge of human nature to Byron. In a sketch of his life she gives Jeaffreson the credit for cleansing his reputation of the foul stains put thereon by " the morbidly brooding rancour of his ill-used wife " ; but remarks that in so doing Jeaffreson rubbed off a good deal of " the Rembrandt-like colour " of the Byron of tradition. She regards the poet as a representative man not of England but of Europe. Admitting the lack of exquisiteness in his prosody, she calls him " a master of monumental expression." A large part of her introduction is an examination of the three periods of his work : the Narrative-lyric ; the Dramatic ; and the Narrative-satiric. Ending with an allusion to Euphorion, she comments upon Byron's

breathless chase after the ideal ; this reckless indifference to the yearning hands and pleading voices fain to restrain him ; this scorn and contempt of all limitations, domestic and social ; this Titanic audacity and spiritual isolation.

In 1887 the same talented woman edited a selection of

Byron's letters for the " Camelot Series."   I note two points in her introduction.   First, she writes :

To make out that his enthusiasm for Greece and active efforts in her behalf were the result of a morbid craving for producing a theatrical effect, is to misapprehend the finest side of [his] character. . . . The expedition to Greece . . . was the crowning sequence of a long chain of previous efforts.

She compares this with his advocacy of Irish claims, " a crucial test of true liberalism " in 1820.   Secondly, she speaks of the lamentable blunder of Carlyle's denunciation of Byron as " a sham strong man."

Truly it would be instructive to institute a comparison between the letters of this weak English lord and those penned by the strong Scotch peasant's son.

She compares Byron's cheerful humour amid the real discomforts of the orient with Carlyle's groanings over crowing cocks and barrel-organs :

Who is the strong man here ?   The sage who, living to be eighty-four, fussed and fumed for over fifty years about such an ordinary complaint as dyspepsia, or the poet . . . who, suffering from wasting fevers and agues, never wrote otherwise than jokingly of his bodily ailments, and who, only too truly foreboding his early death, treated *that* but as a trifling matter compared to the serious issues for which he was prepared to sacrifice life ?

The centenary of Byron's birth passed with no public notice except in Greece.   Mr. Murray seems to have had some thought of preparing a Centenary edition of the poet's works, and H. Buxton Forman, the editor of Shelley and Keats, was considered as a possible editor.[1]   This project,

---

[1] See *N. & Q.*, 7th Series, ix, 8.   That Buxton Forman was not chosen is not to be regretted, for, as various remarks show (*e.g.* Keats's *Works*, iv, 256), he was quite out of sympathy with Byron.   Cf. Taine, *Hist. litt. ang.*, iv, 449.

though nothing came of it at the time, developed into the great definitive edition of Byron.[1]

In 1890 Roden Noel contributed to the " Great Writers Series " a short *Life of Lord Byron* which is, on the biographical side, an epitome of Jeaffreson's work, though it avoids the devastatingly de-pedestalizing processes of Jeaffreson's unsympathetic, unimaginative mind. The critical portion is sane, sound, and robust ; but there is little novelty in it, and the point of view is the same as that of Noel's essay of 1873.[2] In 1891 Noel followed this book with a brief estimate of Byron in Miles's *Poets and Poetry of the Nineteenth Century*.[3] He recognizes Byron's active assistance of " Liberal and National causes against temporal and ecclesiastical tyranny " ; and he singles out, as the really immoral element in Byron, the fact that " he sometimes confounded faith, devotion, and domestic affection with the cant and hypocrisy that he rightly lashed." Byron is " the man of the world's poet " ; the taint of worldliness was both inborn in him and also contracted from the society in which he moved.

In 1891 the English translation of Cesare Lombroso's *The Man of Genius* appeared. This book powerfully affected criticism during the eighteen-nineties ; its influence is very obvious in Max Nordau's *Degeneration*. During seventy years of Byron-criticism there had been occasional suggestions that the poet was not altogether sane ; but Lombroso is chiefly responsible for the view, reaffirmed later by several writers,[4] that there was a definite element of insanity in his nature. For our purposes it is sufficient to note that Lombroso frequently cites the case

---

[1] On April 19, 1888, Mrs. Rose Mary Crawshay put into the hands of trustees a fund to endow annual prizes offered to women for the best essays on Byron, Shelley and Keats. These prizes are still awarded. The only noteworthy estimate of Byron inspired by the centennial was from the American critic, George Edward Woodberry. See *The Nation* (N.Y.), xlvi, January 26, 1888, 66 ; reprinted in *The Makers of Literature*, 1901, pp. 371 f. Compare Woodberry's *The Inspiration of Poetry*, 1910, pp. 85 f.

[2] The special value of this biography is that, following the policy of the series in which it appeared, it reprints the catalogue of editions of Byron and works on Byron in the British Museum.

[3] Vol. ii, 363 f.   [4] See p. 341, *post*, note 1.

of Byron in illustration of various psycho-pathological phenomena.[1]

The disputes between Greece and Turkey which culminated in war (1894–97) again drew attention to Byron. Henry Hayman,[2] J. Gennadius,[3] and F. B. Sanborn[4] retraversed the ground of Byron's last expedition to Greece.

The story of Henley's but partially realized project to edit Byron's works may be introduced by a passage in Mr. Murray's *Lord Byron and his Detractors* : [5]

In 1896 the edition of Byron by the late W. E. Henley was announced. I saw the announcement with great regret, for I knew that even he could not produce a really good work without the documents which I possessed, while it would seriously interfere with the prospects of the edition for which my grandfather and father had been collecting materials for over sixty years. I did not wish to bring out my edition then ; . . . but . . . my hand was forced.

Mr. Murray remarks that the plan inherited from his father " might have been put off till the Greek Kalends " but for Henley's project, which compelled him " to enter at once upon a task which I regarded as a duty handed to me." Mr. Murray had an interview with " a well-known man of letters, an M.P."—the late Harry Cockayne Cust—who was a friend of Henley, to try to arrange some sort of co-opera-tion ; " but no basis of amalgamation could be arrived at."

Henley stubbornly continued his editorial work, and in 1897 published the first volume of *The Works of Lord*

---

[1] Byron's club foot ; his " solidification of the sutures " ; the fact that he was in love when eight years old ; the convulsive attack when he saw Kean act ; his " exquisite and sometimes perverted sensibility " ; his imagining that he was haunted by a spectre ; his diseased egoism ; his treatment of his wife and various mistresses ; his fear of cold ; and his hereditary bias towards extreme eccentricity of character—all are duly catalogued with elaborate comment.

[2] " Lord Byron and the Greek Patriots," *Harper's Magazine*, February 1894, pp. 365 f.

[3] " Byron and the Greeks," *English Illustrated Magazine*, xvii, June 1897, 289 f.

[4] " Odysseus and Trelawny. A Sequel to Byron's Grecian Career," *Scribner's Magazine*, xxi, April 1897, 504 f. ; " Lord Byron in the Greek Revolution," *Scribner's Magazine*, xxii, September 1897, 345 f.

[5] P. 76.

Byron, containing letters of 1804-1813. He was hopelessly handicapped by his inability to make use of the vast stores of unpublished material in the possession of Mr. Murray ; and his publisher, Mr. Heinemann, seeing the uselessness of attempting to compete with the rival edition which began to appear in 1898, retired from the undertaking. Henley's edition remains a one-volume fragment. As editor he showed the same brilliant, trenchant verve that characterizes his *Burns ;* and also the same inaccuracies in minor details. His notes are for the most part brief biographical sketches.[1] The following passage from his brief preface is a good example of his virile somewhat boisterous style :

The years whose voice-in-chief was Byron have always seemed to me among the most personal (so to speak), as certainly they are the worst understood, in the national existence. They were years of storm and triumph on all the lines of human destiny ; and they gave to history a generation at once dandified and truculent, bigoted yet dissolute, magnificent but vulgar (or so it seems to us), artistic, very sumptuous, and yet capable of astonishing effort and superb self-sacrifice. It was a generation bent above all upon living its life to the utmost of its capacity ; and, though there are still those living who can remember when its master-poet—for that, I take it, the singer of Lara and Don Juan was—was gathered to his fathers, so great a change has come upon his England in the interval between the obsequies at Hucknall Torkard and the writing of this Preface, that it is practically not less remote from ours than the England of Spenser and Raleigh.

Henley explains his purpose to collect a series of facts and portraits that will

make for a more intimate understanding of Byron's character and Byron's achievement. . . . Both these are extraordinary ; neither can be explained, or shouted, or sniffed away.

A reviewer in *The Academy,*[2] while finding in Henley's text and notes " a rare combination of vitality, for annotator,

---

[1] Reprinted together as " Byron's World," in Henley's *Works* (1908), iv, 1 f.

[2] Vol. ii, December 19, 1896, 551. See also *The Athenœum,* January 2, 1897, p. 7.

like author, is alive to the finger-tips," and while greeting Henley as the " heaven-sent editor " for whom Byron has waited so long,[1] is thoroughly anti-Byronic, writing :

Being convinced that all the king's horses and all the king's men cannot put Humpty Dumpty together again, we are content to watch with holy indifference the chance of a Byron boom.[2]

In his privately printed reply to *Astarte*, Mr. Murray has told of the arrangement which he effected with Byron's grandson, the Earl of Lovelace, whereby the Earl should become editor-in-chief of the projected definitive edition. It is unnecessary for me to recount the phases of the Earl's change of mood from one of cordial co-operation to one of violent hostility to Mr. Murray and his plan. The outcome was that Mr. Ernest Hartley Coleridge was appointed editor of the Poetry and Mr. Rowland E. Prothero (now Lord Ernle) of the Letters and Journals. The latter had the more interesting and important task, for though Mr. Coleridge was able to supply a great body of *variæ lectiones*, the poems, save for a few short pieces and a number of fragments (notably the opening stanzas of the unfinished seventeenth canto of *Don Juan*), were already all in print, whereas Prothero was able to expand enormously the body of the letters. In both sections of the work great advances were made in the assembling of bibliographical data. The edition of course inspired a great number of new estimates of Byron's achievement. And the tone of reviews changed in many cases as the edition progressed. At first doubt was expressed on many hands as to the necessity of such a

[1] The New York *Nation*, lxvii, August 18, 1898, 131 f., reviewed the " Two New Editions of Byron " together. This notice is said to be by Professor G. L. Kittridge. Mr. Prothero's work is praised, and Henley's is severely condemned. His prepossessions, his hectoring style, his unfairness, his Byron-worship, flippancy and exaggeration and blunders are noted. The reviewer remarks that Henley passes over many points needing elucidation to dwell at length on anything that strikes his fancy. " He is too nearly a genius for that lowlier function " of editorial work.

[2] Much the same view was expressed at about the same time in Professor C. H. Herford's *The Age of Wordsworth* (1897), pp. 235 f. For minor Byroniana of these years see my bibliography *sub* Rosslyn, the Earl of ; and Bancroft, George.

venture ; but the new material, enormous in amount and admirably arranged, was welcomed ever more cordially as the work advanced towards completion.[1] Besides formal reviews there were articles on various phases of Byron's work.[2] But it is manifestly impossible to record all these ephemera, and I must content myself with the principal critiques of the new edition.

I shall begin with one of the most extreme examples of anti-Byronism that I have ever read. This is Lionel Johnson's notice of Coleridge's first volume of the poems.[3] Here are some excerpts :

A beautiful devil of supreme genius—that is the Byron of tradition. . . . Infamous, perhaps : but what a poet, what

[1] An excellent series of reviews appeared in *The Athenæum* (May 14, June 23, 1900 ; April 13, 1901 ; May 24, 1902 ; August 15, 1903 ; June 4, 1904). *The Academy* was at first (*e.g.* May 21, 1898 ; June 30, 1900) very hostile ; but on April 26, 1902, it published " The Persistence of Byron " in which occurs this passage : " Those who lightly tell us that Byron is exploded have not read history aright, or they would know that a man who once moved the world profoundly can never be made little or dull. Macaulay was surely wrong when he wrote of Byron : ' To our children he will be merely a writer.' Who thinks of Byron as merely a writer ? Those writings—his letters and *Don Juan*—which most reveal the man himself most interest us now." See the next note on other articles in *The Academy*.

[2] " Byron as Self-Critic," *The Academy*, August 11, 1900, was suggested by Sir Henry Irving's announcement of his design to produce *Manfred*. This passage is interesting : " Only the other day we heard a critic speak of Byron's poetry as a dead thing. . . . Can poetry that has once profoundly stirred a people, a continent, sink into the nothingness that deserves a shrug ? . . . The present state of Byron's reputation is curious. Broadly speaking, his poetry is not read. Well, that is nothing. . . . Is Shelley widely read ? We think not. But the world calls back its mighty men of song when it has need of them ; and we are by no means sure that such a call is not going forth to Byron. . . . There must be thousands of readers to whom Byron's letters, as they are now being republished with additions, are as lamps to his works. . . . They permit—perhaps for the first time— a really clear estimate to be made of Byron's executive literary powers." In the same journal, May 2, 1903 (pp. 439 f.), there is a fine article on *Don Juan*, entitled " A Poet's Table Talk." From it I quote these sentences : " Why will men not willingly let die a poem so charged with irreverence for things above and contempt for things below ? Is it not because we all savour Byron's opinions in moments and crises of our lives, and are pleased to find them finely phrased, and linked to a splendid personality ? . . . Byron sowed the spirit of questioning, and the courage of denial, deep in the hearts of men. . . . The mere stimulus of his opinions and ejaculations is of value. He is our deputy-rebel, and he has this advantage, that he speaks not as a croaker in a corner, but, with incomparable strength of utterance, as a man who had seen the kingdoms of the world and their glory."

[3] *The Academy*, May 7, 1898, p. 489.

a man ! . . . To me, Byron, with all his pretensions and his fame, seems a very two-penny poet and a farthing man. . . . The vulgar aristocrat, the insolent plebeian, that Byron was, looks ludicrous by the side of his great contemporaries. . . . He did one thing well : he rid the world of a cad—by dying as a soldier. . . . Emphatically, he was not a poet, not if Shakespeare and Milton are poets. . . . A magnificent satirist . . . a poet of infinite tediousness in execrable verse. . . . He turned the lovely speech of English poetry into a hideous noise.

Lionel Johnson calls Byron's love of freedom " a sonorous and impassioned commonplace." He continues :

When Tennyson heard of Byron's death, he went out upon the seashore and wrote upon the sand the words, " Byron is dead ! " Seas of oblivion have swept over Byron, and washed away his fame, as the sea washed away those words.

(The simile is not very impressive, but if we must have it, let it be based on fact : Tennyson wrote the words upon a rock !) And Johnson ends : " The ' poet of passion ' is dead. . . . His wailings and howlings wring no man's heart, stir no man's pulses."

An article evidently prompted by Johnson's abuse is " The Spectre of Byron at Venice," by " H. L." [1] Johnson, however, is not mentioned by name. The writer tells of his remembrances of Byron's verse at Venice and in Greece.

Dwelling upon the vividness of this sudden revival of a forgotten literary thrill, I came to examine our present supercilious attitude towards Byron. Why does the man's magnetism outlive our superior knowledge ? Alas ! he possessed, what none of those who sneer at him to-day possess, in an infinitesimal degree—genius. . . . To-day everybody takes pains ; everybody writes well ; the thinnest minor poet that ever twittered of thrushes and rushes, of saints and altars and dead loves, could teach Byron his ignored business. . . . Spontaneity ! Here was a man who studied

---

[1] *The Academy*, June 24, 1899, p. 685.

neither dictionary nor metre ; who took you by the throat on impulse ; who swore and laughed, and writhed and cursed, as nature impelled him. . . . It will be time to dethrone Byron when we can prove that the world has forgotten him.

Two of the best of the new estimates came from America. Mr. Paul Elmer More's article, " The Wholesome Revival of Byron," [1] is still of value. He considers the recent exaltation of Wordsworth and Shelley "indicative of an effeminate and oversubtilized taste." And with the trivialities to which Tennyson carried " the petty prying nature-cult " of the Romanticists Mr. More contrasts the " breadth and scope " of Byron's treatment of nature. The classic element in his poetry " saves him from shadowy and meaningless words."

I hardly know where in English literature, outside of Shakespeare, one is to find the great passions of men set forth so directly and powerfully as in Byron. . . . I think the [moral] evil of his work has been much exaggerated. . . . His mind was right ; he never deceives himself.

Mr. More contrasts Shelley's perfect confidence in his own right-doing ; " in this glozing of evil lies the veritable danger to morals. There is no such insidious disease in Byron's mind." Admitting Byron's faults as an artist, he says :

We are not likely to learn bad grammar from him, and his dull poems are easily passed over. . . . In these days of pedantic æsthetes it is refreshing now and then to surrender ourselves to the impulse of untrammelled genius.

A similar study of " The Byron Revival " is by Professor W. P. Trent.[2] Beginning with some remarks on the renewed interest in the poet, caused in part by the two new editions of his work, Professor Trent remarks that hitherto textual criticism of Byron has been neglected and that the variant

---

[1] *The Atlantic Monthly,* December 1898.
[2] *The Forum,* **xxvi,** 1898, 242 f. ; reprinted in *The Authority of Criticism and other Essays,* 1899.

readings now published may make students think better of him " as technical artist." Byron's way to great work was embarrassed by a " mass of uniformly immature and mediocre work," which the student must know, but which the general reader may ignore. No popular revival is possible, but cultured readers may turn anew to him because of the force of his personality. Trent places the opinion of critics of judgment above the views of critics of taste (like Swinburne) and of knowledge (like Arnold). The true and competent critic recognizes in Byron the poet of an age, the author of a masterpiece of long and sustained utterance—*Don Juan*, says Trent, " gives me the sense of being in the presence of a spirit of almost boundless capacity " —a versatile genius. He remarks that " the advocates of peace among the nations should hail him as their most effective champion " ; and adds that it is unreasonable to eschew Byron on the score of blasphemy and immorality, when we " tolerate Mrs. Humphry Ward " and read *Jude the Obscure* and *Evelyn Innes*.

A thorough-going and eloquent defence of Byron came from the representative of an un-Byronic school of poetry— Stephen Phillips, in 1898 at the heights of his abilities and short-lived reputation.[1] Phillips has naturally much to say of Byron's prosody. He does not hold with the " usual opinion " that Byron's poetry is at its best excellent rhetoric, at its worst slip-shod and theatrical doggerel. He admits that Byron had no scientific mastery of verse, with care for vowel values, the system of pauses, and so forth ; but he insists that Byron's lack of concern for such matters does not interfere with the consummate metrical ability of his best work, such as *The Vision of Judgment*.

The character of the age in which we live is in itself sufficient to explain the depreciation of such a poet. We are not now, and have not been for many years, under the influence of any great world-movement, or any strong spiritual vision.

[1] " The Poetry of Byron," *The Cornhill*, lxxvii, January 1898, 16 f.

Such times as the present make poets " bend all their energies towards technical perfection." Phillips does not decry such efforts ; but it is inevitable that in such an age and in such conditions

a writer whose excellences are elemental, not technical, who convinces rather by energy and force than by elaborate and long-sought felicity, must undergo a period of detraction. . . . In the present age there is a danger of overpraising literary perfection and of underrating sheer force and natural energy. We have grown accustomed to the laboured felicities of Tennyson, to the pensive perfections of Arnold, and the diffuse technicalities of Swinburne ; and we demand . . . that no verse shall be given to the world that is hasty and ill-considered. There is, however, the greater peril of ignoring creative splendour while we look narrowly for metrical niceties.

Then, after an examination of Byron's various excellences, comes this final paragraph :

Byron, then, is to be estimated chiefly by the range of his power. In satire he is supreme, in description excellent, in power of narration the second of English poets.[1] As a dramatist he is infinitely below the Elizabethans, yet he has dramatic grip ; in imagination he is infinitely below Milton and one or two others, but imagination he has, and of a real quality. I have no intention of " placing " or attempting to " place " Byron in English literature. Undoubtedly there are three English poets who are head and shoulders above the rest : Chaucer, Shakespeare, and Milton. They are so chiefly by a power of sheer conception which no later writer has approached ; and also by a power of execution of altogether higher quality than has since appeared. After these three is a great gulf fixed. Then there is the huge throng of poets, whom it is difficult to class in any accurate order. Among the second throng, however, time will give Byron a high, probably the highest place, by virtue of his elemental force, his satire, and his width of range. He is to be set " a little lower than the angels," but to be " crowned with glory and worship."

[1] Chaucer being the first.

Much of Sir Alfred C. Lyall's essay, " The Works of Lord Byron," [1] is occupied with more or less convincing explanations of the decline of the Byron vogue. He notes that the most intimate details of the poet's life have been laid bare unmercifully ; that the Byronic school exhausted itself ; that at no time since his day has some considerable poet not occupied public attention ; that the discouragement of Byron's period gave way to the prosperity and sanguine activities of the Victorian era ; that Byron's " too exclusively worldly experience identified him with his particular class of society " ; and that his poetry, being incessantly occupied with current events, is removed from the sympathies of a later generation. Lyall finds in Byron a forerunner of the " self-reflecting analytical style that is common in our own day " but warns " the dainty art-critic " that he may burn his hands on " such metal thrown red hot from the forge." A fine comment on Swinburne's later views of Byron must be quoted entire :

The bitter disdain which Mr. Swinburne has poured upon Byron's verse and character, though tempered by acknowledgement of his strength and cleverness, and by approbation of his political views, excites some indignation and a sympathetic reaction in his favour. One can imagine the ghost of Byron rebuking his critic with the words of the Miltonic Satan :

> Ye knew me once no mate
> For you, there sitting where ye durst not soar ;

for in his masculine defiant attitude and daring flights the elder poet overtops and looks down upon the fine musical artist of our own day.

The last of the estimates directly inspired by the Coleridge-Prothero edition that I shall analyse is an article by J. Churton Collins.[2] Collins's opening remark that " there is no corner, no recess, in Byron's crowded life, into which we

[1] *Edinburgh Review*, October 1900 ; reprinted in *Studies in Literature and History*, pp. 179 f.

[2] *Quarterly Review*, April 1905 ; reprinted in *Studies in Poetry and Criticism*.

are not admitted," shows a lack of any suspicion of the
suppression of certain letters or of the new " revelations "
which in that same year, 1905, *Astarte* was to furnish. Much
of the article is occupied with literary parallels of the sort
in which Collins delighted. But the characteristics which
impressed all favourable critics of this period are noted :

Shakespeare excepted, his versatility is without parallel
among English poets. . . . *Childe Harold* and *Don Juan*,
regarded comprehensively, are perhaps the two most brilliant
achievements in the poetry of the world. . . . The greatness
of Byron lies in the immense body and mass of the work
which he has informed and infused with life, in his almost
unparalleled versatility, in the power and range of his
influential achievement.

I have now to pass in rapid review a few other estimates
of the years 1896–1905. Lafcadio Hearn lectured twice
on Byron at Tokio.[1] In the earlier discourse he said :

Byron is now scarcely read. It is true that at the very
moment of this lecture a new edition of Byron's works is
being given out to the public ; but I think that its success
will be only of a limited kind. Byron is almost dead in
our literature. . . . The reason that his work is no longer
read or valued, except by the young, is that it is nearly
all done without patience, without self-control, and therefore
without good taste, or the true spirit of art. . . . Poetry
requires qualities of character that did not exist in the nature
of Byron. . . . The great genius never did its best, never
tried to do its best.

But in his later lecture Hearn contradicts himself, saying :

Any critic can find bad work in Byron ; but scarcely any
poet can show us at certain splendid moments, the same
strength and the same fire of emotional life.

If we are left uncertain as to where Hearn stands, there is
no uncertainty about Henley in his last bold utterance on
his favourite poet : [2]

[1] 1896 and 1902 ; *Interpretations of Literature* (1916), i, 111 f. and 124 f.
[2] *Pall Mall Magazine*, August 1900 ; quoted in *The Academy*, July 21,
1900, p. 45.

And Kaled, Gulnare, Zuleika, Haidee, are they so very much
less interesting, do they touch us so very much less instantly,
are they so very much more remote from reality, than
" faintly smiling Adeline " and these other Tennysonian
beauties ?   And the May Queen —with her Robin and those
" garden tools " and that " Traviata cough " of hers—
are we really to take her to our bosoms now—even now !—
before that thrice excellent Aurora Raby and our " frolic
grace Fitz-Fulke," who have so much to do with the gaiety
and supremacy of the last cantos of *Don Juan?* I trow
not ; for these shams signed " Tennyson " are already dead,
and not dead only but damned.

The comparison extends beyond Tennyson to—

that mass of half-inspired, half-realized, half-uttered, and
wholly perfunctory and futile gabble which—some noble
passages apart— is Browning.

And after a side-blow at Rossetti, Henley turns to Shelley :

In truth, Mr. Coleridge is fully justified in remarking that
Byron's poetry " holds it own." Does Shelley's ? I
wonder ! some lyrics apart, I wonder ! Has *The Cenci*
never been found out ? do people still find sustenance in
The Revolt of Islam and *The Witch of Atlas,* and *Rosalind
and Helen* and *The Sensitive Plant?* Were these things
ever anything to anybody ? I'll not believe it ! Or, if
they were, in the days of their birth, are they anything
to anybody now, after fourscore years and a surfeit of
Tennyson and Browning and Rossetti ? . . . On the whole,
it looks as though Matthew Arnold had but grasped half
the truth when he said that Byron and Wordsworth would
head the procession of Nineteenth Century English poets
into the " mist and hum " of the Twentieth Century. It
may be Shelley and Byron ; it may be Byron and Keats ;
it may be Byron and Coleridge. But, whoever the one,
the other will certainly be Byron.[1]

---

[1] For minor Byroniana of this period see my bibliography *sub* Laurent,
E. and Warner, C. D.   Other items are : *Newark as a Publishing Town,*
by T. M. B. (1898) which tells (pp. 18 f.) of Byron's relations with Newark ;
two articles by J. M. Bulloch—" The Lucky Duffs," (*English Illustrated
Magazine,* June 1898, pp. 235 f.) which traces the rise of the Duff family
and suggests that Byron's love of action came from the Gordons and his
intellect from the Duffs ; and " The Tragic Adventures of Byron's

Theodore Watts-Dunton, for some incomprehensible reason, was selected to write the article on Byron for the revised edition of *Chambers' Cyclopœdia of English Literature* (1903).[1] The article is unsympathetic, sometimes unjust ; and the entire weight of emphasis is misplaced. Watts-Dunton declares that " no competent critic " has ever ranked Byron among the great poets. (It must be remembered that in Watts-Dunton's opinion the only competent critics in England lived at Putney.) His own competence may be judged by his statements that Byron's lameness was the central fact of his life, and that his misery was caused chiefly by fat and shortness of money. Questioning Byron's " sincerity," Watts-Dunton goes so far as to question the licentiousness of Byron's Italian life ; he believes that the extent of his debauchery, as related in Byron's letters, is inconsistent with the huge amount of literary work accomplished. But on this problem, too, the critic's competence may be open to doubt. The highest accomplishment of Byron, Watts-Dunton declares, was the ability to be jaunty while carrying a weight of matter. He ends with a long disquisition intended to prove that Byron was not really the " poet of liberty " (the only genuine one being, we are to assume, the critic's house-mate at The Pines) ; and that he revolted from " those moral curbs and restraints without which society would rapidly fall to pieces." The only lesson that Byron taught " was the sacred rights of fine gentlemanism." On the whole this article is more illuminating as to Watts-Dunton than as to Lord Byron.[2]

Ancestors. The Gordons of Gight. A Study in Degeneration " (*Aberdeen Free Press*, November 11, 18, and 25, 1898), which traces the record of murder, suicide, duels, sudden deaths, executions, sale of estates, imprisonment, scandal, etc., in the Gordon family, and asks : " What chance had . . . Byron with such a pedigree behind him ? " E. Derry's *Rhymes of Road, Rail, and River* [1899 ?] contains a poem called " Six Days at Geneva and Chamonix " in which there are allusions to Byron along with other famous memories of those places. See especially p. 17. Theodore Wratislaw's *Swinburne* (1900) shows frequent evidence of violent anti-Byronism. Henry Murray, in a review of Wratislaw (reprinted in *Robert Buchanan . . . and other Essays*, 1901, p. 116) protests against the view that Byron is " dead," and quotes amusingly the Scotsman : " I'd no bury him just yet—wait till he smells a wee grewsome."

[1] Vol. iii, 118 f.

[2] George Rebec's essay " Byron and Morals " (*The International Journal*

In 1905 English readers unacquainted with the original Danish work (1875) were offered an extended view of the continental estimate of Byron in the English translation of George Brandes's *Main Currents in Nineteenth Century Literature,* in which chapters xvii-xxii of volume four (" Naturalism in England ") are devoted to Byron, while to no other poet are more than two chapters allowed. Brandes's famous and brilliant study, being European, not English, is beyond the limits of this book ; it must suffice to say that he considers Byron as the central and representative figure of the liberal movement in letters not in England only but in Europe at large.[1]

of Ethics, xiv, October 1903, 39 f.) is an impressive estimate, leading to the conclusion that " the essential final influence of Byron is a powerfully moral one. . . . The vindication of Byron's essential morality [lies in] the boundless Byronic despair, and in his holding aloft the uncompromising standard of revolt." Mr. Rebec contrasts Wordsworth, who accepted comfortable illusion, acquiescence, and conformity, with Byron who rejected them.

[1] " Poetry and Rebellion," by George M. Trevelyan (*The Independent Review,* 1905 ; reprinted in revised form in *Clio, a Muse,* pp. 101 f.), is a review of Brandes, volume iv. I quote two sentences. " His [Byron's] service to mankind was this, that in the hour of universal repression and discouragement, he made all England and all Europe hear the note of everlasting defiance. . . . He spake, and the oppressor looked pitiable, and the inquisitor stood stark naked to the scorn of the world." And this : that the deficiency of Byron's liberalism lay in his old-fashioned ideas of women. " He understood the rights of man, but he seems never to have heard of the rights of women." A popular article with many excellent illustrations is " Byron," by J. Wight Duff, in *The Bookman,* October, 1905, pp. 9 f. Duff makes the interesting suggestion that Byron's reputation has been harmed by the sort of selections that have been made for school-books ; " it is useless to pretend that Byron can be judged apart from *Don Juan.*" He notes that Byron's fame stands higher than it did a generation ago ; " a return is at last being made to him by responsible critics." *Good Words* (xlv, 1904, 467 f. and 579 f.) published " The King of the Humbugs," an incomplete and hitherto unpublished satire by Byron.

CHAPTER XV

THE LATEST PHASE

THE perturbed spirit of Byron was not allowed to rest, and in 1905 his own grandson, Ralph Milbanke, Earl of Lovelace, reopened " the Byron mystery " by publishing his extraordinary book, *Astarte*.[1] The generation that had been disturbed and excited by Mrs. Stowe's " revelations " had mostly passed away, and the charges brought against Byron and his half-sister had largely been forgotten when from a clear sky came this renewal of the accusations, supported by documents and formulated officially, as it were, by the head of the Byron family. The Countess of Lovelace's explanation of her late husband's conduct [2] is that Lord Lovelace had all his life brooded indignantly upon the contumely heaped upon his grandmother, Lady Byron, towards whom he had been brought closely in childhood and upon whom all his loyalty and affection were lavished to the exclusion of any loyalty to the memory of his grandfather, the great poet. It was in mistaken zeal to free his grandmother from charges which were in reality not in the least serious that he thus openly accused Lord Byron of the gravest crime. It was a witty Scottish professor who remarked to me that " Lord Lovelace should

[1] *Astarte. A Fragment of Truth concerning George Gordon Byron, Sixth Lord Byron. Recorded by his Grandson, Ralph Milbanke, Earl of Lovelace.* London : Printed at the Chiswick Press, 1905. In order to secure copyright, a few copies of this work were sold, but the majority were given to a strictly selected group of representative people. The " new edition with many additional letters, edited by Mary, Countess of Lovelace " was published by Christophers in 1921. There is also a pirated and much abbreviated American reprint, Buffalo, 1905.

[2] *Ralph, Earl of Lovelace. A Memoir.* By Mary, Countess of Lovelace, 1920.

have learned from his great namesake that he could not love even his grandmother so much without loving honour more." In any case, the insults to his grandmother, a worthy woman of whom the world would never have heard but for her marriage to a great and wayward genius, were largely the figments of the Earl's fancy ; but, be that as it may, his widow's attempt to justify his action is quite comprehensible. But there the matter should have been allowed to rest ; and I see no justification for bringing *Astarte* out from the twilight obscurity of the original edition and republishing it in 1921. In this new edition some matter, partly unrelated to Byron, partly a series of attacks on the Murrays, is omitted ; and thirty-four letters from Byron (thirty-one to his sister ; three to his wife) are published for the first time. These are certainly a great and welcome addition to the correspondence of the most clever of English letter-writers ; and to come upon them, towards the end of *Astarte*, after the sickly motive-finding, conscience-probing epistles of Lady Byron and her set, is to come from a psychiatric clinic out into wide free air. Some are naughty, some are revengeful, some are boisterous, some are sentimental ; but in all we hear the voice of genius. Save one sentence in one letter (an allusion to Lucretia Borgia) there is not a line in them capable of being perverted by the most unhealthy imagination into evidence against Byron and Mrs. Leigh.

I have digressed to notice the new material in the edition of 1921, and must return to Lovelace's work. It is unnecessary to review the controversy between the Earl and Mr. Murray ; [1] it is enough to state that the issues raised and

---

[1] See *Lord Byron and his Detractors*, privately printed for Members of the Roxburghe Club, 1906. This is made up of three articles : " Astarte," by the late E. H. Pember, a reply to Lord Lovelace's charges, revealing the flimsiness of much of the evidence and coming to the conclusion that at worst the verdict in the case must be " not proven " (pp. 3 f.) ; " Lord Byron and Lord Lovelace " by Mr. Murray, a complete refutation of the Earl's account of the relations of the Byron family with the Murrays (pp. 60 f. ; reprinted from *The Monthly Review*, February 1906) ; and " Lord Lovelace on the Separation of Lord and Lady Byron," by R. E. Prothero (pp. 91 f. ; reprinted from *The Monthly Review*, March 1906). See also my article, " The Byron Problem," *The Nation* (N.Y.), cxiii, August 21, 1921, pp. 207 f. In this I go into the matter more fully than

settled between the two are so clear-cut and conclusive as to warrant the assertion that no statement in *Astarte* is to be accepted unless substantiated beyond doubt by documentary evidence. Much is made of the " fact " that Sir Leslie Stephen, an expert in the art of biography, agreed with Lord Lovelace ; but the documents offered in support of this statement show only that Stephen outlined the course of the argument to be followed by Lovelace, not that he agreed with him. It is a great pity that Lovelace did not follow Stephen's outline closely. Such accusations (granting that it was necessary to drag them from the limbo of old, unhappy, far-off things) should have been made as simply and as briefly as possible. But what we have is a reckless medley—a semi-fictitious reconstruction of the circumstances of Byron's life with detailed accounts of actions and speeches of which there can be no possible proof and with a large amount of discussion of subjects extraneous to the theme, supported by long pedantic citations from Hazlitt, Newman, Renan, Chateaubriand, and many other writers. The method employed is rather that of an awkward novelist who has not mastered the technique of his art than of a lawyer or historian. It reminds one of Balzac in his clumsier moments or of Bourget in its extravagantly subtle interpretations of character and motive.

Lord Lovelace did not know how to present a legal argument and he had no literary taste or gift, but he possessed a certain clumsy patience which resulted in the creation of an " atmosphere " or state of mind fitted for the reception of his weighty and atrocious family " secret." That atmosphere is so close and sultry that the light penetrates through it reluctantly. A single reading of the book is apt to carry conviction, and since oxen and wainropes would not drag most people through its dreary length twice,

---

is necessary here ; from it I have taken some sentences in my text. Of reviews of the 1921 edition of *Astarte* see also *The Saturday Review*, July 16, 1921 ; *The Nation and Athenæum*, August 6, 1921 ; and *The Spectator*, August 6, 1921. These well represent opposing views of the question. See also Lord Ernle's article, " The End of the Byron Mystery," *The Nineteenth Century*, xc, August 1921, 207 f.

it has convinced many readers who have not paused to sift and weigh the evidence.[1] But whether it wins acceptance or not, and in spite of its miserable theme and inartistic treatment, *Astarte* cannot but be of intense interest as a " human document " exposing not only the mentality and morality of Byron and of the women whose fates were interwined with his, but also the mentality and morality of the Earl of Lovelace. To the student of the human heart it offers matter for melancholy contemplation. If not a reflection of Byron, or at best a distorted reflection, it is the very mirror of Lord Lovelace, in its mingling of pride, arrogance, miscellaneous scholarship, and strange ingenuousness. It must be insisted upon that it is not an immoral book ; or if there be anything corrupting in it it comes not from Byron but from his grandson. The veiled defence of incest should have been suppressed in the revised edition in mercy to the writer's memory, as should also have been blotted out the shocking passage in which Lovelace expressed the wish that Mrs. Leigh had gone off to Italy with Byron to live openly as his mistress. Then, says this unworthy grandson of a great genius, " Lady Byron's justification would have been complete, and great would have been their rejoicing." It may be questioned whether poor Byron, with all his sins, would ever have stooped so low as to pen that sentence.

The solution of the problem hinged in large degree upon the identification of the woman to whom Byron addressed the famous letter of May 17, 1819.[2] The internal evidence

---

[1] Yet what shall we say of this letter from Lady Gregory to Lord Lovelace (*Memoir*, p. 149) ? " I don't think the true and painful story could have been told with greater reverence—and I feel that Byron's own life-story is in some curious way made better by all the truth being told." I have read *Astarte* through in both editions, and " reverence " seems to me to be a quality peculiarly lacking in it. And what of this letter from Henry James (*ibid*. pp. 151 f.) ? " As I went on I saw your act . . . as a high and grave inevitability absolutely complete in itself, and justified by the very terms in which you perform it." James protests against the large amount of extraneous matter ; he would have preferred " your bundle of precious relics wrapped in a plain white napkin—instead of in your cloth of gold." " Precious relics ! " " Cloth of gold ! "

[2] See my article in *The Nation*, just cited, and Mr. Edgcumbe's book about to be discussed. To re-examine the problem here is needless.

supports the view that that woman was Mrs. Chaworth-Musters ; and working upon this clue [1] Mr. Richard Edgcumbe produced his *Byron : the Last Phase* (1909). That part of his book which really deals with the last, the Grecian, phase of Byron's career is an admirably weighed summary of the evidence as to the conduct and character of Byron during the days when he manifested his energy, his heroism, and his gift of leadership. The complex explanation advanced as an alternative to *Astarte* is not convincing. The external evidence is nearly worthless, but curiously the theory explains a good many mysterious utterances in Byron's writings.[2] The conclusion I draw from his book is that the " mystery " has in it so many contradictory elements that it is incapable of a solution that will satisfy all inquirers.

The baffling contradictions of the evidence become more apparent in Lord Broughton's *Recollections of a Long Life*, which Mr. Murray published in 1909. In these volumes there is much material relating to Byron and to the history of his reputation. The account of the separation and of the destruction of the " Memoirs " is especially noteworthy. The tone, as those who know the character of John Cam Hobhouse would expect, is everywhere loyal, manly and healthy-minded. The narrative of the separation, a contemporary document, is difficult to reconcile with the charges brought against Byron by Lord Lovelace.

Francis Gribble's *The Love Affairs of Lord Byron* (1910) may be passed over with the remark that the author accepts

---

[1] Mr. Edgcumbe had already advanced part of his argument several years before the appearance of *Astarte*. See *The Athenæum*, August 24, 1901, p. 253, for his contention that Byron's *Stanzas to the River Po* relate not to La Guiccioli but to Mary Chaworth. Cf. Bibliography, *sub* Bruce, J. D.

[2] I have discussed the matter at length in my *Dramas of Lord Byron* (1915), pp. 69 f., where I suggested tentatively a new argument, based on parallels between *Manfred* and *The Dream*, in support of Mr. Edgcumbe's thesis. This argument has lately been independently suggested by Mr. R. C. K. Ensor in *The New Statesman*, May 7, 1921. See also Andrew Lang's bitter reply to Mr. Edgcumbe in *The Fortnightly Review*, n.s. lxxxviii, August 1910, 269 g. ; Augustin Filon's " Le Crime de Lord Byron," in the *Revue de deux Mondes*, January 15, 1912, pp. 387 f. ; Miss Mayne's *Byron*, ii, 327 f. ; and other authorities referred to in the pages of my monograph on the dramas.

Mr. Edgcumbe's theory of renewed intimacy with Mary
Chaworth, but rejects Edgcumbe's identification of Medora
Leigh as Byron's child by Mary.[1]

The only full-length biography of Byron written by a
woman is Miss Ethel C. Mayne's (1912). She is a clever
woman of the world who, with the instinct of the novelist,
is an adept at the analysis of character. In her book
literary criticism is introduced only incidentally and though
her taste is sound (as when she recognizes that *Don Juan*
" is one of the incomparable splendours of the human mind ")
she makes no effort to justify her taste on theoretical or
philosophic grounds. As a woman she sees that Byron
was unfair to women ; but she emphasizes by contrast
the loyalty and frankness of his relations with men. " For
friendship, fame, and freedom he could act ; for love he
could only dream." She feels the fascination of the poet's
personality and in her closing words well expresses his
appeal :

Is it his fame, his beauty, his heroism ? None of these.
It is his enthralling humanity. We are mourning for
ourselves.

Miss Mayne accepts Lord Lovelace's charges as proved,
and dismisses Mr. Edgcumbe's theories with unwarranted
contempt.[2]

The tangle of evidence became worse when, in *Lord Byron's
Correspondence*, edited by Mr. Murray (1922), there were

---

[1] It is a frivolous book. Mr. Gribble's qualifications for writing on
Byron are betrayed in his remark (where he forgets the famous lines in
the epistle of Donna Julia to Juan) that Byron's love-affairs " were the
principal incidents of his life, and almost the only ones."

[2] Two reviews of Miss Mayne's book represent opposing opinions of
her acceptance of *Astarte*. *The Nation* (New York ; May 8, 1913, pp.
476 f.) notes her omission of Mr. Edgcumbe's arguments that the most
damnatory letter in *Astarte* can scarcely have been addressed to Mrs.
Leigh, and her suppression of the lines in *Manfred* that tell against *Astarte*.
Moreover, she does not weaken Hobhouse's testimony. " We are bound
to assert our positive conviction," says this reviewer, " that the weight
of available evidence exculpates Byron and Mrs. Leigh." *The Athenæum*
(November 2, 1912, p. 511), on the other hand, agrees with her interpretation of the old scandal, and adds : " Byron, whose genius and whose
sins were alike colossal, is on his greater pilgrimage into the centuries, a
wondrous figure."

published certain letters from Byron to Lady Melbourne which supported Lord Lovelace's charges. In the face of so many contradictory pieces of testimony the only judicial attitude is that of suspended judgment ; the philosophical attitude is to dismiss the problem from the mind and henceforth, disregarding ancient scandals, estimate Byron as poet and as man of letters. Not that I would urge that the passionate personality and romantic career of this fascinating figure of the past be forgotten ; and even did I urge it, the twentieth century would continue to turn oftener to the story of his life than to the pages of his works. But it must be remembered that the great Byron is to be found, not in gossip about his " love-affairs " but in *Childe Harold* and *Manfred, Don Juan* and *Cain*, and the letters.[1]

I have reached the last stage of our long inquiry and am able to turn from the details of biography to literary criticism. The most important of recent estimates of Byron must be examined ; I have selected twelve essays and lectures.

Mr. J. F. A. Pyre's article " Byron in our Day " [2] lures me once more beyond the bounds of English criticism, for this American essay is, I think, one of the most satisfying of all estimates of the poet. It is long and packed with matter, and I cannot do justice to it in a paragraph. Mr. Pyre sketches the decadence of English poetry from the full flower of romanticism in Keats, through the æstheticism of Tennyson and the morbid religious voluptuousness of Rossetti, to the technical extremes of Swinburne, where

---

[1] I relegate to a foot-note some remarks on recent inquiries into the problem of Byron's sanity. His symptoms are discussed in Joseph Grasset's *The Semi-Insane and the Semi-Responsible* (1907 ; English translation, p. 249) and are classed among those indicated by the title of the book. Fulsome praise of Byron's poetry is combined with an excursus into physiology, anatomy, and psychology in *The Last Illness of Lord Byron : a Study in the Borderland of Genius and Madness*, by John Knott, M.D. (St. Paul, Minnesota, 1921). A somewhat similar but better balanced investigation is *In Spite of Epilepsy. Being a Review of the Lives of three great Epileptics—Julius Cæsar, Mohammed, Lord Byron*, by Matthew Wood, M.D. (1913). Dr. Wood believes that Byron's epilepsy, at first psychic, perhaps only emotional, developed into *grand mal*. He examines Byron's own veiled allusions to the disease. Finden's reproduction (a mere caricature, by the way) of Harlowe's drawing of Byron, Dr. Wood considers exhibits the *facies epilepticus*.

[2] *The Atlantic Monthly*, xcix, April 1907, 542 f.

verse merges into music. Thin and quavering imitators
followed him.

We get farther and farther from normal human experience,
into a region where white peacocks wander about, in gas-lit
gardens ; . . . finally we have for gain the patchouli and
lingerie of *London Nights* . . . One would like to hear at
last the large laugh . . . of Rabelais, or even the hearty
blasphemies of *Don Juan*, clearing through this atmosphere
of insipid and effeminate pruriency.

But, says Mr. Pyre, the only people who return to-day
to the natural world are " a plaintive little band of Gælic
minstrels."   " Romanticism has run out.'

The old charges against Byron are met in novel ways.
Of his lack of artistry and of any sense of his mission as a
poet Pyre says :

The professional artist as such he despised. . . . One of
the chief sources of his aversion for Wordsworth was the
smugness with which (as he saw it) that poet assumed the
rôle of professional good man and priestly bard.

Pyre admits the much-debated " insincerity," but

his posing was mostly harmless—as superficial as the swagger
and millinery of the soldier, merely adventitious to the
genuine strength and gallantry underneath.

Of Byron's treatment of women :

It may be doubted if the critics have done justly in treating
his delinquencies less leniently than those of Shelley and
Burns.   There was less of cowardice and cruelty in Byron's
treatment of women than was the case with either Burns
or Shelley.

Byron was often whimsical, unreasonable, ungenerous ;
sometimes revengeful ; he was violent and impatient. But
he was capable of fine magnanimity and affection ; he
was clear-sighted and strong. His was not the mind that
can recreate what it finds in the world in new splendour
and entirety. The law to which he subdues the facts of
the world is his own being. This is the source of his might

as well as of his childishness. Pyre sees something noble and stirring in the arrogance which sees in all nature and all society the prototype of the poet's own life.

One man stands up and says to all the world, " This is I : I am one with the storm! The rolling thunder-storm, reverberating through the abysses of the Alps, is the echo of my own soul! All desolate lands and cities—Greece, unhappy Greece, Venice with her faded grandeurs, and Rome, a plundered ruin—*express me*. But I am greater than these symbols, myself, one and indivisible—a tortured human soul, unconquered, unsurrendering." This it was which made conquest of reviving Europe. To an age of awakening individuality, he proclaimed the dogma of rebellion, of freedom and defiance. And he became as a pillar of fire to superannuated peoples. . . . His sense of the unsatis-factoriness of life is in itself recreative. One does not hate the false, unless his eyes, however bandaged, have had some glimpse of the truth. . . . The total effect is not that of despair but of defiant will.

This suggestive essay is charged with interesting com-ment ; but I must turn from it to one by the author of *London Nights*, a book condemned by name by Mr. Pyre. Yet Mr. Arthur Symons's study of Byron [1] is a model of open-minded appreciation of a poet opposed in many parti-culars to the critic who discusses him. For in criticism Mr. Symons has concerned himself largely with form, shade, subtlety, fine discriminations ; and in his verse emphasis has been abhorrent to him. A feeling for Byron's weaknesses as well as for his elements of strength is visible throughout this appreciation. I have space for but a few extracts.

The strain of commonness which we find in the greatest of those to whom action was more than thought. . . . He speaks to humanity in its own voice, heightened to a pitch which carries across Europe. . . . His mind was never to him a kingdom, but always part of the tossing democracy of human kind. . . . Himself in actual life the least con-trolled of men, . . . a great emergency always found him quietly ready for it.

[1] *The Romantic Movement in English Poetry* (1909), pp. 239 f.

Symons declares that Byron's eagerness for applause does not denote vulgarity of mind ; it was essential to his subject-matter. " An obscure person on his travels," writing such poetry, would have been ridiculous ; but Byron filled Europe with the thought of his presence in the Alps, and added history to Waterloo because *his* " tread was on an empire's dust."

It is not only that he never forgets himself, but he never forgets that he is a lord, and that one of his feet is not perfect.

His self-torture, gloom and pride were given him " lest the world should satisfy him, which is failure in life."

In 1910 the editor of the definitive edition of Byron's Poetry contributed his final estimate of Byron to the eleventh edition of the *Encyclopædia Britannica*.[1] This article is necessarily largely occupied with biographical matter ; but it contains some excellent general observations :

Self-will was the very pulse of the machine. Pride ruled his years. . . . It stands to reason that Byron knew that his sorrow and his despair would excite public interest. . . . It does not follow that he was a hypocrite. His quarrel with mankind, his anger against fate, were perfectly genuine. . . . Cynical speeches . . . need not be taken too literally. Byron talked for effect. . . . There is an increasing tendency on the part of modern critics to cast a doubt on Byron's sanity. . . . Inherited bad blood on both sides, . . . of a neurotic temperament, . . . at one time he maddened himself with drink, but there is no evidence that his brain was actually diseased. . . . He was born with certain noble qualities which did not fail him at his worst. He was courageous, he was kind, and he loved truth rather than lies. He was a worker and a fighter. . . . A great creative artist . . . his canvass is crowded with new and original images. . . . With whatever limitations as artist

---

[1] Vol. iv, 897 f. Mr. Coleridge delivered a charming address on " Lord Byron " before the Royal Society of Literature, May 25, 1904 ; it is printed in the Society's *Transactions*, second series, xxv, 127 f. He gives a delightful account of his editorial labours ; reviews Byron's work by periods ; and speculates upon the causes of his continental fame. To *Poet's Country*, edited by Andrew Lang (1907) Mr. Coleridge contributed some pleasant but insignificant chat on Byron (pp. 46 f.).

or moralist, he invented characters and types . . . real enough and distinct enough to leave their mark on society as well as on literature. . . . He wrote because " his mind was full " of his own loves, his own griefs, but also to register a protest against some external tyranny of law or faith or custom.

Coleridge then attempts to explain Byron's failure to retain his hold on English literature. The knowledge and culture he taught were soon available through other channels. His revolutionary politics neither interested nor concerned middle-class radicalism and liberalism. The religious revival and a sterner moral code turned men's minds to Wordsworth and then to Tennyson. His technique came to be analysed calmly by critics undazzled by his personality. And poetry came to be regarded by many readers as, in some sort, a substitute for religion. " Without doubt," says Coleridge, " there has been a reconsideration of Byron's place in literature, and he stands higher than he did, say, in 1870." His unorthodoxy no longer alarms ; what once shocked and distressed men is now seen to be humorous. As a satirist in the widest sense of the word, as an analyser of human nature, he comes, at whatever distance, after and yet next to Shakespeare.

To the same year, 1910, belongs William J. Courthope's study of Byron in his *History of English Poetry*.[1] Courthope notes two characteristics of Byron's genius : " An intense self-consciousness, joined to a power, probably unequalled, of absorbing the social atmosphere about him and giving imaginative expression to it." *Childe Harold*, he says, " became famous because it was representative " ; because Byron gave poetic expression to the feeling of *ennui* in cultivated society. Because of the mixture of contemplation and action in his genius he was the fullest embodiment of romanticism in English poetry.

Byron at first attempted to give a personal and romantic dress to revolutionary sentiment, and afterwards, when

---

[1] Vol. vi, chapter viii : " Romantic Self-representation : Byron."

his rupture with society was complete, sought for suitable epic and dramatic forms of verse in which to express his contempt for the moral standards of his country.

His " excessive indulgence of individuality . . . betrayed him into moral anarchy." Throughout this study Mr. Courthope is constantly, after his wont, stressing the political and social relations of Byron's poetry.

Two less important estimates of Byron, both of 1910, must be discussed briefly ; and to a foot-note shall be consigned other Byroniana of 1907-1911.[1] In his essay on " The Optimism of Byron," [2] Mr. G. K. Chesterton argues characteristically that Byron's pessimism is an inverted optimism ; that his depreciation of man was for the purpose of exalting nature ; that " his really bitter moments were his frivolous moments " ; and so forth.

[1] There are suggestive remarks in Mr. Charles Whibley's introduction to *Poems by Lord Byron* in " The Golden Poets Series " (1907). The critic describes Byronism as at once melancholy and combative ; dejection giving way to violence. " No one understood the use and meaning of Byronism better than the poet himself." Mr. Whibley notes the striking paradox of " the contempt of this great Romantic for Romance of every kind." " We are told that . . . Byron is no longer read. If that be so, he shares the fate of many masters . . . Byron is paying the common penalty of grandeur." *The Ghosts of Picadilly*, by George E. Street (1907), contains a sketch of Byron's life while he lived at the Albany (pp. 91 f.). Compare Street's *Book of Essays* (1903), which contains two reviews of Prothero's edition of the Letters, reprinted from *Blackwood's*, November 1899 and December 1901. I have not seen Street's *Books and Things*, which has in it, I believe, something on Byron. Nor have I seen A. J. MacDonald's *Star-gazing* (1907) which, according to a bookseller's catalogue, contains poems on Byron, Burns, Shelley, and other poets. W. A. Shaw's article, " The Authentic Portraits of Byron " (*The Connoisseur*, July and August, 1911, xxx, 155 f., and 251 f.) reproduces twenty-five portraits and gives a list of those unvouched for by reliable biographical data. (Compare " The ' Gex ' Portrait of Lord Byron," by C. W. Macfarlane, *The Century*, June 1914, pp. 221 f. which tells of the discovery of a portrait at Gex in the Lower Jura near Geneva. Macfarlane notes the signs of genuineness : the greater massiveness of the left side of the face ; the great size of the left eye ; the faintness of the dimple in the chin, which idealizations exaggerate ; and the general virility and vigour of the head. This accords with contemporary testimony of Hobhouse and Hanson, and in these points the " Gex " portrait resembles the Thorwaldsen bust, etc.) *The Pilgrim Poet : Lord Byron of Newstead*, by Albert Brecknock (1911) has many excellent illustrations. It is written from the " local " point of view, with much about Newstead, Hucknall, etc. *The Diary of Dr. John William Polidori*, edited by W. M. Rossetti (1911), contains many side-lights on Byron but nothing to alter one's general estimate of his character save perhaps that it shows that the accounts of Byron's bad treatment of Polidori have been exaggerated.

[2] *Twelve Types*, pp. 31 f.

The address on the occasion of the foundation of the Byron Chair of English Literature at University College, Nottingham, was delivered by Mr. Whitelaw Reid, at that time American Ambassador to Great Britain, on November 29, 1910.[1] Reid calls Byron " perhaps the greatest poet of the nineteenth century, certainly its most celebrated Englishman." He is thoroughly uncritical, classing *Don Juan* and *The Waltz* together, and talking of the " wearisome pages of mere degradation " in the former poem. After the " sparkling froth and dull, noisome sediment " of his work have been rejected, Reid finds that a body of noble verse, headed by *Childe Harold*, remains. I should not have given this much space to the discourse but for the importance of the occasion on which it was delivered.

Of all the critiques of Byron produced in the twentieth century I should select the chapter in Professor Oliver Elton's *Survey of English Literature* (1912) [2] as, on the whole, the most satisfactory in its sympathetic yet judicious understanding of Byron's character and in the lucid and keen quality of its criticism. The chapter is so carefully articulated that I find it especially difficult to convey any idea of its excellence in brief analysis, and I must content myself with notes on a few of Professor Elton's points and with a few excerpts. To Elton Byron remains " an inspiration and a living force." He finds in Byron's poetry as the years advanced towards his premature death,

if not a steady growth, still a true advance, a gradual shedding of false experiment, a growing realization of beauty, a visible increase of veracity, and, in the long run, victory.

Here is Elton's comment upon the third canto of *Childe Harold* :

When all superficial posturing is allowed for, there remains a vast and warranted egoism, manlier than Rousseau's, and, if less august, nearer to us all than Wordsworth's,

---

[1] *Byron* (1910). The proceedings on this occasion are reported in an appendix, pp. 40 f.

[2] Vol. ii, chapter xvii, pp. 135 f.

by virtue of the suffering involved in it : and this egoism, luckily careless of offending, gave a noticeable and still unexhausted impulse to the enlargement of the European spirit. This it did, not by making current any new and fertile thought, but by the spectacle of a large nature, at issue with itself, and losing itself, at least for passing solace, both in the pageant of the past, and in a vision so splendid of the banded peoples of the world, as should even now steel us against all the allurements of Reaction, that sterile temptress. Carlyle's counsel, " Close thy Byron, open thy Goethe," implies a false contrast. For to open Goethe is to read the song of Euphorion, and the praise of *Cain ;* and thus we are led to see Byron's emancipating power better, and to open him again after all.

Like so many critics, Elton meditates upon the causes of the decline in Byron's reputation ; and makes this suggestion, among others :

The frank, mocking representation of society on a large scale has been taken from poetry and given over to the novel. But the novel, in the hands of Dickens and Thackeray . . . was timid beside *Don Juan*—as timid in comment as in topic. The truth is that no English writer of either verse or prose since Byron has had at once the courage, the zest, and the aptitude for the same task. Poetry may have become franker in the record of casuistical passions and intimate lusts ; but it has never again broadened to the business of depicting battles and seraglios and the high comedy of intrigue.

For the last time I must gather together in a foot-note [1]

[1] Fifteen items must be recorded. (1) *Poems and Letters of Lord Byron*, edited from the original manuscripts in the possession of W. K. Bixby, by W. N. C. Carlton. (Published by the Society of the Dofobs, Chicago, 1912.) Of this handsome volume, which contains fourteen letters not in Prothero's edition, but fifty-two copies were printed. (2) *Poetical Works of Lord Byron. Containing only those Poems which Time has proven Immortal.* (New York : The Clover Press, 1912.) The taste betrayed by the format of this book is execrable, and I mention it only as a curiosity. (3) *A Day with Lord Byron*, by May Byron (n.d. ; 1913 ?), is a graceful but entirely " popular " sketch of a typical " day " in Byron's life, interwoven with excerpts from his poems. (4) *Dandies and Men of Letters*, by Leon H. Vincent (1913), contains (pp. 77 f.) " Episodes in the Life of a Noble Poet." This is quite uncritical, and the writer's interest is in English society rather than in poetry. (5) " To the Spirit of Byron," by Robert

some remarks on less significant Byroniana, while in my text there remain to be considered three discourses on Byron. On February 5, 1915, Miss Marie Corelli delivered a lecture on " Byron, the Man and the Poet," at Nottingham.[1] The famous novelist dwells with generous admiration upon Byron's brilliant gifts and fascinating personality, the handicaps from which he suffered and the triumphs which he accomplished. Yet at the same time Miss Corelli recognizes the limitations of his achievement. Another Nottingham lecture was delivered in 1918 by Sir Arthur Quiller-Couch.[2] After making " some damaging, almost desperate, admissions "—such, for example, as that Byron's lyrical gift was " cheap, almost null," and that he had " small sense for blank verse "—and after remarking that April 25, 1816, divides " what to discard and what to retain " in Byron's poetry, the lecturer suddenly becomes enthusiastic

Underwood Johnson (*The Independent*, December 7, 1914, lxxx, 368). (6) Byron : " Battle of Waterloo " (*ibid*. lxxxii, June 28, 1915, 521). (7) " Byron as a War Poet," by Walter Sichel (*The Fortnightly Review*, cv, January 1916, 120 f.). (8) F. W. Moorman's chapter on Byron in *The Cambridge History of English Literature*, xii. (1916), chapter ii. This is a judicious, impartial, and in the main favourable summary of modern opinion, but though an excellent digest it is not distinguished by any original contribution to Byron-criticism. (9) *Tricks of the Trade*, by J. C. Squire (1917) : " If Lord Byron had written *The Passing of Arthur*." This is a fairly amusing parody ; here is a stanza :

> So, having safely stowed away the sword
>   And marked the place with several large stones,
> Sir Bedevere returned to his liege lord
>   And, with a studious frankness in his tones,
> Stated that he had dropped it overboard ;
>   But Arthur only greeted him with groans :
> " My Bedevere," he said, " I may be dying,
> But even dead I'd spot such bare-faced lying " (p. 73).

(10) The performance of *Manfred* by the London Stage Society, August 1918. (11) The *Times Literary Supplement*, June 6, 1918, p. 254, on manuscripts found at Hydra, Greece, including a letter describing Byron's death. (12) " Byron's *Cain*," by Stopford Brooke, *Hibbert Journal*, October 1919. (13) Nahum Sokolow's *History of Zionism* (1919) ; vol. i, chapter xviii. is on " Lord Byron," especially, of course, the *Hebrew Melodies*. (14) " The Humour of Lord Byron," by Walter Sichel, *The Nineteenth Century*, December 1920, pp. 1026 f. (Cf. *The Fortnightly Review*, lxx, 231). (15) On the very day I have been putting these last notes together there comes to me a volume entitled *Suspended Judgments*, by J. C. Powys (1923), which contains (pp. 279 f.) a loud-voiced, disorderly appreciation of Byron. This is the latest thing I have read on the subject of my book.

[1] Miss Corelli's lecture has never been published, but through her courtesy I have been able to read it in manuscript.

[2] *Studies in Literature*, second series (1922), pp. 1 f.

and gradually leads up to this fine passage upon the ingredients of *Don Juan :*

All his fortunes with his insurgent wrath against them, his knowledge of men and cities, his fatal sensual half-knowledge of women, with that noble damning core of true intuition ever torturing our Lucifer wide-eyed for the best thing missed, for salvation lost—all his facility of wit, his perfectness in the note of conversation among well-bred men and women ; his own very considerable grasp of politics ; his sense of Europe ; his sense of the hypocrisy underlying all received government, all received religion ; his sense of seas and mountains and vast natural forces amid which man may be viewed at will as a controlling engineer or a derisory ape ;—all these (I say) in the end miraculously met together, found the measure and stanza exactly suitable to them and to Byron's genius, and combined in *Don Juan.*

Less eloquent, perhaps, than these two discourses, but better balanced and more scholarly, is Professor H. J. C. Grierson's " Wharton Lecture," *Lord Byron : Arnold and Swinburne* (1920). Starting with some remarks upon the æsthetic and moral conflict between Arnold's and Swinburne's estimates of Byron, Professor Grierson constructs a sane and judicious estimate of his own.

In 1922 Mr. Murray published two volumes of *Lord Byron's Correspondence.* I have already remarked upon the biographical information in this collection ; and here it remains only to call attention to the character of the letters. Those to Lady Melbourne (in volume one) are unpleasant and cast no favourable light upon the youthful Byron ; but once more it becomes apparent that Byron's genius flamed out after his second departure from England, and the letters from Italy (in volume two) are a brilliant addition to his correspondence. This second volume contains, moreover, a large number of letters from Shelley to Byron, now published for the first time. These letters further illuminate the relationship existing between the two great poets. In them Shelley pays to Byron's genius the tribute of unstinted admiration.

Here, then, I bring to a close my survey of the history of Byron's contemporary and posthumous renown. I offer no summary, for my entire book has been in the nature of a summary of a theme which might have been greatly expanded. But though the narrative and critical portion of this essay in the history of criticism is now accomplished, I trust that no reader will close my book without at least glancing at the pages that follow. A bibliography makes dry and tedious reading ; nor is the labour of compiling it the most thrilling of literary tasks. But, as Mr. Coleridge said in the preface to the list of editions, selections and translations which rounds out so admirably his edition of the poems, " a bibliography speaks with authority and it speaks last." Mine supplements my text in support of the contention that Byron has not been, and has never been, forgotten, and that the hundred years since his death, if they heard many a voice of detraction raised, have also been a century of praise.

BIBLIOGRAPHY

This list is arranged alphabetically according to authors. In the case of pseudonymous publications, if the author's name is known a cross-reference points from the pseudonym to the author; if unknown, the item is entered under the pseudonym. Anonymous publications are entered under the first important word of the title. Anonymous articles in magazines and newspapers, however, are grouped together under the title of the periodical. Early reviews of Byron's poems are not generally included. Sufficient lists of such are given by E. H. Coleridge in the various introductions in the definitive edition of Byron's *Poetry* (John Murray). These may be supplemented by the list compiled by Richard Edgcumbe in *Notes and Queries*, 7th Series (1886), ii, 284–5. I have not, as in my text, limited myself to English Byroniana, but, to increase the usefulness of this bibliography, have added a representative selection from the Byroniana of other countries. Items marked with an asterisk I have not seen.

Academy, The. " Byron's Letter on the Separation," October 9, 1870.
—— " The Last Years of Lord Byron," January 24, 1877.
—— " The Spectre of Byron at Venice," June 24, 1899. [Signed " H. L."]
—— " The Persistence of Byron," April 26, 1902.
—— " A Poet's Table Talk," May 2, 1903.
Accepted Addresses, or Praemium Poetarum. To which are added, Macbeth Travestie, in Three Acts, and Miscellanies by Different Hands. London : Thomas Tegg, 1813.
An Account of Lord Byron's Residence in the Island of Mityline. London, 1819.
ACKERMANN, RICHARD. Lord Byron. Sein Leben, seine Werke, sein Einfluss auf die deutsche Literatur. Heidelberg, 1901.
—— *" Byrons Thyrza, Kaluza-Thuraus," *Zeitschrift für französischen und englischen Unterricht,* vii.
—— " Neuere Forschungen über Byron," *Germanisch-romanische Monats-schrift,* i. (1909), 368 f.
—— *" Noch einmal die Ursache von Byrons Ehescheidung," *Allgemeine Zeitung,* 1903, No. 97.
—— " Lord Byrons Verlobung, Ehe und Scheidung," *Englische Studien,* xxxii. (1903), 185 f.
—— " Byron-Literatur," *Englische Studien,* xxxvii. (1907), 252 f.
   [See also *Anglia Beiblatt,* viii, 21 f. ; *Englische Studien,* lxiii, 300 f.]
ADAMS, THOMAS. A Scourge for Lord Byron ; or, " Cain, A Mystery " Unmasked. London : T. Adams, 1823.
ADRIAN, DR. Lord Byrons Erzählungen ; mit einem Versuch über des Dichters Leben und Schriften. Frankfort, 1820.

*ALBRIZZI, ISABELLA TEOTOCHI. Ritratti Scritti. Pisa : Niccolo Capurro. 1826.

ALISON, SIR ARCHIBALD. Scott, Campbell and Byron. [An address at the Burns Festival, 1844 ; reprinted in Miscellaneous Essays, New York : Appleton, 1860. Cf. " On Sir Archibald Alison's Views of Lord Byron," *Fraser's Magazine*, liv. (August 1856), 159 f.]

ALLAIS, G. " Le pessimisme romantique : Byron et Musset," *Revue des Cours et Conférences*, x. (1897).

ALLEN, L. H. Die Persönlichkeit P. B. Shelleys. Leipzig, 1907.

ALLEN, RICHARD. The Home and Grave of Byron. New York, 1824.

Allen's Popular Hand-Book to Newstead Abbey, formerly the Home of Byron, with a descriptive account of Annesley Hall and Hucknall Church, the Last Resting Place of the Poet. Nottingham : R. Allen, n.d.

Alma Mater. A Poetical Epistle from Alma Mater to Lord Byron, occasioned by the following Lines in a Tale called " Beppo " [etc.]. Cambridge : E. Goode, 1819.

ALTHAUS, FRIEDRICH. " Der wahre Lord Byron," *Nord und Süd*, xxvii. (1881), 312 f.

—— " On the Personal Relations between Goethe and Byron," *Publications of the English Goethe Society*, iv. (1888), 1 f.

*Amores Secretos de Lord Byron. Trad. del ingles. Barcelona, 1843.

Amours secrètes de Lord Byron. Traduites de l'anglais. Paris : Renault, 1842.

Analectic Magazine, The. [What seems to be one of the earliest sketches of Byron's life is an article reprinted from this magazine in Byron's Poetical Works, Boston : Cummings and Hilliard, 1814, i, pp. v–xi. I have not found the original article.]

*ANCELOT, M. Lord Byron à Venise, drame en trois actes, en prose. Paris, 1834.

ANDERSON, WILLIAM. " Life of Lord Byron," Works of Lord Byron. Edinburgh : Fullarton, 1850, i, pp. vii.–ccxxiv.

Annual Biography and Obituary, The. For the Year 1825. London : Longman, 1825. Volume ix. [" Byron," pp. 255 f.]

Another Cain. A Poem. London : Hatchard, 1822.

" ANSER PEN-DRAG-ON." See IRELAND, W. H.

*Anti-Byron : A Satire. [1814.]

ANTON, H. S. Byron's Manfred. Naumberg, 1875. [A Lecture.]

ARBAUD, LEON. " Lord et Lady Byron. Une Calomnie rétrospective," *Le Correspondent*, n.s. xlv. (1870), 174 f.

Argosy, The. " An Incident in the Life of Lord Byron," April 1869.

—— " Lord and Lady Byron," October 1869.

—— " Lord Byron's Daughter," November 1869.

ARMSTRONG, J. L. Life of Lord Byron. London : William Walker, 1846.

ARNOLD, MATTHEW. " Preface " to Poems of Byron, chosen and arranged by Matthew Arnold. London : Macmillan, 1881. [Reprinted in Essays in Criticism, Second Series, 1888.]

—— " Memorial Verses," " Haworth Churchyard," and " Stanzas from the Grande Chartreuse," in Arnold's Poetical Works.

ARNOLD, R. F. " Der deutsche Philhellenismus," *Ergänzungsheft zu Euphorion*, ii. (1896), 71 f. [Especially pp. 84–86.]

ASHBEE, H. S. " The Rest of Don Juan," *The Bibliographer*, iv. (July 1883), 25 f.

[ASHBEE, H. S.] Index Librorum Prohibitorum, being Notes . . . on Curious and Uncommon Books. By Pisanus Fraxi. London: Privately Printed, 1877.

ASHPITEL, ARTHUR. The Home and Grave of Byron; An Historical and Descriptive Account of Newstead Abbey, Annesley Hall, and Hucknall-Torkard. . . . Also Remarks on the Architecture of Newstead Abbey. London: Longman, n.d. [1855].

Asiatic Journal, The. " Lord Byron," n.s. i, No. 2.

ASTON, JAMES and EDWARD. Pompeii and Other Poems. London: Longman, 1828.

Athenæum, The. " Byron," April 8, 1828. [One of a series of Sketches of Contemporary Authors.]

—— " Cowper and Byron," August 9, 1834.

—— " A Byronian Ramble," August 23, 1834.

—— " Lord Byron," June 25, 1870. [A review of Elze's Byron.]

—— A letter on the Destruction of Byron's Memoirs, May 24, 1884.

[Other articles and reviews in *The Athenæum* are referred to in my text ; see also the indices to each volume.]

Attic Miscellany, The. " Lord Byron and His Memoirs," i. (October 1824), 26 f.

" AUCTOR." A Lament on the Death of the Noble Poet, Lord Byron. London, 1824.

AUERBACH, B. " Vom Weltschmerz," Deutsche Abende. Stuttgart, 1867.

AUGHER, P. PASCHAL. A Grammar Armenian and English. Venice: Printed at the Armenian Press of St. Lazarus, 1832.

AUSTIN, ALFRED. A Vindication of Lord Byron. London: Chapman and Hall, 1869.

—— The Poetry of the Period. London: Richard Bentley, 1870.

—— " Wordsworth and Byron," *The Quarterly Review,* cliv. (July 1882), 53 f. [Reprinted as " Byron and Wordsworth," The Bridling of Pegasus. London: Macmillan, 1910.]

—— " The Essentials of Great Poetry," The Bridling of Pegasus, 1910.

—— Autobiography. London: Macmillan, 1911.

AXON, W. E. A. " Byron's Influence on European Literature," Papers of the Manchester Literary Club, x. (1884), 323 f. [Reprinted in Stray Chapters in Literature, Folklore and Archæology. Manchester, 1888, pp. 47 f.]

B., F. H. Manfred. An Address to the Right Hon. Lord Byron, with an Opinion on some of His Writings. London: Wetton and Jarvis, 1817.

B., J. M. Newark as a Publishing Town. Newark: For Private Circulation Only, 1898. [Reprinted from *The Newark Advertiser.*]

BADER, FRANZ. Lord Byron im Spiegel der zeitgenössischen englischen Dichtung. Erlangen, 1915.

—— " Lord Byron im Spiegel der zeitgenössischen deutschen Dichtung," Herrig's *Archiv,* cxxxv. (1916), 303 f.

BAGEHOT, WALTER. Literary Studies. London: J. M. Dent, n.d.

BAGNALL, EDWARD. Lord Byron, with Remarks on his Genius and Character. Oxford: D. A. Talboys, 1831. [Cf. *The Athenæum,* 1831, p. 200.]

BAILEY, THOMAS. Hand-Book to Newstead Abbey. London : Simpkin, Marshall and Co., 1855.

BAKER, H. T. "The Sensationalism of Byron," *Modern Language Notes*, xxxii. (April 1917), 249.

BALL, MARGARET. Sir Walter Scott as a Critic of Literature. New York : Columbia University Press, 1907. [Especially pp. 92 f.]

BANCROFT, GEORGE. History of the Battle of Lake Erie and Miscellaneous Papers. New York : R. Bonner's Sons, 1891. [On Bancroft's relations with Byron.]

BARFF, SAMUEL. Letters written by Lord Byron . . . to Mr. Samuel Barff at Zante. Privately printed for members of Mr. Barff's Family : Naples, 1884.

[BARKER, MISS.] Lines addressed to a Noble Lord. (His Lordship will know why.) By One of the Small Fry of the Lakes. London : W. Pople, 1815.

[BARRETT, EATON STANNARD.] The Talents Run Mad ; or, Eighteen Hundred and Sixteen. A Satirical Poem. In Three Dialogues. By the Author of All the Talents. London : Henry Colburn, 1816.

—— Six Weeks at Longs. By a Late Resident. London : Printed for the Author, 1817. [Cf. *Notes and Queries*, 1st Series, viii, 423.]

BATTINE, WILLIAM. Another Cain, A Mystery. London : John Cahuac, 1822.

BAXTER. G. R. W. Don Juan Junior. A Poem. By Byron's Ghost. London : Joseph Thomas, 1839.

Beauties of English Poets. Venice : In the Island of St. Lazarus, 1852.

BEDDOES, THOMAS LOVELL. Letters. Edited by Edmund Gosse. London : Elkin Mathews and John Lane, 1894.

BEDFORD, JOHN HARMAN. Wanderings of Childe Harold. A Romance of Real Life. Interspersed with Memoirs of the English Wife, the Foreign Mistress, and various other Celebrated Characters. London : Sherwood, Jones and Co., 1825.

*BELFAST, THE EARL OF. Poets and Poetry of the Nineteenth Century. London, 1852. [A course of lectures.]

BELLOC, LOUISE SWANTON. Lord Byron. Paris : Renouard, 1824.

BEMBOW, WILLIAM. A Scourge for the Laureate. In Reply to his Infamous Letter of the 13th of December, 1824, Meanly Abusive of the Deceased Lord Byron, etc. London : Bembow, n.d. [1825].

*BENNETT, D. M. The World's Sages, Infidels, and Thinkers. New York, 1876.

Beppo in London. A Metropolitan Story. London : Duncombe, 1819.

*BERNARD, EDWARD. Pedigree of George Gordon, Sixth Lord Byron of the Family of Burun, or Buron, or Byron. London, 1870.

BEST, J. R. Satires and the Beggar's Coin, a Poem. London : Hurst, Chance and Co., 1831.

BETTANY, W. A. L. Confessions of Lord Byron. London : John Murray, 1905. [Introduction " On Byron's Obligation to Johnson."]

BEUTLER, K. A. Ueber Lord Byrons Hebrew Melodies. Leipzig : Hoffman, 1912.

BEYER, PAUL. Der junge Heine. [*Bonner Forschungen*, i.] Berlin, 1911. [Pp. 67–73 on Byron's influence on Heine.]

[BEYLE, MARIE HENRI.] " Lord Byron en Italie et en France. Récit d'un temoin oculaire, 1816," *Revue de Paris*, March 1830. [Appended to some editions of Racine et Shakespeare.]

[BEYLE, MARIE HENRI.] Rome, Naples et Florence. Paris, 1818. [English translation: Rome, Naples and Florence in 1817. Sketches of the Present State of Society, Manners, Arts, Literature, etc., in these Celebrated Cities. By the Count de Stendhal. London : Henry Colburn, 1818.]

BLABY, J. C. "Lines written on perusing Lord Byron's Poem entitled Childe Harold," *Gentleman's Magazine*, lxxxiii, part i. (February 1813), 159.

[BLACK, JOHN ?] Letter to the Right Honourable Lord Byron. By John Bull. London : William Wright, 1821.

Blackwood's Magazine. Review of Don Juan, v. (August 1819), 512 f.
—— "Lord Byron and Pope," ix. (May 1821), 227 f.
—— "Lord Byron," xi. (February 1822), 212 f. [Signed "Siluriensis."]
—— "Lord Byron," xv. (June 1824), 709 f.
—— "Destruction of Byron's Memoirs," xvi. (November 1824), 530 f.
—— "Southey and Byron," xvi. (December 1824), 711 f.
—— "Lord Byron," xvii. (February 1825), 131 f.
—— "Recollections of Lord Byron," cvi. (July 1869), 24 f. [Review of the Countess Guiccioli's Recollections.]
[The above is only a selection from the more important articles in *Blackwood's ;* some others are listed under the authors' names. The earlier volumes contain many more. Consult the several indices.]

BLAIKIE, W. G. "Lord Byron's early school days," *Harper's Magazine*, lxxxiii. (1891), 409 f.

BLAQUIERE, EDWARD. Narrative of a Second Visit to Greece, including Facts connected with the Last Days of Lord Byron. London : Whittaker, 1825.

BLAZE DE BURY, H. "Lord Byron et le Byronism," *Revue des Deux Mondes*, xi. (October 1, 1872), 513 f. [Reprinted in Tableaux romantiques de littérature et d'art. Paris, 1878.]

BLEIBTREU, KARL. Der Traum. Ein Roman. Leipzig, 1880. [Based on Byron's early life.]
—— Lord Byrons letzte Liebe. Leipzig, 1881. [A novel.]
—— Lord Byrons letzte Liebe. Leipzig, 1886. [A drama.]
—— Meine Tochter. Ein Drama. Leipzig, 1886. [Based on Byron's life.]
—— Geschichte der englischen Literatur im 19. Jahrhundert. Leipzig, [1888]. [Pp. 151 f.]
—— Byron der Uebermensch, sein Leben und sein Dichten. Jena : Costenoble, [1896].
—— *Byrons Geheimnis. Ein Drama in fünf Akten. 1900.
—— *Das Byron-Geheimnis. Munich and Leipzig, 1912.
—— *" Das Weib im Leben Goethes und Byrons," *Nord und Süd*, xxxv, Heft 18 (1910).
[Cf. "Psychological Study of Byron," *The Weekly Scotsman*, June 21, 1884.]

BLESSINGTON, THE COUNTESS OF. *Fugitive Pieces. Genoa, 1823.
—— Conversations of Lord Byron. London : Henry Colburn, 1834. [Reprinted from Colburn's *New Monthly Magazine*, 1832. New edition: London : Richard Bentley, 1893 ; French translation : by C. M. Le Tellier, Paris, 1833. Annotated edition, 1893. Cf. *The Gentleman's Magazine*, May 1843.]
—— The Idler in Italy. London : Henry Colburn, 1839.
—— The Lottery of Life. London : Henry Colburn, 1842.

BLIND, MATHILDE. "Introduction" to The Letters of Lord Byron [a selection]. London : Walter Scott, 1887.
—— "Introduction" to The Poetical Works of Lord Byron. London : Walter Scott, 1886.
BLÜMEL, M. Die Unterhaltungen Lord Byrons mit der Gräfin Blessington als ein Beitrag zur Byronbiographie kritisch untersucht. Breslau, 1900.
BLUMENTHAL, F. Lord Byron's Mystery Cain and its Relation to Milton's Paradise Lost and Gessner's Death of Abel. Oldenburg, 1891.
BOGLIETTI, GIOVANNI. "Giorgio Byron. Memoranda Byroniana," Nuova Antologia, xxxix. (May 1, 1878), 51 f. ["Il presente articolo è come la prefazione di un esame completo, che l'autore si propone di fare delle opere di Lord Byron."]
—— "La Solitudine di Byron," Nuova Antologia, li. (September 1, 1878), 5 f.
—— "Il vero Byron," Nuova Antologia, lii. (November 15, 1883), 245 f. [A review of Jeaffreson's The Real Lord Byron.]
—— "Lord Byron : Il Childe Harold e il Don Juan," Nuova Antologia, liv. (March 1, 1879), 39 f.
BORN, STEPHEN. Lord Byron. Basel, 1883.
BORROW, GEORGE. Lavengro. 1851.
—— The Romany Rye. 1857.
BOULAY-PATY, EVARISTE, and LUCAS, HIPPOLYTE. Le Corsaire, poème dramatique en cinq actes et en vers. Paris, 1830. [Reprinted 1901. This piece follows Byron's narrative fairly closely but continues the story beyond the point where the original poem ends.]
*BOURDON, ISIDORE. La Physiognomonie, ou l'Art de connaître les hommes. Paris, 1830. [Especially p. 235 ; see Estève, p. 208.]
BOWEN, ANNA. "Byron's Influence upon Goethe," The Dial (Chicago), xxviii. (1908), 144 f.
BOWLES, W. L. Letters to Lord Byron on a Question of Poetic Criticism. London, 1822.
—— Two Letters to Lord Byron, in answer to his Lordship's Letter to **** ****** on the Rev. W. L. Bowles' Strictures on the Life and Writings of Pope. London : John Murray, 1821. [Cf. The Gentleman's Magazine, xci, part i. (April 1821), 291 f. and (June 1821), 533 f.]
—— A Final Appeal to the Literary Public relative to Pope. To which are added some Remarks on Lord Byron's Conversations. London, 1825.
—— "Childe Harold's Last Pilgrimage" (1824), Poetical Works of W. L. Bowles. Edinburgh : James Nichol, 1855, ii, 284 f.
—— A Letter to Lord Holland, in Vindication of Westminster, Eton, Winchester and the English Universities, in answer to some Strictures of Thomas Moore, Esq., in his late Life of Lord Byron. London, 1830. [Cf. The Devizes Gazette, March 18, 1830.]
BOWRING, SIR JOHN. Autobiographical Recollections. London, 1877.
BRANDES, GEORGE. Main Currents in Nineteenth Century Literature. New York : Macmillan, 1905. New edition. New York : Boni and Liveright, 1923. [Translation by Diana White and Mary Morison of the Danish : Hovedstromninger i det 19de Aarhundredes Litteratur. Copenhagen, 1875. Volume iv, chapters 18–23 on Byron.]

*BRANDES, GEORGE. "Byron," *Fremmede Personligheder*. Copenhagen, 1889.

BRANDL, ALOIS. "Goethe und Byron," *Oesterreichische Rundschau*, i. (1883).

—— Coleridge and the English Romantic School. London : John Murray, 1887.

—— "Goethes Verhältnis zu Byron," *Goethe-Jahrbuch*, xx. (1899), 3 f.

BRANDL, LEOPOLD. "Die Broughton-Papers und ihr Verhältnis zur Byron-Frage," *Englische Studien*, xli. (1909), 267 f.

BRECKNOCK, ALBERT. The Pilgrim Poet : Lord Byron of Newstead. London : Francis Griffiths, 1911.

BREIER, F. "Byron und Southey (Eine literarische Fehde)," Herrig's *Archiv*, v. (1849), 290 f.

[BRENNAN, E.] The Foot-prints of Albé. Part I. Rome and Florence : A. Zanaboni, 1874. [No more published.]

The Bride's Confession, Contained in a Letter to her Friend, Bella. Otherwise entitled The Bridal Night. Poem attributed to Lord Byron. Preceded by Miss Pilton and her Spiritual Adviser and followed by The Reprisals : a Crazy Tale. Paris : Privately Issued, [1916].

BRIFAUT, CHARLES. "Fontanes : Lord Byron ; dialogue lu à la Société des Bonnes-Lettres," *Annales de la littérature et des arts*, xix. (1825), 125 f.

"BRITANNICUS." Revolutionary Causes : with a Brief Notice of some late Publications ; and a Postscript containing Strictures on Cain, etc. London : J. Cawthorn, 1822.

British Controversialist, The. "Was Byron or Scott the Greater Poet ? "

Broadway. "The Tendency of Byron's Poetry," iv, 54 f.

BROCKEDON, WILLIAM. Finden's Illustrations of the Life and Works of Lord Byron, with Original and Selected Information on the Subjects of the Engravings. London, 1833–34.

"BROOKE, ARTHUR." See CLARIS, J. C.

BROOKE, STOPFORD. "Byron's Cain," *The Hibbert Journal*, xviii. (October 1919), 74 f.

[BROUGHAM, LORD.] Critique from the Edinburgh Review on Lord Byron's Poems. Which occasioned English Bards and Scotch Reviewers. London : Sherwin, 1820.

BROUGHTON, LORD. See HOBHOUSE, J. C.

BROWN, FRANK CLYDE. The Literary Influence of Byron on Shelley. Chicago, 1902. [A thesis, in manuscript, in the library of the University of Chicago.]

BROWN, JOHN. The Stage : A Poem. London : Souter and Hatchard, 1820.

BROWNE, J. HAMILTON. "Narrative of a Visit to Greece," *Fraser's Magazine*, September 1834.

—— "Voyage from Leghorn to Cephalonia with Lord Byron in 1823," *Blackwood's Magazine*, xxxv. (1834).

BROWNING, ELIZABETH BARRETT. Letters. Edited by F. G. Kenyon. London : Macmillan, 1897.

BROWNING, ROBERT. Fifine at the Fair, 1872.

—— The Inn Album, 1875.

—— Pacchiarotto, 1876.

BROWNING, ROBERT and ELIZABETH BARRETT. Letters, 1845–46. London : Smith, Elder and Co., 1899.

BRUCE, J. DOUGLAS. "Lord Byron's Stanzas to the Po," *Modern Language Notes*, xxiv. (December 1909), 258 f. ; xxv. (January 1910), 31 f.

BRYDGES, SIR SAMUEL EGERTON. Letters on the Character and Poetical Genius of Lord Byron. London : Longman, 1824. [Cf. *Blackwood's Magazine*, xvii. (February 1825), 137 f.]

—— An Impartial Portrait of Lord Byron, as a Poet and a Man, compared with all the Evidences and Writings regarding him, up to 1825. Paris : Galignani, 1825.

—— A Note on the Suppression of Memoirs announced by the Author in June 1825, containing numerous Strictures on Contemporary Public Characters. Paris : J. Smith, 1825.

—— Autobiography, Times, Opinions and Contemporaries. London : Cochrane and M'Crone, 1834. [Cf. *The Athenæum*, June 14, 1834, p. 443.]

BUBE, ADOLF. "Lord Byron " [a poem], *Gedichte von Adolf Bube*, 1836, p. 97 f. [First published in *Dresdener Abendzeitung*, August 6, 1824.]

BUCHNER, ALEXANDER. Lord Byrons letzte Liebe. Eine biographische Novelle. Leipzig, 1862.

—— *Etude sur Lord Byron. Cherbourg, 1874.

BUCKSTONE, J. B. Don Juan ; a Romantic Drama, in three acts (founded on Lord Byron's celebrated Poem). London : John Dicks, 1828.

—— A New Don Juan ! An Operatical, Poetical, Egotistical, Melodramatical, Extravaganzical, but strictly Moral Burletta, in two acts ; (founded on Lord Byron's celebrated Poem). The Dramatic and Original Music by G. H. Rodwell, Esq. First performed at the Adelphi Theatre, with distinguished approbation. London, n.d. [c. 1828]. [This is included in Richardson's New Minor Drama. vol. i. London : T. Richardson, 1828.]

BUELL, L. M. "Byron and Shelley," *Modern Language Notes*, xxxii. (May 1917), 312 f.

"BULL, JOHN." See BLACK, JOHN.

BULLOCH, J. M. *"The Duffs and the Gordons : Brains, Bravery and Byron," *Scottish Notes and Queries*, xi. (May 1898), 161 f.

—— "The Lucky Duffs," *English Illustrated Magazine*, June 1898, pp. 235 f.

—— "The Tragic Adventures of Byron's Ancestors. The Gordons of Gight. A Study in Degeneration," *Aberdeen Free Press*, November 11, 18, and 25, 1898.

BULWER-LYTTON, EDWARD. The Siamese Twins, 1831. [The edition I have used is : New York : Harper, 1831.]

—— England and the English. London : Bentley, 1833.

—— "The Present State of Poetry," *The Monthly Chronicle*, June 1838, pp. 309 f. [Reprinted in Critical and Miscellaneous Writings. Philadelphia : Lea and Blanchard, 1841, i, 334 f.]

—— " Conversations with an Ambitious Student in Ill-health," *The New Monthly Magazine*, December 1830. [Reprinted in Critical and Miscellaneous Writings, i, 89 f.]

BULWER-LYTTON, HENRY. "Life of Lord Byron," in Galignani's edition of Byron's Works, 1835 ; reprinted in Select Poetical Works of Lord Byron. London : Adam Scott, 1848 ; and in Byron's Works, Bohn edition, London, 1851.

[BURGES, GEORGE.] Cato to Lord Byron on the Immorality of his Writings. London : W. Wetton, 1824. [Cf. *The Gentleman's Magazine*, xciv, part i. (January 1824), 49.]

BYRON, GEORGE GORDON NOEL, LORD. [The spurious pieces and the editions of Byron's Works containing them have been listed in the body of this book. The spurious volumes are listed in this bibliography under their titles or, when ascertainable, the name of the author. The following three items are most conveniently set down here.]

—— Lord Byron's Armenian Exercises and Poetry. Venice : In the Island of St. Lazarro, 1870.

—— Lord Byron's Tales. Consisting of the Giaour, The Bride of Abydos, The Corsair, Lara. With all the Notes : Hebrew Melodies, and other Poems. Halifax : William Miller, 1845.

—— Manfred : a Choral Tragedy in three Acts. London : T. H. Lacy, n.d. [Lacy's Acting Edition of English Plays, vol. lx, n.d.]

BYRON, MAJOR G. G. The Inedited Works of Lord Byron, now first published from his Letters, Journals, and other Manuscripts, in the possession of his son, Major George Gordon Byron. Part I. New York : G. G. Byron and R. Martin, 1849. [No more published.]

BYRON, GERALD NOEL. The New Don Juan. The Introduction by Gerald Noel Byron. And the Last Canto of the Original Don Juan from the Papers of the Countess Guicciolli [*sic*]. By George Lord Byron. Never before published. London : E. Head, n.d. [1880].

BYRON, HENRY J. The Bride of Abydos ; or, The Prince, the Pirate, and the Pearl. An Original Oriental Burlesque Extravaganza. London, n.d. [Lacy's Acting Edition of English Plays, vol. xxxvi.]

[BYRON, ISABELLA, LADY.] Remarks occasioned by Mr. Moore's Notices of Lord Byron's Life. London : Privately printed, n.d. [1830].

—— Another edition of the same : A Letter to Thomas Moore, Esq., occasioned by his Notices of the Life of the Late Lord Byron. London, n.d. [1830].

—— Another edition of the same : The Living and the Dead ; or, Lady Byron's Remarks addressed to Mr. Moore, respecting her Separation from her Husband, n.l., n.d. [1830 ; reprinted from *The Northern Whig*].

BYRON, MAY. A Day with Lord Byron. London : Hodder and Stoughton, n.d. [1913 ?].

*Byron in Greece. London : Privately printed, 1825.

Byron Painted by his Compeers ; or, All about Lord Byron, from his Marriage to his Death, as given in the various newspapers of his day, showing wherein the American novelist gives a truthful Account, and wherein she draws on her own morbid Imagination. London : Samuel Palmer, 1869.

Byroniana : The Opinions of Lord Byron on Men, Manners, and Things, with the Parish Clerk's Album kept at his Burial Place, Hucknall-Torkard. London : Hamilton, Adams and Co., 1834. [Cf. *Notes and Queries*, 3rd Series, xii, 241 ; 6th Series, ii, 125.]

Byroniana. Bozzies and Piozzies. London : Sherwood, Jones and Co., 1825.

Byroniana und Anderes aus dem Englischen Seminar in Erlangen. Erlangen, 1912.

Byroniana. [A scrap-book of miscellaneous clippings from newspapers and periodicals in the British Museum. Two volumes, folio.]

Byroniana. [A similar scrap-book in the Wheildon collection of the Boston Public Library. One volume, folio.]

Byroniana. [A similar collection in the possession of H. C. Roe, Esq., of Nottingham. Three volumes, folio ; the last two entitled " The Byron-Stowe Controversy." These volumes contain much material difficult or impossible of access elsewhere.]

CAINE, T. HALL. Cobwebs of Criticism. A Review of the first Reviewers of the "Lake," "Satanic," and "Cockney" Schools. London : Elliott Stock, 1883. [Cf. The Academy, xxiii, 357.]

*CALCAÑO, J. Tres Poetas pesimistas del siglo xix. Lord Byron ; Shelley ; Leopardi. Estudio critico. 1907.

CAMPBELL, J. DYKES. Samuel Taylor Coleridge. A Narrative of the Events of his Life. London : Macmillan, 1894.

CAMPBELL, THOMAS. Life and Letters. Edited by William Beattie. London : Moxon, 1849.

—— "Lady Byron and Thomas Moore," The New Monthly Magazine, April 1830, pp. 379 f.

Canto xvii. of Don Juan. By One who desires to be a Very Great Unknown. London : James Gilbert, 1832.

CANTÙ, CESARE. Lord Byron ; discorso di Cesare Cantù. Aggiuntevi alcune traduzioni ed un serie di lettere dello stesso Lord Byron, ove si narrano i suoi viaggi in Italia e nella Grecia. Milan, 1833.

—— English translation : Lord Byron and His Works. A Biography and Essay. Edited by A. Kinloch. London : George Redway, 1883.

CARLTON, W. N. C. (Editor). Poems and Letters of Lord Byron. Edited from the original manuscripts in the possession of W. K. Bixby of St. Louis. Chicago : Privately Printed for the Society of the Dofobs, 1912.

CARLYLE, THOMAS. Sartor Resartus. 1833.

—— Critical and Miscellaneous Essays. New York : Scribner, n.d.

CARRY, ARISTIDE. Childe-Harold aux Ruines de Rome. Paris, 1826. [Not mentioned by Estève.]

CASTELAR, EMILIO. Lord Byron. Madrid, 1873.

—— English translation by Mrs. Arthur Arnold : Life of Lord Byron and other Sketches. New York : Harper, 1876.

" CATO." See BURGES, GEORGE.

*CHADWICK, ADAM. Cain and Abel : An Oratorio Poem in Two Parts. London, 1843.

Chambers' Journal, " Last Records of Byron," March 27, 1869.

—— " Byron at Work," October 9, 1869.

CHAMISSO, ADELBERT VON. " Lord Byrons letzte Liebe " [a poem on Byron's death], Der Gesellschafter, 1827, No. 155. [Reprinted in Chamisso's Werke ; Deutsche National-Litteratur, vol. cxlviii. Stuttgart : Union Deutsche Verlagsgesellschaft, n.d., pp. 244 f.]

CHAPMAN, E. M. English Literature in Account with Religion : 1800–1900. Boston : Houghton, Mifflin Co., 1910. [On Byron, pp. 91 f.]

*Characteristics of Men of Genius. London, 1846. [" Lord Byron," i, 245 f.]

*CHASLES, V. E. PHILARÈTE. " Byron," Encyclopédie du xixᵉ siècle, i, 245 f.

CHASLES, V. E. PHILARÈTE. "La Vie et l'influence de Byron sur son époque," Etudes sur la littérature et les Moeurs de l'Angleterre au xix siècle. Paris, n.d. [1850].

CHATEAUBRIAND, FRANÇOIS-RENÉ DE. Essai sur la littérature anglaise. Paris : Furne-Jouvet, 1867.

CHESTERTON, G. K. Twelve Types. London : A. L. Humphreys, 1910.

CHEW, SAMUEL C. The Dramas of Lord Byron : A Critical Study. Göttingen : Vandenhoech and Ruprecht, 1915.

—— "Byron and Croly," Modern Language Notes, xxviii. (November 1913), 201 f.

—— "Notes on Byron," Modern Language Notes, xxix. (April 1914), 105 f.

—— "Did Byron write ' A Farrago Libelli ? ' " Modern Language Notes, xxxi. (May 1916), 287 f.

—— "Unpublished Letters of Lord Byron," Modern Language Notes, xxxi. (November 1916), 446 f.

—— "Byroniana," Modern Language Notes, xxxiii. (May 1918), 306 f.

—— "The Pamphlets of the Byron Separation," Modern Language Notes, xxxiv. (March 1919), 155 f.

—— "An Original Letter of Lord Byron," The Nation (N.Y.), cvi. (April 18, 1918), 473 f.

—— "A Byron-Shelley Hoax," The Nation (N.Y.), cvii. (August 24, 1918), 199 f.

—— "Byron in Fiction," Notes and Queries, 12th Series, iv. (January 1918), 10.

—— "The Byron Apocrypha," Notes and Queries, 12th Series, v. (May and June 1919), 113 f. and 143 f.

—— "The Centenary of Don Juan," American Journal of Philology, xl. (June 1919), 117 f.

CHIARINI, GUISEPPI. Donne e poeti ; appunti critici. Rome : C. Verdesi, 1885. [Contains : " Lord e Lady Byron " ; " Lord Byron e Teresa Guiccioli."]

—— " Lord Byron nella politica e nella letteratura della prima metà del secolo," Nuova Antologia, cxviii. (1891), 103 f. and 245 f.

Child Albert, or the Misanthrope, and other Poems, imitative and original. Edinburgh: John Thomson; London: Baldwin, Cradock and Joy, 1819.

*" Childe Harold in Boetia," The Galaxy, 1820.

Childe Harold in the Shades : An Infernal Romaunt. London : Hookham, 1819.

Childe Harold's Pilgrimage to the Dead Sea ; Death on the Pale Horse, and other Poems. London : Baldwin, Cradock and Joy, 1818.

CHORLEY, HENRY F. The Authors of England. A Series of Medallion Portraits of Modern Literary Characters. Engraved from the Works of British Artists by Achille Collas. With Illustrative Notes. London : Charles Tilt, 1838.

Christian Observer, The. " Lord Byron's Poetry," November 1819.

—— " Character, Opinions, and Writings of Lord Byron," February, March, and April 1825.

CHURCHMAN, P. H. " Byron and Shakespeare," Modern Language Notes, xxiv. (April 1909), 126 f.

—— " Lord Byron's Experiences in the Spanish Peninsula in 1809," Bulletin hispanique, xi. (1909), 56 f. and 125 f.

CHURCHMAN, P. H. "Byron and Espronceda," *Revue hispanique*, xx (1909), 5–210. [Cf. R. Schevill in *Modern Language Notes*, xxvii. (January 1912), 28 f.]
—— "The Beginnings of Byronism in Spain," *Revue hispanique*, xxiii. (1910), 333 f.
*CIPRO, G. B. Lord Byron a Venezia. 1837.
[CLARIS, JOHN CHALK.] Poems. By Arthur Brooke. London: Longmans, 1818. [Contains an "Address to Lord Byron." See *The Gentleman's Magazine*, lxxxviii, part 2 (August 1818), 148 f.]
*CLARK, JOHN. [A continuation of Don Juan, in two volumes, containing twelve new cantos. Volume i. and the title-page of volume ii. are missing in the unique copy in the library of the English Seminar at Erlangen. The date is between 1834 and 1847.]
CLARK, J. C. A Study of American and English Poets. New York: Scribner, 1909.
CLARK, W. J. Byron und die romantische Poesie in Frankreich. Leipzig: Pöschel and Trepte, 1901.
[CLARKE, H. S.] In the Matter of the Stowe Scandal: Lord Byron's Defence. London, 1869.
CLARKE, J. S. Sketches of Character. Downpatrick, Ireland: Office of *The Recorder*, 1873. [Contains: "Lord Byron, His Genius and Character."]
[CLASON, ISAAC S.] *Don Juan, Cantos ix, x, and xi. Albany, N.Y., 1823.
—— Don Juan, Cantos xvii–xviii. New York: Charles Wiley, 1825.
*CLAUS, WILHELM. Byron und die Frauen. Berlin, 1862.
CLINTON, GEORGE. Memoirs of the Life and Writings of Lord Byron. London: James Robins, 1825.
*COATES, HENRY. The British Don Juan. Being a Narrative of the Singular Amours, Entertaining Adventures, Remarkable Travels, etc. of the Hon. Edward W. Montague. London: James Griffen, 1823.
[COCKLE, MRS.] Lines Addressed to Lady Byron. Newcastle: S. Hodgson, 1817.
COGNIARD, H. and BURAT DE GURGY, E. Byron à l'Ecole d'Harrow, épisode mêlé de couplets. Paris, 1834. [Written for performance by school children.]
*Colburn's New Monthly Magazine. "An Event in the Life of Lord Byron," xcix. (1853), 138 f.
—— "Some Account of the Right Honourable George Gordon, Lord Byron," iii. (1815), 527 f.
COLERIDGE, ERNEST HARTLEY. "Lord Byron." An Address before the Royal Society of Literature, May 25, 1904 ; printed in the Society's *Transactions*, Second Series, xxv. London: Asher and Co., 1904.
—— "Byron," in Poet's Country, edited by Andrew Lang. Philadelphia: Lippincott, 1907.
—— "Byron," The Encyclopædia Britannica, eleventh edition, iv, 897 f. (1910).
COLERIDGE, E. H. and PROTHERO, R. E. The Works of Lord Byron. London: John Murray, 1898–1904. [Includes a great amount of new editorial and critical material.]
COLERIDGE, SAMUEL TAYLOR. Biographia Literaria; or, Biographical Sketches of my Literary Life and Opinions. London: Rest Fenner, 1817. [Ed. J. Shawcross. Oxford: The Clarendon Press, 1907.]

COLERIDGE, SAMUEL TAYLOR. Letters. Edited by E. H. Coleridge. Boston: Houghton, Mifflin Co., 1895.
—— Table-Talk. Edited by H. N. Coleridge. New York: Harper, 1833.
COLLER, D. W. The Battle of Oblivion; or, Criticism and Quackery. Chelmsford, n.d. [1831]. [Satirizes Byron's imitators.]
COLLINS, J. CHURTON. Studies in Poetry and Criticism. London: Bell, 1905. [Contains "The Works of Lord Byron," reprinted from *The Quarterly Review*, cii. (April 1905), 429 f.]
[COLTON, CHARLES CALEB.] Remarks, Critical and Moral, on the Talents of Lord Byron and the Tendencies of Don Juan. By the Author of Hypocrisy: a Satire. With Notes and Anecdotes, Political and Historical. London [various booksellers], 1819.
—— Another edition: Remarks on the Talents of Lord Byron, and the Tendencies of Don Juan. London, 1820.
CONANT, MARTHA P. The Oriental Tale in England in the Eighteenth Century. New York: Macmillan, 1908.
Continuation of Don Juan. Cantos xvii. and xviii. London: G. B. Whittaker; Oxford: Munday and Slater, 1825 [actually towards end of 1824].
COOPER, LANE. "Notes on Byron and Shelley," *Modern Language Notes*, xxiii. (April 1908), 118 f.
CORELLI, MARIE. "Byron, the Man and the Poet." Lecture delivered at Nottingham, February 5, 1915. [Not published; exists in manuscript.]
*COTTERILL, H. B. An Introduction to the Study of Poetry. London, 1882.
COTTLE, JOSEPH. An Expostulary Epistle to Lord Byron. London: Cadell and Davies, 1820. [Cf. *The Monthly Review*, xciv. (1821).]
"COUNTRY CURATE." The Living and the Dead. By a Country Curate. London: C. Knight, 1827.
COURTHOPE, W. J. "The Revival of Romance: Scott, Byron, Shelley," *The National Review*, v. (1886). [Reprinted in The Liberal Movement in English Poetry. London: Macmillan, 1885.]
—— History of English Poetry. London: Macmillan. [Volume vi. (1910), chapter viii: "Romantic Self-Representation: Byron."]
*Court Journal, The. "Lord Byron in Italy; specially translated from the Memoirs of a Celebrated French Woman," April 10, 1830, pp. 226 f.
[COWLEY, WILLIAM.] Don Juan Reclaimed; or, His Peregrination continued from Lord Byron. By W. C. Sheffield: Printed for the Author, 1840.
Le Cri de l'Angleterre, au Tombeau de sa Reine. Dithyrambe de lord Byron. Traduit de l'Anglais. Paris: Chez les Marchands de Nouveautés, 1821.
*A Critique on the Address written by Lord Byron, which was spoken at the Opening of the New Theatre Royal, Drury Lane, October 10, 1812. By Lord ——. London [1812 ?].
A Critique on *The Liberal*. London: William Day, 1822.
CRUIKSHANK, GEORGE. Forty Illustrations of Lord Byron. London: James Robins, n.d. [1825]. [These illustrations also appear in Clinton's Byron.]

CUNNINGHAM, ALLAN. "Byron," *The Athenæum*, 1833, pp. 771 f. [One of a series of articles: "Biographical and Critical History of the Literature of the Last Fifty Years."]

*CUNNINGHAM, W. Lives of Eminent Englishmen.

Current Opinion. "Hewlett's Picture of Byron," lvi. (January 1914), 48.

DAGLEY, R. Death's Doings; consisting of numerous Original Compositions in Prose and Verse, the Friendly Contributions of Various Writers; principally intended as Illustrations of Twenty-four Plates, designed and etched by R. Dagley. London: Andrews and Cole, 1826.

DALGADO, D. G. Lord Byron's Childe Harold's Pilgrimage to Portugal Critically Examined. Lisbon: Impresa Nagional, 1919.

DALLAS, R. C. and DALLAS, A. R. C. Recollections of the Life of Lord Byron from the Year 1808 to the end of 1814. Taken from authentic documents. London: C. Knight, 1824.

—— Correspondence of Lord Byron with a Friend, including his Letters to his Mother, written from Portugal, Spain, Greece, and the Shores of the Mediterranean, in 1809, 1810, and 1811. Philadelphia: Carey and Lea, 1825. [Cf. *Blackwood's Magazine*, xvii. (February 1825), 146.]

—— Lord Byron's Correspondence with a Friend. Also Recollections of the Poet, the whole forming an Original Memoir of Lord Byron's Life from 1808 to 1814. And a Continuation and Preliminary Statement of the Proceedings by which the Letters were Suppressed in England at the Suit of Lord Byron's Executors. Paris: Galignani, 1825.

*DALLOIS, J. Etudes morales et littéraires à propos de Lord Byron. Paris, 1890.

*DAMAS-HINARD, J. S. A. DE. Chants sur Lord Byron. Paris: Delaunay, 1824. [Five cantos.]

Les Dames de Byron; or, Portraits of the Principal Female Characters in Byron's Poems. London, 1836.

[DANIEL, GEORGE.] The Modern Dunciad: a Satire. With Notes, Biographical and Critical. London: Effingham Wilson, 1815. [Reprinted in The Modern Dunciad, Virgil in London, and other Poems. London, 1835.]

*DANIEL, H. J. [See *Notes and Queries*, 5th Series, vii, 519, for Daniel's statement that he wrote and published "a seventeenth canto in continuation of Don Juan."]

"DANIELS." "The Death of Byron," *The Mirror*, vii. (1824), 261.

DARLEY, CHARLES. [An article comparing Byron and Beddoes.] *The London Magazine*, December 1823.

DARMESTETER, JAMES. "Lord Byron," Essais de littérature anglaise. Paris, 1883. [Pp. 161 f.]

[DAVENPORT, H. and ROLLS, MRS. HENRY.] The Book of Spirits, and Tales of the Dead; Comprising "Lord Byron in the Other World"; "Weber and the Heavenly Choir"; "Talma in Celestial Spheres"; "The Phantom Ship"; and other Narratives of Deep and Awful Interest, principally original but partly translated from Grecian MSS. London: W. C. Wright, n.d. [c. 1825]. [The authors named are responsible only for the portions of the book dealing with Byron.]

DAWSON, EDGAR. Byron und Moore. Leipzig, 1902.
[DEACON, W. F.] Warreniana, with Notes, Critical and Explanatory, by the Editor of a *Quarterly Review*. London, 1824. [" The Childe's Pilgrimage," pp. 81 f.]
DELAVIGNE, CASIMIR. Nouvelles Messeniennes; Lord Byron. Paris, 1829. [Reprinted in Œuvres complètes. Paris, 1846, v, 118.]
" DELIA." A Poetical Epistle from Delia to Lord Byron. London, 1817.
DENNIS, JOHN. Heroes of English Literature : English Poets. London, 1883. [Pp. 344 f. : " Lord Byron."]
DERBY, E. Rhymes of Road, Rail, and River. Bristol : J. W. Arrowsmith, n.d. [1899].
Despair : a Vision. Derry Down and John Bull : a Simile. Being two political parodies on " Darkness " and a scene from The Giaour by Lord Byron. Together with a Love Letter from John Bull to Liberty and a Farewell Address from the Same to the Same. London : Printed for the Author by R. Hamblin, 1820.
*DEVEY, J. Estimates of Modern Poets. London, 1873.
Devizes Gazette, The. " The Ghost of Byron," September 30, 1830.
DIBDIN, T. F. The Library Companion ; or, The Young Man's Guide, and the Old Man's Comfort, in the Choice of a Library. London : Harding, Triphook and Lepard, 1824. [Cf. *The Gentleman's Magazine*, xciv, part ii. (September 1824), 247.]
DIMOND, WILLIAM. The Bride of Abydos, a tragick play, in three acts : as performed at the Theatre Royal, Drury Lane. London : Richard White, 1818. [Reprinted as : The Bride of Abydos : a Romantic Drama in three acts. From Lord Byron's Celebrated Poem. Lacy's Acting Edition of English Plays, vol. lxx.]
A Discourse on the Comparative Merits of Scott and Byron, as Writers of Poetry. Delivered before a Literary Institution in 1820. Only 50 copies printed, 1824.
DISRAELI, BENJAMIN (Earl of Beaconsfield). Vivian Grey. 1826.
—— Contarini Fleming. 1832.
—— Venetia, or the Poet's Daughter. 1837. [Cf. *The Edinburgh Review*, October, p. 68.]
D'ISRAELI, ISAAC. The Literary Character, or the History of Men of Genius, drawn from their own Feelings and Confessions. Fourth edition, revised. London : Henry Colburn, 1828.
DOBELL, BERTRAM. " A Byron (?) Discovery," *The English Review*, August 1915, p. 1 f. [Article appended to a reprint of A Farrago Libelli.]
DOBELLI, AUSONIO. " Dante e Byron," *Giornale Dantesca*, vi. (1898), 145 f.
DOBOSAL, G. Lord Byron in Deutschland. Zwittau, 1911.
Don Giovanni : a Poem in two cantos. Azim and Lilla. And other Pieces. Edinburgh : Edward West, 1825.
Don Juan. With a Preface by a Clergyman. London : Hodgson, 1823. [Byron's Poem.]
—— Canto the Third. London : Greenlaw, 1821.
—— Canto XI. London : Sherwood, Neely and Jones, 1820.
—— Canto the Seventeenth. London : Cooper ; New York : Scribner, Welford and Co., 1870.
*Don Juan. Canto XVII. Ravonspear, 1830.
Don Juan. Cantos XVII, XVIII. London : Duncombe, 1825.

Don Juan. With a Biographical Account of Lord Byron and his Family ;
Anecdotes of his Lordship's Travels and Residence in Greece, at
Geneva, etc. Including, also, a Sketch of the Vampyre Family.
Embellished with a Portrait of his Lordship, from an Original
Drawing. Canto III. London : Wright, 1819.

Don Juan in Search of a Wife. [c. 1830 ? —— title-page missing in the
copy in the British Museum.]

Don Leon : a Poem by the late Lord Byron, Author of Childe Harold, Don
Juan, etc., and forming part of the Private Journal of his Lordship
supposed to have been entirely destroyed by Thomas Moore. To
which is added Leon to Annabella : an Epistle from Lord Byron to
Lady Byron. London : Printed for the Booksellers, 1866. [The
publisher was probably W. Dugdale.]

Facsimile reprint, Paris, n.d. [c. 1900]. Of the first edition,
" printed abroad " earlier than 1853, I have found no trace save
the reference in Notes and Queries, 1st Series, vii. (1853), 66.

DONNER, J. O. E. Lord Byrons Weltanschauung. Helsingfors, 1897.

The Dorchester Guide ; for a House that Jack Built. With thirteen
Cuts. London : Dean and Munday, n.d. [c. 1820].

"DORMOUSE, DUNSTAN." Rigmarole : a Poem. By Dunstan Dormouse.
London : Cookes and Richards, 1856.

DOWDEN, EDWARD. " The French Revolution and Literature " (1877) ;
reprinted in Studies in Literature. London : Kegan Paul, Trench
and Co., 1889.

—— The French Revolution and English Literature. New York :
Scribner, 1897. [Especially pp. 259 f.]

—— The Life of Percy Bysshe Shelley. London : Trübner, 1886.

—— " Byron," Atalanta, June 1890, pp. 577 f.

DRIVER, HENRY AUSTIN. Harold de Burun : a Semi-dramatic Poem ; in
six scenes. London : Longman, Rees, Orme, etc., 1835.

—— Byron and The Abbey. A few Remarks elicited by the Rejection of
his Statue by the Dean of Westminster. London : Longman, 1838.

*DROUINEAU, GUSTAVE. " Un Chagrin de Lord Byron," Annales roman-
tiques, 1832, pp. 128 f. [A poem introducing Newstead, Marie
Chatworth [sic], and Byron.]

Dublin University Magazine, The. "The Morality of Don Juan," by
" The London Hermit," lxxxv. (May 1875), 630 f.

—— " Manfred : Poem and Drama," by " The London Hermit," lxxxiii.
(April 1874), 502 f.

—— " The Fame of Byron," by "F.R.S.," n.s. v, February 1880, 224 f.

DU CAMP, MAXIME. " Souvenirs littéraires," huitième partie, Revue des
Deux Mondes, January 15, 1882, pp. 301 f.

DUFF, J. WRIGHT. *Byron and Aberdeen. Aberdeen, 1902.

—— " Byron," The Bookman (London), xxix. (October 1905), 9 f.

DUEHRING, E. *" Der Pessimismus in Philosophie und Dichtung : Schopenhauer und Byron," Deutsche Vierteljahrsschrift (Stuttgart,1865),
pp. 189 f.

—— Byron, seine Gesellschaftskritik und Stellung über den Dichtern.
Leipzig, 1910.

DUMAS, ALEXANDRE (père). Mémoires. Paris : Calmann-Levy. [iv,
81 f., on Byron's death.]

DYCE, ALEXANDER. " Plagiarisms of Lord Byron," The Gentleman's
Magazine, lxxxviii, part i. (February 1818), 121. [Cf. ibid., pp. 389 f.]

*Eberty, F. Lord Byron. Eine Biographie. Leipzig, 1862. [Cf. Herrig's *Archiv*, xlv. (1869), 52.]

Eckermann, J. P. Gespräche mit Goethe in den letzten Jahren seines Lebens. Leipzig, 1837. [Especially under date November 16, 1823.]

Edgcumbe, Richard. History of the Byron Memorial. London : Effingham Wilson, 1883.

—— " Byronic Literature," *Notes and Queries*, 7th Series (1886), i, 265, 425 ; ii, 3, 86, 143, 284.

—— Byron : The Last Phase. London : John Murray, 1909.

Eichler, A. John Hookham Frere : sein Leben und seine Werke ; sein Einfluss auf Lord Byron. [*Wiener Beiträge zur englischen Philologie*, xx.], 1905.

Eighteen Hundred and Twenty-Six. Carmen Seculare. By Somebody. London : Effingham Wilson, 1826.

Eimer, Manfred. *" Byron und Crabbe," *Frankfurter Zeitung*, 1903, No. 15.

—— Lord Byron und die Kunst. Strassburg, 1907.

—— Byron und der Kosmos. [*Anglistische Forschungen*, xxxiv.] Heidelberg : Carl Winter, 1912.

—— Die persönlichen Beziehungen zwischen Byron und den Shelleys. [*Anglistische Forschungen*, xxxii.] Heidelberg : Carl Winter, 1910.

—— " Das apokryphe Buch Henoch und Byrons Mysterien," *Englische Studien*, xliv, 26 f.

—— " Byrons Pantheismus vom Jahre 1816," *Englische Studien*, xliii, 406 f.

—— " Neuere deutsche Byron- und Shelley-Literatur," *Englische Studien*, xliii, 130 f. ; xliv, 423 f.

—— " Byrons persönliche und geistige Beziehungen zu den gebieten deutscher Kultur," *Anglia*, xxxvi, 313 f. ; 397 f.

An Elegy on the Death of Lord Byron : intended as an humble but sincere Tribute to the exalted Virtues and brilliant Talents of that much Lamented Nobleman ; to which is prefixed a Dedicatory Address . . . on behalf of Suffering Greece. London : Royal Academy, n.d. [1824].

Elliott, Ebenezer. Love : a Poem in Three Parts. To which is added The Giaour : a Satirical Poem. London : Charles Stocking, 1823.

—— " Byron and Napoleon ; or, They Met in Heaven, by the Author of the Cornlaw Rhymes," *The Monthly Magazine*, 1831.

Elton, Oliver. A Survey of English Literature. London : Edward Arnold, 1912. New edition, 1921. [Vol. ii, chapter xvii : " Byron."]

Elze, Karl. Lord Byron. Berlin, 1870.

—— English translation : Lord Byron : a Biography. With a Critical Essay on his Place in Literature. Translated with the Author's sanction. London : John Murray, 1872.

Engel, Eduard. Lord Byron. Eine Autobiographie nach Tagebüchern und Briefen. Berlin, 1876.

Engel, H. Byrons Stellung zu Shakespeare. Ostern, 1903. [Cf. *Englische Studien*, xxv, 147.]

Englander, D. Lord Byrons Mazeppa. Berlin, 1897.

" Erasmus." The Outlaw : a Tale. Edinburgh, 1818.

Ernle, Lord. See Prothero, R. E.

ESCHWEGE, H. The Knight's Tour. In a continuous and uninterrupted Ride over 48 Boards or 3072 Squares, adapted from Byron's Mazeppa. Shanklin, I.W. : Silsbury Brothers, 1896.

ESTÈVE, EDMOND. Byron et le Romantisme francais. Essai sur la Fortune et l'Influence de l'Œuvre de Byron en France de 1812 à 1850. Paris : Hachette, 1907.

*ESTIENNE, L. Un Retours vers Byron. 1869.

*EVANS, DR. "Lord Byron's Infidelity," The Monthly Repository, January 1825.

"FABIUS." A Letter to the Right Hon. Lord Byron, protesting against the Immolation of Gray, Cowper and Campbell at the Shrine of Pope. London, 1825.

FARRER, J. A. Literary Forgeries. With an Introduction by Andrew Lang. London : Longman, Green and Co., 1907.

FERGUSON, J. C. Lecture on the Writings and Genius of Byron. Carlisle. A. Thurman, 1856.

FILON, AUGUSTIN. "Le Crime de Lord Byron," Revue des Deux Mondes, January 15, 1912, pp. 387 f.

FINLAY, GEORGE. History of the Greek Revolution. London, 1861.

—— History of Greece. Oxford : The Clarendon Press, 1877.

—— Cf. also STANHOPE, L. F. C.

FLAISCHLEN, CÄSAR. "Lord Byron in Deutschland," Centralblatt für Bibliothekswesen, vii. (1890), 455 f.

FLETCHER, WILLIAM. Lord Byron's Illness and Death as described in a Letter from William Fletcher (His Lordship's Valet and Confidential Servant) to Hon. Augusta Leigh. Privately printed, Nottingham, 1920. [From the original in the possession of H. C. Roe, Esq.]

*FORTOUL, H. "De l'Art actuel. Byron, Scott et le Romantisme," Revue encyclopédique, lix. (1833).

FOSTER, VERE. The Two Duchesses : Family Correspondence. London : Blackie, 1898.

*FOURÈS, ELIE. Le Premier Amour de Lord Byron, nouvelle inédite. Paris, 1885.

FRANCE, HECTOR. "Byron," La Grande Encyclopédie, viii, 544 f.

FRANKEL, JONAS. "Zu Heines Uebersetzungen aus Byron," Euphorion, xix. (1912), 647 f.

FRANKL, LUDWIG AUGUST. "Byron am Lethe," Episch-lyrische Dichtungen. Vienna, 1834, pp. 159 f.

Fraser's Magazine. "Remarks on Mr. Hobhouse's and Mr. Galt's Correspondence Respecting Atrocities in the Life of Lord Byron," ii. (1830), 533 f.

—— "Lord Byron's Juvenile Poems," vi. (September 1832).

—— "The Celebrated but Hitherto Unpublished Poem of Lord Byron on Mr. Rogers," vii. (January 1833), 81 f.

—— "Critical Illustrations of Lord Byron's Poetry," vii. (March 1833), 303 f.

—— "The Proposed Byron Memorial," n.s., xiii. (February 1876), 246 f.

—— "The Byron Monument," n.s., xix. (May 1879).

FRAZER, W. The Decay of Literature : a Poem. Glasgow : George Richardson, 1835.

FREDERKING, ARTHUR. "Goethes Euphorion," Euphorion, xv. (1908), 697 f.

FRENCH, B. F. The Beauties of Lord Byron, selected from his Works, to which is prefixed a Biographical Memoir of his Life and Writings. Philadelphia, 1828.

FRICK, R. "Hernani und Byron," *Zeitschrift für vergleichende Literaturgeschichte*, xvii. (1908).

FRIEDRICHS, ERNST. "Lermontov und Byron," *Germanisch-romanische Monatsschrift*, vii. (1915–19), 60 f.

*FRISWELL, JAMES H. Essays on English Writers. London, 1869. [Lord Byron, pp. 317 f.]

FROUDE, JAMES ANTHONY. Thomas Carlyle: A History of the First Forty Years of his Life. London, 1884. [I have used the Scribner edition, 1910.]

—— "A Leaf from the Real Life of Lord Byron," *The Nineteenth Century*, xiv. (August 1883), 228 f. [Cf. J. C. Jeaffreson in *The Athenæum*, September 1 (pp. 273 f.), and 22 (pp. 366 f.), 1883.]

FUESS, C. M. Lord Byron as a Satirist in Verse. New York: Columbia University Press, 1912.

Full Particulars of the Much Lamented Death of Lord Byron, with a Sketch of his Life, Character, and Manners. London: B. Dickinson, 1824.

FUHRMANN, L. Die Belesenheit des jungen Byron. Berlin: Kindler, 1903.

Gallery of Byron Beauties. London, 1866.

GALT, JOHN. The Life of Byron. London: Colburn and Bentley, 1830.

—— "Pot versus Kettle," *Fraser's Magazine*, ii. (December 1830), 533 f. [Cf. *The Athenæum*, September 4, 1830, pp. 149 f.; *Fraser's Magazine*, ii. (October 1830), 347 f.; *The Edinburgh Review*, lii. (October 1830), 230 f.; *The Monthly Review*, December 1830 ; *The Monthly Magazine*, October 1830 ; *The Gentleman's Magazine*, September 1830.]

GAMBA, COUNT PIETRO. A Narrative of Lord Byron's Last Journey to Greece. London: John Murray, 1825.

GANTZER, PROF. "Lord Byrons Manfred nach seinem Gedankeninhalte entwickelt," Herrig's *Archiv*, xix. (1856), 209 f.

GARNETT, RICHARD. "Shelley and Beaconsfield," Essays of an Ex-Librarian. New York: Dodd, Mead and Co., 1901.

—— "The John Bull Letter to Lord Byron," *The Athenæum*, 1903, pp. 304 f.

GENDARME DE BÉVOTTE, GEORGES. La Légende de Don Juan. Son évolution dans la littérature des origines au romantisme. Paris: Hachette, 1906. [Chapter xi. is on Byron's Don Juan.]

GENNADIUS, J. "Byron and the Greeks," *English Illustrated Magazine*, xvii. (June 1897), 289 f.

Gentleman's Magazine, The. "Upon Reading Lord Byron's Reflections on the Battle of Talavera in Childe Harold," lxxxii, part i. (June 1812), 566. [A poem in five quatrains, signed "A. H."]

—— "Sentiments on the first perusal of The Giaour (Infidel)," lxxxiii, part ii. (July 1813), 4. [A letter signed "C. T."]

—— "Remarks Philosophical and Literary on the Poetry of Byron and Scott," lxxxix, part ii. (October 1819), 315 f. [Signed "E. P." Cf. pp. 397 f.]

Gentleman's Magazine, The. "Lord Byron's Plagiarisms," xci, part i. (April 1821), 349 f. [Signed "S." Cf. *ibid.* pp. 601 f., signed "E.B." ; *ibid.* part ii. (September 1821), pp. 228 f., signed "Atticus."]
—— "The Rhetoric of the Infidel School ; or, Points of Resemblance between Lord Bolingbroke and Lord Byron," xcii, part ii. (November 1822), 398 f. ; (December 1822), 511 f. ; 582 f. [Signed "E. P."]
—— "Memoir of the Late Lord Byron," xciv, part i. (June 1824), 561 f.
—— "Lord Byron and his Critics," December 1883.
Georgian Revel-Ations ! or, The Most Accomplished Gentleman's Midnight Visit below Stairs ! A Poem. Reprinted from a suppressed Work entitled "Pindaric Odes and Tales," by Peter Pindar the Younger. London 1821. With Twenty Suppressed Stanzas of "Don Juan," in Reference to Ireland. With Byron's Own Curious Historical Notes. The Whole Written in Double Rhymes from a Manuscript in the Possession of Captain Medwin. Great Titham : Printed at Charles Clark's Private Press, 1838.
—— The Byronic portion of this book was reprinted as : Some Rejected Stanzas of "Don Juan," with Byron's own curious notes. The whole written in Double Rhymes, after Casti's manner, an Italian author from whom Byron is said to have plagiarized many of his beauties. From an unpublished manuscript in the possession of Captain Medwin. A very limited number printed. Great Totham, Essex : Printed at Charles Clark's Private Press, 1845. [Printed on one side of the paper only.]
"Gerard, William." See Smith, W. G.
[Gifford, William ?] The Illiberal ! Verse and Prose from the North ! ! [Motto] Dedicated to My Lord Byron in the South ! ! N.B. To be continued occasionally ! ! viz. as a Supplement to the Liberal. London : Printed by G. Morgan, Published by T. Holt, and Sold by C. Chapple, and all other Booksellers, n.d. [1823 ?].
Giles, Henry. "The Moral Spirit of Byron's Genius," and "The Moral Philosophy of Byron's Life," Lectures and Essays. Boston : Ticknor, Reed and Fields, 1850.
Gilfillan, George. A Second Gallery of Literary Portraits. Edinburgh : James Hogg, 1850. [Cf. "Lord Byron," *Tait's Magazine,* xiv ; and *The British Quarterly,* February 1850.]
Gillardon, Heinrich. Shelleys Einwirkung auf Byron. Karlsruhe, 1898. [Cf. *Englische Studien,* xxvii, 287.]
*[Gillies, R. P.] Childe Alaric and other Poems. London, 1813, [Apparently the earliest imitation of Childe Harold.]
*Gnad, Ernst. "Der Weltschmerz in der Poesie" (1869), Literarische Essays. Vienna, 1891.
Goedeke, K. Grundriss zur Geschichte der deutschen Dichtung. Dresden, 1910. [Contains, iv, 2, pp. 488 f., a bibliography of the relations of Byron and Germany.]
Goerth, A. "Lord Byron. Eine psychologisch-ästhetische Studie," Herrig's *Archiv,* xlv. (1869), 31 f.
Goethe, J. W. von. "Lebensverhältnis zu Byron," *Werke* (1833), xlvi 221 f.
—— Tages- und Jahreshefte, 1817.
—— Ueber Kunst und Alterthum. [Various passages on Byron.] [See also *sub* Brandl, Eckermann, Price, Ticknor, Valentin, etc.]

GOODRICH, S. G. Recollections of a Lifetime. New York, 1857. [Vol. ii, pp. 103 f.]

Good Words. "The King of the Humbugs," xlv. (1904), 467 f. and 579 f. [A hitherto unpublished poem by Byron, with editorial commentary.]

GORDON, SIR COSMO. Life and Genius of Lord Byron. London : Knight and Lacy, 1824.

GORDON, PRYSE LOCKHART. Personal Memoirs or Reminiscences. London : Colburn and Bentley, 1830.

GORDON, ROSE. Childe Archie's Pilgrimage. London: G. Pulman, 1873.

Gordon : a Tale. A Poetical Review of Don Juan. London : Allman, 1821. [Cf. *The Imperial Magazine*, May 1822.]

GOTTSCHALL, RUDOLF. *Lord Byron in Italien, ein Drama. 1847.

—— Porträts und Studien. Leipzig, 1870. [Contains : "Byron und die Gegenwart," i, 3 f. ; reprinted from *Unsere Zeit*, 1866, ii, 480 f.]

—— Der neue Plutarch. Leipzig, 1878. [Contains : "Byron," vol. iv.]

GOWER, LEVESON. "Did Byron write Werner ? " *The Nineteenth Century*, xlvi. (August 1899), 243 f.

GRAF, ARTURO. "La Poesia di Caino," *Nuova Antologia*, cxxxiv. (March 16 and April 1, 1908), pp. 193 f. and 425 f.

Grafenstein. 1826. [A satiric poem containing allusions to Byron.]

GRAHAM, WILLIAM. Last Links with Byron, Shelley and Keats. London : Smithers, 1898. [Contains "Chats with Jane Clairmont" and "The Secret of the Byron Separation."] [The complete unreliability of this book is exposed by W. H. Woolen in an article in *Notes and Queries*, 13th Series, i. (October 27, 1923), 323 f. Cf. *ibid.*, 11th Series, ii, 108 and viii, 228 and 249.]

GRANT, HARDING. Lord Byron's Cain, a Mystery ; with Notes ; wherein the Religion of the Bible is considered in reference to acknowledged Philosophy and Reason. London: William Crofts, 1830. [Cf. *The Monthly Magazine*, May 1830 ; *Fraser's Magazine*, iii, 285 f. ; *Englische Studien*, xvi, 310.]

GRASSET, JOSEPH. Demi-Fous, demi-Responsables. English translation by S. E. Jelliffe : The Semi-Insane and the Semi-Responsable. New York : Funk and Wagnalls, 1907.

GREEF, A. "Byrons Lucifer," *Englische Studien*, xxxvi. (1905), 64 f.

GREVERUS, DR. "Zur Charakteristik Byrons," Herrig's *Archiv*, xii. (1853), 112 f.

GREVILLE, C. C. F. The Greville Memoirs. A Journal of the Reigns of King George the Fourth and King William the Fourth. Edited by Henry Reeve. London : Longmans, 1874.

GRIBBLE, FRANCIS. The Love Affairs of Lord Byron. New York : Scribner, 1910.

GRIERSON, H. J. C. Lord Byron : Arnold and Swinburne. London : Humphrey Milford, n.d. [1921]. [The Wharton Lecture on English Poetry, xi. Reprinted from the *Proceedings of the British Academy*, ix.]

—— *Poems of Lord Byron. With a Preface. London : Chatto and Windus. [Announced as forthcoming.]

*GRISWOLD, HATTIE TYNG. Home Life of Great Authors. Chicago, 1887. [" Lord Byron," pp. 94 f.]

GROAG, J. G. Lord Byron als Dramatiker. Linz, 1877.

GROMIER, EUGÈNE. Byroniennes, élégies. Paris : Delangle, 1827. [Nine poems on Byron.]

374 BIBLIOGRAPHY

*GRONOW, CAPTAIN. Reminiscences. London, 1862. ["Lord Byron,"
pp. 208 f.]
—— Last Recollections, being the Fourth and Final Series of his
Reminiscences. London, 1866. ["Lord Byron and Dan Mackin-
non," pp. 100 f.]
GUICCIOLI, THE COUNTESS OF (MME. DE BOISSY). Lord Byron jugé par
les témoins de sa vie. Paris, 1868.
—— English translation: My Recollections of Lord Byron, and those of
Eye-Witnesses of his Life. Translated by H. E. H. Jerningham.
London : Richard Bentley, 1868.
—— American reprint : Memoirs of Lord Byron by his Mistress. New
York, 1869.
[Cf. The Athenæum, April 5, 1873, p. 439 ; Belgravia, vii. (1869) ;
Daily Telegraph, March 28, 1873 ; Pall Mall Gazette, April 30,
1873 ; Victoria Magazine, November 1873, p. 23.]

HACKWOOD, F. W. William Hone, His Life and Times. London :
Unwin, 1912.
HADLEY, JAMES. Essays Philological and Critical. New York : Holt
and Williams, 1873.
HAHN, GUSTAV. Lord Beaconsfields Roman Venetia ; ein Denkmal
Byrons und Shelleys. Dresden, 1898.
*HALDANE, LORD ; SAINTSBURY, GEORGE ; and others. Byron, the Poet.
Centenary Essays. London: Routledge. [Announced as forth-
coming.]
HALLECK, FITZ GREEN. The Works of Lord Byron . . . with a Sketch
of his Life. New York : Dearborn, 1834. [Reprinted in Byron's
Works, Hartford, 1857.]
HALLER, WILLIAM. " Byron and the British Conscience," The Sewanee
Review, xxiv. (January 1916), 1 f.
HAMANN, ALBERT. The Life and Works of Lord Byron. Berlin, 1895 ;
new edition, 1910.
HAMILTON, H. B. Portrayal of the Life and Character of Lord Byron in
the Novel by Benjamin Disraeli entitled "Venetia." Leipzig :
Gustav Schmidt, 1884.
*HAMILTON, WALTER. Parodies of the Works of English and American
Authors. London, 1886. ["Lord Byron," iii, 190 f.]
HANCOCK, A. E. The French Revolution and the English Poets. New
York : Holt, 1899.
HANNAY, JAMES. Satire and Satirists. London, 1854. ["Byron,"
pp. 241 f.]
HARE, AUGUSTUS and JULIUS CHARLES. Guesses at Truth. London,
1827. [I have used the Boston : Ticknor and Fields, 1851, edition.]
HARNACK, O. "Puschkin und Byron," Zeitschrift für vergleichende
Literaturgeschichte, i. (1888). [Reprinted in Essays und Studien.
Brunswick, 1899.]
HARNESS, WILLIAM. The Wrath of Cain : A Boyle Lecture, delivered at
the Church of St. Martin's-in-the-Fields. London : Rivington,
1822.
HARPER, GEORGE MCLEAN. William Wordsworth : His Life, Works and
Influence. New York : Scribner, 1916.
*HARRISON, JAMES A. A Group of Poets and their Haunts. New York,
1875. [" Italian Haunts of Lord Byron," pp. 31 f.]

" HARROVIENSIS." A Letter to Sir Walter Scott, Bart., in Answer to the Remonstrances of Oxoniensis on the Publication of Cain, A Mystery, by Lord Byron. London : Rodwell and Martin, 1822.

*HAUSSONVILLE, THE COMTESSE DE. La Jeunesse de Lord Byron. Paris, 1872.

—— Les Dernières Années de Lord Byron. Paris, 1874.

HAWEIS, HUGH R. Gems from Byron. With an Introduction. London : Routledge, 1886.

HAYMAN, HENRY. "Lord Byron and the Greek Patriots," *Harper's Magazine*, February 1894, pp. 365 f.

[HAYWARD, ABRAHAM.] "The Byron Mystery," *The Quarterly Review*, cxxvii. (October 1869), 400 f.

—— "Mrs. Stowe's Vindication," *The Quarterly Review*, cxxviii. (January 1870), 218 f.

—— Review of Jeaffreson's The Real Lord Byron, *The Quarterly Review*, clvi. (July 1883), 90 f.

*HAYWARD, ABRAHAM. Sketches of Eminent Statesmen and Writers, with other Essays. London, 1880. [" Byron and Tennyson," ii, 305 f.]

HAZLITT, WILLIAM. Collected Works. Edited by A. R. Waller and Arnold Glover. London : Dent, 1902. [Hazlitt's chief articles on Byron are : a Review of Childe Harold, iv, in *The Yellow Dwarf*, May 2, 1818 ; " Pope, Lord Byron, and Mr. Bowles," *The London Magazine*, June 1821 ; in The Spirit of the Age ; in Lectures on the English Poets ; " Byron and Wordsworth," *The London Weekly Review*, April 5, 1828 ; and " Posthumous Poems of Percy Bysshe Shelley," *Edinburgh Review*, July 1824.]

HEARN, LAFCADIO. Interpretations of Literature. New York : Dodd, Mead and Co., 1916. [Two lectures on Byron, i, pp. 111 f. and 124 f.]

Heath's Book of Beauty. 1847.

HEBER, REGINALD. Review of Byron's Dramas, *The Quarterly Review*, xxvii. (July 1822), 476 f.

HECKEL, HANS. Das Don Juan-Problem in der neueren Dichtung. Stuttgart : J. B. Metzler, 1915. [Especially chapter v.]

HENLEY, WILLIAM ERNEST. Review of Arnold's Poetry of Byron, *The Athenæum*, June 25, 1881, pp. 839 f. [Reprinted in Views and Reviews. New York : Scribner, pp. 56 f. ; and in Henley's Works. London : David Nutt, 1908.]

—— The Works of Lord Byron. Volume I. : Letters, 1804–13. London : William Heineman, 1897. Edited by W. E. Henley. [No more published. Henley's notes are reprinted together under the title " Byron's World " in his Works.]

*HENGESBACH, ——. "Shall we read Lord Byron in our Classes, and which of his Works ? " Fulda, 1888. [I do not know whether this is a book or an article in a magazine.]

HENNIG, PAUL. "Verhältnis von Robert Southey zu Lord Byron," *Anglia*, iii. (1880), 426 f. [Also in pamphlet form, Halle, 1880.]

HERBERT, W. V. The Corsair. Libretto for Grand Opera. London : Evereth and Son, 1906.

HERFORD, C. H. The Age of Wordsworth. London : George Bell, 1897.

HERLOSSOHN, KARL. "Byrons Tod. Elegische Phantasie," *Schriften*, edited by Böttger, xi, i, 15 f.

*HERMANN, —. A Grammatical Inquiry into the Language of Lord Byron. Berlin, 1902.

HERVÉ, CHARLES and CHARLES STANLEY. Don Juan Married. [c. 1833 ; this " continuation " was, apparently, never printed.]

HEWLETT, MAURICE. Bendish: a Study in Prodigality. London: Macmillan, 1913.

—— " Don Q. on Don Juan," The Times, July 22, 1922.

HILLARD, GEORGE STILLMAN. Six Months in Italy. London, 1843. [" Lord Byron," ii, 338 f.]

HOBHOUSE, JOHN CAM (LORD BROUGHTON). A Journey through Albania and other Provinces of Turkey. London: Cawthorn, 1813. [Cf. The Gentleman's Magazine, lxxxiv, part i. (April 1814), 353 f.]

—— Travels in Albania. London: Murray, 1855.

—— Italy from 1816 to 1854. London: Murray, 1861.

—— Historical Illustrations to the Fourth Canto of Childe Harold: Containing Dissertations on the Ruins of Rome ; and an Essay on Italian Literature. London: Murray, 1818.

—— Review of Dallas's Recollections and of Medwin's Conversations, Westminster Review, January 1825.

—— Contemporary Account of the Separation of Lord and Lady Byron ; also of the Destruction of Lord Byron's Memoirs. Privately printed, 1870.

—— Recollections of a Long Life. London: John Murray, 1909–11.

HOCK, STEFAN. " Die Vampirsagen und ihre Verwertung in der deutschen Literatur." [Forschungen zur neueren Literaturgeschichte. Munich (1900), vol. xvii.]

HODGES, CHARLES. Original Poems, Translations [etc.]. Munich: Jacob Bayer, 1836.

HODGSON, FRANCIS. Lady Jane Grey: a Tale, in two books ; with miscellaneous Poems in English and Latin. London: Bensley, 1809.

—— Childe Harold's Monitor ; or, Lines occasioned by the last canto of Childe Harold, including Hints to other Contemporaries. London: J. Porter, 1818. [Cf. The Gentleman's Magazine, lxxxviii, part ii. (August 1818), 137 f. ; The Monthly Review, November 1818 ; Richard Edgcumbe, in Notes and Queries, 7th Series, ii, 3 ; and Franz Bader, "Zu Childe Harold's Monitor," Herrig's Archiv, cxxxviii. (1919), 67 f.]

HODGSON, J. T. Memoirs of the Reverend Francis Hodgson, B.D., Scholar, Poet, and Divine. London: Macmillan, 1878.

HOFFMANN, E. T. A. " Walter Scott und Byron, eine Erzählung " (c. 1820). [A section of the Serapionsbrüder.]

*HOFFMANN, FREDERICK A. Poetry, its Origin, Nature and History. London, 1884. [" Byron," i, 441 f.]

HOFFMANN, KARL. Ueber Lord Byrons The Giaour. Halle: Karras, 1898.

HOGG, JAMES. The Pilgrims of the Sun. London, 1815.

—— The Poetic Mirror. London, 1816.

—— " Ode for Music. On the Death of Lord Byron. By the Ettrick Shepherd," Blackwood's Magazine, xxi. (1827), 520 f.

—— Poetical Works of the Ettrick Shepherd. Edinburgh: Blackie, 1840.

*HOHENHAUSEN, ELISE VON. Rousseau, Goethe, Byron ; ein kritisch-literarischen Umriss aus ethisch-christlichem Standpunkt. Kassel, 1847. [She also wrote several poems on Byron : see Ochsenbein, pp. 31 f.]

HOLL, KARL. "Goethes Vollendung in ihrer Beziehung zu Byron und Carlyle," *Germanisch-romanische Monatsschrift*, ix. (1921), 75 f.

HOLTHAUSEN, F. "Skandinavische Byron-Uebersetzungen," *Englische Studien*, xxv. (1898), 325 f.

—— "Tegnér und Byron," Herrig's *Archiv*, ci. (1899), 141 f.

HOLZHAUSEN, P. Napoleons Tod im Spiegel der zeitgenössischen Presse und Dichtung. Frankfort : Diesterweg, 1902.

—— Bonaparte, Byron und die Briten. Frankfort : Diesterweg, 1904.

—— *"Lord Byron und seine deutschen Biographen," *Beilage zur Allgemeinen Zeitung*. Munich (1903), Nos. 174 and 175.

[HONE, WILLIAM.] Hone's Lord Byron's Corsair. Conrad, the Corsair ; or, The Pirate's Isle. A Tale. By Lord Byron. Adapted as a Romance. London : William Hone, 1817.

—— The Three Trials of William Hone. London : William Hone, 1818. [New edition, with introduction and notes by W. Tegg, 1876.]

—— Don John ; or, Don Juan Unmasked ; being a Key to the Mystery attending that remarkable Production, with a descriptive Review of the Poem and Extracts. London : William Hone, 1819.

—— Don Juan. Canto the Third. London : William Hone, 1819.

HOOK, THEODORE. [Quoted on Byron, without reference to the source whence the quotation is derived, in *The Academy*, February 15, 1902, p. 161.]

HOOPS, JOHANNES. Lord Byrons Leben und Dichten. Frankfort, 1903.

HOVEY, RICHARD. To the End of the Trail. New York : Duffield, 1908.

HOWELL, OWEN. Abel. Written, but with great humility, in Reply to Lord Byron's Cain. London : John Mardon, 1843.

HOWITT, WILLIAM. A Poet's Thoughts at the Interment of Lord Byron. London : Baldwin, Cradock and Joy, 1824.

—— Homes and Haunts of the Most Eminent British Poets. London : Bentley, 1847. [On Byron, ii, 467 f.]

—— A Letter on the Stowe controversy, *The Daily News*, September 4, 1869.

HUGO, VICTOR. "Sur George Gordon, Lord Byron," *La Muse française*, ii. (June 1824), 327 f.

—— "Lord Byron et ses rapports avec la littérature actuelle," *Annales romantique*, 1827–28.

HUNT, LEIGH. Lord Byron and some of his Contemporaries ; with Recollections of the Author's Life, and of his Visit to Italy. London : Henry Colburn, 1828. [Two volumes ; also a one-volume edition in quarto.] [Cf. *The Athenæum*, January 2, 23, and 30, 1828 ; *The Literary Messenger*, January 1828, pp. 18 f. ; *The Quarterly Review*, xxxvii. (March 1828) ; *The Monthly Review*, 1828.]

—— The Autobiography of Leigh Hunt, with Reminiscences of Friends and Contemporaries. London, 1850. [Revised edition, 1860 ; edited by R. Ingpen, 1903.]

—— The Feast of the Poets : with Notes and other Pieces in Verse, by the Editor of *The Examiner*. London, 1814.

[ILEY, MATTHEW ?] The Life, Writings, Opinions and Times of the Right Hon. George Gordon Noel, Lord Byron ; including in its most extensive Biography, Anecdotes and Memoirs of the Lives of the Most Eminent and Eccentric, Public and Noble Characters and

Courtiers of the Present Polished and Enlightened Age and Court of His Majesty George the Fourth. In the course of the Biography is also separately given, Copious Recollections of the lately destroyed MS. Originally intended for post-humous publication and entitled Memoirs of My own Life and Times, by The Right Hon. Lord Byron. "Crede Byron." Motto of the Byron family. [A second motto, from Timon of Athens, eight lines, beginning "I have in this rough work set forth a man," etc.] By an English Gentleman, in the Greek Military Service, and Comrade of his Lordship. Compiled from authentic Documents and from long personal Acquaintance. In three volumes. London : Matthew Iley, 1825.

Illusion ; or, The Trances of Nourjahad, a Melo-drama, by Lord Byron. [Of this I know nothing save a reference to it in *The Gentleman's Magazine*, lxxxiii, part ii. (December 1813), 697.]

Illustrations to the Works of Lord Byron. The Drawings by Chalon, Leslie, Harding ; Engraved under the superintendence of Mr. C. Heath. London, n.d. [c. 1846].

Imperial Magazine, The. "Memoir of Living Poets—Lord Byron." 1822.

*" Imprecations of Lord Byron in Stanzas : Translated from the English," *El Censor*, 1820–22, xiii, 345. [A Spanish hoax noted by Churchman who, however, does not give the Spanish title. Cf. the next item.]

Imprécations : Stances traduits de l'anglais de Lord Byron. Brussels, 1822. [An eight-page pamphlet ; a copy is in the Bibliothèque Nationale, Paris.]

Independent, The. "Byron : The Battle of Waterloo," lxxxii. (June 28, 1915), 521.

INTZE, O. Byroniana. Bremen, 1914. [Valuable bibliography, in part supplementing that of E. H. Coleridge.]

[IRELAND, W. H.] Scribbleomania ; or, The Printer's Devil's Polichronicon. A Sublime Poem. By Anser Pen-Drag-On. London : Sherwood, Neely and Jones, 1815.

Irner. Par Lord Byron. Traduit de l'anglais. Paris : Ponthieu, 1821.

Irregular Ode on the Death of Lord Byron, écrite à Paris par un Anglais. Paris : Didot, 1825.

IRVING, WASHINGTON. The Crayon Miscellany. Philadelphia, 1835. [Includes " Abbotsford and Newstead Abbey."]

*JACOBSEN, F. J. Briefe an eine deutsche Edelfrau über die neuesten englischen Dichter. 1820. [Cf. Price, pp. 518 f.]

JANTZEN, H. "Zu Lord Byrons Giaour," Herrig's *Archiv*, cvi. (1901), 286 f.

JEAFFRESON, JOHN CORDY. The Real Lord Byron. New Views of the Poet's Life. London, 1883 ; Boston : Osgood, 1883. [See *The Athenæum*, May 12, August 18, September 1 and 22, 1883 ; *The Academy*, March 26, 1883 ; *The British Quarterly*, No. 155, 1883 ; *The Fortnightly Review*, April 1883 ; *The Guardian*, August 15, 1883 ; *The Nineteenth Century*, August 1883 ; *The Quarterly Review*, July 1883 ; *The Saturday Review*, June 16, 1883.]

—— "Mrs. Leigh," *The Athenæum*, September 19, 1885.

—— A Book of Recollections. London : Hurst and Blackett, 1894.

JEBB, RICHARD C. Modern Greece. London : Macmillan, 1880. [" Byron in Greece," pp. 143 f.]

JEFFREY, FRANCIS. Contributions to the *Edinburgh Review*. London: Longman, 1846.

*JERNINGHAM, H. E. H. Reminiscences of an Attaché. [On La Guiccioli.]

John Bull Magazine and Literary Recorder, The. "A Supposed Chapter from Byron's Own Memoirs," i. (July 1824), 19 f. [Cf. *ibid.* November 1824, p. 163; *Blackwood's Magazine*, xvi. (July 1824), 115 f. This fabrication may be by Theodore Hook.]

JOHNSON, LIONEL. Review of the Coleridge-Prothero edition of Byron's Works, *The Academy*, May 7, 1898.

JOHNSON, ROBERT UNDERWOOD. "To the Spirit of Byron," *The Independent*, lxxx. (December 7, 1914), 368.

JONES, JOHN. Attempts at Verse, by John Jones, an Old Servant: with some Account of the Writer, written by himself: and an Introductory Essay on the Lives and Works of our Uneducated Poets, by Robert Southey, Esq., Poet Laureate. London: Murray, 1831. [Contains a poem "On the Death of Lord Byron," pp. 306 f.]

JOSENHANS, WALTHER. Lord Byron und die Politik. Stuttgart: J. F. Steinkopf, 1917.

JOWETT, H. Byron. Printed for private circulation, n.d. [1884.]

Juan Secundus. Canto the First. London: John Miller, 1825.

*"JULIA, ÆMILIA." Byron; Salathiel, or the Martyrs; and other Poems. By Æmilia Julia. London: Routledge, 1855. [Cf. *The Athenœum*, May 19, 1855, p. 581.]

"JULIUS." More News from Venice. By Beppo, a Noble Venetian. Translated from the Original. By Julius. Oxford: Printed by W. Baxter, for J. Vincent, 1818. [Another edition: London: Sherwood and Co., 1818.]

*JUNOT, MME. ANDOCHE (DUCHESS OF ABRANTES). Souvenirs d'une ambassade et d'un séjour en Espagne et en Portugal de 1808 à 1811. Brussels, 1838.

KAHN, RUDOLPH. Die Pope-Kritik im 18. Jahrhundert mit Einschluss der Byron-Bowles Controverse. Emmendingen: Dölter, 1910.

KAISER, DR. Byrons und Delavignes Marino Faliero. Dusseldorf, 1870.

KEAN, CHARLES. Sardanapalus. A Tragedy by Lord Byron. Adapted for Representation. [Lacy's Acting Edition of English Plays, vol. xi.]

KEATS, JOHN. "Sonnet to Byron" and "Sleep and Poetry" in any edition of Poems.

—— Letters. Edited by H. Buxton Forman. London: Reeves and Turner, 1895.

KENNEDY, JAMES. Conversations on Religion, with Lord Byron and others, held in Cephalonia, a short time previous to his Lordship's Death. London: John Murray, 1830. [Cf. *The London Magazine*, October 2, 1824; *The Monthly Review*, August 1830; *Fraser's Magazine*, October 1830.]

*KER, W. P. "Byron," *The Criterion*, ii. (October 1923).

[KILGOUR, ALEXANDER.] Anecdotes of Lord Byron, from Authentic Sources; with Remarks illustrative of his Connection with the Principal Literary Characters of the Present Day. London: Knight and Lacy, 1825.

KINDON, J. "Byron versus Spenser," *International Journal of Ethics*, xiv. (1904), 362 f.

KINGSLEY, CHARLES. "Thoughts on Shelley and Byron," *Fraser's Magazine*, November 1853. [Reprinted in New Miscellanies. Boston : Ticknor and Fields, 1860 ; and in Works, 1880, xx, 35 f.]

KLUGE, W. Lord Byron's Werner or The Inheritance. Eine dramentechnische Untersuchung mit Quellenstudien. Leipzig, 1913.

KNOBBE, A. Die Faust-Idee in Lord Byrons Dichtungen. Stralsund, 1906. [Cf. *Englische Studien*, xxxviii, 98.]

KNOTT, JOHN. The Last Illness of Lord Byron : a Study in the Borderland of Genius and Madness, of Cosmical Inspiration and Pathological Psychology. St. Paul, Minnesota : Volkszeitung Printing Co., 1912. [Cf. *The Athenœum*, March 9, 1912, p. 282.]

KOEPPEL, EMILE. Lord Byron. Berlin : Hofmann, 1903. [In the series " Geisteshelden."]

—— " Lord Byrons Astarte," *Englische Studien*, xxx. (1902), 195 f.

—— " Die Engel Harut und Marut in der englischen Dichtung," *Englische Studien*, xxxvii, 461 f.

KÖHLER, ——. A Glance at Lord Byron as a Dramatist. Jever, 1877.

KÖLBING, E. Lord Byron's Werke, in kritischen Texten mit Einleitung und Anmerkungen. Weimar : E. Felber, 1893 (vol. i.), 1896 (vol. ii.). [Cf. review by J. Hoops, *Englische Studien*, xxiii, 135 f.]

—— " Zu Byrons Prisoner of Chillon," *Englische Studien*, xvii, 175 f. ; xxiii, 445 f.

—— " Kleine Beiträge zu einer Byron-Bibliographie," *Englische Studien*, xvii, 327 f.

—— " Lord Byron und Miss Elizabeth Pigot," *Englische Studien*, xvii, 441 f.

—— " Lord Byron und Dupatys Lettres sur l'Italie," *Englische Studien*, xvii, 448 f.

—— " Byron und Shakespeares Macbeth," *Englische Studien*, xix, 300 f.

—— " Zu Byrons Manfred," *Englische Studien*, xxii, 140 f.

—— " Zehn Byroniana," *Englische Studien*, xxv, 147 f.

—— " Byron-Literatur," *Englische Studien*, xxvi, 284 f.

KRAEGER, H. Der Byronische Heldentypus. [*Forschungen zur neueren Literaturgeschichte*, vi.] Munich, 1898. [Cf. *Englische Studien*, xxvi, 92.]

—— " Lord Byrons Beziehungen zu Amerika," *Wissenschaftliche Beilage zur Allgemeinen Zeitung*, 1897, Nos. 58–62.

—— " Lord Byron und Francesca da Rimini," Herrig's *Archiv*, xcviii (1897), 463 f.

KRANZ, ELISABET. Der Prinzregent und spätere Georg IV. als Gegenstand der Satire bei Thomas Moore und Lord Byron. Stuttgart, 1912.

KRAUSE, FRANZ. Byrons Marino Faliero. Breslau, 1897. [Cf. *Englische Studien*, xxvi, 145 ; *Euphorion*, vi. (1899), 585 f.]

KRUMMACHER, M. " Zu Byrons Childe Harold," *Englische Studien*, viii, 411.

KUCHYNKA, J. V. The Influence of Lord Byron on Bohemian Literature. Chicago, 1916. [MS. thesis in the library of the University of Chicago.]

*KUERNBERGER, FERDINAND. " Ein unveröffentlichtes Manfred-Gedicht zu Robert Schumanns Musik," *Oesterreichische Rundschau*, viii. (1906).

*LA BOURDELLÈS, R. G. Leopardi ; Lord Byron en Suisse, en Italie, et en Grèce. Paris, 1901.

*Lady Byron's Reply to her Lord's Farewell, with Referential Notes to the Lines in Lord Byron's Poem particularly alluded to by her Ladyship. London, 1825. [Probably a reprint of one of the numerous " Replies " of 1816.]

Lady Byron's Responsive " Fare thee well." London: Richard Edwards, 1816. [Cf. *The Gentleman's Magazine*, lxxxvi, part ii. (September 1816), 249.]

Lady Byron, The Life of, compiled from the best Authorities. To which is appended a Vindication of Lord Byron. London: Police News Edition, n.d. [1869].

[LAFAYETTE, EMILY.] Maid of Athens. By Lafayette McLaws. New York, 1906.

LAKE, J. W. A Poetical Tribute to the Memory of Lord Byron. Paris: Amyot, 1824.

—— " Life of Lord Byron," in the 16-volume edition of Byron's Works. Paris: Galignani, 1822. [Reprinted separately in London, 1826 ; found also in the 7-volume edition of the Works. Paris: Didot, 1825. See also *sub* Lamartine.]

LAMARTINE, ALPHONSE DE. " L'Homme : A Lord Byron," Méditations poétiques. Paris, 1820.

—— Le Dernier Chant du Pélérinage d'Harold. Paris, 1825. [Cf. *The Monthly Review*, November 1825.]

—— English translation : The Last Canto of Childe Harold's Pilgrimage. Translated from the French of M. de Lamartine, by J. W. Lake. Paris, 1826.

—— Another version : The Last Canto of Childe Harold's Pilgrimage. By Alphonse de Lamartine. London: E. Lloyd, 1827. [Cf. *The London Literary Gazette*, December 2, 1826, pp. 754 f.]

—— *" La Vie de Byron," *Le Constitutionnel*, September 26-December 2, 1865.

[LAMB, LADY CAROLINE.] Glenarvon. London: Henry Colburn, 1816.

—— Reprinted as: The Fatal Passion. London: C. H. Clarke, n.d. [1865].

—— *French translation by " Mme. de P***, née L***." Paris, 1819.

LAMB, CHARLES. Letters. Edited by Alfred Ainger. London: Macmillan, 1888.

LANDOR, WALTER SAVAGE. Imaginary Conversations of Literary Men and Statesmen. London: Taylor and Hessey, 1824.

—— Gebir, Count Julian and other Poems. London: Moxon, 1831.

—— The Last Fruits off an Old Tree. London: Moxon, 1853.

—— Dry Sticks Fagoted by Walter Savage Landor. Edinburgh: Nichol ; London: Nisbet, 1858.

—— Heroic Idyls, with Additional Pieces. London: Newby, 1863.

—— Works. London: Chapman and Hall, 1876.
    [Cf. also Sir Sidney Colvin's Landor (London: Macmillan, 1881), p. 22 ; and Wise and Wheeler's Bibliography of the Writings of Landor.]

LANG, ANDREW. Letters to Dead Authors. London: Longmans Green and Co., 1886.

—— " Byron and Mary Chaworth," *The Fortnightly Review*, n.s. lxxxviii. (August 1910), 269 f.

*LATOUR, A. DE. Memoires de Silvio Pellico. 1837.

382 BIBLIOGRAPHY

*LAUBE, H. Das junge Europa, Roman in drei Büchern : Die Poeten, die Krieger, die Bürger. 1836. [See Porterfield, p. 86.]
—— Lord Byron, eine Reisenovelle. 1835.
*LAURENT, E. Byron. 1899.
A Layman's Epistle to a Certain Nobleman. London : Rodwell and Martin, 1824.
*LEAKE, COLONEL. Historical Outline of the Greek Revolution. [c. 1825.]
LE BAS, C. W. Review of the Life and Character of Lord Byron. London : Rivington, 1833. [Reprinted from The British Critic, April 1831.]
LEGARÉ, H. S. " Lord Byron's Character and Writings " ; " Lord Byron's Letters and Journals " ; Writings. Charleston, S. C. : Burgess and James, 1846, ii, 356 f., and 411 f. [Reprinted from The Southern Review.]
LEIGHTON, ALEXANDER. " Life of Lord Byron," in Poetical Works of Lord Byron, with illustrations by K. Halowelle. Edinburgh : W. P. Nimmo, 1861 ; new edition, 1868. [This " Life " is reprinted in Crowell's edition of Byron's Works, 1884.]
*" LEON." Don Juan in Ireland. By Leon. [See The Athenæum, December 3, 1870, p. 723.]
Leon to Annabella. An Epistle after the Manner of Ovid. Se no e vero, e ben trovato. London : MacJohn, Raymer and Co., n.d. [1865 or earlier].
—— Another edition, included, with separate title-page, in the 1866 edition of Don Leon (q.v.) : The Great Secret Revealed ! Suppressed Poem by Lord Byron, never before published. Leon to Annabella. By Lord Byron. An Epistle explaining the Real Cause of their Eternal Separation and Justifying the Practice which led to it. Forming the Most Curious Passage in the Secret History of the Noble Poet. Influencing the whole of His Future Career.
—— Reprinted : (1) Brussels, 1875 ; (2) with Don Leon, Paris, c. 1900 ; (3) in Poetica Erotica. A Collection of Rare and Curious Amatory Verse. Edited by T. R. Smith. New York : Printed for subscribers by Boni and Liveright, vol. iii. (1922), pp. 243 f.
LEONARD, WILLIAM ELLERY. Byron and Byronism in America. Boston [no publisher], 1905.
*LESCURE, ADOLPHE. Lord Byron. Histoire d'un homme. Paris, 1866.
L'ESTRANGE, A. G. The Literary Life of the Reverend William Harness. London : Hurst and Blackett, 1871. [The substance of this biography is reproduced in Personal Reminiscences, by Barham, Harness and Hodder, edited by R. H. Stoddard. New York : Scribner, Armstrong and Co., 1875].
—— History of English Humour. London, 1878. [On Byron, ii, 184 f.]
L'ETOILE, A. E. DE. Lord Byron : sa biographie et choix de ses poèmes. Paris, 1885.
A Letter of Expostulation to Lord Byron, on his present Pursuits with Animadversions on his Writings and Absence from his Country in the Hour of Danger. [The Pamphleteer, xix. (1822), 347 f.]
A Letter to R. W. Elliston, Esq. . . . on the Injustice and Illegality of his Conduct in representing Lord Byron's Tragedy of Marino Faliero. London : John Lowndes, n.d. [1820].
Lettre de Lord Byron au Grand Turc. Précédé de la Lettre de Sa Hautesse au Noble Lord. Traduit de l'anglais. Paris : Sanson, 1824.

LEVI, EUGENIA. "Byron and Petrarch," *The Athenæum*, July 20, 1901, pp. 95 f. [Cf. reply by W. Irving Way, *The Athenæum*, August 17, 1901, p. 222.]

LEVY, SIEGMUND. "Ueber das Verhältnis von Byrons Hints from Horace zu Horaz und zu Pope," *Anglia*, ii. (1879), 256 f.

LEWES, LOUIS. Lord Byron. Hamburg, 1897.

Light at Last. The Byron Mystery ! Mrs. Beecher Stowe and her True History of Lady Byron's Life. Lord Byron's Half-Sister, Augusta. The Early Life of Lord Byron. Strange Mental Affliction. The Solution of Lord Byron's Connection with his Half-Sister, Augusta. The Real Cause of the Separation between Lord and Lady Byron, his Poems, etc. Price One Penny. [London, 1869.]

Light or Darkness ? A Poem. With Remarks on Lord Byron's Detractors. London : Smart and Allen, 1870.

LINDSAY, LORD. A letter in *The Times*, September 7, 1869.

*Lines on the National Byron Memorial. London, 1876.

*LIPNICKI, E. "Byron in Befreiungskampfe der polnischen National-literatur," *Das Magazin*, 1877, pp. 301 f., 317 f., 334 f.

LISTER, T. H. "Byron," The Encyclopædia Britannica, 8th edition, vi. (1854), 37 f. [Reprinted as "Life of Lord Byron" in the 10-volume edition of Byron's Works. Boston : Little, Brown and Co., 1861, vol. i, pp. xi f.]

*Literary Gazette, The. "Byroniana." *c.* 1828. [A series of articles.]

LLOYD, A. J. A Guide to Newstead Abbey and Gardens. Mansfield : W. and J. Linney, n.d.

LOCKHART, J. G. Peter's Letters to his Kinsfolk. Edinburgh : Blackwood, 1819.

—— Review of Moore's Byron, *The Quarterly Review*, January 1831, pp. 168 f.

—— The Life of Sir Walter Scott. [The edition I have used is : Boston : J. B. Millet Co., 1902, ten volumes.]

LOFORTE-RANDI, ANDREA. Nella Letteratura straniere. [5th Series.] Palermo : Reber, 1903. [On Shakespeare, Goethe, Byron and Shelley.]

LOHMANN, O. "Byrons Manfred und sein Verhältnis zu Dichtungen verwandten Inhalts," *Anglia*, v. (1882), 291 f.

LOMBROSO, CESARE. L'Uomo di genio, 1888. [English translation : The Man of Genius. London : Walter Scott, 1891.]

London Magazine, The. "The Literary Police Office, Bow Street," February 1823, pp. 157 f.

—— "Personal Character of Lord Byron," October 1824.

Lord Byron's Farewell to England ; with three other poems, viz. : Ode to St. Helena, To my Daughter, on the Morning of her Birth, and To the Lily of France. London : J. Johnston, 1816.

Lord Byron's Farewell to England, and other late poems ; Including an entire copy (now first printed) of his Curse of Minerva : Together with an original Biography. Philadelphia : Moses Thomas, 1816.

Lord Byron's Manfred. At Drury Lane Theatre. By a Dilettante behind the Scenes. London : J. W. Last, 1863.

Lord Byron's Pilgrimage to the Holy Land. A Poem. In Two Cantos. To which is added The Tempest : a Fragment. London : J. Johnston, 1817. [After this book had been suppressed by injunction Johnston re-issued it with the title : A Pilgrimage, etc.]

" Lord Byron's Residence in Greece," *The Westminster Review*, ii. (July 1824).

*LORENZO D'AYOT, MANUEL. Shakespeare, Lord Byron y Chateaubriand, como modelas de la juventad literaria. Madrid, 1886.

LOTZE, CURT. Quellenstudien über Lord Byrons The Island. Leipzig : Junghanss, 1902.

LOUNSBURY, THOMAS R. The Life and Times of Tennyson. New Haven : The Yale University Press, 1915.

LOVELACE, MARY, COUNTESS OF. A Portrait Mis-named Lady Byron. 1918. [Reprinted from *The Connoisseur*, October 1917. Cf. LJ, iv, 66.]

—— Ralph, Earl of Lovelace : A Memoir. London : Christophers, 1920.

LOVELACE, RALPH MILBANKE, EARL OF. Astarte. A Fragment of Truth concerning George Gordon, sixth Lord Byron. Recorded by his Grandson. London : Printed at the Chiswick Press, 1905.

—— New edition, revised, with many additional letters, edited by Mary, Countess of Lovelace. London : Christophers, 1921.
[There is also a pirated Buffalo (New York) reprint, with many omissions, 1905.]

[LUCAS, SAMUEL.] The Stowe-Byron Controversy. A Complete Résumé of all that has been written and said upon the subject. Together with an Impartial Review of the Merits of the Case. By the Editor of *Once a Week*. London : Thomas Cooper, 1869.

LUDWIG, E. " Lord Byron und Lasalle," *Neue Rundschau*, xxii. (1911), 931 f.

LUEDER, A. Lord Byrons Urteile über Italien und seine Bewohner, ihre Sprache, Literatur und Kunst. 1893.

LUMBROSO, ALBERTO. " Saggio di un tentativo bibliographico su Lord Byron," *Pagine Veneziane*. Rome, 1900–1905, pp. 126 f.

LUNT, GEORGE. The Grave of Byron, with other Poems. Boston : Hilliard, Gray, Little and Wilkins, 1826.

LUTHER, A. Byron, Heine, Leopardi : Drei Vorträge. 1904. [" Lord Byron und seine Helden."]

LYALL, SIR ALFRED C. Studies in Literature and History. London : John Murray, 1915. [Reprinted from *The Edinburgh Review*, October 1910 ; a review of the Coleridge-Prothero edition of Byron's Works.]

MACAULAY, THOMAS BABBINGTON, LORD. Review of Moore's Byron, *The Edinburgh Review*, liii. (June 1831), 544 f. [Reprinted in Critical and Miscellaneous Essays. Philadelphia : Carey and Hart, 1841, vol. i ; also in other editions of Macaulay's works. Also separately as a biographical sketch. Boston, 1877.]

*MACDONALD, A. J. Star-gazing : Metrical Compositions. Boston, 1907. [Contains a poem on Byron.]

MACFARLANE, C. W. " The Gex Portrait of Lord Byron," *The Century*, June 1914, pp. 221 f.

MACKAY, CHARLES. Medora Leigh ; A History and an Autobiography. Edited by Charles Mackay. With an Introduction and a Commentary on the Charges brought against Lord Byron by Mrs. Beecher Stowe. London : Richard Bentley, 1869.

MACKAY, GEORGE ERIC. Lord Byron at the Armenian Convent. Venice : Office of the *Polyglotta*, 1876.

MACKAY, WILLIAM. The True Story of Lady Byron's Life. Christmas Comic Version. London, 1869.

MACMAHAN, A. B. With Byron in Italy. Chicago : McClurg, 1906.

MACREADY, WILLIAM CHARLES. Reminiscences. London, 1875.

MADDEN, R. R. The Infirmities of Genius illustrated by referring to the Anomalies in the Literary Character, to the Habits and Constitutional Peculiarities of Men of Genius. Philadelphia : Carey, Lea and Blanchard, 1835. [Byron, vol. ii, chapters ix.–xvii.]

—— Memoirs of the Countess of Blessington. London, 1855.

Magazine of American History, The. "Scott, Moore and Byron," xxv. (1891), 501 f.

MAGINN, WILLIAM. The Odoherty Papers. New York : Redfield, 1855.

—— Miscellanies : Prose and Verse. Edited by P. W. Montagu. London : Low, 1885. [Contains : " John Gilpin and Mazeppa," i, 92 f. ; "Lament for Lord Byron," ii, 259 f. ; "Critique on Lord Byron," ii, 327 f.] [Maginn contributed to the Noctes Ambrosianæ, for which see WILSON, JOHN.]

MAGNIEN, EDOUARD. Mortel, Ange, ou Démon. Paris, 1836. [Elze, Life of Byron, p. 330, refers to "Lord Byron, Man, Angel or Devil," which apparently implies an English translation of Magnien's trilogy ; but I have found no other trace of it.]

MALCOLM, JOHN. The Buccaneer and other Poems. London, 1824. [Contains "Lines on the Death of Lord Byron," reprinted in *The Mirror*, No. 99.]

*MALLING, MATHILDA. Manden-Hustruen og Lord Byron. Copenhagen and Christiana, 1912. [A novel.]

Marino Faliero, or the Doge of Venice ; who was Executed for a Conspiracy, in the Eightieth Year of his Age. An Interesting Tale on which is founded the Highly Celebrated Tragedy by Lord Byron. London : Hodgson, n.d. [1821–24 ?]. [This prose narrative attained at least three editions.]

MARSHALL, MRS. JULIAN. The Life and Letters of Mary Wollstonecraft Shelley. London, 1889.

MARTINEAU, HARRIET. Biographical Sketches. London : Macmillan, 1869.

*MASON, EDWARD T. Personal Traits of British Authors : Byron, Shelley, Moore, etc. New York, 1885.

MASSIAH, S. R. ST. CLAIR. Byron : a Poem. 1869. [No place or publisher stated.]

MATTHAIE, O. Characteristics of Lord Byron. [n.d., no place, no publisher stated.]

MAUDE, THOMAS. Monody on the Death of Lord Byron. London : Hatchard, 1824.

MAUROIS, ANDRÉ. Ariel, ou la Vie de Shelley. Paris : Grasset, 1923. [On Byron, part ii, *passim.*]

MAYCHRZAK, F. Lord Byron als Uebersetzer. Altenburg, 1895. [Cf. *Englische Studien*, xxi, 393.]

MAYER, S. R. T. "Lady Caroline Lamb," *Temple Bar*, June 1878.

MAYN, GEORGE. Ueber Lord Byrons Heaven and Earth. Breslau, 1887. [Cf. *Englische Studien*, xi, 145.]

MAYNE, ETHEL C. Byron. New York: Scribner, 1912. [Cf. *The Athenæum*, November 2, 1912, p. 511; *The Nation* (N.Y.), May 8, 1913, pp. 475.]

*MAZURE, A. "Etude morale sur Lord Byron et sur son influence à l'égard de la littérature contemporaine en France," *Revue anglo-française*, vol. i. Poitiers, 1833.

MAZZINI, GIUSEPPE. "Byron e Goethe," Scritti litterari d'un italieno vivente. Lugano, 1847. [English translation in Mazzini's Life and Writings. London: Smith, Elder and Co., 1891, vi, 61 f.]

MAZZONI, G. Storia letteraria d'Italia: Il Ottocento. [On Byron, pp. 710 f.]

McCANN, WALTER E. "Byronism," *The Galaxy Miscellany*, June 1868, pp. 777 f.

"McLAWS, LAFAYETTE." See LAFAYETTE, EMILY.

MEDWIN, THOMAS. Journal of the Conversations of Lord Byron at Pisa. London: Henry Colburn, 1824. [Cf. *Blackwood's Magazine*, November 1824; *The Gentleman's Magazine*, xciv, part ii. (November 1824, pp. 434 f. and p. 546; *The Westminster Review*, January 1825.]

—— French translation: in the sixth edition of Pichot's version of Byron, vol. xvii. (1827).

—— The Angler in Wales. London, 1834.

MEESTER, M. E. DE. Oriental Influences in the English Literature of the early Nineteenth Century. [*Anglistische Forschungen*, xlvi.] Heidelberg: Carl Winter, 1915. [Especially chapter vi.]

*MEGYERY, I. Lord Byron. 1889.

MELCHIOR, F. H. Heines Verhältnis zu Lord Byron. [*Literarhistorische Forschungen*, xxvii.] Berlin: E. Felber, 1903.

MENEGHETTI, NAZZARENO. Lord Byron a Venezia. Venice, n.d. [1910].

MEREDITH, GEORGE. Letters. Collected and edited by his son. New York: Scribner, 1912.

*MÉRIMÉE, PROSPER. "Mémoires de Lord Byron," *Le National*, March 7, 1830.

—— "Réclamation contre les Mémoires de Lord Byron publiés par M. Moore," *Le National*, June 3, 1830.

*MICKIEWITZ, A. "Goethe und Byron," *Mélanges*, 1872, vol. i.

MILLER, BARNETTE. Leigh Hunt's Relations with Byron, Shelley and Keats. New York: The Columbia University Press, 1910.

MILLER, THOMAS. Elegy on the Death of Lord Byron's Mary. London: Simpkin and Marshall; Nottingham: G. Simons, n.d. [c. 1833].

MILLIDGE, F. A. Byrons Beziehungen zu seinen Lehrern und Schulkameraden. Leipzig: Zechel, 1903.

MILLIGEN, JULIUS. Memoirs of the Affairs of Greece . . . with various Anecdotes relating to Lord Byron and an Account of his last Illness and Death. London: John Rodwell, 1831.

MILLIKEN, E. J. Childe Chappie's Pilgrimage. London: Bradbury, Agnew and Co., 1883. [Reprinted from *Punch*.]

MILNER, H. M. *The Italian Don Juan, or Memoirs of the Devil. Translated by H. M. Milner. London, 1820.

—— Mazeppa; or, The Wild Horse of Tartary. A Romantic Drama, in three acts. Dramatized from Lord Byron's Poem. [Lacy's Acting Edition of English Plays, vol. xcvi; French's Standard Drama, No. cxxxiv.]

NETTEMENT, A. F. Histoire de la littérature française sous la Restauration. Paris, 1853. [On Byron, i, 236 f.]

NEUDECK, HEINRICH. Byron als Dichter des Komischen. Karlsruhe, 1911.

A New Canto. London : William Wright, 1819.

New International Encyclopædia, The. New York : Dodd, Mead and Co., 2nd edition, 1914. [" Byron," iv, 243 f.]

New Monthly Magazine and Literary Journal, The. "Lord Byron's Juvenile Poems," February 1819.

—— "Lord Byron," November 1819.

—— "Conversation of an American with Lord Byron," xlv. (1835), 193 f. and 291 f. [Signed " D."]

—— "An Event in the Life of Lord Byron," xcix. (1853), 138 f.

New Readings of Old Authors. Byron. The Giaour. London : Wilson and Tilt, n.d. [A series of comic illustrations perverting the meaning of various lines in the poem. Shakespeare occupies several numbers in the same series.]

NEWMAN, JOHN HENRY. "Poetry with Reference to Aristotle's Poetics," The London Review, i. (1829). [Reprinted in Essays, Critical and Historical. London : Pickering, 1872, vol. i.]

Newstead Abbey and the Relics of Byron. Mansfield : John Linney, n.d.

Newstead Abbey : Lord Byron : Colonel Wildman. A Reminiscence. Leeds : Fenteman and Sons, 1856.

Newstead Abbey : Its Present Owner ; with Reminiscences of Lord Byron. London : Longman, n.d.

NICCOLINI, G. Vita di Giorgio, Lord Byron. Milan, 1835.

NICHOL, JOHN. Byron. [English Men of Letters Series.] London : Macmillan, 1880. [Cf. Harper's Magazine, December 1880.]

NIEJAHR, JOHANNES. "Goethes Helena," Euphorion, i. (1894), 81 f. [Especially pp. 84 f.]

NIESCHLAG, HERMANN. Ueber Lord Byrons Sardanapalus. Halle, 1900.

NIGHTINGALE, J. The introductory matter in : Poems on Domestic Circumstances . . . by Lord Byron. To which are prefixed Memoirs of the Life of the Author, and a Statement of All the Facts that have as yet come before the Public relative to those "Domestic Circumstances" which have ultimately produced a Separation between Lord and Lady Byron. London : J. Bumpus, 1816.

NISARD, D. "Lord Byron et la société anglaise," Revue des Deux Mondes, November 1, 1850, pp. 413 f.

—— Portraits et Etudes d'histoire littéraire. Paris, 1874. [" Lord Byron," pp. 319 f.]

NODIER, CHARLES. "Notice préliminaire " in A. Pichot's translation of Byron's Works. Paris, 1823.

—— *"Lord Byron et Thomas Moore," La Quotidienne, November 1, 1829.

NOEL, RODEN. "Lord Byron and his Times," St. Paul's Magazine, xiii. (1873). [Reprinted in Essays on Poetry and Poets. London, 1886.]

—— "The Grave of Byron," Songs of the Heights and Deeps. London, 1885. [Reprinted in Noel's Life of Lord Byron.]

—— Life of Lord Byron. [Great Writers Series.] London : Walter Scott, 1890. [Contains a valuable bibliography by J. P. Anderson, which supplements the present bibliography along certain lines. See especially pp. xxv f., "Songs, etc. set to Music," and pp. xxix f., " Magazine Articles, etc."]

NOEL, RODEN. "Byron," Miles's Poets and Poetry of the Nineteenth Century. London : Routledge, 1905, ii, 363 f.

"NORTH, CHRISTOPHER." See WILSON, JOHN.

North American Review, The. [For a list of articles on Byron see CUSHING, WILLIAM : Index to the North American Review, 1815–77. Cambridge, 1878.]

NORTHUP, C. S. "Byron and Gray," Modern Language Notes, xxxii. (May 1917), 310 f.

[NORTON, ANDREWS.] A Review of the Character and Writings of Lord Byron. London : Sherwood, Gilbert and Piper, 1826. [Reprinted from The Atlantic Monthly, October 1825.]

Notes and Queries. Passim ; see the several indices.

*NUNEZ DE ARCE, GASPAR. Ultima lamentación de Lord Byron.

Nuova Antologia. "Il Centenario di Byron e la stampa," xcvii. (February 16, 1888), 728 f.

O., W. The Bride of Abydos : A Tragedy in five acts. Founded upon The Bride of Abydos and The Corsair of Lord Byron. London : James Harper, 1818.

OCHSENBEIN, W. "Die Aufnahme Lord Byrons in Deutschland und sein Einfluss auf den jungen Heine," Untersuchungen zur neueren Sprach- und Literaturgeschichte, vi, Berne : Francke, 1905. [Cf. The Modern Language Review, i. (1906), 152 f.]

OEFTERING, W. E. Wordsworths und Byrons Natur-Dichtung. Karlsruhe : F. Thiergarten, 1901.

OESTERLING, A. "Byron und Beyle," Germanisch-romanische Monatsschrift, vi, (1914) 335 f.

"OLD SARBOT." Brum : A Parody. [1860 ?]

OLIPHANT, MARGARET O. Literary History of England. New York : Macmillan, 1882.

D'OLIVET, FABRE. Cain. Mystère dramatique. Traduit en vers français et réfuté dans une suite de remarques philosophiques et critiques, précédé d'une Lettre addressé à Lord Byron, sur les Motifs et le But de cet ouvrage. Paris, 1823.

On Genius. Addressed to Lord Byron. London, 1823.

Once a Week. "The Home and Grave of Byron," July 2, 1860.

"OUTIS." "The True Story" of Mrs. Stowe. By Outis. London : Mann, n.d. [1869].

"OXONIAN." The Radical Triumvirate ; or, Infidel Paine, Lord Byron, and Surgeon Lawrence colleaguing with the patriotic Radicals to emancipate Mankind from all Laws, human and divine. A Letter to John Bull. From an Oxonian resident in London. London : Francis Westley, 1820.

"OXONIENSIS." See TODD, H. J.

PAGET, JOHN. "Lord Byron and his Calumniators," Blackwood's Magazine, January 1870. [Reprinted in Paradoxes and Puzzles, 1874, pp. 283 f.]

Pall Mall Gazette, The. "A Letter from Byron to Teresa," May 28, 1884.

*A Parody on "Modern Greece." Addressed to Lord Byron. London, 1824.

PARRY, THOMAS. The Beauties of Byron, with a Sketch of his Life and a Dissertation on his Genius and Writings. London, 1823.

PARRY, WILLIAM. The Last Days of Lord Byron: with his Lordship's Opinions on various subjects, particularly on the State and Prospects of Greece. London: Knight and Lacy, 1825. [Cf. *The Gentleman's Magazine*, xcv, part i. (June 1825), 517 f.]

The Particulars of the Dispute between the late Lord Byron and Mr. Southey. Edinburgh, 1824.

PAYNE, J. W. H. The Unfortunate Lovers; or, The Affecting History of Selim and Almena. A Turkish Tale; from "The Bride of Abydos" of Lord Byron. London: Dean and Munday, n.d. [The New York edition, published by S. King, is dated 1822.]

PEACOCK, THOMAS LOVE. The Ballad of Sir Proteus. 1815.

—— Nightmare Abbey. London, 1818.

—— Letters. Edited by Richard Garnett. Boston: The Bibliophile Society, 1910.

PEBODY, CHARLES. Authors at Work. London, 1872. [On Byron, pp. 247 f.]

[PEMBER, E. H.] Part author of Lord Byron and his Detractors. See MURRAY, JOHN [IV.].

[PENN, GRANVILLE.] Lines to Harold. Stoke Park, Buckinghamshire: Privately printed, 1812. [Reprinted: (1) in Original Lines and Translations. London: Murray, 1815; (2) with the title changed to "Address to Lord Byron on the Publication of Childe Harold," in The Poetical Album, second series, 1829; (3) separately, with the original title and imprint, in 1843.]

"PEPPERPOD, PETER." The Literary Bazaar; or, Poet's Council. A Grand, Historic, Heroic, Serio-Comic, Hudibrastic Poem. In two cantos. With a Pic-nic Elegy on Richard Brinsley Sheridan, Esq. By Peter Pepperpod, Esq. London: James Harper, 1816.

PERRY, THOMAS SERGEANT. "Recent Criticism of Byron," *The International Review*, vii. (1879), 282 f.

PETERS, ROBERT J. Lord Byron. A Study in Heredity and Environment. Tiffin, Ohio: E. R. Good and Brother, 1894.

PFEIFFER, ANTON. Thomas Hopes Anastasius und Byrons Don Juan. Munich: Schuh, 1913.

PHILLIPS, STEPHEN. "The Poetry of Byron. An Anniversary Study," *The Cornhill*, lxxvii. (January 1898), 16 f.

*PHILLIPS, W. A Review of the Character and Writings of Lord Byron. London, 1826.

"PHILO-MILTON." A Vindication of the Paradise Lost from the Charge of Exculpating Cain: A Mystery. By Philo-Milton. London: Rivington, 1822.

PICHOT, AMÉDÉE. "Notice biographique" and notes to his translation of the Œuvres complètes de Lord Byron. Paris: Ladvocat, 1819 f. [Cf. Estève, pp. 526 f.]

—— "Essai sur le caractère et le génie de lord Byron," in vol. i. (1823) of the fourth edition of his translation.

—— Voyage historique et littéraire en Angleterre et en Ecosse. Orné de Portraits, Vues, Monumens de Sculpture, etc. Et des Facsimiles de l'écriture des principaux Ecrivains anglais de l'époque actuelle. Paris: Ladvocat et Gosselin, 1825. [Especially vol. iii, pp. 66 f.]

The Pilgrimage of Ormond; or, Childe Harold in the New World. Charleston, S. C., 1831.

"PISANUS FRAXI." See ASHBEE, H. S.

Poems by the Right Hon. Lord Byron ; with his Memoirs. London : Jones and Co., n.d. [1825 ; reprinted, 1835].

Poems on his Domestic Circumstances, by Lord Byron. Second edition . . . to which is prefixed Memoirs of his Life. Bristol : W. Shepard, 1816.

Poems on the Death of Lord Byron. [A manuscript volume in the Library of Trinity College, Cambridge. Call number, H. 9. 82.]

Poems written by Somebody ; most respectfully dedicated (by permission) to Nobody ; and intended for Everybody who can read ! ! ! London : Published at the request of several persons of distinction. Baldwin and Co., 1818.

[POLIDORI, J. W.] The Vampyre : a Tale, by the Right Hon. Lord Byron. London : Sherwood, Neely and Jones, 1819. [Reprinted from *The New Monthly Magazine*, April 1819. Cf. *The Monthly Review*, May 1819.]

POLIDORI, J. W. The Diary of Doctor John William Polidori. Edited and Elucidated by William Michael Rossetti. London : Elkin Mathews, 1911.

POLLOK, ROBERT. The Course of Time. London, 1827.

PONITZ, ARTHUR. Byron und die Bibel. Weida i. Th., 1906.

PORTERFIELD, A. W. " Poets as Heroes in dramatic works in German Literature," *Modern Philology*, xii. (1914), 65 f. and 297 f. [This includes several examples of Byron as hero.]

Portfolio, The Political and Literary. " Literary Frauds," No. vi. (December 7, 1816), pp. 121 f.

POWYS, J. C. Suspended Judgments. New York : American Library Service, 1923. [Contains a chapter on Byron.]

PRENTIS, STEPHEN. An Apology for Lord Byron. With Miscellaneous Poems. London : John Macrone, 1836.

PRESTON, ELLIOTT W. Lord Byron Vindicated ; or, Rome and Her Pilgrim. By " Manfred." London : Simpkin, Marshall and Co., 1876.

PRICE, L. M. English-German Literary Influences. Berkley : The University of California Press, 1919. [" Byron," chapter xxi.]

PROCTER, B. W. Miscellaneous Poems. By Barry Cornwall. London, 1822. [Various allusions to Byron.]

PROELSZ, JOHANNES. Das junge Deutschland. Stuttgart, 1892. [Contains much information on Byron's influence.]

PROTHERO, ROWLAND E. [LORD ERNLE]. Introduction, notes, and appendices to the definitive edition of Byron's Letters and Journals. London : John Murray, 1898-1904.

—— Part author of Lord Byron and his Detractors. See MURRAY, JOHN [IV.].

—— " The Goddess of Wisdom and Lady Caroline Lamb," *The Monthly Review*, June 1905.

—— " The End of the Byron Mystery," *The Nineteenth Century*, xc. (August 1921), 207 f.

PUDBRES, ANNA. " Lord Byron, the Admirer and Imitator of Alfieri," *Englische Studien*, xxxiii, 40 f.

PUGHE, G. H. Studien über Byron und Wordsworth. [*Anglistische Forschungen*, viii.] Heidelberg : Carl Winter, 1912.

—— Review of Kolbing's edition of The Prisoner of Chillon [Byron's *Werke*, vol. ii.], *Modern Language Notes*, xii. (1897), 239 f.

PYRE, J. F. A. "Byron in our Day," *The Atlantic Monthly*, April 1907, pp. 542 f.

Quarterly Review, The. Report of the case of Walcot *vs.* Walker, etc., xxvii. (April 1822), 123 f.

Quarterly Review, The. Notice of the proposed Byron Monument. July, 1828 (p. 14 of advertisements).

—— Review of Tennyson's Poems, lxx. (1842), 392 f.

—— Review of Russell's Moore, xciii. (June 1853), 239 f.

—— "Coleridge as a Poet," cxxv. (July 1868), 78 f.

—— "Byron and Tennyson," cxxxi. (October 1871), 354 f.

—— "Byron and Bonaparte," ccxii. (January 1910), 1 f.

[Also many reviews of Byron's poems ; and articles entered under their authors' names.]

QUILLER-COUCH, SIR ARTHUR. Studies in Literature, second series. New York : Putnam, 1922. [Contains a Lecture on Byron delivered at Nottingham in 1918.]

R., N. Essai sur le caractère, les moeurs et l'esprit de lord Byron, traduit de l'anglais par N. R. Paris, 1824. [I know of no English original.]

RAAB, HANS. "Ueber einige Fortsetzungen von Byrons Don Juan," Byroniana und Anderes. Erlangen, 1912.

RABBE, ALPHONSE. "Le poignard du Moyen Age," *Annales romantiques*, 1825, pp. 229 f. [Reprinted in Œuvres posthumes de A. Rabbe. Paris, 1836, i, 238 f. When first published Rabbe passed this off as a translation of a work by Lord Byron.]

RABBE, FELIX. Les Maîtresses authentiques de Lord Byron. Paris, 1890.

RANK, OTTO. Das Inzest-Motiv in Dichtung und Sage. Leipzig : F. Deuticke, 1912.

RAPP, MORIZ. "Studien über das englische Theater," part vi, Herrig's *Archiv*, xx. (1856). [Byron, pp. 397 f.]

RASSOW, MARIA. "Goethe und Byron," *Goethe-Jahrbuch*, xxxiii. (1912), 227 f.

READE, JOHN EDMUND. Cain the Wanderer ; A Vision of Heaven ; Darkness ; and other Poems. By ——. London : Whittaker, Treacher and Co., 1830.

—— Italy : a Poem in six parts. With Historical and Classical Notes. London : Saunders and Otley, 1838.

—— The Deluge. A Drama in twelve scenes. London : Saunders and Otley, 1839.

—— Poetical Works. London : Chapman and Hall, 1852.

REBEC, GEORGE. "Byron and Morals," *The International Journal of Ethics*, xiv. (October 1913), 39 f.

REED, HENRY. Lectures on the British Poets. 1859.

Reflections on Shipboard. By Lord Byron. London : Kirby and Allason, 1816. [Another edition : London : Plummer and Brewis, 1816.]

REID, T. WEMYSS. The Life, Letters and Friendships of Richard Monckton Milnes, First Lord Houghton. London : Cassell, n.d.

REID, WHITELAW. Byron. London : Harrison and Sons, 1910. [Re-printed in American and English Studies. New York : Scribner, 1913, ii, 165 f.]

REIFFENBERG, F. DE. " Le Siège de Corinthe, scènes lyriques," Poésies diverses. Paris, 1825.

Rejected Addresses, The Genuine ; presented to the Committee of Management for Drury Lane Theatre ; preceded by that written by Lord Byron and adopted by the Committee. London : McMillan, 1812. [Cf. *The Gentleman's Magazine*, lxxxii, part ii. (December, 1812) 564 f.]

A Reply to Fare thee Well ! ! ! Lines addressed to Lord Byron. London : Plummer and Brewis, 1816. [Cf. *Englische Studien*, xxvi, 68.]

Reply to Lord Byron's Fare thee Well. Newcastle : S. Hodgson, 1817. [Signed " C."]

RESCHKE, HEDWIG. Die Spenserstanze im neunzehnten Jahrhundert. [*Anglistische Forschungen*, liv.] Heidelberg : Carl Winter, 1918. [On Byron, pp. 88 f.]

REVEIL, ACHILLE, and COLIN, A. M. Historical Illustrations of Lord Byron's Works, in a series of Etchings by Reveil, from original Paintings by A. Colin. London : Charles Tilet, 1834.

[REYNOLDS, G. W. M.] A Sequel to Don Juan. London : Paget and Co., n.d. [c. 1843].

REYNOLDS, JOHN HAMILTON. " Literature. The Quarterly Review— Mr. Keats," *The Alfred, West of England Journal and General Advertiser*, October 6, 1818. [Reprinted by H. Buxton Forman in The Works of John Keats, iii, 373 f.]

RICHARDS, ALFRED B. Ad Byronis Animam. [A poem clipped from a newspaper, dated September 1869, without indication of origin, in the album of Byroniana belonging to H. C. Roe, Esq.]

RICHTER, HELENE. " Zur Frage : Wer war Byrons Thyrza ? " Herrig's *Archiv*, cxii. (1904), 70 f.

RIGAL, EUGENE. " Victor Hugo et Byron," *Revue d'histoire littéraire de la France*, xiv. (1907), 455 f.

RIVES, HALLIE ERMINIE [MRS. POST WHEELER]. The Castaway. Indianapolis : The Bobbs-Merrill Co., 1904.

ROBERTS, W. " Some Poems attributed to Byron," *Walford's Antiquarian*, xii, 101 f. [Cf. *Notes and Queries*, 7th Series, ii, 183 ; iv, 77.]

ROBERTSON, J. G. History of German Literature. Edinburgh : Blackwood, 1902. [See index *sub* " Byron."]

ROBINSON, HENRY CRABB. Diary, Reminiscences, and Correspondence. Edited by Thomas Sadler. Boston : Fields, Osgood and Co., 1870.

[ROBY, JOHN.] The Duke of Mantua. A Tragedy. By ——. [Vignette of Byron with mask.] London : Thomas Davison, 1823. Second edition. London : Whittaker, 1833. [Republished, with the authorship acknowledged, in The Legendary and Poetical Remains of John Roby. London, 1854.]

ROE, FREDERICK W. Carlyle as a Critic of Literature. New York : Columbia University Press, 1910.

ROE, HERBERT C. The Rare Quarto Edition of Lord Byron's " Fugitive Pieces " described by Herbert C. Roe. With a Note on the Pigot Family. Nottingham : Printed for private circulation, 1919.

ROE, JOHN C. Some Obscure and Disputed Points in Byronic Biography. Leipzig, 1893.

Roever, F. Lord Byrons Gedanken über Alexander Popes Dichtkunst. Erlangen, 1886.

Rogers, Samuel. Italy : a Poem. London : Cadell and Moxon, 1830.

—— Table Talk. Edited by Alexander Dyce. New York : Appleton, 1856.

Rose, William Stewart. See LJ, iv, 211 f., for Rose's Verse-epistle to Byron.

Ross, Janet. " Byron at Pisa," *The Nineteenth Century,* xxx. (1891), 753 f.

Rossetti, William Michael. " Critical Memoir " in Poetical Works of Lord Byron. London : Edward Moxon, 1870.

Rosslyn, The Earl of. Sonnets and Poems. London : Remington, 1890. [" Byron," p. 77.]

Rotscher, Dr. Manfred . . . in ihrem inneren Zusammenhang ent-wickelt. Bamberg, 1884.

Ruskin, John. Essay on Literature. 1836. Works, Library Edition, London : George Allan, i, 373.

—— Notes on the Turner Bequest. 1857. *Works,* xiii, 144.

—— " Fiction, Fair and Foul," Part iii, *The Nineteenth Century,* September 1880. *Works,* xxxiv, 322 f.

—— Praeterita. 1883. *Works,* xxxv.

[For a complete list and analysis of Ruskin's references to Byron see the Index to the Library Edition, xxxix, pp. 94 f.]

Russell, Lord John. Memoirs, Journal and Correspondence of Thomas Moore. Edited by Lord John Russell. Boston : Little, Brown and Co., 1853.

Russell, William. Extraordinary Men : Their Boyhood and Early Life. London : Ingram, Cooke and Co., 1853. [On Byron, pp. 211 f.]

" Rutherford, Mark." See White, William Hale.

Saintsbury, George. A History of Nineteenth Century Literature. New York : Macmillan, 1896. [On Byron, pp. 75 f. This is, I believe, Saintsbury's most extended treatment of Byron, but allusions to him occur in many of Saintsbury's other works, *e.g.* the History of English Prosody, the History of Criticism, etc. Cf. also *sub* Haldane, Lord.]

Salvo, C. de. Lord Byron en Italie et en Grèce ; un aperçu de sa vie et de ses ouvrages. Paris, 1825.

Sambourne, Linley. Venice, from Lord Byron's Childe Harold, with thirty lithographs from original drawings made in Venice. London, 1878.

Sanborn, F. B. " Odysseus and Trelawny. A Sequel to Byron's Grecian Career," *Scribner's Magazine,* xxi. (April 1897), 504 f.

—— " Lord Byron in the Greek Revolution," *Scribner's Magazine,* xxii. (September 1897), 345 f.

Sand, George [pseudonym]. " Essai sur le drame fantastique : Goethe, Byron, Miekiewicz," *Revue des Deux Mondes,* December 1, 1839. [Reprinted in Autour de la Table, and in Œuvres complètes. Paris : Lévy, 1876, v, 111 f.]

Satirist, The. " Lord B—n to his Bear," ii. (June 1808), 368 f. [Cf. p. 489.]

Schaffner, Alfred. Lord Byrons Cain und seine Quellen. Strassburg, 1880. [Cf. *Englische Studien,* iv, 335.]

SCHALLES, E. A. Heines Verhältnis zu Shakespeare, mit einem Anhang über Byron. Berlin, 1904.

SCHERER, EDMOND. Etudes critiques de littérature. Paris, 1876. [An important review of Taine's chapter on Byron. Scherer's very adverse opinion of Byron prompted Arnold to reply in his "Preface."]

SCHIFF, HERMANN. Ueber Lord Byrons Marino Faliero und seine anderen geschichtlichen Dramen. Marburg, 1910.

SCHIPPER, J. "Lord Byron und die Frauen," Beiträge und Studien zur englischen Kultur- und Literaturgeschichte. Vienna and Leipzig, 1908, pp. 307 f.

SCHIRMER, W. F. Die Beziehungen zwischen Byron und Leigh Hunt. Freiburg, i, B. : Wagner, 1912.

*SCHMIDT, ELISE. Der Genius und die Gesellschaft, ein Drama. 1850. [Byron is the hero.]

SCHMIDT, IMMANUEL. Byron im Lichte unserer Zeit. Hamburg, 1888.

*SCHMIDT, JULIAN. "Lord Byron," Porträts aus dem 19. Jahrhundert. Berlin, 1878. [Pp. 37 f.]

*SCHMIDT, O. Rousseau und Byron. Ein Beitrag zur vergleichenden Literaturgeschichte des Revolutionszeitalters. 1890.

SCHOLKOPF, ARTUR. Das Naturgefühl in Lord Byrons Dichtungen. 1909.

SCHULTESS-YOUNG, H. S. The Unpublished Letters of Lord Byron. Edited with a Critical Essay on the Poet's Philosophy and Character. London : Richard Bentley, 1872. [Cf. *Notes and Queries*, 7th Series, ii. (1886), 196.]

SCHUMANN, ROBERT. Manfred : A Dramatic Poem by Lord Byron. The Music by Robert Schumann. Op. 115. With connecting text in the form of Prologues by Richard Pohl. Translated from the German and adapted for the use of the N.Y. Philharmonic Society, by J. R. Cornell. New York : Torrey, 1869.

SCOTT, JOHN. Articles attacking Byron in *The Champion*, April 7, 14, and 21, 1816.

SCOTT, SIR WALTER. "The Death of Lord Byron," Prose Works. Edinburgh : A. and C. Black, iv. (1861), 343 f. [Reprinted from *The Edinburgh Weekly Journal*, 1824. The first six paragraphs were reprinted as "The Character of Lord Byron" in *The Pamphleteer*, xxiv. (1824), 169 f. Part of this article also appeared in : Miscellaneous Poems, including those on his Domestic Circumstances, by Lord Byron. To which are prefixed Memoirs of the Author, and a Tribute to his Memory by Sir Walter Scott. London : Bumpus, 1824.]

SCOTT, WILLIAM BELL. "Introduction" to The Complete Poetical Works of Lord Byron. London : Routledge, 1874. [Reissued 1883 and 1890.]

Scribner's Magazine. "The Point of View," September 1896, p. 385.

SÉCHÉ, A. and BERTAUT, J. La Vie anecdotique et pittoresque des grands écrivains : Lord Byron. Paris, 1909.

A Sermon on the Death of Lord Byron. By a Layman. London : Longmans, 1824.

The Seventeenth Canto of Don Juan. In Continuation of the unfinished Poem by Lord Byron. Intended as the First Canto of the remaining Eight which are wanting to complete that Author's original design of extending the Work to Twenty-four. London : W. Wilson, 1829. [No more published.]

The Shade of Byron : A Mock Heroic Poem, containing Strange Revelations not hitherto disclosed, with copious notes, a preface with the author's comments on the " Story " by Mrs. Stowe, and a repudiation of the charges hurled against the memory of Lord Byron and his beloved sister Ada Augusta. Vol. i. London, n.d. [1871]. [No more published.]

Sharpe's London Magazine. " Letters, etc., of Lord Byron," n.s. xxxvi. (July and August, 1869), 14 f. and 70 f.

Shaw, W. A. " The Authentic Portraits of Lord Byron," The Connoisseur. xxx. (July and August, 1911), 155 f. and 251 f.

Shelley, Jane, Lady. Shelley Memorials. From authentic Sources. London : Smith, Elder and Co., 1859.

Shelley, Mary Wollstonecraft. The Last Man. London, 1826.

—— Lodore. By the Author of Frankenstein. London, 1835. [New York : Wallis and Newell, 1835.]

Shelley, Percy Bysshe. History of a Six Weeks' Tour. London : Hookman and Ollier, 1817.

—— Letters. Collected and edited by Roger Ingpen. London : Pitman, 1909.

—— " Julian and Maddalo," " Lines written among the Euganean Hills," and " Adonais " in any edition of the Poems.

Sichel, Walter. " Byron as a War Poet," The Fortnightly Review, cx. (January 1916), 120 f.

—— " The Humour of Lord Byron," The Nineteenth Century, December 1920, pp. 1026 f.

" Sidney." Sidney's Letter to the King ; and other Correspondence connected with the reported Exclusion of Lord Byron's Monument from Westminster Abbey. London : James Cawthorne, 1828.

Sigmann, Luise. Die englische Literatur von 1800–1850 im Urteil der zeitgenössischen deutschen Kritik. [Anglistische Forschungen, lv.] Heidelberg, Carl Winter, 1918. [Especially pp. 93 f.]

Simhart, Max. Lord Byrons Einfluss auf die italienische Literatur. [Münchener Beiträge zur romanischen und englischen Philologie, xlv.] Munich, 1909.

Simmons, James Wright. An Inquiry into the Moral Character of Lord Byron. New York : Bliss and White, 1824. [Reprinted, London : John Cochran, 1826. Cf. The Literary Chronicle, April 29, 1826.]

Sinzheimer, S. Goethe und Lord Byron. Eine Darstellung der persönlichen und literarischen Verhältnisse mit Berücksichtigung des Faust und Manfred. Munich, 1894.

A Sketch from Public Life : A Poem, founded upon recent Domestic Circumstances ; with Weep not for me ! and other Poems. London : William Hone, 1816.

Smiles, Samuel. A Publisher and his Friends. Memoir and Correspondence of the late John Murray with an Account of the origin and progress of the House. London : John Murray, 1891.

Smith, G. B. " Lady Caroline Lamb," The Gentleman's Magazine, December 1883.

Smith, Horatio and James. Rejected Addresses ; or, The New Theatrum Poetarum. London, 1812. [Cf. " Address of Condolence to the Unsuccessful Candidates for the Drury Prize," The Gentleman's Magazine, xxxii, part ii, 471.]

SMITH, HORATIO and JAMES. Horace in London : Consisting of Imitations of the First Two Books of the Odes of Horace. London : John Miller, 1813.

[SMITH, WILLIAM GERARD.] Byron re-studied in his Dramas ; being a Contribution towards a definitive Estimate of his Genius. By William Gerard. London : F. V. White, 1886.

SOKOLOW, NAHUM. History of Zionism, 1600–1918. London : Longmans, 1919.

Sortes Horatianae. A Poetical Review of Poetical Talent. London : T. Hamilton, 1814.

*SOUMET, ——, and BALOCHI, ——. Le Siège de Corinthe. Tragédie lyrique en cinq actes. Musique de Rossini. Paris, 1826.

SOUTHEY, ROBERT. Two letters to The Courier, dated January 5, 1822, and December 8, 1824 ; reprinted in LJ, vi, Appendix I.

—— " Preface " to A Vision of Judgment. London, 1821. [Reprinted in Southey's Poetical Works. Boston : Little, Brown and Co., 1860, x, 195 f.]

—— Life and Correspondence. Edited by C. C. Southey. London, 1849–50. [Especially volumes iv. and v.]

—— The Two Visions ; or, Byron vs. Southey. New York : Borradaile, 1823.

*SPACH, LOUIS. " Byron," Encyclopédie des gens du monde. Paris, 1834. [I suspect, but am not certain, that the author is identical with Ludwig Spach, for whom see the next item.]

*SPACH, LUDWIG. " Byrons Tod zu Missolonghi," Autobiographische Aufzeichnungen. [New edition, 1901.]

A Spiritual Interview with Lord Byron. His Lordship's Opinion about his new Monument. By Quevedo Redivivus. London : Samuel Palmer, 1875.

SPRENGER, R. " Eine Stelle in Byrons Childe Harold, und Geibels Tod des Tiberius," Englische Studien, xxxii. (1903), 179 f.

SQUIRE, J. C. Tricks of the Trade. London : Martin Secker, 1917. [Contains : " If Lord Byron had written The Passing of Arthur."]

[STACY, JOHN ?] A Critique on the Genius and Writings of Lord Byron, with Remarks on Don Juan. Norwich : John Stacey, 1820.

STANHOPE, LEICESTER FITZGERALD CHARLES. Greece in 1823 and 1824 ; being a Series of Letters and other Documents on the Greek Revolution . . . to which are added, Reminiscences of Lord Byron. London : Sherwood, Gilbert and Piper, 1825. [Contains " Reminiscences of Lord Byron," by George Finlay, pp. 499 f. ; " Sketch of Lord Byron," by Stanhope, pp. 530 f. See also passim.]

—— Another edition : Greece during Lord Byron's Residence in that Country in 1823 and 1824 ; being a Series of Letters and other Documents on the Greek Revolution, written during a visit to that country. Paris : Galignani, 1825.

" STENDHAL." See BEYLE, M. H.

STEPHEN, LESLIE. " Byron," The Dictionary of National Biography, vii, 132 f.

STERNDALE, W. H. " Lines addressed to Lord Byron on reading the Stanzas inscribed on a Cup fashioned from a Human Skull," The Gentleman's Magazine, xciv, part i. (June 1824), 449. [Reprinted from The Stafford Iris.]

STIGAND, W. "Byron and the Countess Guiccioli," *Belgravia*, February 1869. 491 f.

STODDARD, F. H. "Lord Byron," *The New Princeton Review*, iv. (1887), 145 f.

—— Editorial material in "The Lyceum Edition" of Byron's Works. Boston: F. A. Niccolls, n.d.

—— "Critical and biographical introduction" to Childe Harold and other Poems. New York: Appleton, 1899.

STOHSEL, KARL. Lord Byrons Trauerspiel Werner und seine Quelle. Erlangen, 1891. [Cf. *Englische Studien*, xvii, 141 f.]

*STOROSCHENKO, N. J. "Byrons Einfluss auf die europäische Literatur," *Oblast literatury*. Moscow, 1902.

STOWE, HARRIET BEECHER. "The True Story of Lady Byron's Married Life," *Macmillan's Magazine*, September 1869, pp. 377 f.

—— Lady Byron Vindicated; a History of the Byron Controversy. London: Macmillan, 1870.

"Strada." Article on Byron, signed "Strada," *The Champion*, May 8, 1814, No. 70, pp. 150 f.

STREET, GEORGE E. The Ghosts of Piccadilly. New York: Putnam, 1907.

STYLES, JOHN. Lord Byron's Works, viewed in Connection with Christianity and the Obligations of Social Life. A Sermon. London: Knight and Lacy, 1824.

The Sultana; or, A Trip to Turkey. A Melodrama in three acts, founded on Lord Byron's Don Juan. New York: N. B. Holmes, 1822.

Sun, The. "Languishing Lyrics, or the Lamentable Loves of the Lacrymose Lord and the Lugubrious Lady," September 23, 1815. [This newspaper contains much Byroniana.]

Sunday Magazine, The. "An Anecdote of Lord Byron," November 1879.

SWINBURNE, A. C. "Preface" to A Selection from the Works of Lord Byron. London: Edward Moxon, 1865. [Reprinted in Essays and Studies. London: Chatto and Windus, 1875.]

—— "Wordsworth and Byron," *The Nineteenth Century*, April and May, 1884. [Reprinted in Miscellanies. London: Chatto and Windus, 1884.]

—— Letters. Edited by Edmund Gosse and T. J. Wise. London: John Lane, 1919.

SYMONDS, JOHN ADDINGTON. "Byron," The English Poets. Edited by T. H. Ward. London: Macmillan, 1880, iv, 244 f.

SYMONS, ARTHUR. The Romantic Movement in English Poetry. London: Constable, 1909.

T., L. F. "Byron," in a series of articles entitled "Stars that have set in the nineteenth century," *The Democratic Review*, n.s. x. (1842), 225 f.

TAINE, HIPPOLYTE. Histoire de la littérature anglaise. [Ed. Hachette, 1911; "Byron," volume iv, book iv, chapter ii, pp. 308 f.]

Tait's Edinburgh Magazine. "The Lady of Annesley," 1836.

—— "Burns and Byron," 1844.

Tales of Chivalry and Romance. Edinburgh: James Robertson, 1826.

TALFOURD, THOMAS N. An Attempt to Estimate the Poetical Talent of the Present Age, including a Sketch of the History of Poetry. London, 1815.

TAYLOR, SIR HENRY. "Preface" to Philip van Artevelde. London, 1834.

TAYLOR, JOHN. Byronna, the Disappointed. A Tale of Lord Byron; or, the Power of the Passions. Part i. A Poem. London: W. Rock, n.d. [No more published.]

—— "On the Portrait of the Late Lord Byron, painted by Richard Westall," The Gentleman's Magazine, xciv, part ii. (1824), 167. [A poem.]

TELLES, ALBERTO. Lord Byron em Portugal. Lisbon, 1879.

Temple Bar. "Lord Byron," February 1869.

—— "Lord Byron's Married Life," June 1869.

—— "Character of Lord Byron," October 1869.

—— "Byron and Shelley," October 1871.

[TENNYSON [-TURNER], CHARLES.] "On the Death of Lord Byron," Poems by Two Brothers. London: Simpkin and Marshall, 1827, pp. 128 f.

TENNYSON, HALLAM, LORD. Alfred, Lord Tennyson. A Memoir. London: Macmillan, 1897.

THACKERAY, W. M. "Memorials of Gormandizing," Fraser's Magazine, xxiii. (June 1841), 710 f. [Reprinted in Ballads and Miscellanies, Works, Biographical Edition.]

—— Notes of a Journey from Cornhill to Grand Cairo. London, 1846. [Works, Biographical Edition, v, 624 f.]

THIERGEN, OSCAR. Byrons und Moores orientalische Gedichte. Leipzig, 1880.

THOMAS, JOHN W. An Apology for Don Juan. London: T. Green, 1824.

—— Second edition, with "Stanzas on the Death of Lord Byron." London: W. Booth, 1825.

—— Third edition, "to which is added a Third Canto, including Remarks on the Times." London: Partridge and Okey, 1850.

—— Fourth edition, with title altered to Byron and the Times; or, An Apology for Don Juan. London: Partridge and Okey, 1855.

THOMPSON, W. G. Lines on the Death of Lord Byron. Newcastle, 1824.

[THOMSON, CHARLES ?] Line on the Departure of a Great Poet from this Country. London: John Booth, 1816. [Cf. The Critical Review, July 1816.]

THORNTON, ALFRED. Don Juan. Volume the First. With fifteen coloured engravings. London: Thomas Kelly, 1821.

—— Don Juan. Volume the Second. Containing his Life in London; or a True Picture of the British Metropolis. With coloured engravings. London: Thomas Kelly, 1822.

Three Weeks at Fladong's. A Novel. By a Late Visitant. London: Printed for the Author, 1817.

Thurston's Illustrations to Lord Byron's Poem, The Corsair. London: Thomas Tegg, 1814.

TICKNOR, GEORGE. Life, Letters and Journals. London: Trubner, 1876. [See entry for October 25, 1816.]

Times, The. On the Destruction of Byron's Memoirs, May 19, 1824.

Times, The. On Disraeli's speech at the Byron Memorial Meeting, July 17, 1875.

—— [*The Times* and its Literary Supplement contain much Byroniana.]

Tinsley's Magazine. "Glimpses of Fashionable Life in the Time of Byron," October 1870.

To the Departed. Stanzas to the Memory of Lord Byron. London: Hatchard, 1825.

[TODD, H. J.] A Remonstrance addressed to Mr. John Murray, respecting a Recent Publication. London: Rivington, 1822. [Signed "Oxoniensis."]

TORRENS, W. McCULLAGH. Memoirs of the Right Hon. William, second Viscount Melbourne. London: Macmillan, 1878. [Cf. S. R. T. Mayer, "Lady Caroline Lamb," *Temple Bar*, June 1878; and *The Quarterly Review*, January 1878.]

TOYNBEE, P. J. Dante in English Literature. London: Methuen, n.d. [1908]. [On Byron, ii, 31 f.]

TOZER, H. F. Introduction and notes to Childe Harold. Oxford: The Clarendon Press, 1885.

TREDE, JOHANN H. Das persönliche Geschlecht unpersönlicher Substantiva (einschliesslich der Tiernamen) bei Lord Byron. Kiel, 1914.

TREITSCHKE, HEINRICH VON. "Lord Byron und der Radicalismus," *Preussische Jahrbücher*, 1863. [Reprinted in Historische und Politische Aufsätze, i, 305 f.]

TRELAWNY, EDWARD JOHN. Recollections of the Last Days of Shelley and Byron. London: Edward Moxon, 1858.

—— Records of Shelley, Byron, and the Author. London: Pickering, 1878.

—— The Relations of Percy Bysshe Shelley with his Two Wives, Harriet and Mary, and a Comment on the Character of Lady Byron. London: Printed for private circulation only, 1920. [A pamphlet issued by T. J. Wise, Esq.]

—— The Relations of Lord Byron and Augusta Leigh. With a Comparison of the Characters of Byron and Shelley and a Rebuke to Jane Clairmont on her Hatred of the Former. London: Printed for private circulation only, 1920. [A pamphlet issued by T. J. Wise, Esq.]

[See also *The London Literary Gazette*, February 12, 1831, for extracts from an unpublished journal by Trelawny.]

TRENT, W. P. "The Byron Revival," *The Forum*, xxvi. (1898), 242 f. [Reprinted in The Authority of Criticism and other Essays. New York: Scribner, 1899.]

TREVELYAN, G. M. Clio, a Muse, and other Essays. London: Longmans 1913. [Contains "Poetry and Rebellion," reprinted from *The Independent Review*, 1905.]

TREVELYAN, G. O. The Life and Letters of Lord Macaulay. New York: Harper, 1877.

TRIBOLATI, FELICE. "Lord Byron a Pisa," *Nuova Antologia*, xxvii. (July 1874), 631 f.

TRICOUPI, M. SPIRIDION. Funeral Oration on Lord Byron. Composed and delivered at Missolonghi, April 1824. London, 1825.

TROWBRIDGE, J. T. My Own Story. Boston: Houghton, Mifflin and Co., 1903. [On Byron, pp. 55 f.]

The True Story of Lord and Lady Byron, as told by Lord Macaulay, Thomas Moore, Leigh Hunt, Thomas Campbell, the Countess of Blessington, Lord Lindsay, the Countess Guiccioli, by Lady Byron, and by the Poet himself, in answer to Mrs. Beecher Stowe. London: J. C. Hotten, n.d. [1869 or 1870].

The True Story of Mrs. Shakespeare's Life. Boston: Loring, n.d. [1869 or 1870]. [A parody on Mrs. Stowe.]

TUCKERMAN, HENRY T. Thoughts on the Poets. New York: Francis, 1848. [" Byron," pp. 165 f.]

TÜRCK, HERMANN. Der geniale Mensch. Third edition, Berlin: Dümmler, 1898.

—— English translation: The Man of Genius. London: A. and C. Black, 1914. [Chapter vi, pp. 179 f. : " Lord Byron's Delineation of the Superman in Manfred."]

TURNER, SHARON. Prolusions on the Present Greatness of Britain ; on Modern Poetry ; and on the Present Aspect of the World. London: Longman, 1819.

*TURNER, W. Journal of a Tour in the Levant. London, 1820.

TURNOUR, E. J. The Warning Voice. A Sacred Poem, addressed to Infidel Writers of Poetry. London, 1818.

UHDE, H. Zur Poetik von Byrons Corsair. Leipzig and Hamburg, 1907.

*Universal Review, The. "Lord Byron," November 1824 ; January 1825.

Uriel, a Poetical Address to the Right Hon. Lord Byron, written on the Continent : with Notes, containing Strictures on the Spirit of Infidelity maintained in his Works ; an Examination of his Assertion that " If Cain is Blasphemous, Paradise Lost is Blasphemous," and several other Poems. London: Hatchard, Burton and Smith, 1822.

URQUHART, H. J. Poems Sacred and Classical. London, 1845. [Pp. 123 f. : " Lines written on Lord Byron, in early youth."]

VALENTIN, V. "Goethes Verhältnis zu Lord Byron," Berichte des freien deutschen Hochstifts zu Frankfurt, xvi. (1900), 239 f.

VAN DOREN, CARL. The Life of Thomas Love Peacock. London: Dent, 1911.

VARNHAGEN, H. Ueber Byrons dramatisches Bruchstück Der umgestaltete Missgestaltete. Erlangen, 1905.

—— De Rebus quibusdam Compositionem Byronis Dramatis quod Manfred inscribitur. Erlangen, 1909.

—— "Zur Textkritik von Byrons Manfred," Byroniana und Anderes. Erlangen, 1912.

Il Venerdì Santo. Scena della Vita di Lord Byron. Turin, 1847.

*VENGESOVA, ——. Byron et le romantisme français. St. Petersburg, 1906.

VERFÈLE, D. J. C. Pèlerinages d'un Childe Harold Parisien. Paris: Dupont, 1825.

VIENNET, I. P. G. " Byron," Minerva littéraire, vol. i. Paris, 1820.

VIGNY, ALFRED DE. "Œuvres de lord Byron," *Le Conservateur littéraire*, Paris, iii. (1820), 212 f.

—— "Sur la Mort de lord Byron (fragment d'un poème qui va être publié)," *La Muse française*, Paris, ii. (1824).

VILLEMAIN, A. F. "Byron," Biographie universelle, ancienne et moderne. Paris : Desplaces, 1843, vi, 279 f. [This first appeared in the "Supplement" to the edition of 1835. The article is reprinted in Villemain's Etudes de littératures anciennes et étrangères. Paris, 1846.]

VINCENT, LEON H. Dandies and Men of Letters. Boston : Houghton Mifflin Co., 1913.

"VINDEX." Captain Medwin vindicated from the Calumnies of the Reviewers. London : William Marsh, 1825.

Vindication of Lady Byron. London : Richard Bentley, 1871. [Reprinted from *Temple Bar*, June 1869.]

VOLPI, ODOARDO. Arnaldo ; Gaddo ; and other unacknowledged poems ; by Lord Byron and some of his Contemporaries ; collected by Odoardo Volpi. Dublin : Wakeman ; London : Groombridge, 1836.

WAGSCHAL, FRIEDRICH. "Goethes und Byrons Prometheusdichtungen," *Germanisch-romanische Monatschrift*, iv. (1912), 17 f.

WARD, MRS. HUMPHRY. The Marriage of William Ashe. New York : Harper, 1905.

WARNER, C. D. The Warner Classics : Poets. New York : Doubleday and McClure, 1899.

[WATKINS, JOHN.] Memoirs of the Life and Writings of Lord Byron with Anecdotes of some of his Contemporaries. London : Henry Colburn, 1822. [Cf. *The European Magazine*, September 1822 ; *The Gentleman's Magazine*, xcii, part i. (February 1823), 149.]

WATTS-DUNTON, THEODORE. "Byron," Chambers' Cyclopædia of English Literature. New edition. London : Macmillan, 1903, iii, 118 f.

WAUGH, ARTHUR. Alfred, Lord Tennyson. A Study of his Life and Work. New York : Macmillan, 1896.

WEBSTER, J. WEDDERBURNE. Waterloo and other Poems. Paris : Didot, 1816. [Pp. 47 f., "Lines on Lord B—n's Portrait."]

WEDDIGEN, F. H. O. Lord Byrons Einfluss auf die europäische Literatur der Neuzeit. Hanover, 1884. [New edition, Leipzig, 1901.]

—— "Lord Byrons Einfluss auf die französische Literatur," Herrig's *Archiv*, lxix. (1883), 89 f.

—— "Lord Byron und die russische Literatur," Herrig's *Archiv*, lxix. (1883), 214 f.

WEISER, C. S. Popes Einfluss auf Byrons Jugenddichtungen. Halle, 1877. [Cf. *Anglia*, i, 252 f.]

WENZEL, G. "Miltons und Byrons Satan," Herrig's *Archiv*, lxxxiii. (1889), 67 f.

WERNER, JOSEPH. "Die persönlichen und literarischen Wechselbeziehungen zwischen Goethe und Byron," *Berichte des freien deutschen Hochstifts zu Frankfurt*, ii. (1886), 181 f.

WESTENHOLZ, F. Ueber Byrons historische Dramen. Stuttgart, 1890.

Westminster Review, The. "Lord Byron's Residence in Greece," ii. (July 1824).

WETTON, H. W. The Termination of the Sixteenth Canto of Lord Byron's Don Juan. London : Trubner, 1864.

WETZ, W. Neuere Beiträge zur Byron-Biographie. Cologne, 1905.

—— "Zu Goethes Anzeige des Manfred," *Zeitschrift für vergleichende Literaturgeschichte*, xvi. (1905).

WHIPPLE, EDWIN P. "Byron," *The North American Review*, January 1845. [Reprinted in Essays and Reviews. New York : Appleton, 1848.]

WHITE, C. Mazeppa. An Equestrian Burlesque, in two acts. Transposed and arranged. New York : Brady, n.d. [c. 1860]. [No. 3 in Brady's Ethiopian Drama.]

[WHITE, WILLIAM HALE.] The Revolution in Tanner's Lane. By Mark Rutherford. Edited by his friend Reuben Shapcott. London : Trubner, 1887. [Cf. *The Academy*, April 26, 1902.]

—— "Byron, Goethe, and Mr. Matthew Arnold," *The Contemporary Review*, lx. (August 1881), 179 f. [Reprinted in Pages from a Journal. With other Papers. London : Unwin, 1901.]

*WIDDER, CÄSAR VON. "Lord Byrons Geliebte" [a poem], Vergissmeinnicht. Taschenbuch für das Jahr 1830.

WIEHR, J. "The Relation of Byron to Crabbe," *Journal of English and Germanic Philology*, vii. (1908), 134 f.

WIFFEN, J. H. Aonian Hours, a Poem, in two cantos, with other Poems. London : Longman, 1819. [Canto ii, stanzas 17–22, on Byron, "the modern Timon."]

—— "The Character and Poetry of Lord Byron," *The New Monthly Magazine and Literary Journal*, May 1819. [Cf. *ibid*. February and November, 1819.]

WILBERFORCE, EDWARD, and BLANCHARD, E. F. Poems. London : Longman, 1857. [Contains "Don Juan, Canto xvii."]

WILDE, OSCAR. Ravenna. 1878.

WILKINSON, HENRY. Cain. A Poem. Intended to be published in parts. Containing an Antidote to the Impiety and Blasphemy of Lord Byron's Cain ; with Notes, etc. Part i. London : Baldwin, Cradock and Joy, 1824. [No more published.]

WILKOMM, ERNST. Lord Byron, ein Dichterleben. 1839. [A novel.]

WILLIAMS, E. E. The Journal of Edward Ellerker Williams, Companion of Shelley and Byron in 1821 and 1822. London, 1902.

WILLIAMS, JOHN. On the Death of Byron. London, 1824. [An elegiac stanza in Greek.]

WILLIS, N. P. Lady Jane. New York, 1844. [See Canto ii, stanzas 10–11.]

WILMINK, ERNST. Lord Byrons Naturgefühl. Leipzig : R. Noste, 1913.

WILMOT, ROBERT. "Lines addressed to Lord Byron, April 1816." [See Astarte (ed. 1905), p. 121.]

WILMSEN, FRIEDRICH. Ossians Einfluss auf Byrons Jugendgedichte. Berlin : Felber, 1903.

WILSON, JOHN ["CHRISTOPHER NORTH."] Noctes Ambrosianae. Edinburgh : Blackwood, 1892.

—— "Christopher among the Mountains," *Blackwood's Magazine*, xliv. (September 1838), 285 f. [See also *Blackwood's Magazine*, March 1825 ; May 1838 ; April 1839 ; etc.]

WINTER, WILLIAM. Shakespeare's England. London: Macmillan, 1892.
[Chapter x: "Relics of Lord Byron."]
—— Gray Days and Gold. London: Macmillan, 1892. [Chapter viii:
"Byron and Hucknall-Torkard."]
WISE, THOMAS J. Catalogue of the Ashley Library. London: Privately
printed. Vol. i. (1922). [Contains list, with descriptions, of
Byron first editions.]
WOLFE, CHARLES. "The Burial of Sir John Moore." [Cf. Archdeacon
Russell's Memoir of Charles Wolfe. London, 1825; and a note on
the "Cynotaph" in The Ingoldsby Legends. London: Bentley,
1869, p. 21.]
WOODBERRY, GEORGE E. "Byron's Centenary," The Nation (N.Y.),
xlvi. (January 26, 1888), 66 f. [Reprinted in Makers of Literature.
New York: Macmillan, 1901.]
—— The Inspiration of Poetry. New York: Macmillan, 1910.
WOODS, MATTHEW. In Spite of Epilepsy. Being a Review of the Lives
of Three Great Epileptics—Julius Cæsar, Mohammed, Lord Byron.
New York: The Cosmopolitan Press, 1913.
WORDSWORTH, WILLIAM. Letters of the Wordsworth Family. Edited
by Charles Knight. Boston and London: Ginn and Co., 1897.
—— "Not in the lucid intervals of life," Poetical Works, ed. Knight.
London: Macmillan, 1896, vii, 402.
WRATISLAW, THEODORE. Swinburne. London: Greening, 1900.
WURZBACH, W. VON. "Lord Byrons Parisina und ihre Vorgängerinnen,"
Englische Studien, xxv, 458 f.
WYPLEL, LUDWIG. "Grillparzer und Byron," Jahrbuch der Grillparzer-
Gesellschaft, xiv. (1904), 23 f. [On Byron's influence upon Ahnfrau.]
—— "Grillparzer und Byron," Euphorion, ix. (1902), 677 f. and x. (1903),
159 f. [On Byron's influence upon Ein treuer Diener seines Herrn.]

"Z." Don Juan. With a short Biographical Sketch of the Author.
London, 1827.
ZABEL, ERNST. Byrons Kenntnis von Shakespeare und sein Urteil über
ihn. Halle, 1904.
ZACCHETTI, CORRADO. Lord Byron e l'Italia. Palermo: R. Sandron,
[1919].
*ZDZIECHOWSKI, M. "Byron und sein Zeitalter." [See Euphorion, ii.
(1895), 423 f.]
—— "Der deutsche Byronismus," Przeglad Polski, cvii. (1892), 513 f.;
cix. (1894), 306 f. [Cf. Euphorion, i. (1894), 417 f.]
ZEDLITZ, J. C. FREIHERR VON. "Todtenkranze" (1827), Gedichte.
Stuttgart and Tubingen: J. G. Cotta, 1832, pp. 221 f. [Poem on
Byron.]
ZIEHEN, J. "Byronstudien zur Geschichte des Philhellenismus," Berichte
des freien deutschen Hochstifts zu Frankfurt, xii. (1896).
[ZITZ, KATHINKA.] Lord Byron. Romantische Skizzen aus einem vielbe-
wegten Leben. 1867.
ZUCH, JOSEF. Thomas Moores The Loves of the Angels und Lord Byrons
Heaven and Earth. Eine Parallele. Vienna, 1905.

INDEX OF NAMES

[This Index does not include the Bibliography]

THE END